SUSE® LINUX®
Enterprise Server 9
Administrator's Handbook

PETER KUO AND JACQUES BELAND

Novell
PRESS™

Novell®

Published by Pearson Education, Inc.
800 East 96th Street, Indianapolis, Indiana 46240 USA

SUSE LINUX Enterprise Server 9
Administrator's Handbook

International Standard Book Number: 0-672-32735-X

Library of Congress Catalog Card Number: 2004096587

Printed in the United States of America

First Printing: July 2005

08 07 06 05   4 3 2 1

Trademarks

All terms mentioned in this book that are known to be trademarks or service marks have been appropriately capitalized. Novell Press cannot attest to the accuracy of this information. Use of a term in this book should not be regarded as affecting the validity of any trademark or service mark.

Novell is a registered trademark, and Novell Press and the Novell Press logo are trademarks of Novell, Inc. in the United States and other countries. SUSE is a registered trademark of SUSE LINUX AG. Linux is a registered trademark of Linus Torvalds. All brand names and product names used in this book are trade names, service marks, trademarks, or registered trademarks of their respective owners.

Warning and Disclaimer

Every effort has been made to make this book as complete and as accurate as possible, but no warranty or fitness is implied. The information provided is on an "as is" basis. The authors and the publisher shall have neither liability nor responsibility to any person or entity with respect to any loss or damages arising from the information contained in this book.

Bulk Sales

Pearson offers excellent discounts on this book when ordered in quantity for bulk purchases or special sales. For more information, please contact

U.S. Corporate and Government Sales
1-800-382-3419
corpsales@pearsontechgroup.com

For sales outside of the U.S., please contact

International Sales
international@pearsoned.com

Acquisitions Editor
Jenny Watson

Development Editor
Emmett Dulaney

Managing Editor
Charlotte Clapp

Project Editor
George E. Nedeff

Copy Editor
Chuck Hutchinson

Indexer
Julie Bess

Proofreader
Juli Cook

Technical Editor
Timothy Boronczyk

Publishing Coordinator
Vanessa Evans

Book Designer
Gary Adair

N
Novell
PRESS™
Novell.

Novell Press is the exclusive publisher of trade computer technology books that have been authorized by Novell, Inc. Novell Press books are written and reviewed by the world's leading authorities on Novell and related technologies, and are edited, produced, and distributed by the Que/Sams Publishing group of Pearson Education, the worldwide leader in integrated education and computer technology publishing. For more information on Novell Press and Novell Press books, please go to www.novellpress.com.

Associate Publisher
Mark Taber

Program Manager, Novell, Inc.
Darrin Vandenbos

Marketing Manager
Doug Ingersoll

Contents at a Glance

Table of Contents

Preface

Linux started life as a "hobby project" of Linus Torvalds in April 1991. He was trying to create an alternative to the minix operating system that runs on Intel 386/486 AT-class machines. Linux has come a long way since its inception. Today, more than a dozen different Linux distributions such as SUSE, Red Hat, Slackware, and so on, are available and run on a variety of hardware, including big IBM irons (such as the S/390 and the zSeries systems).

For the longest time, Linux was mostly used by home users and within educational institutions due to its cost (free!). The availability of Linux kernel source code made it a very attractive operating system to be studied in computer science courses and also helped to further promote its popularity. In the past few years (starting around late 2002 or early 2003), Linux started to make an inroad into businesses, and Linux desktops are slowly being used to replace Windows machines. SUSE and Red Hat are two major players in the Linux server arena. With financial backing from IBM, Novell acquired SUSE in January 2004. In addition to the NetWare server operating system, Novell now also has the Novell SUSE LINUX Enterprise Server (SLES) and a number of Linux desktop products, such as Novell Linux Desktop.

Like NetWare, SLES offers a wide range of network services, ranging from web server (Apache) to file and print (via Samba, for instance) to directory services (such as LDAP or NIS). SLES 9 allows you to leverage Linux and open source products (such as Apache) by delivering a scalable, high-performance foundation for secure enterprise computing. Built for reliability, it offers comprehensive functionality to power today's networks and meet user demands.

No matter what your purpose is, if you implement SLES in your networking environment, it is important for you to have a firm handle on how it works and how to set up the necessary services. You should know how to configure the server environment so that it is easy for users to use, yet secure against intruders. Good network administrators need to take proactive steps to prevent trouble from developing in the first place. This book serves as your handy reference to administrating, configuring, and securing your SUSE LINUX Enterprise Server.

Although this book is written as an administrator's handbook, you'll find that it contains a large number of security-related discussions and references. Topics covered in this book range from the fundamentals of managing users and groups, setting up and configuring essential network services, to securing your server against possible hackers. The information presented in this book will help you maintain and secure your SUSE LINUX Enterprise Server.

What You'll Learn from Reading This Book

This book is written for all system administrators, consultants, and any others who implement and support SUSE LINUX Enterprise Servers. It is especially useful if you have been administrating NetWare servers and would like to explore SLES as an alternative platform or need to implement SLES side-by-side with NetWare systems.

Using this book, you will learn basic to complex concepts and techniques on setting up a secure server. Whether your interest is solely in knowing how to set up an SLES system quickly for a small department or in knowing how to lock down the server against unwanted users, you will find this book to be a handy reference. This book specifically covers SUSE LINUX Enterprise Server 9, which is the latest available at the time of this writing.

How This Book Is Organized

This book is organized into the following four logical parts:

- **Part I, "SUSE Server Installation and Configuration,"** includes a brief overview of the history of Linux. It provides you with enough information so that, after reading it, you're able to "hit the ground running" and painlessly get your first SLES system installed and operating. It also covers how to manage software changes and hardware modifications.

- **Part II, "User Access and Security Management,"** describes in great detail the various security features and system monitoring and management tools available in Linux.

- **Part III, "Installing and Configuring Networking Services,"** provides you with a quick-start approach to setting up the essential networking and support services, such as printing and backups.

- **Part IV, "Securing Your SUSE Server,"** rounds out the many aspects of general Linux security that you will need to know to proactively prevent problems. Topics include establishing a corporate security policy, learning about intrusion detection tools, and hardening your operating system and network infrastructure against unwanted visitors. By proactively managing your network security, you can prevent many problems; this section will show you how.

Appendix A, "Security Certifications" includes a detailed rundown of security certifications, ranging from Orange Book and TCSEC certification to the most recent CAPP compliance standards. **Appendix B, "Resources,"** includes a list of websites and mailing lists available on the Internet that offer information about general Linux security as well as SUSE-specific security topics.

All the information and techniques presented in this book have been gathered from hands-on, real-world experiences learned from working with Linux and various flavors of Unix, and networking in general, over a period of more than 20 years. In this book, we share with you a selected number of the most frequently encountered problems and steps toward determining and fixing them.

Dedication

I dedicate this book to Belle, a most wonderful horse who is
always willing to lend me her sympathetic ears when Tasha is
busy making snow tunnels.

Peter Kuo

To my parents,
who are still teaching me about life,

and

Carol and Eric,

the two best friends a guy could ask for.

Jacques Béland

Acknowledgments

Writing a book about a server operating system, specifically the SUSE LINUX
Enterprise Server, requires not only knowing the current information that
needs to be put into print, but also in knowing the right people who can either
provide or nudge us in the direction of the correct information. We appreciate
the backing we received from the various support groups at Novell.

Peter Kuo: I am grateful that Kim Groneman (Chief Grasshopper Herder,
Novell Product Support Forums) and John Cox (Chief Grasshopper Herder,
Novell Developer Support Forums) tolerated my disappearance from the
Forums for weeks at a time when busy meeting this book's schedule.

I am especially honored to have Jacques as the co-author on this particular
book project. A big hug goes to his lovely wife, Carol, for allowing me to badg-
er Jacques senseless until he agreed to write the book. I would also like to
thank my parents for periodically sliding pieces of cold pizza under the office
door to keep me writing. Special thanks go to SAB for calling me a "glutton for
punishment" *again* when she was told that another Novell Press book was in
the works. Finally, a nice juicy T-bone goes to Tasha, my beloved Golden
Retriever, for tagging along for long walks in the knee-deep snow at Bruce's
Mill Conservation Area (how come book projects *always* start in winter?!) when

I needed to do some quiet thinking, and for tirelessly listening to all my complaints about book deadlines and RPM package dependencies.

Jacques Béland: As co-author of this book, I would like to express my thanks to Peter for his invitation into the world of technical writing. Over the years, Peter has been a mentor and a guide into the wonderful world of computing. Having the opportunity to collaborate on this work is something quite special. As Peter elaborated above, the support from my family has been wonderful. Both Carol and my son Eric have been quite patient as I horded computers and resources, testing and retesting applications. I would also like to take the opportunity to thank Ted for his friendship and support. As the third member of the infamous Computer Room Crew from our university days, Ted has always been available as a sounding board, a computer resource and, when writing got really tough, a psychoanalyst. For that, I am truly grateful.

The folks at Pearson/Novell Press who were involved with this project provided much-needed guidance throughout the project. George Nedeff (our Project Editor) and Emmett Dulaney (our Development Editor) and Timothy Boronczyk (our Technical Editor) did an outstanding job in providing the much-needed prodding, shaping, and formatting of the book. This book would never have gotten off the ground if not for our Acquisitions Editor, Jenny Watson, for recognizing the need for it. A big hand goes to Timothy Boroncyzk, our Technical Editor, whose helpful comments and suggestions were invaluable to the accuracy of the material presented in this book.

We Want to Hear from You!

As the reader of this book, *you* are our most important critic and commentator. We value your opinion and want to know what we're doing right, what we could do better, what topics you'd like to see us cover, and any other words of wisdom you're willing to pass our way.

You can email or write me directly to let me know what you did or didn't like about this book[md]as well as what we can do to make our books better.

Please note that I cannot help you with technical problems related to the topic of this book and that due to the high volume of mail I receive I may not be able to reply to every message.

When you write, please be sure to include this book's title and author as well as your name and email address or phone number. I will carefully review your comments and share them with the author and editors who worked on the book.

Email: feedback@novellpress.com

Mail: Mark Taber
            Associate Publisher
            Novell Press/Pearson Education
            800 East 96th Street
            Indianapolis, IN 46240 USA

Reader Services

For more information about this book or others from Novell Press, visit our Web site at www.novellpress.com. Type the ISBN or the title of a book in the Search field to find the page you're looking for.

SUSE Server Installation and Configuration

## CHAPTER 1

Installing SUSE LINUX Enterprise Server

In the beginning, the Linux operating system was mostly used as a teaching tool at colleges and universities and by home hobbyists. Over the years, however, Linux has evolved from a "Unix kernel clone/hobby project" into a robust, full-featured commercial product that is sold to millions of users around the world every year. Yet, to this day Linux remains an open system: Its source code is freely available, and Linux development is open to anyone who has the expertise and the energy to become involved.

Starting around 2002, Linux began receiving a great deal of attention as an alternative to the security-plagued Microsoft Windows operating system, both at the desktop and at the server level. Although Linux is solely an operating system, it is typically bundled with various applications and utilities. These bundles are commonly known as *Linux distributions*. These distributions vary quite a bit in the way they are packaged, the way the installation programs work, the third-party software they include, their documentation, the hardware they support, and the technical support offered by the vendor.

SUSE LINUX was created in 1992 by SUSE GmbH, of Nuremberg, Germany. SUSE is an acronym for "Software-und System Entwicklung," which is German for "Software and System Development." "SUSE" is officially pronounced as "Soo-Sah"—although many people also pronounce it "Soozie." The SUSE distribution is the oldest of all Linux distributions in the world and is noted for its reliability, ease of installation, and useability. Novell acquired SUSE in January 2004, so in addition to the NetWare server operating system, Novell now also has as part of its server operating system family the Novell SUSE LINUX Enterprise Server (SLES) product.

Like NetWare, SLES offers a wide range of network services, ranging from web server (Apache) to file and print (via Samba, for instance) to directory services (such as Lightweight Directory Access Protocol [LDAP] or Network Information Services [NIS]). SLES allows you to leverage Linux and open source products by delivering a scalable, high-performance foundation for secure computing, no matter the size of your network. SLES 9 was released in August 2004 (and Service Pack 1 was released in January 2005) and is the shipping version at the time of this writing.

There is nothing better than hands-on learning. The same is true when it comes to software, including operating systems. Therefore, rather than taking up precious page space with marketing and product feature information, we guide you right to installing SLES so you have a working system to experiment with as you follow the topics in the rest of this book. You can find the most up-to-date product data sheet and related information about SLES on Novell's website at www.novell.com/products/linuxenterpriseserver/.

Installation Methods and Overview

SUSE has long been known for providing quality documentation, and SLES 9 is no exception. The manual is broken into installation and administration sections. The installation section offers clear and useful advice on topics such as remote installation (SLES offers a VNC-based installation option to allow for installs on "headless" or blade servers) and simple topics, such as hard drive partitioning.

The installation itself can be handled in an automated fashion reminiscent of the default Windows approach, as well as in a hands-on fashion with numerous options to fine-tune the installation in terms of hard drive partitioning and package selection. We performed some simple installation tests of each method and found that while the more automated installation did a fine job of covering almost every contingency, it took a "kitchen sink" approach to package selection. Table 1.1 illustrates the amount of disk space required for the four installation types, ranging from a bare-bones base install with no graphics at all nor any exotic packages such as Apache to a full install in which relatively *everything* gets installed.

TABLE 1.1
SLES 9 Disk Space Requirement

INSTALLATION TYPE	DISK SPACE REQUIRED
Base system without graphics	400–500MB
Minimal graphical system without KDE	600–700MB
Standard (default)	1.5GB
Full	2.5GB

The less automated installation path gave us near-total flexibility, and that's the approach we recommend when the machine has a predetermined purpose: Select either the base system or the minimal graphical system and then manually select only the desired packages for installation. This results in a more streamlined, economic installation with fewer moving parts and less potential for extraneously running services and the security liabilities they incur.

TIP

Linux veterans will find almost every choice in the installation process familiar (regardless of previous distribution they may have used), and less-experienced administrators will probably receive all the help they need from hints provided by the installer. However, Linux novices will find the installation manual a useful tool while navigating an installation the first few times. If you don't have a printed manual, you can download the Adobe PDF document files located at www.novell.com/documentation/sles9/index.html.

Another installation option is to use AutoYaST, which allows for a one-time configuration to be recorded in an XML file and reused across multiple installations. The following sections provide a brief outline on performing SLES 9 installation using various methods.

NOTE

In the manual installation option, you have total control over the choice of drivers and settings. However, we have found that the automatic hardware detection performed by YaST is usually reliable. Therefore, the manual installation process using the Linuxrc program is not covered here. To learn more about Linuxrc, refer to Chapter 3 of the SLES 9 installation and administration guide (www.novell.com/documentation/sles9/pdfdoc/sles_9_admin_guide/sles_9_admin_guide.pdf).

CD-ROM–Based Installation

The traditional installation method is to use the software CD-ROM set. SLES 9 consists of six CD-ROM discs. CD1 is bootable, so you simply insert it into the CD-ROM drive and boot the server from it. The rest of the discs contain software packages, documentation, and source code.

TIP

CD2 uses a 2.88MB diskette image instead of the bootable ISO image used on CD1. If you have trouble booting from CD1, give CD2 a try.

If your machine is not capable of booting from a CD, you can create a set of three boot diskettes. The necessary diskette images and instructions are in the boot directory of CD1. Refer to the README file if you are already on a Linux system or to README.DOS if you are on a DOS or Windows system. To create these diskettes on a DOS or Windows system, you will need the rawrite utility found in the rawrite directory under dosutils of CD1; a Windows version is located in rawwritewin under dosutils.

TIP

Because of limited space on the boot diskettes, additional device drivers are placed in five separate module diskette images. Therefore, you may want to create these five module diskettes at the same time you create the boot diskettes. The install script will prompt for the appropriate module disk if the driver is not found on the boot diskette.

During the CD-ROM–based installation process, YaST prompts you to change CDs when necessary (see Figure 1.1).

VNC-Based Installation

The VNC-based installation method is designed mainly for the IBM's POWER processor-based systems, zSeries, and S/390 machines. These IBM systems can be configured to run a VNC host, so you can connect remotely using a VNC client to perform the installation.

NOTE

Virtual Network Computing (VNC) is a remote control software (see www.realvnc.com) program that allows you to view and interact with one computer (the "server") using a simple client program (the "viewer") on another computer anywhere on the network or even across the Internet. The beauty of VNC is that the two computers don't even have to be the same type or be running the same operating system. For example, you can use VNC to view an office Linux machine from your Mac at home (see sourceforge.net/projects/cotvnc). VNC is freely and publicly available and is in widespread active use by millions throughout industry and academia; it also is used extensively in private situations. You also can find a VNC server for NetWare at forge.novell.com/modules/xfmod/project/?vncnw.

FIGURE 1.1
YaST prompts for the next CD required in the installation process.

To perform a VNC installation, you need to pass certain parameters to the kernel. This must be done before the kernel is launched. To do this, you need to include the following information in the Initial Program Load (IPL) configuration of the IBM server prior to starting the Linuxrc program:

vnc=1 vncpassword=*password* install=*source*

vnc=1 indicates that the VNC server should be launched on the installation system. vncpassword= specifies the password that a client needs to supply when connecting to the host. The password *must* be at least six characters in length; otherwise, an error is generated when the VNC host starts up, and you will not be able to authenticate. The installation source (install=) can either be specified manually (by specifying the protocol and URL for the directory concerned, such as ftp://sles9.universalexport.ca/install_files or nfs://10.6.7.9/install_files), or it can be install=slp. In the latter case, the installation source is automatically determined by SLP query.

CAUTION

If install= is not specified, the server's local CD-ROM drive is used, which may not be what you want when doing a remote install.

The specific steps and syntax for setting up the VNC host on the IBM servers vary depending on the model, so you should refer to the system-specific documentation for details.

WARNING

The parameter keyword examples shown in section 3.1.7, "Passing Parameters to linuxrc," of the SLES 9 installation and administration guide do clearly reflect that the equal sign (=) is used to separate the keyword and its value when entered at the command line, and not a colon (:), as shown in the examples.

TIP

By default, a VNC-based install uses DHCP to obtain the IP information for the host. However, you can specify a static IP address by including hostip=x.x.x.x netmask=x.x.x.x as part of the Linuxrc parameter. You *must* specify netmask along with hostip; otherwise, DHCP will be used.

SLES 9 includes a Windows 32-bit VNC client (TightVNC) in the dosutils/tightvnc directory on CD1. You can also obtain the latest TightVNC client from www.tightvnc.com or use any one of the other VNC clients, such as the ones from www.realvnc.com.

The VNC server also has a small built-in HTTP server. With this, you can connect to the VNC server using a Java-enabled web browser. The VNC server listens for HTTP connections on port 5801; for example, the URL to use is http://server_name_or_ip_address:5801. The Java applet prompts you for your password (see Figure 1.2) and then displays the desktop.

FIGURE 1.2
Accessing the VNC server via HTTP.

A word of caution: VNC is unencrypted by default, so anyone who has access to the network path between you and the server and a packet sniffer can capture your sessions and extract passwords, server settings, or other entered data. Therefore, if you are performing a remote install, it is highly recommended that you perform only unsecured VNC installations over a trusted network or in a VMWare-like environment. If you must perform a VNC install across a nonsecured network (such as the Internet), we suggest you change the root password and any other password you entered during the unsecured session as soon as you finish the installation via an SSH or similar secure connection method.

Network-Based Installation

Often, it is much more convenient to place all the necessary installation files on a central server and perform the install across the network. This is generally faster than using the "disc jockey" method. Furthermore, files on a server can be easily updated. A side benefit of having such an installation server is the ease with which you can install packages at a later time; you can simply point YaST at this server instead of having to find the CDs and hope that the server's CD-ROM drive is not filled with dust bunnies. There are two ways in which you can set up the directory structure necessary for a network-based installation. One method is to copy the contents of each CD into a separate directory. This has the advantage of having a cleaner directory structure and makes updating specific CDs easier. The drawback is that when YaST needs to access contents on a different CD, you will be prompted to enter the name of that corresponding directory, thus slowing down the installation process a little. The other method is to copy the contents of all the CDs into a single directory. Using this setup, YaST will not prompt you to "switch" CDs.

Instead of setting up an ad hoc central installation server (such as an FTP server running on NetWare), SUSE LINUX provides an Installation Server module for YaST that supports installation across FTP, NFS, and HTTP connections. Consult Chapter 4, "Central Software Installation and Update," of the SLES 9 installation and administration guide for more details.

The Linuxrc installation process supports FTP, NFS, Samba, HTTP, TFTP, and SLP protocols for network-based installation.

AutoYaST-Based Installation

If you are rolling out servers using similar hardware that are similarly configured with the same set of basic services, you can make use of AutoYaST. AutoYaST relies on the hardware detection mechanism of YaST and normally uses default settings, but it can also be customized to suit your particular needs. Therefore, installation hosts need not be strictly identical. It is sufficient for them to have a similar hardware setup. You still need to take into account the limitations of the hardware itself, which cannot be circumvented by AutoYaST.

YaST includes an AutoYaST module, which can be used to create the necessary configuration. This configuration is then written to an XML file, so it can also be edited or even created manually. When you have the contents of the XML file to your satisfaction, copy it to a diskette so it can be used to install new systems. On the new server, pass the following in the boot options field

`autoyast=floppy:///filename.xml`

where `filename.xml` is your configuration file.

CAUTION

Notice the *three* slashes in the "URL" used to perform the AutoYaST-based install.

Further information and extensive documentation for AutoYaST are included in the `autoyast2` package. You can find online documentation, including many examples, at `www.suse.de/~nashif/autoinstall`.

Pre-Installation Planning

Before you undertake the actual task of installing the software, take a few minutes to do some pre-installation planning. Some aspects of your server configuration (such as the hard disk partitioning scheme and filesystem type selection) can be hard to change after SLES 9 has been installed. A few moments of planning, therefore, can save you hours of reconfiguration work later.

You should first make sure the server hardware meets the minimum system requirements for SLES 9 listed in Table 1.2.

TABLE 1.2
SLES 9 System Requirements

REQUIREMENT	NOTES
Minimum system memory requirements for installation	If you are performing a local installation, you need 256MB; an SSH-based network graphical installation requires 256MB; and a VNC-based network installation via FTP requires 512MB.
Minimum system requirements for operation	Server-class computer with Pentium II or ADM K7 450 MHz processor with 384MB RAM. Depending on the package selection, 500MB hard disk space for system software (a bare-bones, no graphical interface, base installation takes 400MB, while a full install takes up 2.5GB of disk space) with another 500MB hard disk space for user data. A 4X CD-ROM drive if installing from CD media, or a floppy drive if the CD-ROM drive does not support booting.

TABLE 1.2

SLES 9 System Requirements (continued)

REQUIREMENT	NOTES
Recommended system requirements for operation	Server-class computer with Pentium 4 or ADM K8 or higher-end (such as Intel Xeon EM64T) processor with 512MB to 3GB RAM; you should have at least 512MB RAM per CPU. Allow 4GB hard disk space for system software and 10GB (or much more) for user data. A 48X CD-ROM drive if installing from CD media, or a floppy drive if the CD-ROM drive does not support booting.

SLES 9 supports the Intel x86, ADM, AMD64, Intel Xeon EM64T, and Itanium processor family. It also runs on IBM POWER processor (formerly IBM iSeries and IBM pSeries systems), IBM zSeries, and IBM S/390 systems. For more detailed requirements such as those specific to the IBM zSeries 64-bit systems, refer to the SUSE LINUX Enterprise Server 9 documentation located at www.novell.com/documentation/sles9/index.html.

NOTE

Novell's Open Enterprise Server (OES) software ships with both the NetWare kernel as well as the Linux kernel (SLES 9). Therefore, if you plan to add OES services to your server later, make sure you take into account the additional RAM and disk space requirements when configuring your server initially.

If your system is a "server class" machine, it will more than likely work with SLES 9. If the system is classified as a "desktop system," it will likely work, but some nonstandard devices (such as certain integrated sound cards and integrated modems) may not work properly. If you try to install SLES 9 on laptop systems, there could be compatibility issues. If, however, you stay with the name brands such as IBM or Dell, it will most likely work. You can find a list of certified hardware for SLES 9 at Novell's YES CERTIFIED Bulletin Search page (developer.novell.com/yessearch/Search.jsp). From the Search page screen (see Figure 1.3), select Network Server from the drop-down list. In the Novell Product list box, select SLES 9 for the appropriate platform, such as SUSE LINUX Enterprise Server 9 for x86; then click Search at the bottom of the page.

The next order of business is to obtain the SLES 9 software. You can purchase the SLES 9 box set (which includes CDs, printed documentation, and one year of support) from one of the Novell partners (see www.novell.com/products/linuxenterpriseserver/howtobuy.html), or you can download the evaluation from Novell at www.novell.com/products/linuxenterpriseserver/eval.html.

The download is available as ISO image files that can then be used to create your own CDs.

FIGURE 1.3
Searching for an SLES 9-certified network server.

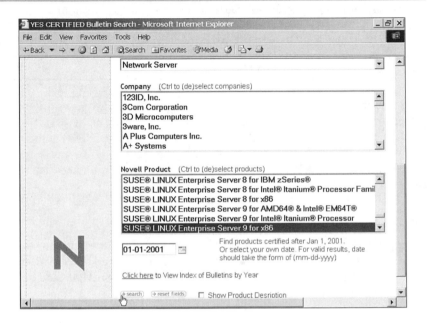

NOTE

If you download the evaluation, about halfway down the HTML page, you will find the evaluation serial number. You will need it to activate the free 30-day installation support and upgrade protection following the procedure listed under "Step 2—Support" at www.novell.com/products/linuxenterpriseserver/eval.html. If you purchased SLES 9 from a Novell partner, you can find the serial number inside the product box. And if you purchased the product online, you will receive an email with the serial number and related information.

TIP

You do not need to create CDs for all six ISO images because you can install SLES 9 via a number of other methods such as FTP or NFS. But you must always create CD1—the boot disk.

When you have the basic components on hand, you need to do a little planning. The following are some topics you should consider before installing SLES 9:

- **The role of the system**—The role of your system determines what software packages (thus, what amount of RAM and disk space) it may require. For instance, if the server is to be a dedicated Domain Name System (DNS) server, there is no need to put a 120GB hard disk in it unless you expect a huge DNS database. Furthermore, a dedicated DNS server would not require a GUI desktop because you can generally perform all necessary configurations using the text-based YaST (Yet another Setup Tool) or using a simple text editor like vi. You should make a list of network services that your server will be offering and then install *only* the required packages, their dependencies, and nothing more.

TIP

We strongly recommend against installing any GUI desktop on production servers. The extra overhead takes away the necessary CPU cycles and RAM from important network services.

NOTE

Software packages can be easily added and removed after the server is up and running. However, experience has taught us that, more often than not, after a package is installed, it is rarely removed, either due to laziness or lack of time. Furthermore, any installed software can be a source for security vulnerability. You will learn later in this book that one of the best ways to secure a system is to run the minimum amount of services required, which means installing only what you need for fear that rogue services may be started without your knowledge.

- **Hard disk partitioning scheme**—For a production server, all the available hard disk space should be devoted to Linux. However, you may want a test server to dual-boot or multi-boot with a number of different operating systems. Even if all the hard disk space is used for Linux, you still need to decide how to "break" up the disk space for the various filesystems, such as root (/), /home, and so on. For example, a standard SLES 9 install takes up about 1.5GB of disk space. This means you should allocate perhaps 2GB to the root filesystem to allow room for expansion. A rule of thumb is, if you have 4GB or less of total disk space, create one partition for swap (typically twice the physical RAM size) and one root partition. If you have more than 4GB of disk space, create a swap partition, a 1GB root partition, a 4GB /usr partition, a 4GB /opt partition, a 1GB /var partition, and assign the remaining space to /home.

TIP

Some (mostly commercial) packages put their data in /opt while the applications themselves are placed in /usr/bin; one example is Mozilla. Therefore, you may either want to create a separate partition for /opt or make the root partition large enough.

- **Hard disk configuration**—SLES 9 supports industry standard hard drives, such as IDE and SCSI (including iSCSI devices). Often, servers use RAID disks for fault tolerance, so you should give some thought to the RAID level you want to use. SLES 9 offers the option of combining several hard drives into one "soft RAID" system with the help of YaST, as an alternative to hardware RAID. SLES's software RAID can be configured as RAID-0, RAID-1, or RAID-5. Note that SUSE products with the 2.6 kernel do not currently support SATA RAID. Either use the SATA drives as a straight block device or a block device with Linux software RAID.

NOTE

A block device (such as a hard disk) is one that sends blocks of data with each read or write, as opposed to a character device (such as a keyboard), in which only one character can be sent or received at a time.

- **Filesystem type selection**—SUSE LINUX supports a variety of filesystem types, ranging from the legacy ext2 to Reiser to JFS. If you require secure file deletion, use ext2. And if you need performance and fault tolerance, Reiser is a good choice. Refer to Table 1.3 to ensure the filesystem type you select supports your file size requirements. You should also decide whether you want to encrypt the filesystem for security purposes. Find out more in Chapter 6, "Filesystem Security."

- **Bootloader selection**—Two industry standard bootloaders are available for most Linux distributions: LILO (**LI**nux **LO**ader) and GRUB (**GR**and **U**nified **B**ootloader). The matter of using one over another is mostly a personal choice (not too different from the notorious vi versus emacs or KDE versus GNOME verbal battles). Because LILO has been around for a much longer time than GRUB, many seasoned Linux administrators prefer LILO. However, GRUB is more powerful than LILO in that you can edit its entries on the fly and update the kernel without having to reinstall GRUB; with LILO, kernel changes and MRB modifications require you to reinstall LILO. SLES 9 uses GRUB by default unless the root filesystem's partition is installed on a RAID system, either a hardware-based RAID or software RAID or a Logical Volume Manager (LVM). You can change the bootloader type at installation time or later using YaST.

CAUTION

Although technically possible, a combination of GRUB with JFS is not recommended by Novell.

- **Password hashing algorithm**—Linux supports a number of different password hashing algorithms to safeguard user passwords. You should select an appropriate hashing algorithm based on the role of your server, its CPU power, and the level of security you desire. For instance, for compatibility with older Unix systems, you should use the default selection of DES hashing algorithm. For a moderate level of password security, select MD5. You can easily change the password hashing algorithm after the system is up and running. Refer to Chapter 4, "User and Group Administration," and Chapter 11, "Network Security Concepts," for more information.

- **Network information**—Unless you are installing a standalone server that is not connected to the network, you should have on hand the following information: the server's IP address and its net mask, default gateway, server's DNS name, and your DNS server address(es).

- **Software support information**—If you want to download the latest SLES 9 software updates during installation, ensure you have the YaST Online Update activation information obtained using the procedure listed at www.novell.com/products/linuxenterpriseserver/eval.html, as discussed earlier. Alternatively, you can perform this function later.

Additional planning and preparation work is required if you are using IBM POWER, zSeries, or S/390 as your SLES 9 server platform. Refer to the IBM-specific documentation located at www.novell.com/documentation/sles9/index.html for additional information.

TABLE 1.3
Maximum Sizes of Filesystems

FILESYSTEM	MAXIMUM FILESYSTEM SIZE	MAXIMUM FILE SIZE
ext2 or ext3 (1KB block size)	2TB	16GB
ext2 or ext3 (2KB block size)	8TB	256GB
ext2 or ext3 (4KB block size)	16TB	2TB
ReiserFS 3.5.x	16TB	4GB
ReiserFS 3.6.x (under Linux kernel 2.4.1 and later)	16TB	1 Exabyte (EB)
XFS	8EB	8EB
JFS (4 KB block size)	4 Petabytes (PB)	8EB
NFS v2 (client side)	8EB	2GB
NFS v3 (client side)	8EB	8EB

LARGE FILE SUPPORT (LFS) IN LINUX

Traditionally, the largest file size supported by a 32-bit system, such as x86, PowerPC, and MIPS, is either 2GB (2^{31} bytes) or 4GB (2^{32} bytes), depending on the implementation. To support files larger than 4GB on 32-bit systems, Linux added Large File Support (LFS) to its kernel and C library (a.k.a. glibc). LFS raises the limit of maximum file size for 32-bit systems to that of 64-bit systems: 2^{63} bytes or 8EB, unless limited by the filesystem itself. On the other hand, 64-bit systems like Alpha, IA64, and x86-64 don't have problems with large files but do support the new LFS interfaces also. In this case, the new interface is mainly an alias to the normal API interface.

The LFS APIs support files up to 8EB in size, but the Linux kernel imposes its own limits on the sizes of files and filesystems it handles:

- On 32-bit systems, Linux kernel 2.4.x limits files and block device sizes to 2TB (2^{41} bytes). However, using Logical Volume Manager, you can combine several block devices to enable the handling of larger files.

- On 64-bit systems, a filesystem and a file may be up to 8EB (2^{63} bytes), but hardware driver limitations may not support such large sizes.

- On 32-bit systems with Linux kernel 2.6 or later with LFS enabled, and on 64-bit systems, filesystem sizes may be up to 9 Zettabytes (ZB; 2^{73} bytes) in size. However, this limit is still out of reach for the currently available hardware.

SUSE LINUX has supported LFS since SUSE 7.0.

An Internet connection is not required to complete the server installation. However, if you want to download SLES 9 updates during the installation process, then an Internet connection is needed.

Ten Easy Steps to SLES 9 Installation

SUSE LINUX products are among the most easily installed Linux distributions available. After you have done your upfront planning homework, as discussed earlier in this chapter, you can complete the actual installation of your first SLES 9 server in less than an hour (subject to the speed of your hardware and installation method chosen) using the 10 simple steps discussed in the following sections.

NOTE

YaST performs all the configuration and installation work. It works by collecting all the necessary information from you and building a to-do list *without* actually touching anything on your system until you click Accept at the last installation dialog box. Given this, if you change your mind halfway through, you can easily abort the installation process and start all over again.

Selecting an Installation Method

When you boot your machine either using CD1 or the boot diskettes, a welcome splash screen is displayed. You are then presented with the boot menu, as shown in Figure 1.4.

If you don't select an option within 20 seconds, the first entry in the menu (Boot from Hard Disk) is automatically selected, and this is not what you want during an installation. Press the Tab key once to cancel the countdown.

At this screen, use the F2 key to change the screen resolution. Typically, 800×600 works well, but some people prefer 1024×768; any higher resolution would make the text displayed during installation difficult to read. If you are to perform a network-based installation, use F3 to select the desired network protocol, and you will be prompted to enter the necessary information, such as the IP address/DNS name of the source server and so on.

TIP

If the graphics screen does not display correctly, select Text mode for the installation. This does not impact the use of your GUI desktop at a later time. As a matter of fact, if you are installing SLES 9 under VMWare Workstation 4.x or 5.x or VMWare ESX Server 2.x (www.vmware.com), you must use Text mode.

FIGURE 1.4
SLES 9 boot menu.

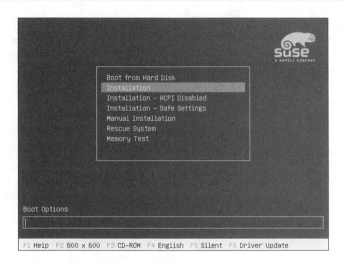

Use the arrow key to highlight Installation and press Enter. You are required to accept the Novell Software Licensing Agreement by clicking on I Agree before you can continue.

Selecting the Language

After you accept the license agreement, the graphical installation tool, YaST, runs. Select your preferred language from the list that appears on the screen, as shown in Figure 1.5, and then click Accept to continue.

Choosing Installation Settings

YasT probes and analyzes your system hardware, makes some automatic installation decisions, and displays them on the following screen (see Figure 1.6). You can change each choice by clicking the Change button and selecting the item you want to modify. For example, to change the software selections, click Change and select Software from the menu.

From the Software Selection screen (see Figure 1.7), you can change the system type that governs what packages are to be installed. The Default system is suitable in many cases, but it tends to also include software that you don't necessarily run. Instead, select Minimum System or Minimum Graphical System and then click on Detailed Selection to select the specific packages you want to run on this server. (You did create a list of packages as suggested in the earlier "Pre-Installation Planning" section, didn't you?)

FIGURE 1.5
Selecting your language.

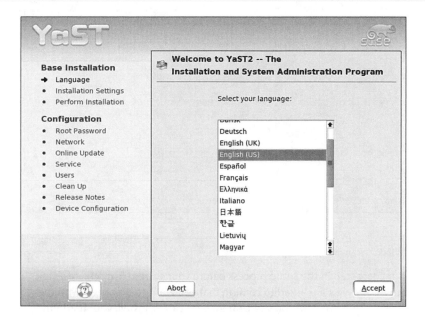

For this step, the following settings generally need changing or customizing:

- Software selections
- Time zone setting

Seasoned users would generally want to change the hard disk partitioning schemes to better suit their needs. They would also change the selection of filesystem type and whether encryption is to be enabled.

Click Accept after all desired changes are made and to continue to the next step.

FIGURE 1.6
Installation Settings screen.

WARNING

This is the last step in the setup process before your system is modified. After clicking Accept, you are asked to confirm that you want to go ahead with the installation using the data collected. After you click Yes, Install, your hard drives will be partitioned and formatted, which means *no* turning back.

Preparing the Hard Disks

After you click Yes, Install, YaST partitions and formats the hard disks. Subsequently, the installation of the system and the software packages begins. During the installation, information about the package that is currently being installed is displayed, along with time-remaining estimates (see Figure 1.8). You will be prompted to change the CD if necessary.

Following the installation of the base system and the application software packages, the bootloader (GRUB or LILO, depending on what you selected in the previous step) is installed, and then the system restarts.

FIGURE 1.7
Software Selection screen.

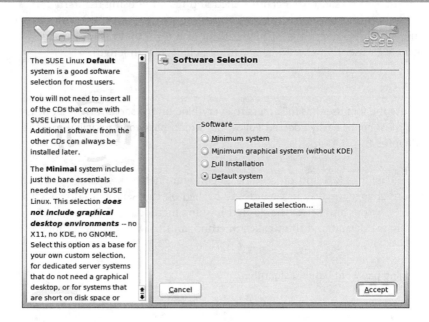

FIGURE 1.8
Software package installation progress screen.

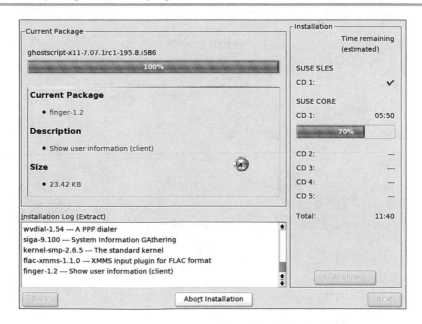

Configuring the System

After the basic system has been installed and restarted using the kernel installed on your hard disk (instead of the one off the boot disk), you can configure some system settings. The first thing you need to do is to set a password for the root user that should be *at least* six characters in length.

CAUTION

Because the root user has full access to everything on the server, his or her password must *not* be easily guessed. Follow the strong-password guidelines outlined in Chapter 4.

Before clicking Next and proceeding to configure network settings, you may want to change the way passwords are hashed on this server. To do so, click Expert Options and select the desired hashing method, as shown in Figure 1.9. (DES is the default and the weakest method, and Blowfish is the strongest.)

FIGURE 1.9
Changing password hashing algorithm.

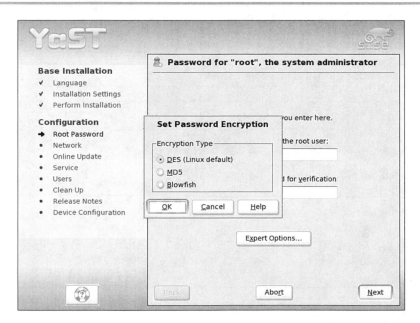

Specifying Network Settings

The next step is to configure your network connectivity. YaST will probe for and auto-detect network cards, modems, ISDN cards, and DSL devices (see Figure 1.10). In most cases, unless you use DHCP to assign a server's network information, the network card configuration would need to be modified.

FIGURE 1.10
Network Configuration screen.

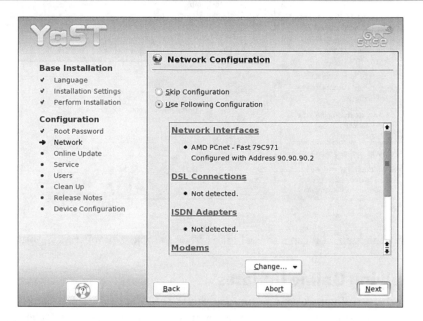

Click Change and select Network Interfaces. Next, select the card you want to modify and click its Change button. Finally, highlight the network card and click Edit. By default, YaST sets up the network card for DHCP, but you may want to use statically assigned values instead:

- To use a static IP address, change the setup method and enter the server's IP address and netmask (see Figure 1.11).

- When not using DHCP, you need to configure a hostname and DNS server information for the server. Click Host Name and Name Server to make the changes; the default hostname is `linux` and its default domain name is `site`.

- Click Routing and enter the IP address of your nearest router in the Default Gateway field.

FIGURE 1.11
Network Address Setup screen.

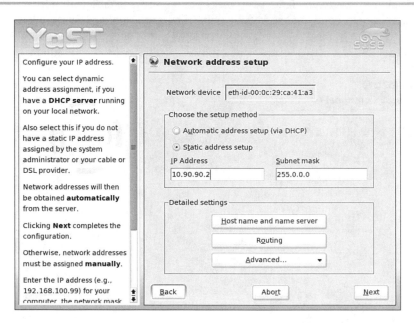

During this step, you can also enable the VNC Remote Administration option.

Applying Online Updates

If you have an Internet connection, you can test the network configuration made in the preceding step and update your system with the online update service. The connection-to-Internet test is performed by attempting to download the SLES release note from SUSE. The success of the Internet connectivity test operation provides confirmation of your correctly configured network card(s).

Configuring Services

The Service Configuration step allows you to configure two services: Certificate Authority (CA) Management and LDAP services (see Figure 1.12). CA management can create a default CA and certificate that can later be used with services, such as Apache, to provide secure connections between the server and its clients. The LDAP service setup creates an LDAP database so you can support LDAP-enabled applications on this server. If you chose not to include the LDAP server during software selection earlier, its setup will not be performed during this step.

FIGURE 1.12
Configuring CA management and LDAP.

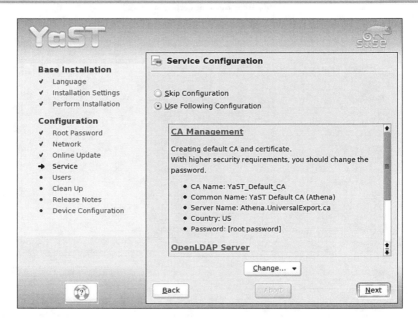

If you choose not to set up these services at this time, you can easily do so later using YaST. Any other services you have selected (such as mySQL) will need to be set up later using YaST or their specific configuration tools.

Configuring User Information

The next step allows you to configure some user-related settings. First, you need to select how a user to your server will be authenticated: via an NIS server, an LDAP server, or using locally stored /etc/passwd information (see Figure 1.13). The default selection is LDAP. If you don't have an NIS or LDAP server on your network or if the users for this server are to be locally managed, select Local as the authentication method; this setting can be easily changed later using YaST.

If you choose NIS or LDAP as the user authentication method, a screen to set up the client is displayed next. Figure 1.14 shows the LDAP client configuration screen.

FIGURE 1.13
Selecting a user authentication method.

FIGURE 1.14
LDAP client configuration.

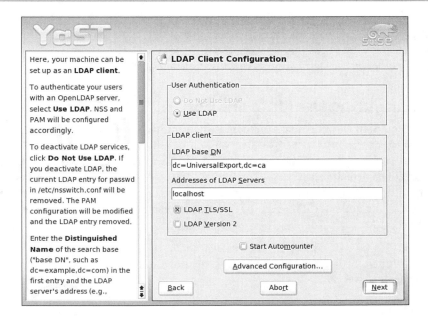

The next screen (see Figure 1.15) asks you to create a new local user (that is, the information will be stored in **/etc/passwd** even though you may have set up NIS as the user authentication method). If you want to create more than one new user at this point, click User Management instead. You can simply click Next and not create a nexnew user for the time being but create users later.

FIGURE 1.15
Adding a new local user.

YaST then updates some configuration files, performs some cleanup, and displays the release note for yournex information.

Configuring Hardware

Finally, YaST performs a hardware probe for graphics cards, monitor, printers, sound, and so on. You can simply accept the results of this check by clicking Next. The next screen (see Figure 1.16) shows that the installation is complete and the server is ready for use.

FIGURE 1.16
Installation completed.

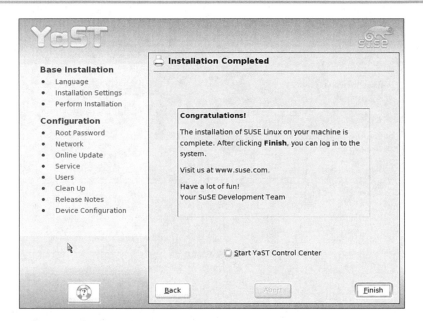

If you have additional hardware to configure or want to jump right into configuring some services, check the Start YaST Control Center check box before clicking Finish.

NOTE

If you perform the installation via VNC, the last configuration module in YaSt (Hardware Configuration) does not probe for the video card or monitor; thus, you will not get the GUI login screen (if you installed GUI support). To remedy this, log in as root at the server console, run init 3, run sax2, and then configure the monitor. Restart the server, and you will now get the GUI login screen.

Troubleshooting

In most instances, SLES 9 installation is trouble-free. However, sometimes things don't go the way you expect. Although any number of things could cause problems, the following are a few of the most common ones and possible workarounds:

- Installation using CD-ROM hangs at about 10–15% when loading data into a RAM disk. The problem seems to occur when using high-speed (52X) CD-ROM drives; the workaround is to switch to a DVD drive or a slower CD-ROM drive (32X, for instance). Alternatively, try a network-based install instead.

- The video screen is unreadable or has multiple ghost images. YaST seems to have trouble determining certain video cards correctly; the workaround is to use Text mode.

- Unexplainable errors occur when the kernel is loading or during the installation. In this case, the problem could be RAM-related. Ensure the memory speed is supported by the motherboard and its timing is set correctly. Use the Memory Test option found in the installation boot menu or the Linux Memtest96 package (`portal.suse.com/sdb/en/2001/05/thallma_memtest86.html`) to perform a prolonged test of your RAM.

- Installation fails to start. Ensure you have at least 256MB of RAM installed. Also try to use the Installation—ACPI Disabled or the Installation—Safe Settings selection instead. The problem could also be caused by bad media.

- The installation process stops abruptly. Try to use the Installation—ACPI Disabled or the Installation—Safe Settings selection instead. The problem could also be caused by bad media.

If you encountered an issue not covered by the preceding workarounds, there are many Internet resources you can consult to see whether anyone else has experienced the same problem and has uncovered a solution. A good place to start is the Google search engine (`http://www.google.com`). Listed in Appendix B, "Resources," are some SUSE-specific Internet newsgroups and websites that you will find useful.

Summary

This chapter covered the necessary steps to install your first Novell SUSE LINUX Enterprise Server 9, starting with the preplanning process, followed by an overview of the various installation methods (such as VNC-based and network-based installs) and then an outline of the actual installation process in 10 simple steps. Finally, some commonly encountered installation errors and workarounds were presented.

Now that you have a new server up and running, the next chapter will guide you through the process of updating the server hardware configuration and modifying software packages.

## CHAPTER 2

Updating the Server

Rare is the system that remains static over its lifetime. Invariably, a server will be assigned to different tasks, moved from location to location, or either upgraded or replaced as more resources are required to perform its current duties. This chapter walks you through the various techniques required to maintain your systems throughout their life cycle.

The main focus of this chapter is to introduce techniques required to perform the following tasks:

- Navigate the two interfaces available for the YaST configuration tool

- Add and remove software components to your base server installation

- Manage critical disk space resources through the addition of additional hardware

- Maintain the network interface

Before we explore the intricacies of YaST, a brief explanation of the way SUSE maintains configuration settings is in order.

Maintaining Your System Configuration

SUSE LINUX Enterprise Server (SLES) maintains information about your system's configuration in the directory /etc/sysconfig. The files and directories present in this location dictate the behavior of the various hardware and software components that make up your server.

When the time comes to reconfigure your server, the files in /etc/sysconfig have to be updated to reflect the change in resources. A proper understanding of the mechanisms involved in making such modification is necessary to allow you to quickly diagnose any difficulties that arise.

SuSEconfig

It is possible to maintain your system manually by editing files residing under /etc/sysconfig and then alerting the system's services of the changes by running SuSEconfig. However, this approach is not recommended unless you have in-depth knowledge of the service you are maintaining and the syntax of its configuration files.

The same configuration files are often required for a number of services. Conversely, one service may depend on multiple configuration files in numerous distinct directories. Making manual changes to one service may have negative effects on others. If you choose to edit the configuration files, make sure to store backup copies first in case of an emergency.

The changes to the static setup files will not affect the functioning of the system until after their services have been restarted. The SUSEconfig utility is invoked to implement the changes.

WARNING

Manual editing of some files is required to gain access to certain advanced configuration features because they are not accessible using the GUI tools. For this reason, you may decide that you would like to maintain some configuration files manually.

It is important that you allow yourself a method for rolling back changes. Making a pre-edit snapshot, or backup copy, of the file you want to change is crucial. In the event of unexpected behavior, the offending configuration file can be quickly replaced without having to rely on the previous days' backups. Depending on the significance of the change, the previous backup media might not be accessible!

Being paranoid is an integral part of system management. Having a quick restore point will save hours of frustration and downtime. Trading a little bit of disk space for peace of mind is a good investment at any time.

SUSEconfig is located in /sbin. This high-level utility invokes the necessary secondary scripts to implement configuration parameters defined in /etc/sysconfig. These scripts, located in the /sbin/conf directory, are named Suseconfig.subsystem-name. Each SuSEconfig script manages one of the subsystems currently installed on the server.

A drawback with SuSEconfig is that it is not the master of all the configuration files found in `/etc/sysconfig`. SuSEconfig does not handle a number of configuration files, notably the ones containing your machine's IP address and volume information.

Limitations in the scope of the SuSEconfig utility, coupled with the intricate nature of modifying multiple files in multiple directories for a single change, make the manual reconfiguration of servers a daunting task. Though servers have been maintained this way for quite some time, a more consistent and efficient automated tool offered with SLES is YaST.

YaST (Yet another Setup Tool)

YaST, as its name implies, is a setup tool for configuring SUSE systems. This utility has been built to present a more intuitive GUI-based environment for maintaining system configuration files. YaST also organizes information drawn from multiple files in different directories into a simple, consistent presentation. This allows you to concentrate on the changes you are trying to make and removes the underlying complexities. Whenever possible, YaST leverages the SuSEconfig utility to manage subsystems.

The YaST configuration tool is accessible through two separate GUI interfaces. The Qt interface is present under the X Windows System, whereas the other uses ncurses and allows a GUI interface in a terminal environment. Both implementations allow you access to the full functionality of the application.

YAST INTERFACES

Both YaST interfaces can be invoked from a terminal session. In an X Windows System terminal session, you invoke the Qt version of YaST by typing yast2 at the command line. Navigation within yast2 is done with the mouse. In non-X terminal sessions, you invoke YaST by simply typing yast. The ncurses version of YaST is navigated using the arrow keys as well as Alt-*letter* combinations, where the letter required is highlighted within the keyword for each menu option.

You might wonder why both interfaces were created. The simple answer is that for a number of server environments, the X Windows System interface is simply not required. Keep in mind that it is imperative to run only the applications required to support a server's tasking. Additional applications can potentially contain vulnerabilities that could compromise the environment.

Also, running these additional applications requires system resources. If the X Windows System interface is not used, the resources it and its associated routines consume would be better dedicated to the server's applications.

On most servers, it is considered prudent not to install the X Windows System or run the server at runlevel 3. On such systems, the ncurses version of YaST allows you to quickly reconfigure the machine with minimal impact on system resources.

You can see the initial YaST menu for both interfaces in Figures 2.1 and 2.2. The main menu for the YaST tool subdivides maintenance into the following main categories:

- **Software**—This section allows you to control what modules are installed on your system, the location of the installation media, as well as how you keep the applications and services up to date. From this selection, you can configure User Mode Linux (UML) as well as your YaST Online Update Server.

- **Hardware**—This section allows you to maintain the different hardware components of your system. Menu options found here cover your server's controller cards for video, sound, and disk. You also can use this section to define peripheral devices such as printers and joysticks.

- **System**—This section of YaST covers your system configuration. It allows you to fine-tune how your system will behave through startup, disk volume, and power management.

- **Network Devices**—This section defines how your server interacts with the outside world. Included in this submenu are server-network interfaces as well as service/appliance connections such as FAX and answering machines.

- **Network Services**—In this section, you maintain the applications that define your server's tasking. You should find configuration options that allow you to customize the services your machine offers. Included are the modules you installed in the Software menu option earlier in this list.

- **Security and Users**—This section allows you to define your password policies, users, groups, your server's internal firewall settings, and the way your server will manage its certificates.

- **Misc**—This catch-all option allows you to view your startup and systems logs in a GUI environment. You can also use this section to define your server as a source server for installations.

The YaST tool provides command-line shortcuts for accessing the configuration options of the various modules. As an example, you can access the firewall configuration screen by starting YaST, selecting the Security and Users menu, and then selecting the Firewall option. Alternatively, you can go directly to the firewall configuration routines by invoking YaST with the "firewall" command-line parameter. The man pages for yast2 discusses the -list option, which, when invoked, reveals a list of the shortcuts to the different submenu options. Though at first navigating from the main YaST screen will be more comfortable, quickly accessing what is required directly will become second nature.

FIGURE 2.1
The ncurses YaST main menu.

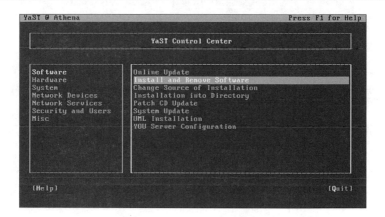

FIGURE 2.2
The X Windows System's YaST main menu.

NOTE

You can find the man page documents for the non-X terminal version of YaST under the yast2 man pages.

SuSEconfig and YaST are tools bundled with SLES that help you configure and maintain your server. Together, the utilities provide a consistent approach and reduce the chances of a forgotten step when multiple changes are required. Now that you have a basic understanding of the YaST tool, it is time to apply this knowledge to everyday system management.

Adding and Removing Packages

Proper maintenance of the different modules that reside on your system helps ensure the reliability of the services you offer. An important step in the configuration of a server is to ensure that only required packages are installed on a system. This has the dual benefit of minimizing resources consumed as well as reducing the possible exposure to exploits in unused packages that tend to be forgotten and therefore not adequately maintained.

How do you know what minimal subcomponents are required to support the main tasking of your server? As a first approximation, this is handled for you by the YaST utility. YaST and the underlying subsystems maintain a list of interdependencies between different packages. If an attempt is made to install or remove a component that is required by a module you need, YaST will warn you.

Installing a Package

The process of adding and removing packages using YaST is fairly simple. As an example, the following walks through the creation of a Domain Name Services (DNS) server. The first step is to build an SLES server and then install the DNS software. Configuring the DNS service is somewhat more complicated and will be covered in Chapter 8, "Network Services."

Continuing with the desire to run only applications that are absolutely necessary, install a server with SLES and choose to install a minimum system. This installs SLES, YaST, and a number of other utilities that make the system easier to administer. To convert this base system into a DNS server, you must add the DNS server software (Bind).

Because the newly installed system is running a base install of SLES, the X Windows System is not available. Sign onto the machine using the root account and start YaST by typing **yast** at the command line. Figure 2.1 shows the ncurses main menu for the YaST tool. You navigate through the tool by using the tab and arrow keys, and when available, highlighted characters represent Alt-keystroke shortcuts. In Figure 2.1, the Install and Remove Software option has been selected.

Pressing Enter at this stage brings up the Install and Remove submenu. By default, the selection screen is filtered by RPM groups. Because the leftmost column for these items is blank in Figure 2.3, you know that they are not installed on this system. If an item is already installed on one of your servers, a lowercase *i* will appear on the left side.

FIGURE 2.3
YaST installed software filtered by RPM group.

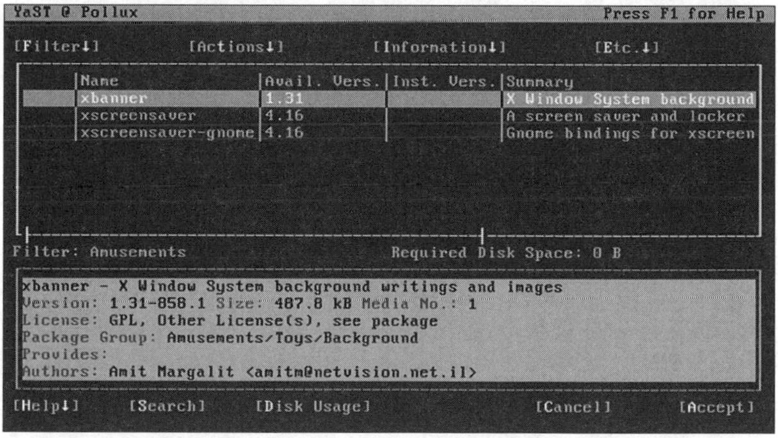

To find the packages already installed on this system, change the filtering option. You can change the filter to show the packages by Selection group by pressing Alt-F and choosing Selections from the drop-down menu, as in Figure 2.4.

After you choose Selections and press Enter, a window appears showing the package groups currently installed (see Figure 2.5). As you can see from the figure, only the base SLES system and YaST are installed on this system.

To install the DNS components required, use the arrow keys to scroll down to the appropriate option and press the plus sign (+) or spacebar to select the package (see Figure 2.6). You can then tab over to the OK button or press Alt-O to continue.

FIGURE 2.4
Changing the Filter setting to present items by choosing Selections.

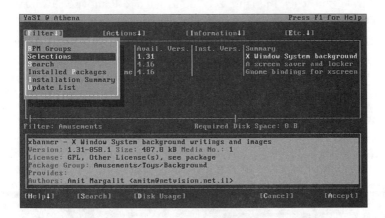

FIGURE 2.5
Installed components for a minimum configuration of SLES.

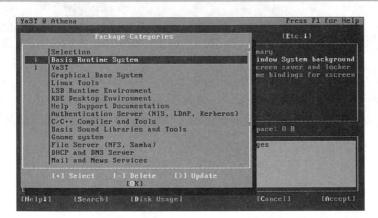

You are then presented with the items contained in the package, as shown in Figure 2.7. If required, it is possible to scroll through these items and remove those not needed. In the current example, simply accept the whole package, select Accept (Alt-A), and continue the installation.

From this stage on, you are prompted for the appropriate media required for the packages selected (see Figure 2.8). If the media is not readily available or if you decide to stop at this point, you can abort the installation by pressing

Alt+R. If you do this, the requested changes will not be committed to the current configuration.

FIGURE 2.6

The DHCP and DNS Server option is selected for installation.

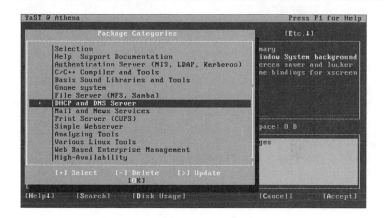

FIGURE 2.7

YaST installation package subcomponent listing.

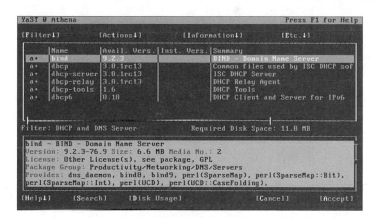

Figure 2.9 shows the progress information of the installation. As each subcomponent is installed, the size, description, and files are displayed.

After all the required components are copied to the server, the appropriate changes are made to the configurations files. As explained earlier, YaST delegates these tasks to the SuSEconfig tool. As each subsystem is affected, YaST logs SuSEconfig's progress, as you can see in Figure 2.10.

FIGURE 2.8
YaST prompt for the appropriate installation media.

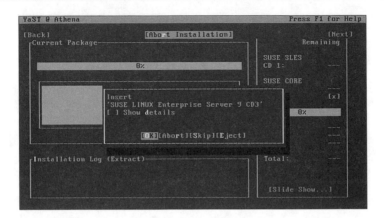

FIGURE 2.9
YaST installation progress screen.

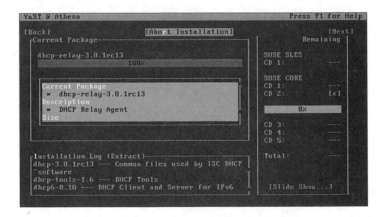

You have now successfully installed the DHCP and DNS package on the server. Before these services can be used, they must be configured. These tasks will be explained in Chapter 8. We will now investigate how unwanted applications can be removed.

FIGURE 2.10
YaST delegates configuration changes to SuSEconfig.

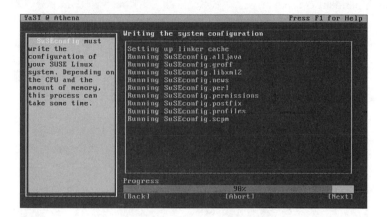

Removing a Package or Subcomponents

The steps required to remove components of the server are similar to those used to install them. In the previous example, you installed the software required for creating a DNS server. At the same time you installed the DNS software, you also installed a DHCP server environment. Due to their interoperability, it is not uncommon to host these applications on the same server. However, since you expect to place this DNS server so that it is accessible from the Internet at large, it would not be prudent to host the DHCP environment on the same server.

To remove the DHCP components, start YaST and navigate to the Install and Remove Software submenu. Change the filtering option to Selections (as you did during the install phase). In addition to the software listed in Figure 2.5, you now have the DHCP and DNS server package installed, as indicated by the letter I in the left column (see Figure 2.11).

To remove the DHCP components, mark the package for update. Highlighting the DHCP and DNS menu option allows you to type a greater-than sign (>) or press the spacebar and select the Update function (see Figure 2.12).

Selecting OK from this screen reveals the list of subcomponents making up the package. This same screen was presented during the install (refer to Figure 2.7). In this case, however, you can select any of the subcomponents for removal. This can be done by entering a hyphen (-) next to the package.

The question of which one to remove first is handled by YaST itself. As components are selected for removal, YaST checks for any dependencies and presents an appropriate warning if necessary. In Figure 2.13, the *DHCP common components* were chosen first for removal. After you select them, YaST presents a list of the dependent components. As you can see, *dhcp-relay* and *dhcp-server* require that the common components be present. By canceling this step and choosing the other dependent packages, you can ensure a clean uninstall.

FIGURE 2.11
Verification that the DHCP and DNS server packages are installed.

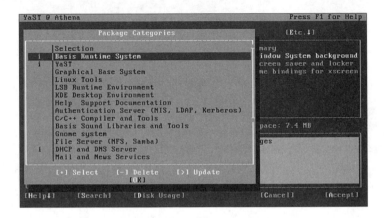

FIGURE 2.12
The Update option is selected for the DHCP and DNS Server package.

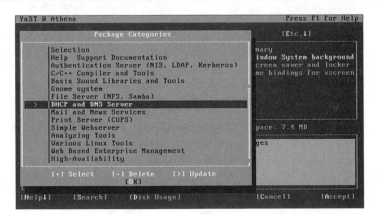

After all the appropriate DHCP components have been marked for removal (see Figure 2.14), you can select the Accept option. YaST then proceeds to remove the identified software and invokes SuSEconfig to manage the changes in the system configuration. At this stage, you should now have a minimum system configuration hosting a single network server process: DNS. We will discuss the configuration of DNS in Chapter 8.

FIGURE 2.13
Component removal dependency warning.

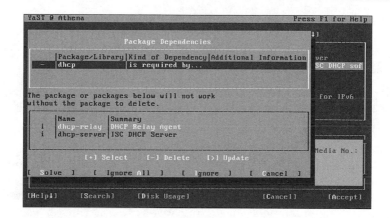

FIGURE 2.14
Identification of components to be removed.

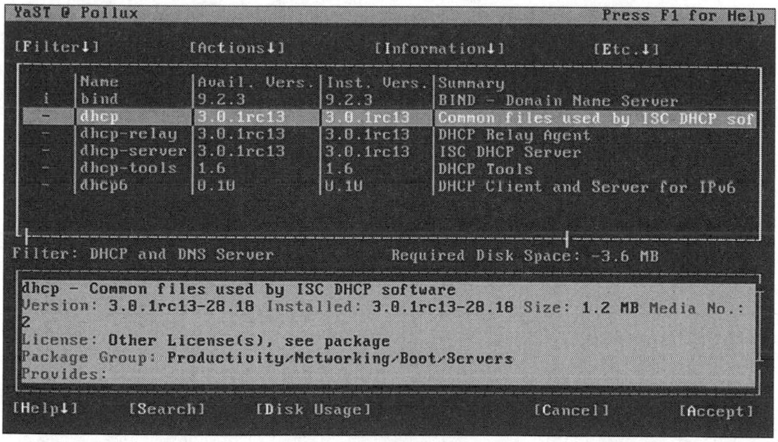

You have seen how YaST can simplify the process of adding and removing application packages on a system. When a system environment is properly configured for its tasking, few changes will be made.

As a system matures and the user community's use of a machine increases, it is not uncommon for a system to run low on resources. The following section examines how you can add devices to a system to solve some of these issues.

Adding and Removing Hardware

The acquisition stage of a new server should include preliminary growth estimates. Capacity planning is an ongoing process and can usually monitor long-term resource consumption. Eventually, either through aging or through the creation of unexpected projects, servers become resource bound.

When possible, a new server will be purchased, with significantly larger capacity, and the functionality transferred to the new machine. In many cases, however, budget or, more typically, time constraints make this impossible.

The most common resource problem is disk space. As users become accustomed to a system or service, they tend to use it more. They copy their local workstation files to the server for proper backups and disaster recovery purposes. In some cases, an individual or department significantly increases its website with new and improved features. Either way, as system manager, you will be required to increase the system's capacity.

The following section examines how additional disk space can be added to a system and targeted to a specific solution. It is understood that additional disk space will have backup and disaster recovery implications. These topics will be covered in Chapter 10, "Data Backup and Disaster Recovery."

Preparations

The most common hardware added to a system is disk space. Other devices you might want to add to your system usually come with vendor-specific instructions for SLES and will not be covered here. Many are peripherals such as scanners, webcams, and audio gear that are not typically incorporated into servers.

For the purpose of this section, we will discuss the concept of a disk as a single physical unit of storage. We will ignore the underlying complexities of how the unit of storage is generated. The "disk" could be simply a single IDE spindle of fixed capacity, or it could be a partition of a larger RAID array managed at the firmware level. In the current discussion, we will treat these as identical in terms of how they are presented to the operating system.

In smaller servers such as a DNS or small web server, it is sometimes simpler to use many of the default install options for SLES. One of the implications of such an installation is that the Logical Volume Manager (LVM) software is not used to configure the environment. LVM allows for the dynamic addition of disk capacity and targets the new disk to specific volume sets on a live system. Though very powerful, such configurations can get very complex and will not be addressed in this section. Additional information on LVM can be found as a series of whitepapers on the SUSE website (`http://www.suse.com/en/whitepapers/lvm/lvm1.html`).

Before you add a disk device to a system, it is important to know where you are going to target the device. When you're building a system, it is good practice to separate, on different devices or partitions, various portions of the directory structure. If, at any point, your / partition becomes 100% used, your system will not be able to operate.

Segregation of the major branches of the / directory help mitigate accidental consumption of critical disk space. Typically, the / level directory on your SLES server contains the entries in the following listing:

```
Athena:~ # ls  /
.   bin   dev   home   lost+found   mnt   proc   sbin   sys   usr
..  boot  etc   lib    media        opt   root   srv   tmp   var
Athena:~ #
```

When you are building a server (see Chapter 1, "Installing SUSE LINUX Enterprise Server"), you have the opportunity of allocating these directories to different locations. On a simple one-disk device system, the default install splits the volume into a swap and a / partition. A more robust approach would be to further partition the single volume into distinct areas to contain the more volatile directory structures. On servers that allow end-user content, placing the /home (user files) and /srv (web content) directories on their own device will balance disk consumption across multiple volumes. If individual devices are not available, placing /home and /srv in separate partitions is still a good idea. The segregation will prevent consumption on one partition from impacting the other. Though you can minimize the risks of a disk-full event through quota management, making the system failsafe is simply the smart thing to do.

Adding a Disk

In our example, a disk will be added to the web server Athena. The current web server will be asked to store a large number of corporate documents instead of the original contact information pages it was originally designed for. A suggested methodology could be as follows:

- A secondary disk is purchased.
- A valid full backup of your system must be performed.
- The disk must be physically added to the machine.
- A valid partition table must be created on the disk.
- The partition(s) must be formatted.
- The formatted partitions must be made live.
- Data must be transferred to the new disk space.
- Reboot and sanity checks are performed.
- User access is restored.

The backup of the system is important because a number of steps in this process could lead to significant data loss or an unbootable system. The physical installation of the disk hardware is machine and interface dependent and will not be covered here. Before the system is shut down, it is important to know the configuration of the disk(s) currently in use on the server. You can accomplish this by using the df command or by looking at the /etc/fstab file:

```
Athena:~ # df -h
Filesystem              Size  Used Avail Use% Mounted on
/dev/sda1               9.4G  2.2G  6.8G  25% /
tmpfs                    93M  8.0K   93M   1% /dev/shm
Athena:~ #
```

Or

```
Athena:~ # cat /etc/fstab
/dev/sda1       /               ext3    acl,user_xattr          1 1
/dev/sda2       swap            swap    pri=42                  0 0
devpts          /dev/pts        devpts  mode=0620,gid=5         0 0
proc            /proc           proc    defaults                0 0
usbfs           /proc/bus/usb   usbfs   noauto                  0 0
sysfs           /sys            sysfs   noauto                  0 0
/dev/dvd        /media/dvd      subfs
➥fs=cdfss,ro,procuid,nosuid,nodev,exec,iocharset=utf8 0 0
/dev/fd0        /media/floppy   subfs
➥fs=floppyfss,procuid,nodev,nosuid,sync 0 0
Athena:~ #
```

fstab **FORMAT**

The fstab file relates physical partitions and information regarding where and how they will be added to a system. Each record in fstab is split up into six distinct sections:

1. The first field identifies the block device to be mounted. This is usually the name of the partition you want to mount (for example, /dev/sda1).

2. The second field indicates the name of the mount point the partition will be associated with (for example, /home).

3. The third field identifies the file system format of the partition. SUSE can recognize a large number of filesystem types such as MS-DOS, ext2, ext3, reiserfs, the CD format iso9660, and many others.

4. The fourth column contains options for the mount command. You can specify that a partition is mounted read-only (ro), mounted read-write (rw), accepts access control lists (acl), and supports user-based quotas (usrquota). Many more options are available—some filesystem dependent. More information on these values can be found in the man pages for the mount command.

5. The fifth field represents a numeric value that is passed to the dump utility. The dump command is used to back up the data on the partition. The value specified here is normally 1 for a level 1 incremental backup. This value can be overridden using your actual backup tool.

6. The sixth and last field controls how the filesystem is checked at boot time. The number represents the order in which partitions are checked. The / partition should be checked first and has a value of 1. Subsequent partitions should have values greater than 1. Because of the parallel nature of the check, partitions on the same device are verified concurrently.

From these listings, you can see that there appears to be only one SCSI disk in the system (*sda*), and it is split into two partitions—namely, / and a swap partition. When the new disk is added, it is given a unique SCSI ID, in this case, 1, and will appear as the second SCSI disk in the system, *sdb*. Had we used an IDE-based system, the disks would appear as *hda* and *hdb*, respectively.

The first procedure is to decide on the low-level configuration of the disk. A partition table contains information on how the disk is subdivided. The simplest way to create a partition table is to use the fdisk utility. You invoke this tool at the command line by using the fdisk verb, followed by the target device name, as shown in Listing 2.1. It is crucial to ensure that you point this utility to the proper device. Failure to do so can result in the corruption of the partition table on an existing device. Detailed information on this utility can be found in the man pages. Once this verb is invoked, the menu m command can be used within fdisk to list the set of internal commands. The possible values available at this time are shown in Table 2.1.

TABLE 2.1
The fdisk Internal Command Set

COMMAND	PURPOSE
a	Toggles a bootable flag
b	Edits bsd disklabel
c	Toggles the DOS compatibility flag
d	Deletes a partition
l	Lists known partition types
m	Prints this menu
n	Adds a new partition
o	Creates a new empty DOS partition table
p	Prints the partition table
q	Quits without saving changes
s	Creates a new empty Sun disklabel
t	Changes a partition's system ID
u	Changes display/entry units
v	Verifies the partition table
w	Writes table to disk and exits
x	Provides extra functionality (experts only)

WARNING

A properly configured and intact partition table is mandatory for a system to function. It is best to be overly paranoid at this stage and triple-check what you are doing. A mistake here can make your server a boat anchor and set you back a considerable amount of time. Ensure that you have a proper disaster recovery plan and have valid backups before going any further.

The following will create a proper partition table for the new disk being added:

Step 1: Look at the existing partition table.

It is not expected that a new disk will contain a valid partition table. If it does, it may be an indication that you have pointed the utility at the wrong volume or you may be using a disk containing data that could be accidentally destroyed. At the console prompt, type fdisk followed by the name of the new volume (**sdb**):

LISTING 2.1

An Example of an fdisk Tool Session

Athena:~ # **fdisk /dev/sdb**
```
Device contains neither a valid DOS partition table, nor Sun,
➥SGI or OSF disklabel Building a new DOS disklabel.
Changes will remain in memory only, until you decide to write
➥ them. After that, of course, the previous content
➥won't be recoverable.


The number of cylinders for this disk is set to 5221.
There is nothing wrong with that, but this is larger than
➥1024, and could in certain setups cause problems with:
1) software that runs at boot time (e.g., old versions of LILO)
2) booting and partitioning software from other OSs
   (e.g., DOS FDISK, OS/2 FDISK)
Warning: invalid flag 0x0000 of partition table 4 will be
➥corrected by w(rite)
Command (m for help):
```

Print out a copy of the current partition table for this disk:

```
Command (m for help): p

Disk /dev/sdb: 42.9 GB, 42949672960 bytes
255 heads, 63 sectors/track, 5221 cylinders
Units = cylinders of 16065 * 512 = 8225280 bytes

   Device Boot      Start         End      Blocks   Id  System

Command (m for help):
```

The **print** command reveals a device with no preexisting partition table. You can now proceed and subdivide the disk. In this case, a partition will be created to contain the user's home directories (**/home**) and another partition to hold the root directory for the web content folders (**/svr**). For this purpose, subdivide the disk in two roughly equal halves.

Step 2: Create the partitions.

Use the **n** verb in fdisk to create a new primary partition. It is essential to create proper Linux-specific entries in the partition table and define the partition types. Failure to do so may generate a scenario in which the disk thinks a partition is vfat but the formatting of the structure is ext3. This will cause con-fusion for the kernel and possibly data loss.

NOTE

The original specification for partition tables allowed a single device to contain up to four partitions. In some instances, such as restricting access to structures, more than four partitions are desirable.

Extended partitions allow for the creation of additional partitions, within a pre-existing partition. When created, the last primary partition can be subdivided into a number of subunits. Each subpartition can then be presented to the operating system and recognized as a real partition.

Adding extra layers of complexity should be discouraged. Large-capacity drives are relatively inexpensive. It is recommended that additional partitions be provid-ed by additional devices instead of using extended partitions.

The software indicates the geometry of the disk. In this case, split it roughly in half:

```
Command (m for help): n
Command action
   e   extended
   p   primary partition (1-4)
p
Partition number (1-4): 1
First cylinder (1-5221, default 1): 1
Last cylinder or +size or +sizeM or +sizeK (1-5221, default
➥5221): 2600

Command (m for help): n
Command action
   e   extended
   p   primary partition (1-4)
p
Partition number (1-4): 2
First cylinder (2601-5221, default 2601):
Using default value 2601
Last cylinder or +size or +sizeM or +sizeK (2601-5221, default
➥ 5221): Using default value 5221

Command (m for help):
```

It is always a good idea to double-check the configuration. This way, you can verify that the type designation for each partition is correct. The partitions are being added to the system to contain standard Linux files. Hence, a type ID of

83 (Linux) is correct. Had you been adding RAM to the system and were required to change the amount of available swap space, you would need to use the type command to change the partition type ID to 82 (Linux Swap). A list of the available partition types can be generated by using the l command shown in Table 2.1.

Though it is possible to place a filesystem of one flavor into a partition marked as a different partition type, doing so is not recommended. By creating the appropriate type of partition, you can verify the nature of a partition before it is mounted into a live system. Mounting a partition with an inappropriate filesystem type will result in data loss and corruption. This is especially true if the mount forces a filesystem check and discrepancies in formatting are interpreted as corruption.

Step 3: Confirm the selections.

Print out the current in-memory version of the partition table before committing the changes to the physical device:

```
Command (m for help): p

Disk /dev/sdb: 42.9 GB, 42949672960 bytes
255 heads, 63 sectors/track, 5221 cylinders
Units = cylinders of 16065 * 512 = 8225280 bytes

   Device Boot      Start         End      Blocks   Id  System
/dev/sdb1               1        2600    20884468+  83  Linux
/dev/sdb2            2601        5221    21053182+  83  Linux

Command (m for help):
```

Now that you have the geometry of the disk as you want it, you need to write the information back to the disk.

Step 4: Commit the new partition information.

The in-memory configuration of the partition table is applied to the physical device through the w (write) command:

```
Command (m for help): w
The partition table has been altered!

Calling ioctl() to re-read partition table.
Syncing disks.
Athena:~ #
```

The last procedure that is required before the disk can be brought online for content is to prepare the partitions for the operating system. To do this, you must configure the partition to obey certain rules governing file structures and the way files are accessed and written. You perform this task by creating a file system on the disk. In the Windows and DOS world, this is known as "formatting."

Step 5: Make a file system for the /home directory structure.

For this step, use the mkfs command. A number of different file systems are available for SLES; they can be found in the man pages. Choosing the correct one for your situation depends on individual corporate policy. For the sake of this example, use ext3.

A good practice is to apply a label to the device partition as you apply the file system. This approach has several benefits. In this case, it could be used to confirm that you allocated the appropriate partition to the intended target before restoring any data.

It is also possible to define a number of additional characteristics for your filesystem. One important consideration is the number of files you expect the partition to contain. Each physical file on the disk is referenced through a structure called an inode. When a filesystem is created, the number of inodes created is based on typical average file size and the size of the partition. If, in your situation, you know that there will be a significant number of very small files, you may need to force a specific inode count. More information on specifying the number of inodes can be found in the man pages for your specific filesystem.

```
Athena:~ # mkfs.ext3 -L HOME -v /dev/sdb1
mke2fs 1.34 (25-Jul-2003)
Filesystem label=HOME
OS type: Linux
Block size=4096 (log=2)
Fragment size=4096 (log=2)
2611200 inodes, 5221117 blocks
261055 blocks (5.00%) reserved for the super user
First data block=0
160 block groups
32768 blocks per group, 32768 fragments per group
16320 inodes per group
Superblock backups stored on blocks:
        32768, 98304, 163840, 229376, 294912, 819200, 884736,
➡ 1605632, 2654208,
        4096000

Writing inode tables: done
Creating journal (8192 blocks): done
```

```
Writing superblocks and filesystem accounting information: done
```

```
This filesystem will be automatically checked every 39 mounts or
180 days, whichever comes first.  Use tune2fs -c or -i to override.
Athena:~ #
```

Step 6: Make a file system for the /srv directory structure.

```
Athena:~ # mkfs.ext3 -L WEB -v /dev/sdb2
mke2fs 1.34 (25-Jul-2003)
Filesystem label=WEB
OS type: Linux
Block size=4096 (log=2)
Fragment size=4096 (log=2)
2632672 inodes, 5263295 blocks
263164 blocks (5.00%) reserved for the super user
First data block=0
161 block groups
32768 blocks per group, 32768 fragments per group
16352 inodes per group
Superblock backups stored on blocks:
        32768, 98304, 163840, 229376, 294912, 819200, 884736,
➥ 1605632, 2654208,
        4096000
```

```
Writing inode tables: done
Creating journal (8192 blocks): done
Writing superblocks and filesystem accounting information: done
```

```
This filesystem will be automatically checked every 29 mounts or
180 days, whichever comes first.  Use tune2fs -c or -i to override.
Athena:~ #
```

The final processes required to incorporate the new device and partitions into the server demand a significant amount of attention to detail. They also require a significant amount of scheduled downtime. To minimize the service outage, you can perform a number of steps before you take down the system.

First, you can create temporary mount points for the new partitions. They are renamed /home and /srv while the system is in single user mode. In addition, you can prepare a new version of **fstab** to mount the new partitions on their proper mount points. This way, you can test the **fstab** file while the system is in single user mode and not have any surprises when the system reboots.

Step 7: Create temporary mount points and check permissions.

```
Athena:~ #
Athena:~ # cd /
```

```
Athena:~ #
Athena:/ # mkdir /new_home
Athena:~ #
Athena:/ # mkdir /new_srv
Athena:~ #
Athena:~ #
Athena:/ # ls -ld *home* *srv*
drwxr-xr-x  7 root  root  4096 Jan 20 08:23 home
drwxr-xr-x  2 root  root  4096 Jan 20 10:40 new_home
drwxr-xr-x  2 root  root  4096 Jan 20 10:40 new_srv
drwxr-xr-x  4 root  root  4096 Jan  5 04:42 srv
Athena:/ #
```

The permissions shown here are correct for files in the root of the filesystem. Users will need read access to the directories. Write access will be granted into subdirectories and below. For the /home structures, users will have write access to their $HOME directory. In the /srv structures, users will be granted access based on the websites they maintain.

Step 8: Clone and add appropriate lines to /etc/fstab.

Clone the fstab file using the cp (copy) command:

```
Athena:/ # cp /etc/fstab /etc/new_fstab
```

Add the new device partitions, their target mount points, their filesystem types, and some default attributes to the new_fstab file. You can do this in any text editor, such as vi.

```
/dev/sdb1    /home       ext3      acl,user_xattr        1 2
/dev/sdb2    /srv        ext3      acl,user_xattr        1 2
```

Step 9: Move to single user mode.

The next step requires that you remove all user access to the file system. This step prevents loss of data in the case of users actively changing content on the server during the switchover. It also has the added benefit of releasing the files used by the web services in the /srv structure. The simplest method for removing all but console access is to bring the system down to single user mode by changing the current runlevel.

Runlevels are covered in more detail in the next chapter. In the current context, a multiuser server is typically at runlevel 3 or runlevel 5 if the X Windows System is active. In single user mode, runlevel 1, the system will have only a minimum number of services running and no interactive sessions other than console access.

For maintenance purposes, the server needs to be transitioned to runlevel 1. You can achieve this by using the init command:

```
Athena:/ # init 1
```

NOTE

Bringing the machine down to single user mode disables all network services on the server. You need physical access to the console environment to continue on from this point.

You can also query the current runlevel of a server by using the runlevel command. The who -r command indicates the current runlevel as well as the previous state.

As an additional precaution, remove the server's network cable from the NIC. If the machine has multiple NICs, ensure that they are labeled and associated with the appropriate card before you remove them. When you are ready to bring your machine back online, you will want to have a few moments for a sanity check on the work performed.

USER MANAGEMENT

You can rest assured that the user community, especially in the case of an Internet-facing web server, will be waiting to pounce on services, even within the downtime window. Any difficulties encountered during the rebuild will generate distracting phone calls from irate users. It is a good idea to take an extra few minutes to check everything first before you reconnect the server to the real world.

Step 10: Switch directories.

This step must be completed in a systematic fashion to ensure that no information is lost and with a minimum amount of downtime. When the system is in single user mode, you must reenter the root password at the console prompt. When you are logged on, you are ready to do the following:

   a. Rename the current directories to a backup version and move the prepared mount points to the appropriate names:

```
Athena:/ # cd /
Athena:/ # mv /home /old_home
Athena:/ # mv /srv  /old_srv
Athena:/ # mv /new_home  /home
Athena:/ # mv /new_srv  /srv
```

b. Back up the active **fstab** and move the new one into position:

```
Athena:/ # mv /etc/fstab /etc/old_fstab
Athena:/ # mv /etc/new_fstab /etc/fstab
```

c. Mount the new disk partitions and attach them to the mount points. For this, you use the **mount** command with the -a parameter. This forces all partitions in /etc/fstab to be mounted. This emulates the state of the mount points after a clean reboot. The **mount** command used here should be the following:

```
Athena:/ # mount -a
```

d. Check to see everything is mounted properly:

```
Athena:/ # df -h
Filesystem          Size  Used Avail Use% Mounted on
/dev/sda1           9.4G  2.2G  6.8G  25% /
tmpfs                93M  8.0K   93M   1% /dev/shm
/dev/sdb1            20G   33M   19G   1% /home
/dev/sdb2            20G   34M   19G   1% /srv
```

Notice the addition of the /home and /srv entries as individual entities and that they both represent 20GB of disk space each.

Step 11: Move the data.

Move the data from the old_ directories to the new disk space:

```
Athena:/ # cd /old_home
Athena:/home # tar cf - * | ( cd /home ; tar xfp -)

Athena:/ # cd /old_srv
Athena:/home # tar cf - * | ( cd /srv ; tar xfp -)
```

You have completed the migration of the data from a directory structure to individual mount points associated with the original names. You are now ready to reboot.

Step 12: Reboot and perform sanity checks.

All the work has been completed at this stage. You now need to confirm the behavior of the system after a restart. This step validates that you did not perform a manual task that is not reflected in the system's normal startup procedures. It also provides a clean shutdown and reinstates the machine to its operational runlevel.

At the console prompt, type **reboot**:

```
Athena:/ # reboot
```

After your system has rebooted, ensure that the new versions of /srv and /home reflect the new configuration. Because they are now mount points instead of traditional subdirectories of /, a df command should show a value for the amount of available disk space for each mount point. An additional quick check would be to test services that depend on the contents that were migrated:

```
Athena:/ # df -h
Filesystem            Size  Used Avail Use% Mounted on
/dev/sda1             9.4G  2.2G  6.8G  25% /
tmpfs                 93M   8.0K   93M   1% /dev/shm
/dev/sdb1             20G    34M   19G   1% /home
/dev/sdb2             20G    34M   19G   1% /srv
```

In one of the preceding steps, you removed the network cables from the server. In some instances, the network environment will not initialize properly without live network cables connected to each NIC. To test, you may need to connect to a test network or simply to a laptop with a crossover cable. This should provide the appropriate signals for the card to initialize properly. You may have to restart the network services before continuing with testing. You accomplish this by rebooting the server or, more gently, by issuing the following command:

```
Athena:/ # /etc/init.d/network restart
```

In the case of Athena being a web server, checking the default server web page as well as accessing a few user public_html directories should suffice. This would verify that the Apache service found both environments and that the permissions associated with the locations are correct. Secondary checks should include testing the users' publishing access to the server through FTP or Samba shares. At this point, you can place the machine back in service. Users should be able to connect to their environment, and all service should be running.

Changing Network Configuration

There are several reasons why you might need to change the network configuration of your server: Your company has changed ISPs, and the server is moving from your intranet to the Internet are possible scenarios.

One of the more frequent reasons is that you have built your server in a test environment behind a firewall. Servers are typically built from original distribution CDs that, over time, become outdated. This has the drawback of generating a first cut of the machine that could present several critical vulnerabilities to the network.

It is essential to mitigate the exposures before the machine can be compromised. As we will see in Chapter 12, "Intrusion Detection," detecting breaches on a server requires having a proper uncompromised image of the system environment. If the machine is exploited before the snapshot has been taken, you may never expose the threat. Building servers behind a paranoid NAT-capable firewall provides additional protection while the system is vulnerable.

Network Parameters

Typically, a machine relies on four main items to enable it to have conversations on a network: a TCP/IP address, subnet mask, routing address, and name server information. Additional information such as the network domain name and domain search order facilitate name resolution but are not essential locally within the server.

In the workstation world, much of this information is provided by DHCP. Servers are usually configured with static information to provide more control over their access and their behavior. In many cases, servers accept connections on specific ports, have a conversation, and close the port. Servers typically do not initiate conversations.

Communications within a subnet depend on a machine's address residing within a common address space defined by a mapping of the TCP/IP subnet and the associated subnet mask. If the matching bit patterns are compatible and machines are on a common network segment, conversations are possible. As an example, machines present behind a NAT firewall are often given a network subnet in the 192.168.x.0 with a network mask of 255.255.255.0, where the NAT device is usually 192.168.x.1. Servers and workstations behind the device are able to communicate with each other using bare TCP/IP addresses without the need to define a gateway address or a name server.

A default gateway, or routing node address, is required only if the machine in question requires access to other machines outside the current network subnet. This is true for answering to conversations initiated outside the current subnet as well. Though a packet can reach a server from the other side of the routing node, the return packets require a hand-off address if the outbound target TCP/IP address is not within the server's own subnet space.

Domain name, domain name search order, and DNS server definitions are all related to the way machines resolve human-legible addresses back into network addresses. They provide the opportunity of managing outbound conversations.

Using YaST to Manage the Network Configuration

YaST provides a graphical method for modifying network settings. When changes are made, YaST ensures the necessary updates are made to the appropriate files throughout the system. You can invoke the X Windows System version by clicking on the YaST icon in the menu system or by invoking `yast2` from the command line. You can also use the LAN shortcut with either `yast` or `yast2` to go directly to the network setup menu.

DEMILITARIZED ZONES (DMZS)

A DMZ is a network that is surrounded on all sides by firewalls. This prevents any traffic from reaching the machines within the DMZ unless they are specifically allowed.

Permissions for TCP/IP conversations to traverse the firewalls are called *firewall rules*. These rules require that the source and target TCP/IP addresses, the protocols, and ports be specified for each allowed conversation.

Typically, a firewall is placed between a hostile network (usually the Internet) and Internet-facing machines such a mail, DNS, and web servers. Traffic within the DMZ is controlled with the local server firewall configuration.

The DMZ machines are in turn considered hostile hosts and are further separated from a company's network by yet another series of firewalls. This back-end firewall controls what, if any, protocols are allowed to access the production network environment. Often web servers require access to a production database. This database server should be in a separate DMZ to further protect its content.

In short, a DMZ is an implementation of a layered defense. The more layers of properly configured protection you have, the better you are protected.

Before proceeding, you need to know what you are changing, why you are changing it, and the new values for each parameter. Table 2.2 shows a typical network configuration change form.

TABLE 2.2
Athena Network Configuration Worksheet

SETTING	OLD VALUE	NEW VALUE	COMMENTS
Server Name	Athena	N/C	Name is unique and ready in external DNS server

TABLE 2.2
Athena Network Configuration Worksheet (continued)

SETTING	OLD VALUE	NEW VALUE	COMMENTS
TCP/IP Address	192.168.1.242	10.1.2.13	DMZ address reserved for web server
Subnet Mask	255.255.255.0	255.255.255.128	DMZ is a Class C
Default Gateway	192.168.1.1	10.1.2.1	Address of outbound firewall
ADDITIONAL INFORMATION			
Domain Name	UniversalExport.ca	N/C	No change
Domain Search 1	universalexport.ca	UniversalExport.ca	Consistency change
Name Server 1	24.226.1.93	10.1.2.10	Managed DNS collection in DMZ
Name Server 2	24.226.1.146	N/A	Only required on the DNS server in the DMZ

The current configuration screen for a server is shown in Figure 2.15. The upper portion of the window shows that there are no unconfigured network cards. The lower portion shows the network cards that have been previously configured and available for changing.

Clicking the Change button brings up an intermediary window showing the network cards resident within the machine. In the case of servers with a single NIC, the required card is already highlighted, and you can select Edit to continue with the reconfiguration. If your server has additional interfaces, select the one you want to change; then select the Edit button.

You are presented with a window similar to that shown in Figure 2.16. The basic TCP/IP information is there for you to edit. At this stage, you can replace the configured IP address with the server's new permanent address. Ensure that the appropriate subnet mask is also configured.

Selecting the Routing button presents you with the window shown in Figure 2.17. At this stage, complex routing is not required, and you can simply update the unique address for the current default gateway and replace it with the DMZ firewall address as per Table 2.2. The firewall will filter outbound packets to ensure that they are of the appropriate type over known and allowed protocols. Select OK to accept the change and return to the network configuration window.

FIGURE 2.15

Initial LAN configuration screen in YaST.

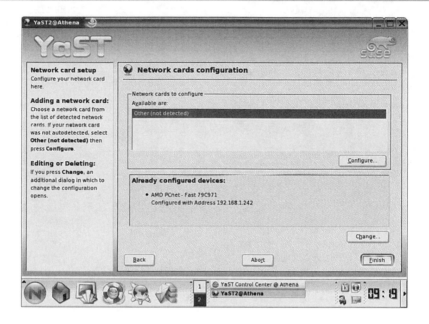

FIGURE 2.16

YaST network configuration window.

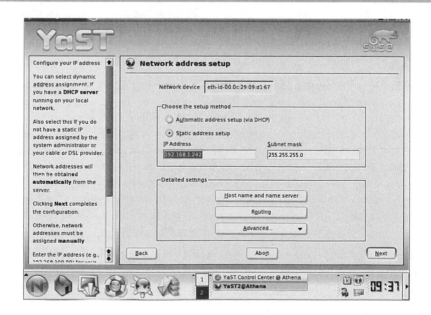

FIGURE 2.17
YaST Default Gateway configuration screen.

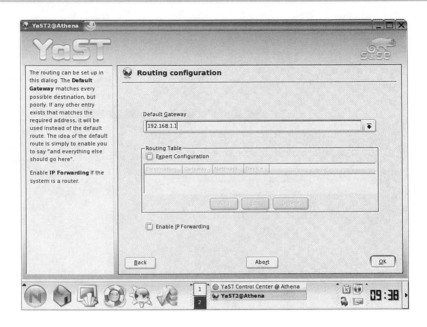

The final step in the reconfiguration is to define the Domain Name Services accessible from this machine. In some configurations, it is acceptable to have servers able to resolve names Internetwide. In most circumstances, having tight control over name resolution can quickly help you identify an improper config-uration, an unidentified requirement or, more importantly, suspicious traffic that might indicate a compromised server.

By pointing name resolution to a single DNS server that does not look beyond itself for name resolution, you have better control over the resulting conversa-tions. In the case of the sample web server, it responds to conversations direct-ly by IP address through ports initiated by requests outside the firewall. The restrictive DNS configuration in the DMZ will prevent any unexpected server-generated conversations from name-resolving hosts and potentially exposing data externally. You can achieve the same effect through a local hosts file and not specifying a DNS server. The current approach, however, allows for consis-tency within the DMZ and a single location to maintain for updates.

You can incorporate the changes identified in Table 2.2 by making the appro-priate modification to the window presented by clicking the Host Name but-ton. You can see an example of the configuration window in Figure 2.18. After you have completed modifications, click OK.

FIGURE 2.18

Host name and name server configuration.

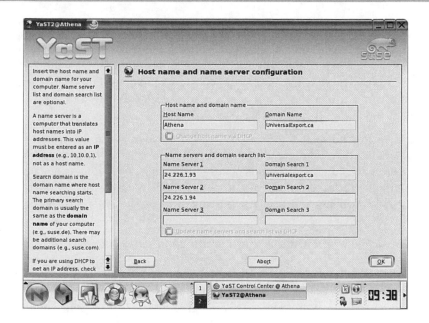

You can apply the combined changes to the system by selecting the Next button on the Network Configuration screen and the Finish button on the resulting network Card Configuration window.

YaST then applies the updates to the appropriate files across the server. YaST will then automatically restart your network services to incorporate the change.You should then be in a position to test access to the server from the new network as well as the name resolution restrictions incorporated in the design.

Summary

Updating servers can be quite a complex task. It is, however, mandatory in order to maintain a secure and robust environment. This chapter touched on a number of the more common configuration tasks. We explored examples of

- Navigating the two interfaces available for the YaST tool
- Adding and removing software modules

- Adding additional storage resources
- Maintaining the network interface

SUSE LINUX provides the YaST tool that can be leveraged to make server configuration tasks easier and consistent across an enterprise. The YaST utility is provided in both an X Windows System and ncurses interface, allowing the use of this tool on even the most minimal of configurations. In the following chapters, YaST will be the tool of choice used to maintain the various services available on SUSE.

This chapter also explored the various steps required to add additional storage capacity to a server. In doing so, we covered a number of topics ranging from disk partitions, filesystems, mount points, and permissions. In moving data from old directories to the new mount points, we have, in essence, covered methods for backing up data and preserving directory structures and permissions.

One of the most important concepts introduced in this chapter revolves around the network connectivity of servers. We introduced the concept of a secure environment for servers to prevent compromises as we build them. We touched on the importance of keeping systems offline as we are maintaining them. The concept of a DMZ was introduced as a standard practice for securing environments exposed to potentially hostile networks.

## CHAPTER 3

Booting and Shutting Down the Server

This chapter explores the various states a server goes through during startup and shutdown procedures. We first examine the path a machine takes from the moment power is applied to a fully running system and how it can be shut down safely.

We also discuss the concept of runlevels and how they are used to control the various applications available on a server. We then explore the preparations required to facilitate system recovery should the server experience difficulties.

As with all things, it is best to start at the beginning: boot loaders.

Boot Loaders

A systematic chain of events is triggered when power is applied to a machine. Commonly, this is called *cold booting* or simply *booting*. As power is applied to the system, a process called the Power On Self Test (POST) is initiated. This stage verifies that the hardware present within the system is operating properly and the saved configuration for the detected hardware within the system matches what is actually preset.

At the end of the POST, control is passed to the Basic Input Output System (BIOS). This small set of instructions loads the stored configuration setting for the various pieces of hardware present within the server. These settings include the date, time, hard drive geometry, and the memory mappings of the various devices.

When this stage has successfully completed, the BIOS loads and executes the instruction found in the Master Boot Record (MBR) of the primary boot device. The MBR is relatively small and is in essence a pointer to the location of the next routine to be executed.

At this point, the SUSE LINUX install passes control over to a piece of software in the MBR that permits the loading of the system kernel. This type of program is called a *boot loader*.

BIOS BOOT DEVICES

Many modern BIOSes allow for a number of boot devices. It is important to ensure that the boot volume for your SUSE server be identified as the first boot device following the install process. This prevents a driver floppy or CD from booting your server into an unknown state in the event of an unscheduled restart.

"The Installation Overview" section of Chapter 1 presented two separate boot loaders available with the default install of SUSE Enterprise Server: LILO and Grub. Both of these routines allow for the targeting of the boot process to a specific boot device, kernel, and unique collection of kernel parameters.

PASSWORDS AND SYSTEM RESTARTS

Passwords can be applied at several levels within a computer. Most modern servers allow for passwords at the BIOS level to prevent unauthorized modification of parameters such as the boot device sequence. This is excellent if you want to prevent someone with physical access to a machine from booting an alternate operating system from removable media. The downside is that you then have another password to keep track of in your disaster recovery password file (see Chapter 10, "Data Backup and Disaster Recovery").

Another level of password protection is available with both boot loaders distributed with SUSE LINUX. This level prevents the selection and execution of a boot process until the proper password is entered. Used in conjunction with the BIOS password, this level offers an attractive protection against a quick local intrusion into the system.

On the downside: This level of password protection will not stop a local attacker with a screwdriver from resetting the BIOS and removing the password. If this is achieved, booting off additional media could lead to a password bypass on the rest of the disk subsystem. Also, having a password on the boot loader will keep the system from rebooting in the case of an unscheduled restart. This may or may not be an attractive feature at 2 a.m.

As always, physical security is a must. If an intruder has access to the machine for an extended period of time, password security, to a first approximation, is moot.

Both LILO and Grub are two-stage boot loaders. The first stage is small enough to be made resident within the Master Boot Record of the volume. Its sole purpose is to properly load the second stage. Though both of these boot loaders have the same goal, there are significant differences in their capabilities. The YaST configuration utility should be used to configure the behavior of both boot loaders.

LILO

The LInux LOader (LILO) is a more static boot loader than its counterpart Grub. The LILO application keeps track of the physical location of the kernel on the volume and stores the reference in a file. At boot time, the application can pass control to the kernel by loading it directly by reference.

LILO maintains a list of possible boot targets in its configuration file. The file /etc/lilo.conf contains both parameters that affect LILO's behavior as well as a list of valid boot targets and kernel options for each.

In the case of a SUSE server, the default configuration includes

- The SUSE kernel and the appropriate parameters that take full advantage of the detected hardware
- A failsafe SUSE kernel with most advanced functions such as ACPI and SVGA turned off
- An 8-second clock for selecting which kernel configuration to use to boot the machine

Listing 3.1 shows a sample LILO configuration from an SLES install. In this example, the header information shows the 8-second (80 tenths of a second) timeout and the default boot option label of Linux. You can also see the removal of APM, ACPI, and other facilities in the Failsafe option. Further details on the options available in lilo.conf can be found in the SLES Administrator's manual as well as on the following web page: http://www.novell.com/documentation/oes/index.html?page=/documentation/oes/sles_admin/data/sec-lilo-overview.html.

LISTING 3.1
Sample LILO Configuration

```
# Modified by YaST2. Last modification on Thu Jan  6 11:40:50
➡2005


message = /boot/message
timeout = 80
prompt
```

LISTING 3.1
Sample LILO Configuration (continued)

```
default = Linux
boot = /dev/sda

image = /boot/vmlinuz
    label = Linux
    initrd = /boot/initrd
    optional
    root = /dev/sda1
    append = "selinux=0 splash=silent resume=/dev/sda3
➥showopts elevator=cfq"

image = /boot/vmlinuz
    label = Failsafe
    initrd = /boot/initrd
    optional
    root = /dev/sda1
    vga = normal
    append = "showopts ide=nodma apm=off acpi=off noresume
➥selinux=0 barrier=off nosmp noapic maxcpus=0 3"

image = /boot/memtest.bin
    label = Memory_Test
    optional
    append = ""
```

At boot time, the boot loader relies on the physical location of the kernel on the device. This location is identified by the actual Cylinder, Head and Sector (CHS) where the kernel resides on the disk. When a kernel is defined in the /etc/lilo.conf file, it is not immediately available for access through LILO. To enable the new kernel, the LILO routine must be run with the -C option. This option will cause the lilo.conf file to be read; the identified kernels will be located on the device and their physical location (CHS) updated in the LILO map file. Failure to perform this extra step will render the new kernel inaccessible at boot time.

Though it may seem a serious limitation to limit kernel accessibility at boot time, it does provide assurance that the selections are those produced through the appropriate routines.

Grub

The GRand Unified Bootloader is more commonly called Grub. This boot loader program is significantly more dynamic than LILO. As you can see in Listing 3.2, there are many similarities between the formatting and information contained in both boot loader configuration files.

In addition to the boot options available through LILO, Grub adds the capability of redirecting the boot to a floppy. Keep in mind that even if you removed the system's capacity to boot off a floppy in the BIOS, this boot loader, once loaded from the primary boot device, presents the floppy as a valid alternate boot device.

NOTE

LILO can be used to boot a system from a floppy if the kernel is also present on the same floppy.

LILO requires a map file to locate the kernel it wishes to boot from. Because the kernel location is not necessarily constant from floppy to floppy, if the boot loader on the primary hard drive is used, the map file stored on the hard drive may not point to the appropriate location should the incorrect floppy be entered in the drive.

GRUB, on the other hand, does not require a map file. Pointing a boot configuration to a known good kernel on a floppy is therefore possible.

Though this is technically possible, you might want to wonder about the validity of doing this. Starting a system from an incorrect kernel could yield disastrous results. Booting from an up-to-date rescue floppy would be the only scenario in which this should be considered acceptable.

LISTING 3.2
Grub menu.lst

```
# Modified by YaST2. Last modification on Wed Jan  5 10:16:38 2005


color white/blue black/light-gray
default 0
timeout 8
gfxmenu (hd0,0)/boot/message

###Don't change this comment - YaST2 identifier: Original
➥name: linux###
title Linux
    kernel (hd0,0)/boot/vmlinuz root=/dev/sda1 selinux=0
➥splash=silent resume=/dev/sda2 elevator=cfq showopts
    initrd (hd0,0)/boot/initrd

###Don't change this comment - YaST2 identifier: Original
➥name: floppy###
title Floppy
    root (fd0)
    chainloader +1
```

LISTING 3.2
Grub `menu.lst` (continued)

```
###Don't change this comment - YaST2 identifier: Original
➥name: failsafe###
title Failsafe
    kernel (hd0,0)/boot/vmlinuz root=/dev/sda1 showopts
➥ide=nodma apm=off acpi=off vga=normal noresume
➥selinux=0 barrier=off nosmp noapic maxcpus=0   3
    initrd (hd0,0)/boot/initrd
```

Grub is different from LILO in that the information in the file is interpreted dynamically as the machine is being booted. This has the benefit of allowing new kernels to be quickly added to the system. The Grub `menu.lst` file can be updated with any text editor, and unlike LILO, no further steps are necessary to make the option available at boot time. Additional information on GRUB can be found in the `man` pages or at the GRUB home page at `http://www.gnu.org/software/grub/grub.html`.

An additional feature available through Grub is the capability to modify the menu entries. Pressing Esc when the graphical Grub menu is present triggers Grub to offer the ncurses version of the boot menu. In this version of the menu, you can edit individual lines controlling the kernel parameters. Instructions on how to do this are provided at the bottom of the boot option screen, as shown in Figure 3.1.

FIGURE 3.1
GRUB edit options available a boot time.

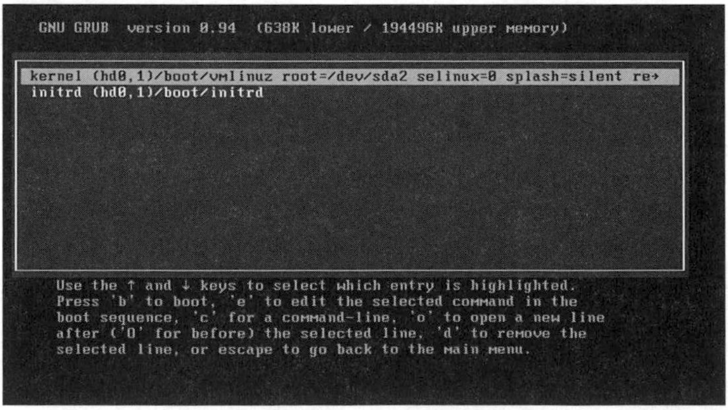

One of the benefits of this option is that you can boot directly into single user mode. In the case of a machine going down for an unknown reason, you can carefully bring up the system in single user mode by dynamically editing the kernel line and adding the word `single` to the end of the line. Boot the system at this point, and you will have a minimally booted environment in which you can perform some diagnostics before trying to bring up the whole system.

Of course, this extra flexibility is also a double-edged sword. Individuals with access to the system can also modify the kernel parameters during the boot sequence. Securing the console should mitigate against this exposure. This can be done through configuring the BIOS, GRUB, or both to require a password at boot time. This approach must be balanced against the physical security of the server and the requirements of having the machine in service. A power failure or unexpected reboot with these options configured would leave the server unable to boot until manual intervention was provided.

Kernel Boot

The next stage in the startup process involves loading the Linux kernel. The boot loader places the kernel in memory as well as `initrd`. As the kernel begins to execute, it unpacks `initrd` into a portion of memory specifically created at runtime to act as a physical disk drive. This new "disk" is then mounted as an initial root partition. This is done to facilitate the identification loading of modules the kernel will need to access the actual system / partition. Building all vendor and architecture disk device drivers right into the kernel would make it unacceptably large and inefficient. This preliminary look-ahead step using `initrd` allows for the dynamic loading of the appropriate module at boot time.

When the proper drivers are available to the kernel, the `initrd` RAM disk is unmounted, the memory reclaimed, and the proper / partition mounted. Before passing control over to the `init` routine, the kernel performs a series of steps to identify and load additional modules it will need.

To see the messages generated by the kernel when the system was started, you can use the `dmesg` command. This will list several hundred lines of device discovery and status information as the server starts up. The following is a synopsis of kernel messages generated during a typical boot sequence:

- Checks the BIOS for a memory configuration
- Turns on ACPI and other kernel parameters as described by the boot loader parameters
- Starts CPU 0 and looks at its properties
- Initializes the console to 80x25 characters
- Checks the various busses for device and IRQ assignments
- Scans for devices on the IRQs (serial ports, floppies, audio, and so on)

- Detects disk drives and network cards
- Loads appropriate modules for the system
- Starts the `init` process

As the kernel loads, it dynamically loads the appropriate modules for the detected hardware. A careful review of the `dmesg` output will identify any serious errors that must be resolved.

After the kernel has finished loading all appropriate modules, it then passes control over to the `init` process. In the next section, we examine how this new startup process loads the remaining portions of the SLES install and makes it ready for use.

`init` and Understanding Runlevels

It is difficult to discuss the `init` program without first having an understanding of what it controls. The `init` process is invoked by the kernel itself and becomes the parent of all other processes on a machine. At startup, the `/etc/inittab` file is interpreted by `init` and all identified routines are processed. The default runlevel for the system is maintained within `inittab`.

You can think of a Linux operating system runlevel as the "application state" of the machine. For each distinct state, select processes are functional. Table 3.1 displays the known list of runlevels and their impact on user access.

TABLE 3.1
RunLevels

RUNLEVEL	SCRIPT DIRECTORY	DEFINITION
0	rc0.d	System is stopped
S	rc1.d	Single user mode accessed from the boot prompt
1	rc1.d	Single user mode
2	rc2.d	Multiuser mode but no network available
3	rc3.d	Multiuser mode with full network access
4	rc4.d	N/A, an unused runlevel
5	rc5.d	Multiuser network enabled including the X Windows System
6	rc6.d	Forces a machine to reboot

You initiate transitions between states by running the `init` routine followed by the runlevel. Each transition, in turn, changes which processes are running. The application startups or shutdowns triggered by a change in the runlevel are managed through a series of script files. The directory `/etc/init.d` is the base directory for a collection of directories, each of which, represents a distinct runlevel. Within each level's directory resides a collection of appropriate scripts for the applications required for the specific runlevel.

When the system enters a particular state, it initiates all the appropriate routines for that state by executing all the script files that begin with the letter `S` (Start) in the corresponding directory.

Similarly, when the system is leaving a source level for another, the scripts residing in the source directory beginning with the letter `K` (Kill) are processed. This ensures that all applications that are supposed to run only in a particular level are shut down properly before the system moves onto the next runlevel.

The one exception is one of efficiency. If a start script for a specific application exists in the target level, the stop (Kill) script in the source level is ignored.

As an example, you can examine the change of state from runlevel 3 and runlevel 5 on the `xdm` application. `Xdm` is the X Windows System display manager. Referring to Table 3.1, X is available only at runlevel 5. Listing 3.3 show the files associated with `xdm` in the `/etc/init.d/rc5.d` directory.

LISTING 3.3
`xdm` Files Associated with Runlevel 5

```
Castor:/etc/init.d # ls -l rc5.d | grep -e xdm
lrwxrwxrwx   1 root root    6 Jan  5 04:53 K06xdm -> ../xdm
lrwxrwxrwx   1 root root    6 Jan  5 04:53 S16xdm -> ../xdm
Castor:/etc/init.d #
```

From Listing 3.3, it is possible to see that `xdm` is both started and stopped as the system enters or leaves runlevel 5. What is also apparent is that both the startup and shutdown scripts are simply links to the same script residing in `/etc/init.d`. This linking minimizes duplication of the scripts, ensuring a consistent application startup and shutdown independent of target runlevel.

The `init` process can therefore be defined as a tool used to control which applications are active on a system. You can identify which applications are active within a runlevel by looking at content of the subdirectory for the level in question.

System Shutdown

One of the most important factors in the health of a system is ensuring that the data and configuration it contains are protected from corruption. It is therefore important to ensure that all applications have terminated successfully and that all their respective files are properly closed. All this must happen before the system unmounts the associated drives and powers off.

Most device input/output is handled in a similar matter across the server. Improperly closed files will not contain the information expected. This could lead to the improper functioning of applications dependent on said files.

One of the most common mistakes on Linux/Unix systems is to manually eject removable media before it is dismounted (`umount`). When this is done, data still stored in the buffers of the device driver cannot be written to the device. Even immediately reinserting the media might not maintain the proper machine state, and the data is therefore lost. To make matters worse, in many cases, the directory structure itself is memory resident. Not writing this structure back to the device properly could mean compromising the directory's contents as well.

The same phenomenon happens with nonremovable media if the system is shut down abruptly. Great strides have been made with new file systems to protect from such losses. Consistency checks at boot time can also repair some of the damage. It is best, however, to perform an orderly shutdown at all times.

Two methods can be used to properly shut down a server. The first method is to use the `init` command with a parameter of zero, as shown in Table 3.1. Though this method stops all processes, it should be used only in extreme circumstances because the shutdown is rather abrupt.

A more graceful way to bring down the system is to use the **shutdown** command. This command brings down the system in a more orderly fashion, gives end users a proper notification of the shutdown, and forewarns other running applications to close open files. Once **shutdown** has been invoked, new login sessions are refused. A simplified format of the **shutdown** command is

```
shutdown [-h or -r] time [shutdown message]
```

In this example, the **-h** implies that the system will be halted after the shutdown and **-r** indicates that you would like to reboot. The **time** parameter in the command is a required field and can be the keyword **now**, a time specified in **hh:mm** format, or a specific number of minutes from now in **+mm** format. When a delay is specified in the command, **shutdown** will create an `/etc/nologin` file. Users will also be reminded of the shutdown every time half of the remaining uptime has expired. As an example, a time period of 10 minutes will see a message broadcast to interactive sessions at one-minute intervals. If the keyword now is used on the command line, no warnings, other than the first, are issued.

The last parameter is an optional message that will be sent to all currently logged-on users informing them of the shutdown. The content of the message is at your discretion.

Listing 3.4 shows a comment entered at the console by the root user as well as a notification received by all logged-on users.

LISTING 3.4
Comment Entered at the Console

```
Athena:/etc # shutdown -h +10 "Memory upgrade. Please log off"

Broadcast message from root (pts/1) (Mon Mar 21 10:38:58 2005):

Memory upgrade. Please log off
The system is going DOWN for system halt in 10 minutes!
```

The proper shutdown of a system is necessary to minimize difficulties when you restart it. Using init 0 to shut down the system does not allow other running processes sufficient time to apply any pending changes and close their files properly. This can lead to file corruption and data loss. The preferred method would be to use the shutdown command.

The interpretation of keystroke sequences is dependent on physical access to the server as well as which version of Linux is being run. In SUSE LINUX, it is possible to use YaST to configure a response to the Ctrl+Alt+Del sequence. This should be disabled as it is preferred, in almost all cases, to control the shutdown through software instead of hardware.

Emergency Boot and Recovery

The events that orchestrate a proper, clean boot sequence are numerous. Proper daily care of your server prevents many of the potential pitfalls. Murphy's Law, which states that if anything can go wrong, it will at the most inopportune time, certainly applies to the computing environment. Before this happens, you should have a plan.

Backups and disaster recovery will be covered in depth in Chapter 10. Before recovery can happen, you will need a bootable system and access to the devices. In most cases, you will need to get access to the system to investigate the cause of the outage before you worry about possible recovery.

The simplest cases are usually self-inflicted. For example, a kernel name was mistyped in the Grub configuration file (see Figure 3.2) . Because you can edit this information at boot time, you can correct the information, boot the system, and edit the proper files to ensure the correction is made permanent. Though GRUB is gaining in popularity, LILO is not subject to this type of misconfiguration. With LILO, the kernel file must be accessible in order for it to be added to the map file. This eliminates the chance an invalid kernel will be presented at boot time.

FIGURE 3.2
Mistyped kernel name in the GRUB configuration file.

```
        Booting command-list

kernel (hd0,1)/boot/vmlinu root=/dev/sda2 selinux=0 splash=silent resume=/dev/s
da1 elevator=cfq showopts

Error 15: File not found

Press any key to continue..._
```

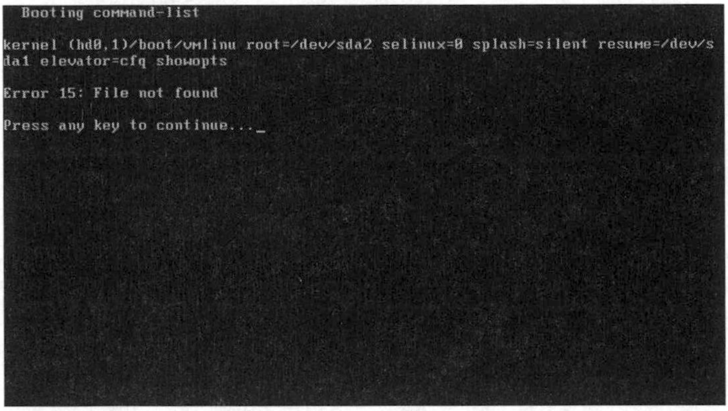

In more difficult cases, something has happened to impede the normal boot process, and the server cannot invoke the normal boot loader. More commonly, the boot process does not complete successfully. In these instances, a separate boot environment is required. The YaST configuration tool can be used to create a rescue floppy, module floppies for nonstandard drivers, as well as a set of standard SUSE boot floppies.

It is strongly suggested that once a system is properly configured, a rescue floppy is created. The recovery process for your server will depend on it. Every time a significant change is made to your system configuration, it is important to create a new rescue floppy. It is a good idea to retain the original should your new configuration prove problematic.

Similarly, if your configuration requires specialized drivers or additional modules to function properly, you will need to make floppy versions of them as well.

NOTE

Because you can boot your system directly from DVD or the first install CD should your boot floppies become inoperable, you will still be able to access your drives.

In such circumstances, you will have bypassed your normal boot routine. Configuration settings such as TCP/IP address and services to start at boot time will have been ignored.

Having an additional set of rescue floppies will allow you to start your system properly.

In the event of a disaster, booting from the distribution DVD/CD or the YaST boot floppies should be possible. During the boot process, you are prompted for the type of installation you would like to perform. One of the options presented is to rescue the system. Once initiated, the rescue system prompts for the rescue disk and additional module disks as required.

At the conclusion of this phase, access to the disk subsystem of the server should be accessible. Investigating the cause of the failure can now begin. In the simplest case, you can get into the appropriate configuration file and fix your error. In most cases, however, things tend not to be so simple.

Boot failures on static, stable systems are caused by hardware failures. It is beyond the scope of this chapter, and possibly this book, to explore the various causes of a system outage. Chapter 10 will explore in more detail the recovery process.

Summary

In this chapter, we examined the processes involved in booting up an SLES server. The major steps are the POST, BIOS, `initrd`, the boot loader, the kernel load, and the `init` process. A proper understanding of the role of each process will facilitate the diagnostic phase should a failure occur.

When a system shutdown is required, it is important to ensure that the shutdown is performed in a controlled manner to avoid file corruption and data loss. There are several options available for halting a system. The preferred method is to use the `shutdown` command. This utility provides for the proper notification of the shutdown to system users.

We also introduced the steps necessary to provide alternate access to the system should a problem arise in the startup process. Additional techniques for recovery are discussed in Chapter 10.

PART II

User Access and Security Management

## CHAPTER 4

User and Group Administration

As the system administrator of a multiuser system, you are responsible for, among many other tasks, managing and controlling user access to system resources. Because SLES is a multiuser system, this chapter provides you with an understanding of how users and groups are identified, how this information is used to determine access privileges to data and applications, and how you can effectively manage user and group information. The following topics are covered in this chapter:

- User and group IDs
- System users versus regular users
- The /etc/passwd, /etc/shadow, and /etc/group files
- Ways to create and update user and group information using YaST and command-line tools
- User account security considerations

User and Group IDs

Each user and group in SLES is assigned a unique numeric value because it is much easier for the operating system to deal with numbers than text strings. The number associated with a user is called a *user ID (UID)* and the number assigned with a group is called a *group ID (GID)*. By default, SUSE LINUX (all versions) assigns UIDs to regular (nonsystem) users starting at 1000, and GID assignments starting at 100.

The Linux standard reserves the UID range from 0 through 99 for the system itself, and the range 100 through 499 for special system users (such as services and applications). To allow room for future expansion, SUSE LINUX thus starts regular user ID values at 1000 (and ends at 60000, by default; the maximum upper limit is 65535). Table 4.1 shows the SLES-created system users, their UIDs, and their primary GIDs.

NOTE

Every Linux (and Unix) system has a special, privileged user called **root**. The root user always has a UID of 0 (zero). There are no special or reserved group names in Linux.

WARNING

Because the operating system identifies users by their UID, different usernames with the same UID are considered to be one and the same. Consequently, you can set up additional root users by assigning a UID of 0 to these users. By the same token, if you accidentally (or someone maliciously) made a user's UID equal to 0, you have granted that person unlimited privileges over the system. As a precaution, you should periodically audit /etc/passwd (and your LDAP/NIS databases, if you are using them for authentication) to ensure only root and designated users have a UID and GID set to 0. Bastille, mentioned in Chapter 13, "System Security," can be used to automatically detect unauthorized duplicate root accounts.

If you need to set up multiple administrators, it is best to either assign these users to a special group (such as the root group) that has been granted the necessary rights or preferably use sudo (as discussed in Chapter 5, "User Environment Management and Security."

TABLE 4.1
SLES Default System User Settings

USERNAME	UID	PRIMARY GID	DESCRIPTION
root	0	0	The root (super) user
bin	1	1	Used by system services, such as lpd
daemon	2	2	Background service
lp	4	7	Printing daemon
mail	8	12	Mailer daemon
news	9	13	News system
uucp	10	14	Unix-to-Unix CoPy system

TABLE 4.1

SLES Default System User Settings (continued)

USERNAME	UID	PRIMARY GID	DESCRIPTION
games	12	100	Games account
man	13	62	Manual pages viewer
at	25	25	Batch jobs daemon
postgres	26	26	PostgreSQL Server
mdom	28	28	Mailing list agent (Majordomo)
wwwrun	30	8	WWW daemon apache
squid	31	65534	WWW-proxy squid
amanda	37	6	AMANDA (backup utility) admin
irc	39	65534	IRC (Internet Relay Chat) daemon
ftp	40	49	FTP account FTP server daemon
named	44	44	Name server (DNS) daemon
gdm	50	15	Gnome Display Manager daemon
postfix	51	51	Postfix daemon
mysql	60	2	MySQL database admin
vscan	65	102	Vscan account used by samba-vscan
pop	67	100	POP admin
sshd	71	65	SSH daemon
Mailman	72	67	GNU mailing list manager
Snort	73	68	Snort network monitor
Ntp	74	65534	NTP (Network Time Protocol) daemon
Ldap	76	70	User for OpenLDAP
Hacluster	90	90	High-Availability cluster heartbeat processes
Cyrus	96	12	User for cyrus-imapd
Stunnel	100	65534	Daemon user for stunnel (universal SSL tunnel)
quagga	101	101	Quagga routing daemon
dhcpd	102	65534	DHCP server daemon
radiusd	103	103	Radius daemon
nobody	65534	65533	Special user for assigning NFS permissions

When you log in to Linux, your active, or current, GID is set to the primary (or default) GID as specified in the user database (such as /etc/passwd), even though you may be a member of multiple groups. The operating system calculates a user's access permissions to files based on the current GID. You can change your active GID to a new one by using the newgrp command, as follows:

```
newgrp groupname
```

NOTE

Although usually used to switch your UID to that of the root user, the su command may be used to switch your active UID to that of another user (su *username*). If you're currently root, no password is required; otherwise, you will need to supply the password of that user.

If *groupname* is not given, the GID is switched back to the primary GID. After you switch to a new group successfully—you must be a member of the group, or be root, to do so—all your actions from then on will have the permissions of that new group. For example, if you create a new file or directory, the group of the new file or directory will be "*groupname.*"

Upon executing the newgrp command, you remain logged in, the current directory is unchanged, and a new shell is created. Some implementations of newgrp *always* replace the current shell with a new shell, even if the command terminates with an error (such as when an unknown group was specified). Consider the confusion that may result: Are you in a new shell and need to use the exit command to return to your original shell, or are you still in your original shell where the exit command would terminate your current session? SUSE's implementation avoids this problem by not creating a new shell should the command fail.

To return to the previous GID and shell, use the exit command and not newgrp; otherwise, you start yet another shell. The following illustrates the effects of the newgrp command:

```
Athena:/home/admin # #display my UID, GID, and groups I belong to
Athena:/home/admin # id
uid=0(root) gid=0(root) groups=0(root),64(pkcs11)
Athena:/home/admin # #show my currently running processes
Athena:/home/admin # ps
        PID TTY          TIME CMD
       7853 pts/1     00:00:00 bash
```

```
           7875 pts/1    00:00:00 ps
Athena:/home/admin # #change group to wheel
Athena:/home/admin # newgrp wheel
Athena:/home/admin # #check my current settings:
Athena:/home/admin # #wheel is now my current GID
Athena:/home/admin # id
uid=0(root) gid=10(wheel) groups=0(root),10(wheel),64(pkcs11)
Athena:/home/admin # #and I have one extra bash shell running!
Athena:/home/admin # ps
       PID  TTY           TIME CMD
       7853 pts/1    00:00:00 bash
       7877 pts/1    00:00:00 bash
       7885 pts/1    00:00:00 ps
Athena:/home/admin # #return to previous setting
Athena:/home/admin # exit
exit
Athena:/home/admin # #and the extra bash shell is gone too
Athena:/home/admin # id
uid=0(root) gid=0(root) groups=0(root),64(pkcs11)
Athena:/home/admin # ps
       PID  TTY           TIME CMD
       7853 pts/1    00:00:00 bash
       7886 pts/1    00:00:00 ps
```

When you return to your original shell, its previous environment (such as shell variables and working directory) is preserved; you are returned to the exact state you were in just before you started the new shell.

NOTE

The user is prompted for a password if the group has a password and the user is not listed in the /etc/group file as being a member of that group. The only way to create a password for a group is to use the passwd utility and then cut and paste the password from /etc/shadow to /etc/group. Group passwords are antiquated and not often used, but they provide a means for a user who is not listed as a member to take on the identity of that group.

Linux reserves the GID range from 0 through 10 for system groups. Similar to UIDs, by default, user-created groups start with a GID of 1000, and the GID value can be as high as 60000. Table 4.2 shows the SLES-created system groups and their GIDs.

TABLE 4.2

SLES Default System Groups and Their GIDs

GROUP NAME	GID	COMMENTS
Root	0	This is the set of privileged users who are granted special powers in the system. By default, root is the only member of this group. On some Linux distributions, the wheel group is used instead.
Bin	1	This group exists for historical reasons, and some programs (such as shutdown) won't run without it. SUSE LINUX does not use this group.
Daemon	2	This group is used by various services and applications, such as mySQL, that do not run with root privileges.
Sys	3	This group exists for historical reasons, and some programs won't run without it.
Tty	5	The terminal devices with names beginning with /dev/tty are group accessible to the tty group. Programs such as write and wall need access to /dev/tty* and they set their group id (sgid) to tty.
Disk	6	The disk device nodes are group accessible to the disk group. Programs that need access to them set their GID to disk.
Lp	7	Jobs associated with the lp (printer) daemon (lpd) are group accessible to the lp group so that lpd can access them without being root.
www	8	This group is generally used to assign rights to folders containing HTML documents.
Kmem	9	This group is mostly used by programs that need access to /proc/kmem (kernel memory).
Wheel	10	Some Linux distributions use the wheel group instead of the root group for users with systems privileges.
Mail	12	The mail spool directories are group accessible to the mail group. Programs that need access to them set their GID to mail.
News	13	The Usenet news spool directories are group accessible to the news group. Programs that need access to them set their GID to news.
Uucp	14	Group members can initiate uucp jobs.
Shadow	15	Group members have rights over the shadow password file, /etc/shadow.
Dialout	16	Group members are allowed to initiate dialout connections using ppp or ISDN device nodes.

TABLE 4.2

SLES Default System Groups and Their GIDs (continued)

GROUP NAME	GID	COMMENTS
Audio	17	Members in this group have rights over the sound card/device.
Floppy	19	Users in this group can use the floppy drive (generally /dev/fd0, the first drive).
Cdrom	20	This group can use the CD-ROM drive.
Console	21	
Utmp	22	Members in this group can access user login and logout records.
At	25	This group is used by at, a system task scheduling program.
Postgres	26	This group is used by the Postgres SQL database daemon.
Mdom	28	This group is used by the Majordemo mailing list daemon.
Public	32	This group is used by the ProFTP daemon to control file access when a client is logged in as anonymous.
Video	33	Members in this group have rights over the video card/device.
Games	40	This group is used by games that store user-independent high-score values in /var/lib/games.
Xok	41	Members in this group may run X Windows System applications.
Trusted	42	Members of this group can execute the ncpfs binaries.
Modem	43	This group can use the modem device.
Named	44	This group is used by the DNS daemon.
ftp	49	This group is used by the FTP daemon.
Postfix	51	This group is used by the Postfix mail daemon.
Maildrop	59	This group is used by the Maildrop mail daemon.
man	62	This group is used by the manual page facility.
pkcs11	64	Members of this group can manage security certificates. The root user is the default member of this group.
Sshd	65	This group is used by the SSH daemon.
Mailman	67	This group is used by the GNU mailing list daemon.
Snort	68	This group is used by the Snort network monitor.
Ldap	70	This group is used by the OpenLDAP daemon.
Ntadmin	71	This group is used by the Samba daemon.
Haclient	90	This group is used by the High-Availability cluster daemon.

TABLE 4.2
SLES Default System Groups and Their GIDs (continued)

GROUP NAME	GID	COMMENTS
Users	100	This is the default group that **all** users are added to (unless you change the setting in /etc/default/useradd). All the members of this group are provided basic privileges in the system as defined by the system administrator. You place files that all users should have access to in this group.
Quagga	101	This group is used by the Quagga routing daemon.
Vscan	102	This group is used by the vscan daemon.
Radiusd	103	This group is used by the radius daemon.
Nobody	65533	This group is used by NFS.
Nogroup	65534	This group is used by NFS.

User and Group Data Files

Linux stores local user and group information in text files in the /etc directory. Traditionally, user information (including passwords) is stored in the /etc/passwd file, and group information is found in the /etc/group file. However, the /etc/passwd file contains information (such as the comment field, which generally contains the user's full name and the UID of a user) that has to be readable by anyone. At the same time, you don't want passwords world-readable because this capability gives would-be crackers a good place to start (for example, using a password-cracking tool as discussed in the "Be a Cracker Jack" section later in this chapter). So the passwords in newer implementations of Linux (such as SLES) are kept in the shadow file (/etc/shadow), which is readable only by root, and everyone's password is entered into the /etc/passwd file as "x."

WARNING

You should *not* directly edit any of the /etc/passwd, /etc/group, and /etc/shadow files—especially /etc/shadow. Any error in these files may lead to the affected user, including root, no longer being able to log in. Instead, you should use the supplied system tools, such as YaST and the user* utilities (such as useradd) discussed later in this chapter.

NOTE

The three files discussed in this section are used only for users and groups that are *local* to the system. If you use LDAP or NIS authentication methods, users and groups created under these protocols are not stored in these three /etc files, but in the LDAP or NIS database instead.

Next, we examine the record structure of each of these three data files.

The /etc/passwd File

Each line in the /etc/passwd file corresponds to an entry for one person, and fields on each line are separated by a colon. The following is a sample record:

```
eric:x:1000:100:Eric the Webmaster, Room 215a, 555-1212, N/A,
➥other info:/home/eric:/bin/bash
```

The fields, from left to right, are the login name, hashed password, user ID, primary group ID, comment field (officially referred to as the GCOS field), home directory, and default or login shell. The presence of an "x" in the password field indicates that the shadow password file is used; some implementations use an asterisk (*) instead.

WHAT IS THE GCOS FIELD?

The GCOS field has no defined syntax and is generally used for personal information about the user, such as full name, phone number, room number, and so on. Often, the finger utility uses the information stored in this field.

Delimited by commas, finger interprets the information in the GCOS field as follows: user's full name, office location, office telephone number, home phone number. Any additional fields are considered as "other information," and this Other field is not displayed by finger. The following is sample output from finger for user eric:

```
Athena:/home/admin # finger eric
Login: eric                        Name: Eric the Webmaster
Directory: /home/eric              Shell: /bin/bash
Office: Room 215a, 555-1212        Home Phone: N/A
Last login Mon Sep 20 23:10 (EDT) on :0 from console
No Mail.
No Plan.
```

The acronym GCOS comes from GECOS, or General Electric Comprehensive Operating System, a mainframe operating system. This was later changed to

---

General Comprehensive Operating System (GCOS) when GE's large systems division was sold to Honeywell. The name is mostly a nostalgic residue from using the comment field in the /etc/passwd file to store identification data for submitting print jobs or batch jobs from Unix to GCOS machines.

As a security measure, some sites populate the GCOS field with the user's full name and phone numbers but disable the `finger` daemon (see Chapter 8, "Network Services," on how to enable/disable various services). Or, TCP/UPD port 79 is blocked at the perimeter firewall so the GCOS information is only available internally but not to an external query. In most cases, only the user's real name is listed in the GCOS field.

CAUTION

For backward compatibility with older applications and Linux/Unix implementations, the login name should be eight or fewer characters even though Linux can handle longer names.

The /etc/passwd file can contain a line (usually the last line in the file) beginning with a plus (+), which means to incorporate entries from Network Information Services (NIS). There are two styles of + entries. A single + means to insert the entire contents of an NIS `passwd` file at that point:

```
+::::::
```

A line of the form *+name* means to insert the NIS entry (if any) for that username. If a + entry has a non-null field (such as the default shell), the data in that field overrides what is contained in NIS. In the following example, user ted's UID, primary GID, GCOS data, and home directory information will come from NIS, but he will be assigned a default shell of /bin/csh regardless of the setting in NIS:

```
+ted::::::/bin/csh
```

NOTE

All fields in the + entry may be overridden *except* for the user ID.

The /etc/passwd file can also contain lines beginning with a minus (-). These entries are used to disallow user entries. There is only one style of - entry; an entry that consists of *-name* means to disallow any subsequent entry (if any) for *name*. These entries would disallow the specified users from logging in to the machine. For example,

```
-jacques::::::
```

does not allow user jacques to log in to the local system.

You can also use *+@netgroup* or *-@netgroup* to specify entries for all members of the (NIS) network group *netgroup* into /etc/passwd.

CAUTION

The /etc/passwd file must not contain any blank lines. Blank lines can cause unpredictable behavior in system administration software that uses the file.

For more information about the /etc/passwd file, use the man 5 passwd command.

The /etc/shadow **File**

Similar to the /etc/passwd file, each line in the /etc/shadow file is an entry for one person, and the fields are separated by colons. The following is a sample record:

```
eric:$1$w1bsw/N4$UWLu2bRET6YyBS.CAEp7R.:12794:0:90:5:30:12989:
```

This record has the following nine fields:

- Login name.
- Hashed password. By default, passwords are hashed using the crypt function that is based on the Data Encryption Standard (DES) algorithm. (For more information about the crypt function, use the man 3 crypt command.) The resulting DES-hashed password is *always* 13 characters in size. You can change the encryption method to use either MD5 (Message Digest number 5) or Blowfish; see Chapter 11, "Network Security Concepts," for more details.
- Date that the password was last changed. This is given in number of days since the *Epoch* (January 1, 1970).
- Minimum number of days that a password must be in existence before it can be changed.
- Password's life span. This is the maximum number of days that a password can remain unchanged. If this time elapses and the user does not change the password, the system administrator must change it for him or her.

- Number of days before password expiration the user will begin receiving notifications about changing the password. A value of -1 means no warning will be issued.

- Number of days after the password expires that the account is disabled and the user can no longer log in. A value of -1 means access is allowed even if the password has expired.

- Date after which the account is disabled. This is given in number of days since the Epoch. This information is useful for setting up temporary accounts.

- A reserved flag field, and is not currently used.

SLES PASSWORDS: ENCRYPTED OR HASHED?

Encryption is a method of using a mathematical algorithm and a key to scramble data into gibberish. If you know the key and the algorithm used, you can decrypt the gibberish to arrive back at the original information. SUSE (and indeed all Linux and Unix distributions) converts the (cleartext) password into a scrambled text string through a mathematical algorithm called a *cryptographic hash*. The resulting string, in a form that is very different from the original string, is called a *hash* or *hash value*. The way these hash algorithms work is that one cannot recover the original password from the hash value. Because Linux/Unix passwords cannot be converted back into their original text, the term *encrypted Linux/Unix passwords* is a misnomer. The more correct term is *hashed passwords*, and this term is used throughout this book.

The previous sample record shows the following information for user eric:

- The password was last changed on January 11, 2005.

- No minimum amount of time is required before the password can be changed.

- The password must be changed every 90 days.

- The user will get a warning 5 days before the password must be changed.

- The account will be disabled 30 days after the password expires if no login attempt is made.

- The account will expire on July 25, 2005.

TIP

You can use chage -1 username to examine a user's password-aging information. The output for eric looks like this:

```
Athena:/home/admin # chage -1 eric
Minimum:      0
Maximum:      90
Warning:      5
Inactive:     30
Last Change:            Jan 11, 2005
Password Expires:       Apr 11, 2005
Password Inactive:      May 11, 2005
Account Expires:        Jul 25, 2005
```

A nonroot user will be prompted for *username*'s password for security reasons,
even if the user is querying his or her own password-aging data.

NOTE

You can also use passwd -S username to display the password status of a user
or passwd -Sa to display status for all users. The output for user eric looks similar
to this:

```
eric PS 01/11/2005 0 90 5 30
```

The status follows directly after the username: PS means existing or locked password, NP means no password, and LK means the account is locked. As you can see,
the output is not as descriptive as that from chage -1. Furthermore, passwd -S
works only with local users; for all other types of users (such as LDAP), it returns a
status of LK, regardless of the actual status. The remaining fields show the password last changed date, minimum password days, maximum password days,
number of days before warning is issued, and number of days after password
expiration that the account will be disabled, respectively.

The /etc/group **File**

The /etc/group file contains the names of valid groups and the usernames of
their members. This file is owned by root and only root may modify it, but it is
world-readable. When a new user is added to /etc/passwd, information on
what groups that user is a member of must be added here. Group IDs (GIDs)
from the /etc/passwd file are mapped to the group names kept in this file.
Similar to users in the /etc/passwd file, the groups are listed one per line. For
example,

```
audio:x:17:eric,tasha,carol
```

Each entry consists of four fields separated by a colon:

- **Group name**—The name of the group, used by various utility programs to identify the group.

- **Group password**—If set, this allows users who are *not* part of the group to join the group by using the `newgrp` command and typing the password stored here. If a lowercase "x" is in this field, shadow group passwords (stored in `/etc/gshadow`) are being used. However, although earlier versions of SUSE LINUX make use of `/etc/gshadow`, SLES 9 and later do not and any group password hashes are stored in `/etc/group`.

- **Group ID (GID)**—The numerical equivalent of the group name. The system and applications use it when determining access privileges.

- **Member list**—A comma-delimited list of users in the group.

NOTE

Some Linux distributions use /etc/groups to hold passwords that let a user join a group. SUSE does not use this file.

The preceding sample entry from `/etc/group` shows the audio group is using shadow passwords; has a GID of 17; and that eric, tasha, and carol are group members.

CAUTION

The group members in /etc/group should be separated from each other by a single comma and *no* whitespaces. Otherwise, any users listed after the whitespace are not recognized as members.

Similar to `etc/passwd`, the `/etc/group` file can contain a line (usually the last line in the file) beginning with a plus (+), which means to incorporate group entries from NIS. A line with a single + means to insert the entire contents of the NIS `group` file at that point:

```
+:::
```

A line with *+name* means to insert the group entry (if any) for *name* from NIS at that point. If a + entry has a non-null field (such as the group membership), the data in that field overrides what is contained in NIS.

NOTE

All fields in the + entry may be overridden *except* for the user ID.

An entry of the form -*name* means that the group is disallowed. All subsequent entries for that group name, whether in the NIS **group** file or in the local /etc/group file, are ignored.

CAUTION

As is the case with /etc/passwd, the /etc/group file must not contain any blank lines. Blank lines can cause unpredictable behavior in system administration software that uses the file.

For more tinformation on /etc/group, use the man 5 group command.

User Account and Group Management Applications

There are two basic types of applications you can use when managing user accounts and groups on SUSE systems:

- The graphical system assistant application, YaST
- A suite of command-line tools

NOTE

For more information about YaST, refer to Chapter 2, "Updating the Server."

While both YaST and the command-line utilities perform essentially the same task, the command-line tools have the advantage of being scriptable and, therefore, more easily automated. On the other hand, YaST provides a wizard-like graphical interface that walks you through the necessary steps.

Table 4.3 describes some of the more common command-line tools used to create and manage users.

TABLE 4.3
User Management Command-Line Tools

APPLICATION	FUNCTION
/usr/sbin/useradd	Creates a user account using default values from /etc/default/useradd. This tool is also used to specify a user's primary and secondary group memberships.
/usr/sbin/userdel	Deletes user accounts.
/usr/sbin/usermod	Updates account attributes including some functions related to password aging, as well as primary and secondary group membership. For more fine-grained control, use the passwd command. usermod can be used to make changes to LDAP users with the help of the -D and -r LDAP options.
/usr/bin/passwd	Sets passwords. Although primarily used to change a user's password, it also controls all aspects of password aging. It is really the "Swiss-army knife" password utility.
/usr/sbin/chpasswd	Batch changes user passwords by reading in a file consisting of username and password pairs.
/usr/bin/chage	Changes the user's password-aging policies. The passwd utility can also be used for this purpose.
/usr/bin/chfn	Changes the user's GCOS information. Can also use passwd -f instead.
/usr/bin/chsh	Changes the user's default shell. Can also use passwd -s instead.
/usr/sbin/pwck	Checks the integrity of the /etc/passwd and /etc/shadow files.

Table 4.4 lists some of the more common command-line tools used to create and manage groups.

TABLE 4.4
Group Management Command-Line Tools

APPLICATION	FUNCTION
/usr/sbin/groupadd	Creates new groups, but does not assign users to those groups. The useradd and usermod programs should then be used to assign users to and remove them from a given group.
/usr/sbin/groupdel	Deletes groups.

TABLE 4.4
Group Management Command-Line Tools (continued)

APPLICATION	FUNCTION
/usr/sbin/groupmod	Modifies group names or GIDs, but does not change group membership. The useradd and usermod programs should be used to assign users to and remove them from a given group.
/usr/bin/gpasswd	Changes group passwords (stored in /etc/group) to allow nongroup members who know the group password to join the group. Only root may change group passwords. (You can also use passwd -g to change the group password.)
/usr/sbin/grpck	Checks the integrity of the /etc/group file. (On older versions of SUSE LINUX, such as SLES 8, grpck also checks the /etc/gshadow file; SLES 9 and later no longer use a group shadow file.)

To learn more about the utilities in Table 4.4, refer to the man page for each (for example, man grpck).

NOTE

The applications listed in Tables 4.3 and 4.4 do not determine what resources these users and groups have control over. For this, you must use applications that deal with file permissions, some of which are discussed in Chapter 6, "Filesystem Security."

Creating and Editing User Accounts

When you need to create or modify a single user account or a small number of accounts (say, fewer than five), it is usually more convenient to use YaST for the task because of its GUI interface. Otherwise, you may want to consider creating some shell scripts for the task using command-line tools discussed later in this section.

TIP

Many user-creation scripts are available on the Internet. A sample skeleton bash script for creating new users (using the useradd command) can be found at http://www.osix.net/modules/article/?id=577.

Use the following steps to create a new user account using YaST:

1. Launch YaST using one of the following methods:

- From the KDE desktop, click on the YaST icon. Enter the root password if prompted.

- From the KDE desktop, select Applications, System, YaST. Enter the root password if prompted.

- From a terminal window, first run **sux** to become root (if not root already) and then run **yast2** (the GUI version).

- From a terminal window, first run **su** to become root (if not root already) and then run **yast** (the ncurses version).

2. From the YaST Control Center, select Security and Users, Edit and Create Users to launch the User and Group Administration module. (If the NIS, LDAP, Samba, or Kerberos authentication is configured, you will be prompted for additional passwords.)

TIP

You can run yast and yast2 with the parameter users (for example, yast users) so YaST automatically launches the User and Group Administration module instead of displaying the Control Center menu.

3. From the User and Group Administration screen (see Figure 4.1), select Set Filter and choose the type of user accounts (such as Local Users, System Users, or LDAP Users) you want to manage. A list of current users of the selected type is displayed. You may only see Local Users and System Users available as selections under the Set Filter drop-down list. Additional selections (such as LDAP Users) will be available only after you have configured and started the services on the server.

TIP

You can combine multiple user types (such as Local Users and LDAP Users) to be displayed under the Custom filter by editing the selections in Set Filter, Customize Filter, Custom view.

4. Select the Add option, and a screen similar to Figure 4.2 is displayed.

FIGURE 4.1

The User and Group Administration module screen in YaST.

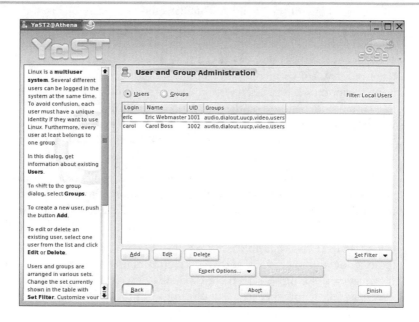

FIGURE 4.2

Adding a new local user.

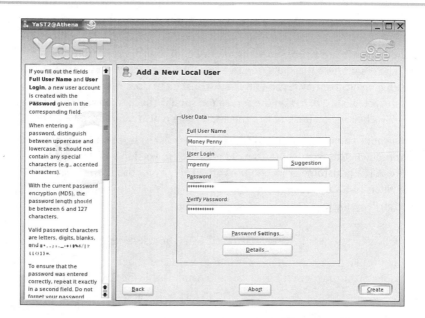

5. Fill in the user's name, login ID, and password. Keep in mind that both login names and passwords *are* case sensitive. Valid passwords can be composed of any of the (7-bit) ASCII characters, including digits and upper- and lowercase letters. However, you should use only *printable* ASCII characters whose decimal values are between the range of 33 and 126. Spaces (dec. 32) do work if you have a pure Linux/Unix environment but may fail with connections from an X emulator or SSH client from a Windows client. Therefore, you should avoid spaces in passwords. Furthermore, depending on the encryption algorithm (such as DES, which is the default), you may be limited to use only up to eight alphanumeric characters. (See "Use a Strong Password-Hashing Algorithm" later in this chapter.)

6. Click Password Settings if you want to change the settings (such as password expiration date) for the new user to something other than the defaults. In many cases, the default settings are sufficient and don't need to be modified.

7. Click Details if you want to change settings such as UID, home directory location, default login shell, and group memberships; the Additional User Information field in this screen corresponds to the GCOS field in /etc/passwd. (Remember that if you plan to run the finger daemon, the information in this field must be in the particular form required by finger; see the earlier "What Is the GCOS Field?" sidebar.) The UIDs are assigned automatically, based on the previously used value, and default settings are read from /etc/default/useradd.

TIP

The shells shown in the drop-down list of the Login shell are read from the /etc/shells file. Edit this file to remove any entry that you don't want to show up. Keep in mind that having an entry in /etc/shells does not necessarily mean the actual shell exists on the server. You should check to ensure the program exists before you include it in the list. This file is also referenced by chsh.

You may notice an entry called /bin/bash1 in /etc/shells, but it is not listed in the drop-down list. /bin/bash1 is an old reference to version 1 of bash, and /bin/bash is a general reference to the current version of bash, which is version 2. YaST filters out /bin/bash1 using the /usr/share/YaST2/modules/ Users.pm Perl script.

8. Click Create when you are satisfied with the user's settings.

9. Repeat steps 4 through 8 to create more users. Click Finish when you are done. You must click Finish for the databases to be updated. Otherwise,

if you click Abort, any changes made (including new users "added") will be discarded.

TIP

You can select Expert Options, Write Changes Now to save the changes made thus far, without exiting the module.

The procedure for updating and deleting a user is similar: Instead of Add, select Edit or Delete after highlighting the desired user.

TIP

If you change a user's UID, YaST will normally change all file ownerships in the user's home directory. If for some reason YaST fails to do this automatically, you can use the chown -R *username* /home/*username* command to change the ownerships.

TIP

When a user's UID is changed using YaST, only the ownership permissions for files in the home directory are adjusted. Changes to the permissions on files that may be located elsewhere on the system are not made.

To find all files on a system owned by a particular user, you can use the find command:

```
find / -uid id_number -print
```

find is a very powerful and useful program that can perform specific functions (via the exec switch) on found files. For instance, the following command will change all files belonging to UID 1000 to UID 1002:

```
find / -uid 1000 -exec chown 1002 {} \;
```

Being familiar with it will add a great tool to your bag of tricks. See man find for more information.

When you use YaST, you can manage most aspects of the user account within the single application, except you cannot use YaST to enable or disable a user account—you must do this using command-line tools. In addition, because YaST is a menu-driven utility, it does not lend itself to batch creation or modification of user accounts easily. Therefore, we highlight the multistep user-creation process necessary when using the command-line tools.

The following steps illustrate what happens when you issue the command /usr/sbin/useradd -m carol:

- A new entry for carol is created in /etc/passwd. The line begins with the username carol, and an "x" is placed in the password field indicating that the system is using shadow passwords. A UID at or above 1000 is created, and the primary GID is set to 100 (group users). The optional GCOS information is left blank. The home directory is created (because of the -m switch) and set as /home/carol, and the default shell is set to /bin/bash as specified by /etc/default/useradd.

NOTE

If you need to create a system user (that is, one with a UID between 0 and 499), include the -r and -u switches. For example,

    useradd -m -r -u 200 -c "db admin user" -g 0 db_admin

creates a user called db_admin whose UID is 200 and primary GID is 0 (that is, the root group), sets the GCOS field, sets the default shell to /bin/bash, and creates /home/db_admin as the home directory. In some cases, you may not want to include the -m switch to create a home directory, such as when the account is used by a daemon instead of a real-life user.

- A new entry for carol is created in /etc/shadow. The line begins with the username carol, and an exclamation point (!) is placed in the password field, which locks the account. The related password policy (such as expiration date) is set according to the values found in /etc/default/useradd.

- Group memberships in /etc/group are updated to include carol in the appropriate groups, such as dialout, uucp, video, and audio. User carol is *not* added to the group users because it is her primary group.

- A directory for carol is created in the /home directory. This directory's ownership is set to user carol and group users. Full privileges (read, write, and execute) are granted to carol, while group and others have only read and execute privileges.

- The files (including subdirectories) within the /etc/skel directory (which contain default user settings, such as .bashrc) are copied into the new /home/carol directory. If useradd is used without the -m option, the home directory is not created; thus, files from /etc/skel are not copied. You can override settings in /etc/default/useradd using additional command-line switches, such as -g and -d. Refer to man useradd for more information.

TIP

You can define additional actions to be performed when useradd and userdel are used. For example, before removing a user using userdel, execute a script—for example, find / -uid *id_number* -exec rm {} \;—to remove all files owned by the user. Refer to the USERADD_CMD, USERDEL_PRECMD, and USERDEL_POSTCMD directives in /etc/login.defs for more information.

At this point, a locked account called carol exists on the system. To activate it, you must next assign a password to the account using the `passwd` command and, optionally, set password-aging guidelines.

It is also possible to configure the account so that during the first login, the user is asked to change his or her password. To configure a user account in this manner, follow these steps:

1. Create the user account using the `useradd` command. At this point, the account is created but locked (with an invalid password assigned).

2. Use `chage -d0` *username* or `passwd -e` *username* to force immediate password expiration. This step sets the value for the date the password was last changed to the Epoch. This value forces immediate password expiration no matter what password-aging policy, if any, is in place.

3. Unlock the account by setting a valid password using `passwd`. You can assign an initial password that will be given to the user, or you can assign a null password (the user just needs to press Enter at the password prompt):

   `passwd -d` *username*

CAUTION

You can also change a user's password by using usermod. However, when using usermod, you need to *first* hash the password before using it. Unlike passwd, usermod does *not* perform the hashing.

In either case, upon initial login, the user is prompted for a new password.

CAUTION

Although using a null password is convenient for both you and the user, there is a slight risk that a third party can log in first and access the system. To minimize this threat, you can lock the account from being accessed by using the procedure discussed in the following paragraphs and unlock it just before the user is ready to log in.

In some instances, you may need to temporarily disable some accounts and reenable them at a later time. You can both disable an account and reenable it with `passwd` (but not with YaST). To disable an account, do the following:

```
passwd -l carol
```

This command inserts a ! character at the beginning of carol's password, making it unmatchable to any hashed value. Then, to enable the account with the original password, do the following:

```
passwd -u carol
```

The previously inserted ! character is removed, so carol can log in again using the assigned password.

TIP

If you have to manage LDAP user passwords, it is best to use YaST, or some LDAP-based tools (such as `ldapmodify`), instead of `passwd`. `passwd` can change only local passwords, even though the -D option can be used to specify binding to LDAP—it cannot authenticate to the LDAP server.

CAUTION

You should train your nonadministrator users to use `passwd` or the desktop password utility (Applications, System, Change Password) to change their passwords, and not to use YaST. When nonprivileged users use YaST to make changes, even to their own accounts, they receive errors indicating some values cannot be updated (for example, "The directory /home is not writable.").

Some Linux distributions, such as Red Hat, use a so-called *user private group (UPG) scheme*. The UPG scheme does not add or change anything in the standard Linux/Unix way of handling groups; instead, it offers a new convention. Under UPG, whenever you create a new user, by default, a unique group with the same name as the user is created and is assigned as the user's primary group. This group contains only this particular user, hence, the name "private group." Usually, this group has the same name as the user login name, and its GID is the same as the user's UID; this can be a bit confusing at times. UPG is meant to make file permission management a little easier. You can find additional discussion of the pros and cons of UPG in Chapter 6. SUSE LINUX does *not* make use of UPG; therefore, you do not see any groups created concurrently when you create new users.

Setting Default User Account Properties

As discussed in the preceding section, default values for the user account are stored in **/etc/default/useradd**. Both **useradd** and YaST use this file. Additional settings, such as password-aging policies, are stored in **/etc/login.defs**. These two files, however, govern only local users—those defined in **/etc/passwd**. The files have no effect when you are creating LDAP or other nonlocal users because settings for those users are stored in their respective databases.

NOTE

Refer to Chapter 8 for information about setting up and configuring services such as LDAP and NIS.

Shown in Listing 4.1 is the default **/etc/default/useradd** file. The default settings for a new user are as follows:

- The primary GID for the user is 100 (group users).
- The user is made a member of the dialout, uucp, video, and audio groups.
- The user's home directory will be created under **/home**.
- The user can log in using the expired password, indefinitely.
- There is no preset account expiration date.
- The user's default shell is **/etc/bash**.
- Files and subdirectories in **/etc/skel** will be copied to the user's home directory after it has been created.

LISTING 4.1

The Default /etc/default/useradd File

```
GROUP=100
HOME=/home
INACTIVE=-1
EXPIRE=
SHELL=/bin/bash
SKEL=/etc/skel
GROUPS=dialout,uucp,video,audio
```

You can customize this file to suit your specific requirements. For instance, if you need the new user to be a member of video, audio, helpdesk, and support groups, change the **GROUPS=** line to read:

```
GROUPS=video,audio,helpdesk,support
```

If some site-specific configuration files (such as a configuration file containing the name of the SQL database server) need to be placed in the user's home directory, simply place them in **/etc/skel**, and they will be copied when the home directory is created.

TIP

Settings in /etc/default/useradd can be edited using YaST. From the User and Group Administration screen, select Expert Options, Defaults for New Users.

Default user account, group, and password-aging policy settings, such as the life span of a password, are found in the **/etc/login.defs** file. This file also contains settings used by the login process (such as the amount of time delay before being allowed another attempt after a failed login). Shown in Listing 4.2 are user account and group-related directives.

LISTING 4.2
User and Group-Related Directives in /etc/login.defs

```
#
# Password aging controls (used by useradd):
#
# PASS_MAX_DAYS
# - Maximum number of days a password may be used.
# PASS_MIN_DAYS
# - Minimum number of days allowed between password changes.
# PASS_WARN_AGE
# - Number of days warning given before a password expires.
#
PASS_MAX_DAYS     99999
PASS_MIN_DAYS     0
PASS_WARN_AGE     7


#
# Min/max values for automatic uid selection in useradd
#
# SYSTEM_UID_MIN to SYSTEM_UID_MAX inclusive is the range for
# UIDs for dynamically allocated administrative and system
# accounts.
# UID_MIN to UID_MAX inclusive is the range of UIDs of
# dynamically allocated user accounts.
#
SYSTEM_UID_MIN         100
SYSTEM_UID_MAX         499
UID_MIN               1000
UID_MAX              60000
```

LISTING 4.2
User and Group-Related Directives in /etc/login.defs (continued)
```
#
# Min/max values for automatic gid selection in groupadd
#
# SYSTEM_GID_MIN to SYSTEM_GID_MAX inclusive is the range for
# GIDs for dynamically allocated administrative and system
# groups.
# GID_MIN to GID_MAX inclusive is the range of GIDs of
# dynamically allocated groups.
#
SYSTEM_GID_MIN          100
SYSTEM_GID_MAX          499
GID_MIN                 1000
GID_MAX                 60000


#
# User/group names must match the following regex expression.
# The default is [A-Za-z_][A-Za-z0-9_.-]*[A-Za-z0-9_.$-]\?
#
CHARACTER_CLASS             [A-Za-z_][A-Za-z0-9_.-]*[A-Za-z0-9_.$-]\?


#
# Umask which is used by useradd and newusers for creating
# new home directories.
#
UMASK                   022


#
# If defined, this command is run when adding a user.
# It should rebuild any NIS database etc. to add the
# new created account.
#
USERADD_CMD         /usr/sbin/useradd.local


#
# If defined, this command is run before removing a user.
# It should remove any at/cron/print jobs etc. owned by
# the user to be removed.
#
USERDEL_PRECMD      /usr/sbin/userdel-pre.local


#
# If defined, this command is run after removing a user.
# It should rebuild any NIS database etc. to remove the
# account from it.
#
USERDEL_POSTCMD     /usr/sbin/userdel-post.local
```

CAUTION

It is best not to change the SYSTEM_UID_* and SYSTEM_GID_* directive settings as that may cause some application not to function properly.

The UMASK directive in /etc/login.defs is used by useradd and YaST to set the proper file permissions on the home directory. Refer to Chapter 6 for information about file ownership and permissions. The USERDEL_PRECMD and USERDEL_POSTCMD directives point to two templates that you can customize for your particular needs. For instance, you may want to copy the user's home directory elsewhere before you delete the user ID. The default script for the USERDEL_PRECMD directive deletes any cron jobs belonging to the user, whereas the default USERDEL_POSTCMD does nothing.

TIP

Settings in /etc/login.defs can be edited using YaST. From the YaST Control Center, select Security and Users, Security Settings. If the Current Security Setting is one of Level 1 through Level 3, click Details. If the selection is Custom Settings, click Next. You are then presented with a series of screens, each dealing with a different set of directives found in /etc/login.defs.

Where redundancy exists between /etc/login.defs and /etc/default/useradd, the settings in /etc/login.defs take precedence.

Creating and Editing Groups

The process for managing groups is similar to that for users. Rather than listing many of the same steps again, we've listed the salient differences here instead:

- From the YaST Control Center, select Security and Users, Edit and Create Groups to launch the User and Group Administration module. If you are already in the User and Group Administration module, click on the Groups radio button near the top of the screen; you can use the Users and Groups radio buttons to switch back and forth between managing users and groups.

- When launching YaST from a terminal session, you can use yast groups or yast2 groups to skip over the YaST Control Center and go directly to the User and Group Administration module.

- Shown in Figure 4.3 is the screen for adding a new local group. You need to provide a group name and optionally select one or more users who will be members of this group.

FIGURE 4.3
Adding a new local group.

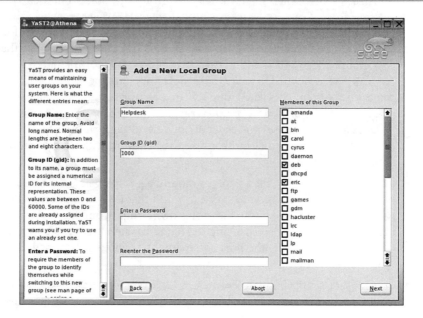

NOTE

The list of users available in the Add New Local Group screen includes *all* known users, which includes those from local, LDAP, NIS, and so on. However, if you are adding, for instance, a new LDAP group, only LDAP users are shown for selection.

- The GID is automatically assigned, using the lowest non-used GID. You can change it to a different value if you like. YaST will warn you if the newly specified value is already in use.

- Group passwords are optional. They allow users who are not members of the group to use `newgrp` to switch their active GID to that group—if they know the group's password.

- When editing an existing group, you will also see a list of users for which this group is their default. You *cannot* modify this list in YaST. To remove a user from this list, you need to assign a different primary GID to that user.

There are three commonly used command-line utilities for managing groups:

- groupadd—This application creates a new group by adding a new entry to /etc/group. Common usage is simply groupadd *groupname* where the next available GID will be assigned. If you want to use a specific GID for the new group, include the -g *id_number* switch; for a system group (that is, a group whose GID is within the range of SYSTEM_GID_MIN and SYSTEM_GID_MAX as defined in /etc/login.defs), include the -r switch. You can assign a group password using the -p *password* switch; or you can add it later using passwd -g *groupname*, gpasswd *groupname*, or groupmod -p *password groupname*. It is generally preferred that you use passwd -g or gpasswd to set the password because the password will not be seen on the command line.

- groupmod—This utility allows you to modify a group's name, GID, its list of members, and its password. Keep in mind that if you change the GID, you need to manually change the group ownership of any files owned by the old GID using chgrp; changing the name has no effect on the group ownership. You can use the find command as previously discussed in "Creating and Editing User Accounts."

- groupdel—Use this utility to delete a group from /etc/group: groupdel *groupname*. Note that you can delete a group only when no user has this group as his or her primary group.

You will not find a /etc/gshadow file on SLES 9 and later systems because it is no longer used.

Security Considerations

The first step in securing any operating system is to secure the user and group accounts. This includes, but is not limited to, the following:

- Enforcing strong password selection
- Restricting user access to only those files, directories, and shells that are absolutely necessary
- Safeguarding system accounts (especially root)
- Closing any potential backdoors, such as disabling unused or dormant accounts

These steps are discussed in the following sections. Other precautions, such as securing a user's working environment, handling filesystem security, preventing and detecting intruders, as well as system hardening are discussed in later chapters in this book.

Using Strong Passwords

Like having good and secure locks on your house, you want users to pick passwords that are difficult to guess yet easy enough to remember so the users will not write down their passwords for the world to find. Difficult-to-guess passwords means they should not be associated with the user personally, such as the name of his or her spouse, names of children, pets, or the user's address. Strong passwords should also not include dictionary words. Many password-cracking programs make use of word lists to brute-force crack passwords. Many of these programs are freely available over the Internet; two of the most popular password-crackers are Crack and John the Ripper. We will discuss how you can use John the Ripper to detect weak passwords on your system in Chapter 11.

One way to select a difficult-to-guess password is to use a randomly selected string of characters, such as *i2#yA9%3r*. This is not a word found in any dictionary, nor is it remotely connected to a user. Unfortunately, your user probably wouldn't be able to remember such a password. The likely result is that the user will write it down on a sticky note and paste it underneath his or her keyboard!

A better way to select a strong password is to use a short phrase (commonly referred to as a *passphrase*) such as *I missed hockey!* Alternatively, you can derive a password from a long sentence such as *The Adventures of Buckaroo Banzai across the Eighth Dimension!* One derivation is to simply take the first letter from each word, except for the word *Eighth*, which is replaced by the number 8, and you get *TaoBBat8D*. Or you can take the second letter of each word, except again for the word *Eighth*, and you get *hdfuach8i*. As you can see, you can use many variations to come up with difficult-to-guess but rather easy-to-remember passwords.

NOTE

Given the ever-increasing computing power and the ready availability of utilities such as John the Ripper and packet sniffers (such as Ethereal), even the most difficult-to-guess passwords are fast becoming worthless. If a hacker obtains a list of your usernames and hashed passwords, he can run Crack or John the Ripper against the list until a match is found. If the user is logging in over a network, both username and password are sent in cleartext (unless the session is encrypted such as when using SSH instead of Telnet). This makes it even easier for the bad guy because all he needs is a sniffer to capture all the network traffic and look for "Login:" and "Password:" in the packets. No need for John the Ripper at all! You can take many steps discussed throughout this book to minimize the impact and even prevent these types of attacks from happening in the first place.

The standard industry recommendations on selecting strong passwords and enforcing password security are summarized in the following sections.

PROTECT YOUR PASSWORDS

The first rule of password security is that you don't *ever* write down your password; memorize it instead. In particular, don't write it down and leave it somewhere that is publicly or easily accessible by others, and don't place it in an *unencrypted* file! If you can't memorize it, you didn't choose a good password. If you *must* write it down, keep it on your person at all times!

If you have access to different systems and a centralized authentication mechanism (such as NIS or LDAP) is not used, use unrelated passwords on these machines. This also applies to your access to systems controlled by different organizations: You don't know how well they protect their systems and don't want to help any bad guys to get into your servers using information hacked from those other systems.

Don't give or share your password, in particular to someone *claiming* to be from computer support or a vendor, *especially over the phone*! Often, a hacker uses deception or misdirection to obtain information from an unsuspecting user— especially a new user. The hacker often pretends to be someone in authority, such as someone from IT Security or a vendor's customer support group that needs to verify a user's identity. Consider the following telephone conversation:

Hacker: Good morning! This is John at the corporate IT Security division. Are you Susan James?

Susan: Yes, this is she.

Hacker: We are in the process of setting up your mainframe access. To make things simple for you, we will make your mainframe's username and password the same as your LAN's so you don't have to memorize multiple logins.

Susan: That's great!

Hacker: Your LAN username is Sjames, correct?

Susan: Yes.

Hacker: All I need is your password so I can enter that into mainframe.

Susan: Sure; it is…

This method is referred to as *social engineering*. The hacker simply carries out a seemingly innocent conversation with the victim in a social setting and obtains the necessary information without having to spend days trying to crack a single MD5- or Blowfish-hashed password!

CAUTION

In recent years, such social engineering ploys (known as *phishing*) have been used on the Internet. The bad guys send out an email to a user falsely claiming to be an established, legitimate enterprise in an attempt to scam the user into surrendering private information that will be used for identity theft. The email directs the user to visit a website where he or she is asked to update personal information, such as passwords and credit card, Social Security, and bank account numbers that the legitimate organization already has. The website, however, is bogus and set up only to steal the user's information. Visit `http://www.ftc.gov/bcp/conline/pubs/alerts/phishingalrt.htm` for more information.

Don't let anyone watch you enter your password and don't enter your password into a computer you do not trust. If the password is needed only for a limited time, change it periodically. When it comes to safeguarding your password, the golden rule is *practice perseverance and vigilance*.

CHOOSE HARD-TO-GUESS PASSWORDS

A strong password should be something you would *not* find in a dictionary (in any language or jargon). You shouldn't use a name (including that of a spouse, parent, child, pet, and so on) or any variation of your personal or login name. Don't use publicly accessible information about you (such as your phone number, car license plate, or employee number) or your environment (such as office address) as part of your password. Don't use a birthday or a simple pattern (such as spelling the username backward, following the name with a digit, or preceding the name with a digit).

A good, hard-to-guess password consists of a mixture of upper- and lowercase letters as well as digits or punctuation. When choosing a new password, make sure it's unrelated to any previous passwords (such as by adding a digit to an old password). Use long passwords (say, eight characters or more). You might use a word pair with punctuation inserted (such as *greAT:@Book*), a passphrase, or selected letters of each word in a long sentence, as discussed previously.

BUTTON DOWN THE HATCHES!

You should *never*, ever, allow an account without a password. Such an account is an open invitation begging some bad guy to compromise your system. Lock all unused accounts—for users who are away for an extended period of time or users who have left your organization but you need to retain their environments—using the `passwd -l` command. You will also find many of the system accounts to have an invalid password assigned (a *single* * or ! in the password field in `/etc/shadow`). These accounts exist to allow programs to be run as the UID associated with that account; they are not direct login accounts. If you ever need to create such an account, ensure you disable its login access.

TIP

In addition to locking dormant accounts by disabling the passwords, you should also remove (or rename) all `.rhosts`, `.netrc`, and `.forward` files in their home directories to prevent remote access as those users via FTP or any of the r- commands (such as `rlogin` and `rexec`).

You should also change these users' shells to a dummy shell such as `/dev/null`, `/bin/false`, or `/sbin/nologin`. This way, even if someone is able to log in as one of these users, an immediate exit will be the result. You may not want to use `nologin` because it informs the user that the account is not available—a giveaway to hackers that the account does exist but is disabled.

USE PASSWORD AGING

No matter how hard a password is to guess, if it has been used for an extended period of time, someone is going to figure it out. It is not uncommon for users to brag with each other about how secure or how clever their passwords are: "I used all my three children's middle names. How's that for a tough password?" "You know the color that I really, really hate?" or "Hey, I used my wife's favorite Italian dish as my password. Try to guess that!"

Given enough talk, and some luck, a bad guy may just figure out what the password is. Therefore, it is a good idea to force the users to periodically change their passwords. Password aging may be implemented on a system-wide basis or on a per-user basis. Password-aging policy in Linux is controlled through the shadow password file and is configured automatically by SLES during installation.

BE A CRACKER JACK

Use a password-cracker yourself to audit for weak passwords. SUSE LINUX implements Pluggable Authentication Module (PAM) by default to provide flexible user authentication. One of the side benefits of PAM is its ability to help enforce strong passwords (through the `pam_pwcheck` module, for instance). (You can find more details about PAM in Chapter 5, "User Environment Management and Security.") There is always a possibility that another system administrator assigned a weak password without realizing it. To find out, you should periodically use a password-cracker, such as John the Ripper, to self-audit and see whether any weak passwords are reported.

CAUTION

When nonroot users change their passwords, PAM ensures a "good" password is chosen; otherwise, the password is not changed. However, for the root user, PAM gives the warning when a weak password is detected but allows it to be used.

TIP

A set of cron scripts called seccheck is included and installed by default as of SuSE 6.3. Seccheck performs daily, weekly, and monthly checks of your system's security and compares them to the last run. The results are emailed to the root account. Weak password checks are performed weekly using John the Ripper. For more information, refer to /usr/share/doc/packages/seccheck/README.

USE A STRONG PASSWORD-HASHING ALGORITHM

The previous recommendations of using passphrases and long passwords are fine *if* the password-hashing algorithm you use supports long strings. By default, SLES 9 (and many other Linux distributions) uses a DES-based algorithm, which supports passwords up to eight characters in length; any string longer than eight characters is *truncated* to eight characters in size. Fortunately, SUSE ships with the option of encrypting passwords with the stronger MD5 hash algorithm or with Blowfish. (For more information on the MD5 hash algorithm, consult RFC 1321; see http://www.schneier.com/blowfish.html for more information about the Blowfish encryption algorithm.) Although MD5 and Blowfish passwords do not eliminate the threat of password cracking, they do make cracking your passwords much more difficult.

NOTE

SLES uses DES as the password-hashing method by default. However, you can change it to either MD5 or Blowfish during install as discussed in the "Detailed Installation Steps" section in Chapter 1, "Installing SUSE LINUX Enterprise Server." Or you can change it any time after the server is up and running, as discussed next.

If you didn't change the password-hashing algorithm from DES to MD5 or Blowfish during install, you can easily change it at a later time. This is easily done using YaST because it will make changes to all the related configuration files for you (such as `/etc/security/pam_unix2.conf` and `/etc/security/pam_pwcheck.conf`). You can make the change either via the User and Group Administration module or the Local Security Configuration module as follows:

- From the YaST Control Center, select Security and Users, Edit and Create Users to launch the User and Group Administration module. Click Expert Options, Password Encryption. From the displayed Set Password Encryption dialog box (see Figure 4.4), select the desired method and click OK. Click Finish for the change to take effect.

FIGURE 4.4
Changing the password-hashing method.

- From the YaST Control Center, select Security and Users, Security Settings to launch the Local Security Configuration module. If the Current Security Setting is one of Level 1 through Level 3, click Details. If the selection is Custom Settings, click Next. The first screen is Password Settings (see Figure 4.5). From the Password Encryption Method drop-down list, select the desired method. Make any other changes if desired. Click Next until the Miscellaneous Settings screen is displayed. Click Finish for the new change(s) to take effect. (From a terminal session, you can launch the Local Security Configuration module directly using `yast security` or `yast2 security`.)

WARNING

There appears to be a cosmetic bug with the User and Group Administration module when setting passwords. Regardless of your current password-hashing algorithm, when you try to use a password longer than eight characters, YaST *always* warns you that the password is too long and asks if it should be truncated. When you click Yes, it is truncated when using DES. However, with MD5 and Blowfish, the password is *not* truncated even though you are led to believe it will be after you click Yes; if you click No, you're returned to the screen to enter the password again.

FIGURE 4.5

Changing the password-hashing method via the Local Security Configuration module.

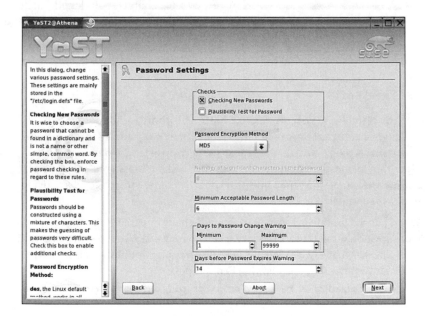

CAUTION

Changing the password-hashing method used does *not* change the existing password hash values to the new one. For instance, switching from the default DES to MD5 leaves existing password hashes as DES. However, new passwords will be hashed using MD5. Therefore, if you want all user passwords to be hashed using the new algorithm, change the method and then expire all passwords. This way, the next time a user logs in, that user will be prompted to change his or her password, and it will be hashed using the new method.

You can determine what hashing algorithm was used for a given password hash by examining /etc/shadow—another reason why this file is accessible by root only because you don't want to give any hackers hints on what hashing algorithm you are using:

- DES-hashed passwords are *always* 13 characters in length, where the first two characters are the salt.

- MD5-hashed passwords can be up to 34 characters in length, including the salt. The salt for an MD5 hash begins with the prefix *1*, and the salt itself is a string that can be up to eight characters and is followed by a dollar sign to indicate the end of the salt (for example, 1abcdefgh$).

- Blowfish-hashed passwords can be up to 60 characters in length, including the salt. The salt for a Blowfish hash begins with the prefix $2a$, and the salt itself is just a two-character string followed by a dollar sign to indicate the end of the salt.

KEYS AND SALTS

On Linux (and Unix) systems, different hash algorithms are supported through the crypt library call. Crypt takes two parameters, a key and a salt, and returns the hashed value. A *salt* is simply a text string (whose length depends on the algorithm in question) that is combined with the key ("password") to generate the hash value. Hashing the same password with different salts results in different hashed values.

When passwd (or one of the many password-changing utilities) changes a password, a random salt is used. This way, even if two users have the same password, they will likely have two different salts, thus two different hash values. This is easily illustrated using the following Perl snippet:

```
Athena:/home/admin # perl -e 'print crypt("password", "s1"),
➥"\n"' s1bASGcvcc/W.
Athena:/home/admin # perl -e 'print crypt("password", "s2"),
➥"\n"' s21GZTaOBHOFc
```

The algorithm used depends on the salt used. The preceding example shows the result of hashing the same text string (*password*) with two different salts (*s1* and *s2*) using the DES algorithm: The two hashed values are radically different. Note that the salt itself is prefixed to the resulting hash, which indicates what hashing algorithm was used. This allows applications, such as passwd, to use the same salt and algorithm to verify a password at a later time.

Each of the DES, MD5, and Blowfish algorithms has its pros and cons, and you should give them some careful thought before picking one. For instance, the Linux (and Unix) implementation of the DES hashing method limits the password to only eight characters, but because all versions of Linux/Unix and most other Unix-like operating systems support it, it is a good choice for cross-platform compatibility. On the other hand, MD5 and Blowfish allow for much longer passwords (127 characters for MD5 and 72 characters for Blowfish), but the algorithms are computational-intensive. So if you have an underpowered server that needs to perform many user authentications per second (such as an LDAP authentication server), performance will suffer. There are also some networking protocols that do not play well with passwords longer than eight characters. For example, only the first eight characters are significant in NIS+ passwords because the underlying secure-RPC protocol uses DES.

Consider the following suggestions when choosing a password-hashing algorithm for your system:

- When using DES, set the minimum password length to be at least six; use an eight-character password for root.

- If all interconnected systems support MD5, use MD5 as the password-hashing algorithm and set the minimum password length to be at least six.

- Consider using Blowfish for all system accounts that require a password. (However, this means you need to switch the password-hashing method from the current setting to Blowfish, change the password, and restore the setting. An alternative is to install the Blowfish-aware version of Perl—the version included with SLES 9 supports only DES and MD5—so you can use a simple script to first generate the hashed value using Perl and then set the password using usermod -p *hashed_value*.)

TIP

You can find the RPM for a version of Perl that supports Blowfish at `http://rpmfind.net/linux/RPM/contrib/libc6/i386/perl-Crypt-Blowfish-2.09-1.i386.html` and at `http://rpmfind.net/linux/RPM/suse/8.2/i386/suse/i586/perl-Crypt-Blowfish-2.09-188.i586.html`. The Perl crypt home page is at `http://cpan.org/modules/by-module/Crypt`.

In most cases, MD5 provides the best balance between performance and security.

Auditing Default Accounts

As mentioned earlier, a number of system accounts exist to allow programs to be run as the UID associated with that account; they are not direct login accounts. FTP, named (for DNS), mail, and news are some examples of such system accounts. Make sure such accounts are prevented from a terminal login by setting their shell to `/bin/false` or similar.

If the services for these accounts are not in use, uninstall them and remove the accounts—or at the very least, disable unused services (see Chapter 8 for more information). Periodically, you should check the contents of `/etc/passwd` and `/etc/shadow` to ensure that the removed system accounts didn't "spontaneously resurrect" themselves or new system accounts were not added without your knowledge, and nonlogin system accounts don't "suddenly" get assigned valid password hashes and shells.

The Root Account

The root account is the key to your entire server kingdom (and to your entire network if the server in question serves as the central authentication server). Nothing is more important than the password to the root account in the Linux/Unix world. For this reason, you will not want to make your root password known to anyone else but yourself. Well, this is often easier said than done.

As you may already have found out, many of the administrative tasks, such as resetting a user's forgotten password, changing system configuration, and so on, require you to be root. If you're the lone ranger who looks after the system(s) at your organization, keeping the root password safe is relatively easy: Follow the recommendations given earlier in this chapter about selecting strong passwords, change it often, never write it down, and so on. However, it is not uncommon in a company for system administration tasks to be shared by two or more people. In such cases, how do you safeguard the root password effectively? The more people who know it, the higher the likelihood it will be leaked to someone who shouldn't know about it!

TIP

If you are the sole system administrator at your organization, it might be a good idea to record the root password in a sealed envelope and keep it in a secure location where only trusted company officers (such as the accountant or CTO) have access to it; a bank safety deposit box is a good choice. The idea here is that although you would want to keep the root password secret from others, you need to provide a way for "continuity" should you be unavailable, due to illness or any other reasons.

There are a number of ways to address the multiple administrator requirements, and we discuss two of them here:

- **Setting up multiple root users**—Instead of providing the root password to the people who need access, you can set up multiple root accounts. Suppose, for example, both Tasha and Carol require administrative access as part of their job. One way to track their root activities is to set up two separate accounts, say tasha-root for Tasha and carol-root for Carol, each with a unique (strong) password and each with a UID of 0. Whenever Tasha needs root privileges, she would log in as tasha-root or su as tasha-root. Carol would do so as carol-root. This method has the advantage of having an audit trail in the forms of process accounting and system logging for each administrator and without having to share the root password. The disadvantage is that each duplicate UID 0 account is another potential vulnerability.

Because adding another UID 0 account is also a common hacker practice, you should review /etc/passwd frequently to check for illegal UID 0 accounts. You can also use Bastille (see Chapter 13) to automatically detect unauthorized duplicate root accounts.

CAUTION

You should not name the root-equivalent accounts with "-root" as that makes it easy for the hackers to zero in on accounts to attack.

- **Using sudo**—The best way of granting multiple users root access is via the sudo (superuser **do**) utility. sudo allows you to grant certain users (or groups of users) the ability to run some (or all) commands as root while logging *all* commands and arguments used, regardless of whether the command was successful. All sudo commands are logged in the log file /var/log/messages, which can be very helpful in determining how user error may have contributed to a problem. All the sudo log entries have the word sudo in them, so you can easily get a thread of commands used by using the grep command to selectively filter the output accordingly. sudo operates on a *per-command* basis, and it is not a replacement for the shell.

NOTE

Further discussion about sudo can be found in Chapter 5.

Running as root *all the time* is not a very good idea. Because it grants you all-powerful, unlimited access to the server and its files, one little mistake may render the whole system useless. For example, before you execute rm -r * (or even just rm *), make very sure you are in the right directory! In general, think twice before you perform certain actions as root. Here are some tips regarding using the root account:

- Become root only when absolutely necessary.
- Gain root access only through su or sudo.

- Restrict from which terminal console(s) root can log in. (See man securetty and refer to the "Authentication Using PAM" section in Chapter 5 for more information.)

- Exercise extreme care when executing potentially destructive commands (such as rm) while being root.

- Use absolute pathnames when invoking commands. This helps to eliminate executing a Trojan Horse program that may have been installed in one of the nonsystem directories that is pointed to by the PATH environment variable.

TIP

When setting up root's environment, do not put user-writable directories in root's PATH. This reduces the chance of running a Trojan Horse program placed (knowingly or not) by a user.

- Whenever you need to remotely administer a system as root, use SSH (discussed in the "Securing Network Services" section in Chapter 13) and sudo.

User in Too Many Groups?

Linux and most other recent Unix systems support at least 32 groups per user. However, because the NFS protocol supports only 16 groups, most of them (SUSE included) have imposed a soft limit of 16 groups per user. There are very rarely circumstances that require more than 16 groups, but it is usually possible to use more if the system will not be exporting or using NFS-mounted filesystems; NFS has a hard-coded limit of 16 groups in its underlying RPC protocol. The first 16 groups are passed to the NFS server for permission checking, while the others are ignored. In other words, a user might appear to belong to a group, but if the 16-group limit is exceeded, the user might not have the access privileges of that group.

Summary

This chapter provided information on how users and groups are identified in Linux and how you can effectively manage user and group information using

YaST and command-line tools. The following topics were covered in this chapter:

- User and group IDs
- System users versus regular users
- The `/etc/passwd`, `/etc/shadow`, and `/etc/group` files
- Ways to create and update user and group information using YaST and command-line tools
- User account security considerations

The next chapter will provide you with information and tips on how best to secure your users' working environment. For instance, you can restrict users to be able to log in using only certain terminal consoles and apply disk quotes so the server does not run out of disk space, resulting in what is sometimes known as "self denial of service" (SDOS).

CHAPTER 5

User Environment Management and Security

All process-based activity on a server is governed by the rights and privileges assigned to the user account under which it is running. The preceding chapter discussed how SLES reserves specific ranges of user IDs (UIDs) and group IDs (GIDs) for system accounts, special accounts, and standard user accounts.

In many operating systems, elevated system access is granted through the assignment of rights by the system administrator. If a specific privilege is not granted deliberately, the user account does not experience an elevation in access rights. In Linux, however, an account can obtain intrinsic rights simply by being placed in a specific UID/GID range. Arguably, mistakes can be made in any operating system environment. Attention to detail and proper auditing of account management would catch such mistakes. In the Linux world, a number in the UID or GID field should be verified for two properties: uniqueness and intrinsic rights.

In this chapter, we investigate user access one level beyond the simple granting of an account. Many of the topics covered here allow you, as the system administrator, to restrict users to allowed patterns of usage. Some users may see this as an obstacle to productivity. In most cases, a corporate IT policy dictates many of the guidelines for each restriction. Implementing these options in a proactive way will enhance your capacity for providing a robust and secure environment.

Account Auditing

The first step in securing a server is to determine what level of presence it must have. A server sitting on a network can be accessed in a variety of ways. Some methods require a username and password, and others do not require any form of authentication.

You can run network services that use a simple query-response scenario that does not require authentication. In this type of environment, a query is sent to a server, the server interprets the information, and when required, it passes information back to the client. Examples include DNS, DHCP, web server traffic, and PING. This type of access is controlled through managing services in the different run levels (see Chapter 3, "Booting and Shutting Down the Server"), the local account the service is run under, and firewall management (see Chapter 11, "Network Security Concepts").

Most services that are of interest to the end user require authentication. Examples are file sharing, remote logins, and access to secured websites. Numerous methods can be used to authenticate users. In this chapter, we concentrate on the authentication processes available on the local server.

Local access to a system is governed by the use of a username and password typically stored in **/etc/passwd**. Chapter 4, "User and Group Administration," introduced the concept of the **/etc/passwd** file as the repository of all user accounts that have access to a system. Listing 5.1 contains a copy of the **/etc/passwd** file from the DNS server installed in Chapter 2, "Updating the Server." If you recall, the DHCP-DNS software components were installed on top of a minimum SLES install. Referring to Listing 5.1, you may observe an interesting fact: A number of accounts created during the install are not required for the proper functioning of DHCP.

LISTING 5.1
/etc/passwd File from the DHCP Server Pollux

```
root:x:0:0:root:/root:/bin/bash
bin:x:1:1:bin:/bin:/bin/bash
daemon:x:2:2:Daemon:/sbin:/bin/bash
lp:x:4:7:Printing daemon:/var/spool/lpd:/bin/bash
mail:x:8:12:Mailer daemon:/var/spool/clientmqueue:/bin/false
news:x:9:13:News system:/etc/news:/bin/bash
uucp:x:10:14:Unix-to-Unix CoPy system:/etc/uucp:/bin/bash
games:x:12:100:Games account:/var/games:/bin/bash
man:x:13:62:Manual pages viewer:/var/cache/man:/bin/bash
at:x:25:25:Batch jobs daemon:/var/spool/atjobs:/bin/bash
wwwrun:x:30:8:WWW daemon apache:/var/lib/wwwrun:/bin/false
ftp:x:40:49:FTP account:/srv/ftp:/bin/bash
```

LISTING 5.1
/etc/passwd File from the DHCP Server Pollux (continued)

```
postfix:x:51:51:Postfix Daemon:/var/spool/postfix:/bin/false
sshd:x:71:65:SSH daemon:/var/lib/sshd:/bin/false
nobody:x:65534:65533:nobody:/var/lib/nobody:/bin/bash
hart:x:1000:100:Hart:/home/hart:/bin/bash
named:x:44:44:Name server daemon:/var/lib/named:/bin/false
dhcpd:x:100:65534:DHCP server daemon:/var/lib/dhcp:/bin/false
```

Echoing the policy that a system should contain only the minimum set of applications for its tasking, a proper account policy should dictate that unused accounts not be permitted on any system. There is no need for accounts such as *games* on a production server unless they are explicitly required. Such accounts, especially those with a UID in the reserved system space, should be removed. Though unlikely, they could provide access to the system if they are compromised. Because they are "standard" account names, modification to the default setup for these accounts could go undetected, allowing inappropriate access to the system. If the accounts are not present, the opportunity for exploit is not present either.

On a typical system, there are three types of accounts: local accounts with elevated access, local accounts used to run the various services, and unprivileged user accounts. In the remainder of this chapter, we examine how to further refine the access given to accounts.

Configuring the User Environment

An organization typically has two types of servers. One type has relatively static content, such as a DHCP or DNS server. The second type of server contains user files. In both cases, providing a consistent work environment for the end user is a must.

Uniformity of behavior over the server environment permits tool sets and scripts to be used cross-platform. Additionally, users do not have to remember multiple command syntaxes to achieve the same goal. In the following sections, we look at how this can be achieved in SLES first by defining a consistent command interpreter and then by selecting a standard set of variables the user can use.

Default Shell

Previously, we detailed the structure of the /etc/passwd file and identified that the last field on each record identifies the default, or login, shell. A login shell is a fancy name for a command interpreter and its associated environment.

Simply put, a *shell* is a program. A shell can be run interactively, spawned off as a child process, or run in the background through `cron`. As with any other program, a shell expects a predetermined syntax for commands and parameters. Within the lifetime of the shell process, the program allows for interaction with the operating system, other processes, and the file system.

Unlike some operating systems, Linux offers a variety of different shells such as `ksh`, `zsh`, `bash`, and others. Each shell supported by SLES incorporates its own syntax and command set. By specifying an initial shell for each user, you can define the type of environment a user experiences when interacting with the system.

A standard should be set for each organization to identify the default shell for all accounts. Each shell type uses a different set of configuration files. To facilitate system management, restricting changes to a single set of configuration files reduces the chances of errors. Choosing a standard shell allows scripting efforts by one individual to be shared with other users.

Selecting which shell to standardize on will invoke various arguments from the different camps as to which is best. For the purpose of this book, we restrict ourselves to describing the `bash` shell.

BUT I DON'T WANT BASH!

`bash` is not the only game in town. SLES comes bundled with a variety of other shells. In some cases, required third-party utilities use the scripting capabilities of other shells. In other cases, users with experience on other systems have tool sets of scripts.

In Linux, the first line of a shell script determines the interpreter for the script. If you look around your server at scripts in /etc/init.d, you will find the first line of many scripts showing

`#!/usr/bin/sh`

Similarly, scripts written in the programming language Perl start with a comment line like

`#!/usr/bin/perl`

The active shell under which the script is initiated interprets this first line of the script and passes the content of the script off to the identified interpreter. Hence, users who need to run specific shells for their scripts need only point their tools to the appropriate interpreter.

bash is a hybrid shell that is compatible with the original Unix sh shell but contains some features originally present only in the Korn and C shells. The following is a quick summary of what bash makes available:

- **Standard command set**—bash invokes the standard Linux commands such as ps, df, mount, man, and so on.

- **Script language**—bash is actually a fully scriptable language including variable, complex looping structures and if-then constructs.

- **Command-line completion**—You can use the Tab key to trigger bash to examine the current command line and expand the provided input to an appropriate value.

AUTOCOMPLETION

Completely typing long names or commands is often unnecessary. bash is aware of what you are typing and can autocomplete filenames for you. As an example, type the following at a command prompt:

Hermes> **cat /etc/serv[TAB]**

bash autocompletes the filename, and the command line becomes

Hermes> **cat /etc/services**

You can also traverse complex directory trees by using the Tab key. Each time the Tab key is pressed, the bash shell interprets what it has found and autocompletes the command for the first target matching the current pattern of text. If the shell detects multiple targets, the cursor will not autocomplete. Pressing Tab again lists the available targets. Typing in enough text to allow bash to uniquely identify a path permits the Tab key to continue traversing the various targets.

- **Command history**—Previously used commands can be recalled and edited using the arrow keys.

COMMAND HISTORY

bash allows for command-line recall and command editing using the cursor keys because bash keeps a history of past commands. Pressing the up- or down-arrow keys allows you to scroll through past commands. Pressing the left- or right-arrow keys allows you to edit the command currently present at the prompt.

Commands can also be retrieved through a search function. If you type the first few letters of a command and press Ctrl+S, bash will retrieve the first previously used command that matches the pattern. In some ssh clients, control characters are handled differently and not passed along to the server side. In such instances, the Ctrl+S sequence may not be accessible.

■ **Redirection of input and output**—The input for commands can be redirected from a file by using the less-than sign. Also, the output from commands can be redirected to a file by using the greater-than sign.

REDIRECTION

Redirection at the command-line level allows the user to redefine the source of STDIN, STDOUT, and STDERR. For input redirection, the single less-than symbol followed by a filename tells the command interpreter to read keystrokes from the identified file rather than from the console keyboard.

In the case of output, two channels exist. STDOUT is the default and can be represented by using 1> followed by a filename or, as a short form, by using a single greater-than sign because the numeric 1 is optional. When this is done, all non-error message output written to the console STDOUT is placed in the identified file. Double greater-than signs cause the output to be appended to the target file.

Error messages, STDERR, are written through the second channel and can be redirected by using 2> followed by a target file for error messages.

You can also combine the standard redirect to a file (for example, > out.txt), with the 2>&1 suffix. This forces STDOUT and STDERR to the same filename. This command would look like this:

Command > alloutput.txt 2>&1

■ **Command-line pipelines**—Using the pipe (|) symbol, you can pass the STDOUT from one command directly to the STDIN of a second command without having to worry about temporary files to host the content.

■ **Environment variables**—bash maintains a list of predefined variables that can be used at the command line or in scripts. This list includes parameters passed between shells, local host information, the path searched when commands are invoked, as well as the prompt presented during interactive sessions. You can also define your own variables in your scripts.

Using a standard shell across the enterprise is important. It provides consistency of interface and allows for the porting of scripts from server to server. In the following section, we examine another benefit of a consistent default shell: controlling login-generated information.

Login Scripts and Environment Variables

In the preceding section, you saw that a shell is simply an instance of a program or command interpreter. This is true whether it is controlling an interactive session or running a script. A login shell is a special case of such an instance, and it triggers a number of additional events.

A login shell executes a number of additional scripts when it is invoked. These additional scripts are used to tailor the environment the user will experience. You, as the system administrator, can customize these scripts to your advantage. These login scripts can modify search paths pointing to customized resources or set up environment variables specific to third-party software. The names of the logon scripts depend on the flavor of the default login shell. If all the users on a system share the same default login shell, maintenance of login scripts will be greatly simplified.

In the case of the **bash** shell, the system-wide login script executed at login is stored as **/etc/profile**. SUSE LINUX suggests that you maintain a customized version of your login script in **/etc/profile.local** instead. This is done to prevent the overwriting of any customizations at upgrade time. At login, the **/etc/profile** script will be run followed by **/etc/profile.local**. One of the benefits of using a managed login script is allowing control over the setting of environment variables that can be used in other scripts or applications. Typical examples would be setting an environment variable **ORACLE_HOME** to point to the base directory for your Oracle install or a **BACKUP_DIR** variable to specify a target location for your backups.

Within the **/etc/profile** script, you will also find numerous calls to other scripts. One such script, **/etc/bash.bashrc**, creates a number of aliases that can be used as shortcuts for other commands. Listing 5.2 shows a few of the aliases provided. If you want to add a number of system-wide aliases, SLES recommends that you place them in the local version, **bash.bashrc.local**. This script will be run following **bash.bashrc**.

LISTING 5.2

Some of the Aliases Generated in /etc/bash.bashrc

```
alias +='pushd .'
alias -='popd'
alias ..='cd ..'
alias ...='cd ../..'
alias dir='ls -l'
alias la='ls -la'
alias ll='ls -l'
```

The default aliases created in **bash.bashrc** allow users to type plus (+) to save their current working directory and minus (-) to return to that directory without the need for typing **pushd** and **popd**. Setting system-wide environment variables and aliases can make the system more comfortable for the users. A case in point would be the **dir** alias in Listing 5.2 that allows for DOS-type commands to appear to work in Linux.

To allow user-based customizations, **bash** also interprets scripts in the user's directory. At login, **bash** runs the first of the following files it finds in the user's directory: **.bash_profile**, **.bash_login**, or **.profile**. These local scripts can be used to set or override variables to better suit the end user's requirements. A typical snippet of a **.bash_profile** would look like Listing 5.3. In this snippet, you can see that two environment variables, **BACKUP_DIR** and **WEB**, are created, as well as an alias. The alias **st**, short for *status*, yields information on the current logged-on process, disk quota usage, as well as a summary of disk space in the user's home directory. When the user is logged in, the variables have the username of the current session in the proper locations, as shown in Listing 5.4. It is important to note that an alias is not evaluated at login; it is evaluated when invoked.

LISTING 5.3
Content of a Typical ./bash_profile

```
BACKUP_DIR=/backup/$USER ; export BACKUP_DIR
WEB="/home/$USER/public_html" ; export WEB
alias st='finger $USER ; quota $USER ; du --si -s $HOME'
```

LISTING 5.4
Verification of Environment Variables After Login

```
eric@Athena:~> env | grep -e BACKUP
BACKUP_DIR=/backup/eric
eric@Athena:~> env | grep -e WEB
WEB=/home/eric/public_html
eric@Athena:~> alias -p | grep -e st=
alias st='finger $USER ; quota $USER ; du --si -s $HOME'
eric@Athena:~>
```

When the $USER symbol is placed in the definitions in Listings 5.3 and 5.4, the .bash_profile script is more portable from machine to machine and user to user. A user with a privileged account on one machine, such as WEBMASTER, should have a regular account, such as eric on other servers. By using standard variables provided by **bash**, the login script becomes user-independent.

Upon logout, the bash shell calls one final script: .bash_logout. If this file exists at logout time, it will be executed. Users can set up routines to back up files or force a cleanup of temporary files. Here is the content of a sample .bash_logout:

```
eric@Athena:~> cat ./.bash_logout
mv Documents.tar.gz old_Documents.tar.gz
tar -zcvf Documents.tar.gz ./Documents
eric@Athena:~>
```

This script makes a copy of the current archive and then creates a backup of the content of the **Documents** subfolder in the account's root directory. If required during an interactive session, this routine can be invoked as ./.bash_logout.

A number of automated script processes take place on login and logout. By defining environment variables and aliases, the system administrator can provide the user with a more consistent environment from server to server.

User Resource Management

In the preceding section, we saw how to define a default shell for local user processes. In doing so, we also introduced scripts that will be executed automatically upon login and logout. These scripts can be used to customize the user environment, provide for common environment variables, and allow for a common system-wide configuration. In the following sections, we examine how to further refine a client's access to system resources.

Authentication Using PAM

Historically, application developers were burdened with developing their own methods for user authentication. This application-by-application approach has led to a multitude of disparate authentication schemes, resulting in individual users having multiple accounts and multiple passwords.

SUSE LINUX uses a system called the Pluggable Authentication Module, or PAM, to standardize the authentication process. With PAM, a programmer can rely on a series of predefined routines to properly identify users. This places the burden of authentication outside the program, resulting in a more portable and flexible architecture for the application.

In SLES, PAM is involved with all aspects of authentication. The main application-specific configuration files for PAM are located in **/etc/pam.d**. Each one of these files contains the rule sets used by PAM to establish the validity of a user for a specific application.

PAM rules are defined by combining four different module types or families:

- **authentication**—Uses challenge-response to verify the user.
- **account**—Determines whether the account is valid or expired.

- `password`—Verifies passwords and the strength of passwords.
- `session`—Processes session setup or teardown.

Each module family can contain multiple member modules. Each member module can be used to validate a specific characteristic required by the application being invoked. As an example, a collection of modules could check the group membership of an account, which terminal the account is being used from, as well as time of day. If all conditions are met, control is passed to the next family of modules. If not, the user session can be terminated.

In the simplest of cases, a family of rules can be satisfied by a single check. In most cases, however, applications require the validation of multiple aspects of an authentication request before a user is granted access.

Each module can be further tweaked by passing parameters that modify its behavior. These passed values override preset default characteristics. The configuration files that store the default behaviors are stored in **/etc/security**. We examine them more closely in the next section.

For each member of each family, it is possible to define a "level of compliance" the rule must satisfy. This metric is called a *control flag* within PAM. Four different levels of control flags are currently recognized:

- **Required**—Individual veto for the module family. Unless this test returns a valid result, the family will refuse access.
- **Requisite**—Immediate veto of access. If this test fails, the authentication request will be immediately denied.
- **Sufficient**—If this test passes, no other steps need take place. Failure of this rule does not terminate the authentication process. Rule evaluation resumes with the next member or family.
- **Optional**—This rule is used to trigger events that do not directly affect the authentication process. It is usually used to provide the client with additional status information.

The permutations and combinations of the modules types (family), the control flags (compliance), and the individual modules available make PAM a granular method of authentication. The variations available also make understanding PAM configurations somewhat daunting. To get a better understanding of a typical PAM configuration, let's examine an out-of-the-box configuration. Located in the **/etc/pam.d** directory is a PAM configuration file for the login process. Listing 5.5 shows the content of this file.

LISTING 5.5

Content of /etc/pam.d/login

```
#%PAM-1.0
auth requisite   pam_unix2.so  nullok      #set_secrpc
auth required    pam_securetty.so
auth required    pam_nologin.so
#auth required   pam_homecheck.so
auth required    pam_env.so
auth required    pam_mail.so
account required    pam_unix2.so
password required   pam_pwcheck.so  nullok
password required   pam_unix2.so        nullok use_first_pass use_authtok
session required    pam_unix2.so        none     # debug or trace
session required     pam_limits.so
```

This first family of modules is the group of *auth*entication modules. Within this family, no fewer than five separate tests are done to validate authentication. The **auth** family calls the following modules:

- **pam_unix2.so** verifies that this is a valid username in the /etc/passwd and /etc/shadow files.

- **pam_securetty.so** verifies that the user root is allowed to access the system from the current terminal.

- **pam_nologin.so** verifies the existence of /etc/nologin. If it is present, the content of the file is displayed to the user, and the authentication is refused.

- **pam_homecheck.so** checks to see whether there are dangerous world-writable files/directories in the user's default login tree and issues a warning. (This option is commented out in the example.)

- **pam_env.so** sets or forces particular environment variables to specific values.

- **pam_mail.so** provides a "New Mail" notification to the user.

The second family of modules is of the **account** type. In this example, only one rule exists, and it references a module used previously in the **auth** type. In this instance, the **pam_unix2.so** rule checks the account to verify that the account is valid: not locked, has not expired.

The third rule type used pertains to the **password** family. The rules are applied as follows:

- **pam_pwcheck.so** prompts for the user password and verifies it. In the case of an expired password, this rule prompts for a new one and checks it against a series of rules to ensure it is appropriately complex. In the example, NULL passwords are acceptable.

- `pam_unix2.so` updates the session authentication token using the password provided from the previous rule.

The final set of rules that are checked during a login are the rules governing the `session`. They are mostly used for the setup and teardown routines that are invoked at process creation and removal. In the example, we have these two rules:

- `pam_unix2.so` is responsible for preparing the session environment for the client.
- `pam_limits.so` verifies resource consumption by the account in question against predetermined limits.

The preceding example illustrates how something as simple as a login can look quite complex. It is important to remember, however, that this complexity has been removed from the application level. The benefits of this approach allow for a common and flexible authentication rule set to be applied across multiple applications. In this way, you can ensure that applications such as `login`, `rlogin`, and `ssh` all follow the same methodology when authenticating access. This removes the opportunity for one application, such as POP3, to accidentally present a weaker authentication mechanism to an attacker.

PAM Module Configuration

In the example in Listing 5.5, a number of the modules are passed parameters that affect how they behave. It is possible to preconfigure certain modules to dictate their behavior should a parameter not be passed. These configuration files are stored in `/etc/security`.

The `pam_unix2.so` module used in the example has a corresponding `pam_unix2.conf` file. This file contains default values, and hence specific behavior, for each of the rule families that call it. In the current configuration, because MD5 hashes are used for the account passwords, the password family has a default parameter value of MD5 in `pam_unix2.conf`. Similarly, the `pam_pwcheck.so` module's configuration file defines that it should use the `cracklib` tool and `md5` to verify passwords.

If parameters are passed to the module from within the PAM configuration file, the passed values will supersede those in the configuration.

Resource Management

An additional benefit to the PAM approach is that a number of additional layers of system management can be directly tied into process creation. In the previous example, the final required module reference in the session group refers to a module called `pam_limits.so`.

The limits module allows the system administrator to limit the resources an account can consume on a system. On individual workstations, resource contention affects only the currently logged-on user. On larger servers, individuals can have an impact on performance if they are allowed to consume any and all available resources.

The `pam_limits.so` module holds its configuration in `/etc/security/limits.conf`. An example of this file is shown in Listing 5.6.

LISTING 5.6
A Typical PAM `limits.conf` File

```
# /etc/security/limits.conf
#
#Each line describes a limit for a user in the form:
#
#<domain>        <type>  <item>  <value>
#
#Where:
#<domain> can be:
#        - an user name
#        - a group name, with @group syntax
#        - the wildcard *, for default entry
#        - the wildcard %, can be also used with %group syntax,
#                for maxlogin limit
#
#<type> can have the two values:
#        - "soft" for enforcing the soft limits
#        - "hard" for enforcing hard limits
#
#<item> can be one of the following:
#        - core - limits the core file size (KB)
#        - data - max data size (KB)
#        - fsize - maximum filesize (KB)
#        - memlock - max locked-in-memory address space (KB)
#        - nofile - max number of open files
#        - rss - max resident set size (KB)
#        - stack - max stack size (KB)
#        - cpu - max CPU time (MIN)
#        - nproc - max number of processes
#        - as - address space limit
```

LISTING 5.6

A Typical PAM `limits.conf` File (continued)

```
#          - maxlogins - max number of logins for this user
#          - priority - the priority to run user process with
#          - locks - max number of file locks the user can hold
#
#<domain>        <type>   <item>          <value>
#
#
eric    soft    nproc    12
eric    hard    nproc    20
eric    hard    maxlogins      2
hart    hard    maxlogins      1
# End of file
```

In this example, limits have been placed on Eric's account. Though there are many other possibilities for limiting an account, **maxlogins** and **nproc** will most certainly be used the most often. With the current configuration, the account eric is limited to two concurrent login sessions. Because each session can spawn a number of child sessions, a process limit has been set significantly higher. Keep in mind that a command that contains a number of pipes creates numerous concurrent children to process the information. The **nproc** value must therefore be large enough to satisfy the process nesting that will occur.

What happens when the resource has been exhausted depends on how the limit was reached. In the case of a Telnet session to the host, the account eric will receive a simple permission denied message, as shown here:

```
Athena login: eric
Password:

Permission denied


Connection to host lost.
```

The **nproc** limit is experienced quite differently. As you can see in the following example, if the number of login sessions is less than the limit, the user is able to log in. If, during the login process, the number of processes exceeds the allowed hard limit, the system is unable to create a session for the user, and the connection is dropped.

```
Athena login: eric
Password:
Last login: Tue Feb 15 07:03:56 from console


Connection to host lost.
```

We have seen in this section that we are able to control the resources consumed by an end user. Application of such measures is required only in cases of abuse, but it is good to know that this can indeed be achieved. Keep in mind that these limits are on a per-account basis and are not restricted to simple logins. Other applications that use PAM can also make use of the `pam_limits.so` module.

Access Time Management

In many mission-critical applications, it is important to restrict application and content changes to specific well-controlled change windows. A method for enforcing such an environment is to use the `pam_time.so` module. This module allows you to control the access to specific services based on where the access is being requested from, the account requesting the access, as well as the time the request is being made.

Because you are now introducing time restrictions into the login process, you must inform PAM that this additional step is required. To do this, you must add a line to the PAM login configuration file `/etc/pam.d/login`. The new version of this file should now look like Listing 5.7.

LISTING 5.7

A Typical PAM `pam_time.so` Module Configuration File

```
#%PAM-1.0
auth requisite  pam_unix2.so     nullok       #set_secrpc
auth required   pam_securetty.so
auth required   pam_nologin.so
#auth     required        pam_homecheck.so
auth required   pam_env.so
auth required   pam_mail.so
account required  pam_time.so
account required  pam_unix2.so
password required pam_pwcheck.so  nullok
password required pam_unix2.so     nullok use_first_pass
➥use_authtok
session required  pam_unix2.so     none
session required  pam_limits.so
```

Listing 5.8 shows a snippet of a configuration file for the time module `/etc/security/time.conf`. In this example, the login application is denied to users eric and hart during the evenings.

LISTING 5.8
Login Time Restriction Example for `time.conf`

```
#service;ttys;users;times
login;*;eric | hart ;!Wk1800-0700
```

Connecting using Telnet to Athena yields the following:

```
Athena:~> telnet 192.168.1.242
Trying 192.168.1.242...
Connected to 192.168.1.242.
Escape character is '^]'.
Welcome to SUSE LINUX Enterprise Server 9 (i586) - Kernel
➥2.6.5-7.97-smp (2).

Athena login: eric
Password:

Permission denied
Connection closed by foreign host.
```

This result is what you would expect. The twist, however, is that it leaves the following back door available during the time window:

```
Athena:~> ssh -l eric 192.168.1.242
Password:
Last login: Tue Feb 15 18:04:35 2005 from 192.168.1.247
eric@Athena:~> date
Tue Feb 15 18:06:48 EST 2005
eric@Athena:~>
eric@Athena:~>
```

It is important to remember that Telnet uses the login process to gain access to the machine while **ssh** uses the **sshd** program. Both use different modules for PAM, and both have their own separate configuration modules. If you want to restrict access using **sshd** as well, the **/etc/security/time.conf** file must include

```
sshd;*;eric | hart ;!Wk1800-0700
```

As well, the **/etc/pam.d/sshd** PAM module configuration file must include an account verification step for time as well. It would now become

```
#%PAM-1.0
auth required     pam_unix2.so # set_secrpc
auth required     pam_nologin.so
auth required     pam_env.so
account required      pam_unix2.so
account required      pam_nologin.so
account required      pam_time.so
```

```
password required        pam_pwcheck.so
password required        pam_unix2.so      use_first_pass use_authtok
session required         pam_unix2.so      none        # trace or debug
session required         pam_limits.so
# Enable the following line to get resmgr support for
# ssh sessions (see /usr/share/doc/packages/resmgr/README.SuSE)
#session  optional       pam_resmgr.so fake_ttyname
```

This now closes the **sshd** access method, as shown in the following. As with **login** and **ssh**, a user could use a number of other methods to access the system: **ftp**, **xdmcp**, and so on. All of them will have to have their own **pam.d** configuration checked for time restrictions as well.

```
Athena:~ # ssh -l eric 192.168.1.242
Password:
Password:
Password:
Permission denied (publickey,keyboard-interactive).
Athena:~ #
```

We have seen in this section that it is possible to define limits for resource consumption on a system. As a first control, the PAM time module allows you to selectively restrict the times at which certain applications are available to select users or groups. Also, using the PAM limits module, you can control the resources certain users can consume. The application of these limiting tools must be taken into consideration for each and every application that uses PAM. Failure to do so could allow access to the system through alternate means.

Quota Management

Previously, we introduced the concept of managing volatile system resources such as RAM and CPU utilization consumed by end-user processes. By limiting the number of interactive sessions and the number of child processes, you are able to control the resource impact of each user. In this section, we address the other consumable that is often abused by individual users: disk space.

Storage subsystems have become larger and larger. With this increase has come an insatiable appetite for storage from the user community. In a server environment, it is imperative to keep resource consumption down to the level of what is appropriate for the tasking of the machine. This is done to ensure that maintenance tasks such as backups are completed in a timely fashion and that resources are available for new initiatives. Invariably, however, servers are subject to "scope creep" and sometimes abuse. It is not uncommon for a user to store a backup of his or her local system on the corporate file server just because it is a safe place.

SLES is capable of monitoring and limiting disk space. This functionality is not active by default on a server, however. A certain amount of overhead is involved, and in most cases, quotas are not necessary. In this section, we walk you through the necessary steps to invoke quotas on a server.

Quotas are administered on a per mount point basis. On a typical server, user content directories are segregated from the system partition by placing them on separate disk partitions. Dynamic environments such as /home and /srv are typically mount points for such partitions. These locations are prime candidates for quotas.

NOTE

Quota support is a kernel-level function. By default, the SUSE kernel supports disk quotas. If you recompile your kernel to include or remove functionality, you will have to ensure that quota support is included if required.

CAUTION

Before you modify any disk or partition information, it is imperative to ensure that you have a valid recent backup of your system.

The disk configuration for Athena is shown in Figure 5.1. You can reach this YaST screen by starting YaST, selecting the System program group, and then selecting the partitioner icon. Here, you can see that the servers have three main disk areas: /, /swap, and /home. To enable quotas on the /home partition, select the partition and click the Edit button.

After you click Edit, the edit screen shows up for the /home partition (see Figure 5.2). You engage the quota system by placing an additional option on the partition information within **fstab**. Select the Fstab Options button to assign the quota parameter.

Selecting the Fstab Options button activates a window similar to the one in Figure 5.3. At the bottom of the window is a text box labeled Arbitrary Option Value. In this field, type **usrquota**. This tells the kernel that this partition needs to keep track of disk usage whenever files are written or removed from the disk. You can activate the change by clicking OK and then Apply to return to the main partitioner window.

NOTE

You also can enable quotas on a partition by manually editing /etc/fstab. It is prudent to make a backup copy of fstab just in case you make a mistake. Editing the file directly is quite safe and will yield the same result. Simply add the usrquota qualifier to the mount options for the partition in question. Of course, changing these options will require the partition in question to be remounted to acquire the new characteristics.

FIGURE 5.1

The YaST Partitioner main menu.

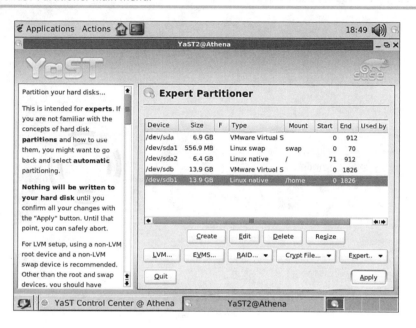

FIGURE 5.2

Editing the /home partition fstab options.

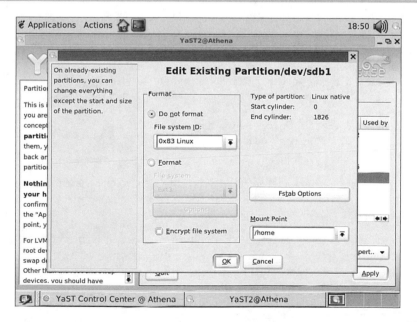

FIGURE 5.3

Adding the usrquota option to the /home partition.

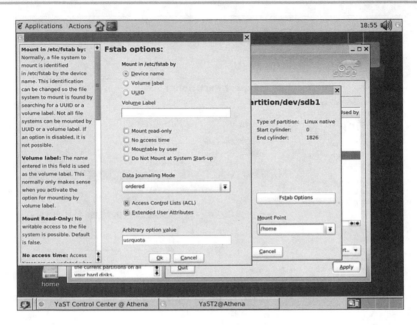

You can now create the initial files for the quota system by invoking the quotacheck command. This command looks at all partitions mounted on the system and creates, or verifies the consistency of, the files required for keeping track of disk usage and limits:

```
Athena:~ # quotacheck -auvg
quotacheck: Scanning /dev/sdb1 [/home] quotacheck:
Cannot stat old user quota file: No such file or directory
quotacheck: Old group file not found. Usage will not be
➥subtracted. done
quotacheck: Checked 92 directories and 220 files
quotacheck: Old file not found.
Athena:~ #
```

In this case, **quotacheck** recognized that on this system only the **/home** mount point had quotas turned on. It also noticed that there were no previous copies of the quota files and hence created new versions.

The next step is to activate the quota monitoring service. It is important to ensure that this service starts when the system itself restarts. Using the YaST Runlevel Editor, select the **quotad** service to run on reboot.

At this point, it is prudent to reboot the system. Doing this remounts all the partitions with the appropriate parameters. When the system comes back up, you are ready to enable and set quotas.

You are now ready to assign quotas to individuals. The amount of disk space allowed for an individual will be left up to a corporate policy, a service-level agreement, or simply good judgment. The total amount of quota allocated to the users should not exceed the disk capacity. Doing so allows the disk to be filled even though a number of users are below quota. It also makes monitoring the quota more difficult. Disk space allocation in SUSE is done in 1KB blocks. Quota limits can therefore be directly related to the amount of disk space, in kilobytes. Similarly, there is a one-to-one relationship between inodes and files. Specifying an inode limit fixes the number of files a user can have independently of how large they become.

The command used to set a quota for a user is called **setquota**. This command takes the following syntax:

```
Setquota -u user #blocks_soft #blocks_hard #inodes_soft
➥#inodes_hard mount_point
```

In this command, the soft limits generate over-quota warnings, and the hard limits cause the system to prevent the consumption of additional resources. A policy should exist that users on a device receive a fixed quota. Stating the policy up front permits the users to police themselves and not lose important information when their quota is exhausted.

Current disk usage for a user can be determined using the **du** command:

```
Athena:~ # du -s /home/hart
116      /home/hart
Athena:~ # du -s /home/eric
548      /home/eric
```

In this example, you can see that the user hart has consumed only 116 blocks and eric has consumed 548. When this file system was created, each block was associated with a size of 1KB. The other parameter you need to understand is the inode value you want to use. An *inode* is a structure that keeps track of file information. In addition to size and access time stamps, an inode points to the string of blocks that make up the content of the file. The inode itself does not contain the data portion of the file. There is a one-to-one relationship between the number of inodes allocated and the number of files a user can generate. To find out how many inodes are available on the partition with quota, use the **df** command:

```
Athena:~ # df -i /home
Filesystem              Inodes    IUsed   IFree IUse% Mounted on
/dev/sdb1              1835008      322 1834686    1% /home
```

You have now collected enough information for setting quotas. Allow your users to consume 10 megabytes of disk space, which is the equivalent of 10,000 1KB blocks, and create 20,000 files. Because you don't want users to hit the wall without any warning, place the soft limits at their target quotas and the fixed limits slightly above. First, check to see what quotas are in force for each user:

```
Athena:~ # quota eric
Disk quotas for user eric (uid 1001): none
Athena:~ # quota hart
Disk quotas for user hart (uid 1002): none
```

Now set limits:

```
Athena:~ # setquota -u eric 10000 11000 20000 21000 /home
Athena:~ # quota eric
Disk quotas for user eric (uid 1001):
     Filesystem blocks  quota   limit   grace   files
➥quota   limit   grace
        /dev/sdb1    548   10000   11000                   130
➥20000   21000
Athena:~ # setquota -u hart 10000 11000 20000 21000 /home

Athena:~ # quota hart
Disk quotas for user hart (uid 1002):
     Filesystem blocks  quota   limit   grace   files
➥quota   limit   grace
        /dev/sdb1    116   10000   11000                    23
➥20000   21000
Athena:~ #
```

The final step is to configure the system to send out warning messages when users are approaching their limits. The quota subsystem contains a procedure called warnquota. This routine checks all user quotas and dispatches messages to those who are over their quota. The configuration file containing the warnquota message is called /etc/warnquota.conf. A stripped-down version of this file is shown in Listing 5.9.

LISTING 5.9
Disk Quota Warning Configuration File

```
/etc/warnquota.conf
# this is an example warnquota.conf
#
MAIL_CMD         = "/usr/bin/mail -t"
FROM             = "quota_cop@localhost"
```

LISTING 5.9
Disk Quota Warning Configuration File (continued)

```
# but they don't have to be:
SUBJECT          = Hey, user, clean up your account!
CC_TO            = "root@localhost"
SUPPORT          = "HelpDesk@UniversalExport.ca"
PHONE            = "Ext. HELP or (4357)"
# Text in the beginning of the mail # This way text can be split to
more lines
# Line breaks are done by '|' character
MESSAGE          = Hello, I've noticed you use too much space\
 on my disk|Delete your files on following filesystems:|
# Text in the end of the mail # is created)
SIGNATURE        = See you!|                          Your admin|
```

It is important to modify this file for your system configuration. By default, the
MAIL_CMD variable does not point to a valid entry.

As an example, user hart has been busy collecting files in his directory.
Checking his quota reveals the following:

```
Athena:/home/hart # quota hart
Disk quotas for user hart (uid 1002):
    Filesystem  blocks   quota   limit   grace   files
➡quota   limit   grace
    /dev/sdb1   10828*  10000   11000   6days      99
➡20000   21000
```

Running warnquota generates an email similar to the following:

```
From root@Athena.UniversalExport.ca  Wed Feb 16 04:36:14 2005
Date: Wed, 16 Feb 2005 04:36:13 -0500
To: hart@Athena.UniversalExport.ca
Cc: root@localhost.UniversalExport.ca
Subject: Hey, user, clean up your account!
From: root@Athena.UniversalExport.ca (root)

Hello, I've noticed you use too much space on my disk
Delete your files on following filesystems:

/dev/sdb1


                        Block limits              File limits
Filesystem              used   soft   hard  grace  used  soft
➡   hard   grace
/dev/sdb1       +-    10828  10000  11000  6days    99 20000
➡ 21000

See you!
                    Your admin
```

As a system administrator, you have to decide how often to check quotas. Once the policy has been set, you can include the `warnquota` command in a `cron` entry so that it is run on a consistent schedule.

User hart can then choose to reduce his consumption, ask for more disk space, or ignore the warning. If he chooses the latter, eventually the grace period will expire, and the user will not be able to create additional files. A sample login session 10 days later will yield this result:

```
hart@Athena:~>
hart@Athena:~>
hart@Athena:~> date
Sat Feb 26 08:45:48 EST 2005
hart@Athena:~>
hart@Athena:~> quota
Disk quotas for user hart (uid 1002):
     Filesystem blocks    quota   limit    grace   files
➥quota    limit    grace
        /dev/sdb1   10828*  10000   11000    none      100
➥20000    21000
hart@Athena:~>
hart@Athena:~>
hart@Athena:~> ls -la > files.txt
/bin/ls: write error: Disk quota exceeded
hart@Athena:~>
```

In this section, we have seen that it is possible under SLES to limit the amount of disk space consumed by a user. Though quota management is not a module within YaST at this time, it is fairly simple to configure and police. The `warnquota` utility should be placed in a `cron` job to run nightly just before or after the backup procedures. This gives the users ample warning of their non-compliance. Limiting the amount of disk space available to users ensures that resources are available across the board. Monitoring resource consumption allows you to better forecast the need for system upgrades.

su **or** sudo

In Unix, there are two types of users: root and the rest. The root account, also known as the *super user*, is required for performing system maintenance tasks. If a user requires an account on a machine, the machine needs to be shut down for maintenance, or an application requires direct access to the Ethernet interface, the root account must be used. This constant demand on the holder of the root account can lead to inefficiencies in the management of the system.

There are two solutions to this problem:

- Share the root password.
- Grant privileged access to others.

The first option is unacceptable. From an audit standpoint, generic accounts are typically frowned upon. It is essentially impossible to track which distinct individual accessed a generic account and performed a particular task. Though it may be possible to correlate who was in the office and had access to a partic-ular terminal, the exercise is often futile. If the account in question has com-plete access to all the files on the system, sharing the password to that account places all the information on the system at risk.

A sound security policy always includes that access is granted on a need-to-have basis. When a system is production ready, most of the requirements for the root account have already been satisfied. In the case in which additional access is required, alternative solutions should be employed. This brings us back to the second option: granting additional privileges.

The **su**, substitute user, command allows an individual to start a shell under the account context of another user. This allows complete access to the target account, including files, mail, and applications available. The transition can be made for a simple command or an entire session depending on the command-line parameters. Here are a couple of variations on the **su** command and the resulting environment:

```
hart@Athena:~>
hart@Athena:~> pwd
/home/hart
hart@Athena:~> ls
bin          login.txt                      photos        su
Documents    ls                             public_html   t2.html
exit         make_teams.good                pwd           test.html
key.txt      Monoalphabetic Crypto.txt      sheila.pdf    t.t
hart@Athena:~>
hart@Athena:~> su -l eric
Password:
eric@Athena:~> pwd
/home/eric
eric@Athena:~> ls
bin Desktop Documents  exit  ls public_html  pwd su
eric@Athena:~> exit
logout
hart@Athena:~> pwd
/home/hart
hart@Athena:~>
```

In this example, a shell is created running under the eric account exactly as it would be if a Telnet or ssh session had been invoked.

In this second example, the ls -l command is executed in the context of the eric account, and control is passed back to the original shell belonging to hart:

```
hart@Athena:~> su -l eric -c 'ls -l ; pwd'
Password:
total 16
drwxr-xr-x   2 eric users 4096 2005-02-15 06:48 bin
drwx------   3 eric users 4096 2005-02-15 07:04 Desktop
drwxr-xr-x   2 eric users 4096 2005-02-15 06:48 Documents
-rw-r--r--   1 eric users   12 2005-02-26 09:55 exit
-rw-r--r--   1 eric users  192 2005-02-26 09:55 ls
drwxr-xr-x   2 eric users 4096 2005-02-15 06:48 public_html
-rw-r--r--   1 eric users   16 2005-02-26 09:55 pwd
-rw-r--r--   1 eric users  517 2005-02-26 09:55 su
/home/eric
hart@Athena:~> pwd
/home/hart
hart@Athena:~>
```

The su command provides the ability for users to access information and resources through other accounts. It does, however, require that individuals share passwords. When this happens, they are invariably written down or shared beyond the originally intended recipient. In the case of the root account, all the functionality of the root account would be available to whoever acquires the password. All the activities of the su command are logged in /var/log/messages as expected, providing a measure of auditing. In many environments, however, the sharing of passwords is against corporate IT policies. Luckily, another utility resolves many of the issues encountered with the su command: sudo.

The sudo utility provides the equivalent functionality of su but with an extra level of granularity. The configuration file for sudo, /etc/sudoers, can be used to limit which users can use sudo and which accounts they are allowed to target. In addition, sudo can be used to limit the verbs available to the new shell.

Listing 5.10 shows a possible configuration for the /etc/sudoers file. In this listing, you can see sample definitions for the various alias types available. A User_Alias can be used to group like users. The current example defines POWERUSER and command aliases to define groups of commands.

The final portion of the sudoers file contains the granting of rights to users and user aliases. In the current example, eric and hart are able to perform most functions commonly associated with an operator type position. In addition, eric has been granted the right to manage disk quotas. Because of the defaults configured in the **sudoers** file, eric and hart must know the root password to obtain the necessary privileges.

In contrast to this, the user belandja can have direct access to the **shutdown** command without the need to know the root password. This capability is often convenient when a user, such as an Oracle DBA, needs to reboot the machine during an install. Because such users do not need the root password for day-to-day tasks, this allows them the freedom to restart the server without requiring additional support staff.

LISTING 5.10
Sample /etc/sudoers File

```
# sudoers file.
#
# This file MUST be edited with the 'visudo' command as root.
#
# Defaults specification
Defaults targetpw # ask for the password of the target user
#%users ALL=(ALL) ALL # WARNING! Only use this together
➥with 'Defaults targetpw'!

# User privilege specification
# You should not use sudo as root in an SELinux environment
# If you use SELinux, remove the following line
root    ALL=(ALL) ALL

User_Alias    POWERUSER  = eric, hart

Cmnd_Alias    MNT = /bin/mount, /bin/umount
Cmnd_Alias    KILL = /bin/kill
Cmnd_Alias    USERMGMT = /usr/sbin/useradd, /usr/sbin/groupadd
Cmnd_Alias    PRINTING = /usr/sbin/lpc, /usr/bin/lprm
Cmnd_Alias    SHUTDOWN = /sbin/shutdown
Cmnd_Alias    REBOOT   = /sbin/reboot

POWERUSER     ALL = (root) MNT, USERMGMT, KILL, PRINTING,
➥SHUTDOWN, REBOOT
belandja ALL= NOPASSWD: /sbin/shutdown
eric      ALL= (root) /usr/sbin/setquota
```

With this configuration in effect, members of the POWERUSER group can perform all the tasks they are required to perform, but no more than that. For the user hart, it is possible for him to manage groups but not affect system services even though he can **sudo** to root. This can be seen in the following excerpt from an online session:

```
hart@Athena:~>
hart@Athena:~> sudo /usr/sbin/groupadd websales
Password:
hart@Athena:~> grep -e websales /etc/group
websales:!:1000:
hart@Athena:~>
hart@Athena:~> sudo /etc/init.d/xinetd stop
Sorry, user hart is not allowed to execute
➥'/etc/init.d/xinetd stop' as root on Athena.
hart@Athena:~>
```

After all the rules are sorted out and access is given to those who need it, the su utility can be retired. The easiest way to do this is to change the permission on /bin/su not to allow Other to have execute access to the program. Replacing the su command with sudo—in conjunction with restricting sensitive accounts to known workstations using PAM—greatly reduces the risk exposure of a server. Locking down root to the console further protects the account from external access.

Summary

In this chapter, you saw that numerous things can be done to make the server environment more secure. In harmony with the concept of running only services that are necessary, accounts must be audited and maintained even on freshly installed servers.

On the user environment side, the chapter examined the Pluggable Authentication Module (PAM) and discussed how it can be used to control system access. PAM is a powerful tool that can be used to control system access, resource consumption, as well as standard approaches to authentication. In terms of consumable resources, this chapter touched on the disk quota system and examined how it can be used to prevent running out of disk space.

To further protect the environment, you saw that it is possible to reduce the number of users who have access to elevated privileges. At the same time, you saw that, for those individuals who do need powerful commands, you can grant them a command set tailored to their needs.

## CHAPTER 6

Filesystem Security

A simple description of the Linux system (which is also true for Unix) is "On a Linux system, everything is a file; if something is not a file, it is a process." Some entities are more than just files (named pipes and sockets, for instance); the Linux operating system and Linux commands treat them as files. Therefore, to simplify discussions, it is fair to say that everything is a file. A Linux system, just like Unix, does not distinguish between a file and a directory because a directory is just a file containing names of other files. Programs, services, texts, images, and so forth, are all files. Input and output devices, and generally all devices, are considered to be files, according to the system.

Linux systems support multiple users, and to let users share or protect their files, a permissions system is implemented. This protection mechanism has some odd twists. For example, to rename or remove a file, you need write permission for the *directory* where the file is located. A thorough understanding of how permissions work lets you make your system more secure, share data easily with other users, and protect files from accidental changes. This chapter reviews the basics—and sheds light into some of the dark corners—of Linux filesystem permissions as well as some advanced topics such as access control lists (in addition to permission settings) and filesystem encryption.

A Review of File and Directory Permissions

In the Linux/Unix world, access permission to a file or directory is determined by whether you are the owner of the file or directory, a member of a specific group assigned, or none of the above (otherwise known as "other" or "world"). In other words, there are three *trustee* assignments (using a NetWare term) possible for each file and directory.

NOTE

A directory is just a special file that contains files and other directories; therefore, for the following discussion, the term *file* is used to refer to both *file* and *directory* unless otherwise specified.

The command `ls -1` displays, among other information, the file type and permission settings of a file. Figure 6.1 shows an example of such a listing and identifies the permission applicability. As you can see, each permission setting consists of three fields (a *triplet*) and is displayed for each of the three trustees. The possible permission value of each field is listed in Table 6.1; the permissions are always in the same order: read, write, and execute for the user, the group, and the others (a.k.a. the world).

FIGURE 6.1
File type and permissions.

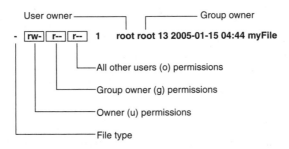

TABLE 6.1
Symbolic Permission Values

PERMISSION	SYMBOL	DESCRIPTION
Read	r	On a file, this means the file is readable. On a directory, it means the contents of the directory may be accessed. It is located in the first position of a triplet.
Write	w	On a file, this means the file may be modified. On a directory, it means that files in the directory may be created, renamed, or deleted. It is located in the second position of a triplet.

TABLE 6.1
Symbolic Permission Values (continued)

PERMISSION	SYMBOL	DESCRIPTION
Execute	x	On a file, this means the file is executable. On a directory, it means that the directory may be traversed and searched for a file (such as using `ls` *directory*). It is located in the third position of a triplet.
Sticky	t	On a directory, the sticky bit means users other than the owner or root *cannot* delete or rename (but can modify) files in this directory, even if they have write permission to the files and the directory. This permission applies only to "others" and is located in the third position of a triplet. On a file, the symbol appears as T and has *no* effect.
		A lowercase t means both the sticky *and* the execute bits are set; an uppercase T means the sticky bit is set, but execute is not.
Set UID (SUID) or Set GID (SGID)	s	Applicable only to the owner or group permission triplet. When found in a file's owner triplet, It means that, when executed, this file will execute with the UID of the owner of the file instead of the UID of the user executing the program; it has no effect if set on the owner triplet of a directory.
		If set in the group triplet of a file, the executed file will assume the GID of the group owner instead of the primary GID of the user executing the program. When set on the group triplet of a directory, all *new* files and subdirectories will inherit the same GID as the directory itself—directories will also inherit the SGID bit—and not the GID of the user who created them; existing files and subdirectories are left unchanged.
		A lowercase s means the SUID or SGID bit is on, and the corresponding user or group execution bit is also on; an uppercase S means the SUID bit is set, but the corresponding execution bit is not set.
		This setting is located in the third position of a triplet.
No permission	–	If this symbol appears in any position in the permission triplet, it means that no permission is assigned in that position.

NOTE

The sticky and SUID/SGID permission bits are further discussed in the "Special File Permissions" section later in this chapter.

The 1s listing in Figure 6.1 shows the following information, from left to right:

- The character in the first column reflects the file type and can be one of the following:

  -, as shown in the example, means this is a regular file.

  b is a block (buffered) special file (such as a tape drive or floppy drive— for example, /dev/fd0).

  c or u is a character-oriented (unbuffered) special file (such as a terminal device—for example, /dev/ttyp0).

  d means it's a directory.

  l is for a symbolic link.

  p is a special FIFO (first in, first out) file (such as a named pipe).

  s is a socket file that provides interprocess networking.

- The first triplet of permission settings (rw-) indicates the file owner can read and write to the file but not execute it (as a binary program or a shell script).

- The second triplet (r--) indicates the members of the file's group can only read the file.

- The third triplet (r--) indicates everyone else (often referred to as world, as in "rest of the world") can only read the file.

NOTE

If a + is displayed after the "others" permissions (such as r--+), it means an access control list (ACL) is assigned to the file. See the "Extended File Attributes" section later in this chapter for details.

- The number of (hard) links to the file; only one link in this example.
- The file owner is user root.
- The file group owner is the root group.
- File size in bytes (13 bytes in this case).
- The modification time.
- Name of the file, myFile.

NOTE

For a shell to execute a file containing shell script commands, the file must have the proper x permission bits set. For instance, for both the file and group owners to be able to run the script file, the x permission must be set on the corresponding triplets. Similarly, if a binary executable, such as the vi editor, is not set with the x permission, you cannot run it.

On the other hand, without the execute bit set, you can still execute the script by typing sh *filename* for a shell script, perl *filename* for a Perl script, and so on. The difference is that the running shell doesn't recognize the script as being executable, but the script interpreter (such as /usr/bin/perl) will happily parse the content of the script file and execute the commands, even if the x bit is not set.

FILES WITH NO OWNER OR GROUP

Ownerless files can be an indication that someone has gained access to your system—created a backdoor user, modified or created some files, and then removed this backdoor user without completely covering his or her tracks. Sometimes these files may just be files created by package installations. You should check regularly for such files using the find command:

Athena:/home/admin # **find / -nouser -o -nogroup**

If you detect any ownerless files, either delete them, or, if you know what they are and want to keep them, assign them to an appropriate user and group using chown.

Bear in mind that the find command can take awhile to run because it needs to check *every* single file on your system. You may consider using a combination of the -path and -prune options to limit the search scope. For example, the following find command will skip checking files and directories in /home/shared directories and below:

Athena:/home/admin # **find / -path '/home/shared' -prune -nouser -o -nogroup**

The meaning of the rwx permissions to files is rather straightforward. However, it is not so obvious when it comes to applying them to directories. The read (r) permission bit on a directory allows you to access its files using ls or similar tools. The reason is that a directory is a special type of file that contains, among other things, the names of files that are stored "in" the directory. So, being able to read a directory lets you access the files stored in it.

In the same way, write (w) permission to a directory lets you modify the directory's contents—such as to change the names of the files stored in that directory. To add, remove, or rename a file, you need write permission *on the directory that contains the file's name*. If a directory is write-protected, the list of entries in that directory cannot be changed—accidentally or on purpose.

The execute (x) permission on a directory lets you search for entries in that directory. Even if you have read permission on a directory (which lets you access files that are in it), you can't *search for* any of its entries unless you also have the execute permission. This may sound a little confusing, but the example shown in Listing 6.1 demonstrates this concept succinctly.

LISTING 6.1
Effect of the Execute Permission Bit on a Directory

```
# md test
# #just to make sure only the owner has rights
# chmod go-rwx test
# ls -ld test
drwx------  2 peter users 48 2005-01-19 01:21 test
# echo "This is a permission test" > test/file.txt
# ls -l test
total 4
-rw-r--r--  1 peter users 26 2005-01-19 01:21 file.txt
# #remove user's execute bit
# chmod u-x test
# ls -ld test
drw-------  2 peter users 72 2005-01-19 01:21 test
# #Hey, can't see directory listing without 'x'!
# ls -l test
/bin/ls: test/file.txt: Permission denied
total 0
# #does tell me filename but wouldn't give file info!
# ls -l test/file.txt
/bin/ls: test/file.txt: Permission denied
# #and can't read file even I have 'r' to the file itself
# cat test/file.txt
cat: test/file.txt: Permission denied
# #put 'x' back on the directory
# chmod u+x test
# #can see the file now
# ls -l test/file.txt
-rw-r--r--  1 peter users 26 2005-01-19 01:21 test/file.txt
# #What if no 'r' to directory, but have 'x'?
# chmod u-r test
# ls -ld test
d-wx------  2 peter users 72 2005-01-19 01:21 test
# #can't do "wildcard" search without 'r'
# ls test
/bin/ls: test: Permission denied
# #but okay if I know the exact filename!
# ls -l test/file.txt
```

LISTING 6.1
Effect of the Execute Permission Bit on a Directory (continued)

```
-rw-r--r--  1 peter users 26 2005-01-19 01:21 test/file.txt
# more test/file.txt
This is a permission test
```

Without execute permission on a directory, you can't access any of its subdirectories. That means you can't access a directory unless you also have execute permission on *all* its *parent* directories, all the way up to the root directory!

NOTE

The root user is not affected by any of the rwx permission restrictions.

Some graphical applications may not handle Linux permissions very well. Because applications such as Nautilus usually show dialog boxes with icons for the files in a directory, they have to be able to "execute" the directory. So, in the example shown in Listing 6.1, if you try to reach a subdirectory under test by clicking through permission.test, you will not be able to. Furthermore, because Nautilus cannot determine the correct file types, subdirectories are displayed (in most cases) using document icons.

Changing Permissions

Although it is a lot easier to change the permission settings using a graphical interface, such as Nautilus (see Figure 6.2), knowing how to perform the task "the hard way" leads to your better understanding the information presented in a GUI dialog box, but the reverse does not hold true. Therefore, to be an effective administrator or power user, you should have an understanding of what takes place "under the hood."

Each of the three sets of permissions is stored as a three-bit digit, and each bit corresponds to one of the read, write, and execute permissions. For easy use with commands, both access permissions and user groups have a code, as shown in Tables 6.2 and 6.3, respectively.

TABLE 6.2
Access Mode Codes

TEXTUAL PERMISSION SYMBOL	NUMERIC VALUE	DESCRIPTION
-	0	No permission granted
r	4	Read access
w	2	Write access
x	1	Execute access

FIGURE 6.2

Changing file permissions using Nautilus.

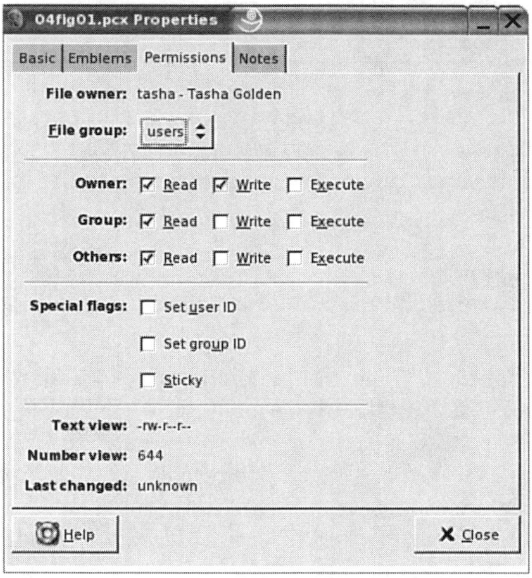

TABLE 6.3

User Group Codes

CODE	DESCRIPTION
u	User permission triplet
g	Group permission triplet
o	Others, or world, permission triplet
a	A shortcut for all three triplets

The chmod utility is used to change the access mode of a file or a directory. You can use it with numeric code or alpha code values—whatever works best for you. The general command syntax is

chmod *access_mode_options target_file_or_directory*

NOTE

Within the Linux/Unix world, the term "to chmod" has become an almost acceptable English verb, meaning the changing of the access mode.

The *access_mode_options* uses the +, -, and = operators to add, remove, or assign permissions to a given group. Combinations separated by commas are allowed. The following example grants the owner of **test** full access while removing all accesses from the group owner and the world:

Athena:/home/admin/demo # **chmod u=rwx,go-rwx test**

NOTE

If you specify more than one mode option, as is in the preceding example, ensure there are *no* spaces before or after the comma. For example, if you used chmod u=rwx, go-rwx test, chmod considers what comes after the space (go-rwx test) as filenames and results in a "No such file or directory" error when trying to access go-rwx.

If a file's owner currently has the rw permission, for example, chmod u=rx will overwrite the current access rights with the new ones, while chmod u+rx will add the execute permission (because the read permission already has been granted).

When you use chmod with numeric arguments, the values for each granted access right have to be counted together per group. Thus, you get a three-digit number, which is the symbolic value for the settings chmod has to make. For example, for rw- permission, the corresponding numeric value (see Table 6.2) is (r=4) + (w=2) = 6. Therefore, the numeric value for rw-rw-rw- is 666. Table 6.4 lists the most commonly used numeric permission combinations to protect files and directories.

NOTE

There is actually a fourth digit, which precedes the first three and sets special access modes, namely the sticky bits and the SUID/SGID bits. These settings are further discussed in the "Special File Permissions" section later in this chapter. To simplify discussion here, you can consider that leading digit to be zero and can omit it when specifying values for chmod.

TABLE 6.4
Common chmod Settings

COMMAND	TEXTUAL VALUE	MEANING
chmod 400 *file*	r-- --- ---	To protect a private file from being accidentally deleted or modified by the owner.

TABLE 6.4

Common chmod Settings (continued)

COMMAND	TEXTUAL VALUE	MEANING
chmod 500 *directory*	r-x --- ---	To protect the owner from accidentally removing, renaming, or moving files from this private directory.
chmod 600 *file*	rw- --- ---	A file that can only be accessed and modified by the owner. A common setting for private files.
chmod 644 *file*	rw- r-- r--	A publicly readable file that can only be modified by the owner.
chmod 660 *file*	rw- rw- ---	The owner and members of the group owner have access, but not the world. A common setting for shared files.
chmod 700 *file*	rwx --- ---	Only the owner has full access to the file, and the file can be executed (such as a shell script). A common setting for a private shell script or program.
chmod 701 *directory*	rwx --- --x	Generally set on the "outgoing" directory on an FTP server where users can download a file only if they know the exact filename.
chmod 703 *directory*	rwx --- -wx	Generally set on the "incoming" directory on an FTP server where users can upload to files but cannot browse for or download existing files.
chmod 755 *directory*	rwx r-x r-x	For files in a directory that should be readable and executable by others, but only changeable by the owner.
chmod 775 *file*	rwx rwx r-x	Standard file-sharing setting for a group.
chmod 777 *file*	rwx rwx rwx	Everybody can do everything to this file.

CAUTION

If you enter a number with fewer than four digits as an argument to chmod, omitted characters are replaced with zeros starting *from the left*. In other words, chmod 77 is the same as chmod 0077.

Changing User and Group Ownership

If the wrong user or group or no owners own a file or directory, the error can be repaired using the chown (change owner) and chgrp (change group) commands. Changing file ownership is a frequent system administrative task in environments where files need to be shared within a group.

The chown command can be applied to change both user and group ownership of a file/directory, while chgrp changes only the group ownership. Of course, the system will check if the user issuing one of these commands has sufficient permissions on the file(s) to be changed. The general syntax of chown is

chown [*options*] *newuser*[:*newgroup*] *file*

Instead of names, numeric UIDs/GIDs may be used instead.

If a colon is used after the username and no group name is given, group ownership will be changed to the primary group of the (administrative) user issuing the command. If no username is provided but a :*newgroup* is specified, chown changes the group owner, performing the same function as chgrp, whose general syntax is

chgrp [*options*] *newgroup* *file*

NOTE

With SLES, instead of a colon in the chown/chgrp commands, you can use a period instead. However, it is a more standard convention to use a colon.

Both chown and chgrp can be used to change ownership recursively, using the -R option. In that case, all underlying files and subdirectories of a given directory will belong to the given user and/or group.

TIP

You can use the --from=*user*[:*group*] option with chown so that only those files and directories whose current owner and/or group match those specified will be assigned a new user and/or group owner. This capability is useful in reassigning ownership if the files and directories are scattered across a number of branches of a filesystem.

Security Considerations

Incorrect file permissions may allow some users to read or modify files that they don't supposedly have access to. The following are two incorrect file permission exploits a hacker will take advantage of: world-accessible (read and/or write) files and group-owned files.

Many system-related files are stored in /etc. Some are world-readable, such as the xinetd configuration files. However, some /etc files should not be world-readable. For example, the /etc/shadow file contains hashed user passwords that should be restricted from world access. Anyone with access to this file may brute-force crack passwords using tools such as John the Ripper. You can easily locate world-readable files using the following find command:

```
$ find / -type f -perm -4 -print 2> /dev/null
```

It is not uncommon for an administrator to make a backup copy of an important system file (perhaps /etc/shadow) before making modifications or testing a procedure. Perhaps due to an oversight on the umask setting (discussed in the "Default Access Permissions" section later in this chapter), the newly created backup file will be world-readable, even if the original file was not! And when that happens to something sensitive like the shadow password file, your system could be compromised.

World-writable files or directories can result in Denial of Service (DoS) attacks or a Trojan horse installation. For instance, it is fairly easily to fill up a filesystem with data when a world-writable file or directory is found. Similarly, a world-writable binary can easily be turned into a Trojan horse; a world-writable xinetd/inetd configuration file can become the source of a backdoor. For example, if /etc/xinetd.d or one of its configuration files (such as vnc) is world-writable, someone could add or modify an existing service and launch an alternate binary. As is the case with world-readable files, you can easily locate world-writable files using the following find command:

```
$ find / -type f -perm -2 -print 2> /dev/null
```

SERVICES BACKDOOR

Say your /etc/xinetd.d/telnet file is writable by someone other than root. Some malicious user or hacker may come across it and make two small modifications: change /usr/sbin/in.telnetd to /bin/bash and enable it to service if it is disabled. Now, when you connect via Telnet, it drops you into a "root shell" (because the service runs as root) *instantly*! No username prompt; no password prompt. The catch here is that you can't run any interactive program, such as vi, and each command you send must be appended with a semicolon (;) or ampersand (&). (For each successful command executed, you will see a "command not found" message displayed by the shell.)

With Linux being open source software, just about all its components are freely available in source code format. A hacker would just need to modify some SUID program, such as ping or passwd, and wait for it to spawn a hidden root SUID shell when executed.

As an administrator, you should check frequently to see whether any previously disabled service is suddenly active and review the contents of the configuration files for unfamiliar changes. The popular targets are services that use privileged ports (ports lower than 1024) because they generally run as root. Any service that runs as root, however, is a potential target.

Often, an application's configuration file is set to be group-readable and -writable. At the same time, some applications store passwords in cleartext in their configuration files. Furthermore, human nature suggests that the probability of someone (such as the system administrator) using the same password for server login and application login is high. Therefore, if a hacker gains access to the unprivileged account named eric, there is a chance that the hacker can locate the root password in one of the group-owned files that Eric has access to.

First, after the hacker logs in using account eric, he can find out the groups Eric belongs to by using the id command:

```
$ id
uid=1001(eric) gid=100(users) groups=100(users),201(web)
```

After noticing Eric belongs to the group named web, the hacker can then use the find command to locate all files owned by that group:

```
$ find / -group web -print 2> /dev/null
/projects/web/README
/projects/web/passwd.txt
/projects/web/index.html
/projects/web/passwd.txt.backup
```

And the two passwd.* files may prove interesting!

From the information in the password files, the hacker may gain access to other accounts, which may in turn lead to more passwords. As the cycle goes on, the hacker may eventually gains root access. Therefore, it is very important that good security procedures be devised *and* enforced. (Refer to the "Corporate Security Policies" section in Chapter 11, "Network Security Concepts," for more information.)

Default Access Permissions

When a user creates a file or directory, a permission *mask*, known as the umask setting, controls the final permissions assigned. The umask is a built-in shell function that *removes* ("masks out") certain permission bits set by a program. A file or directory ends up with its permission bits as follows: When a file is newly created, the kernel assigns it a permission mode of 666 (rw-rw-rw-), and a directory gets 777 (rwxrwxrwx). But before the permissions are actually set, the umask value is applied. The umask value is specified the same way as chmod: first, the user mask; then, the group mask; finally, all others (the special mode mask is skipped for now). So, if the umask value is 022, the final file permission setting is 644 (rw-r--r--). It is often stated that this is as a result of subtracting the umask value from the default permission setting. While the final result in this example reflects such an assertion—and makes it easier to remember the process—the actual mechanics do not work exactly like this. (For example, what if the umask is 027?)

What actually happens is that the requested permission setting (666 in the example) is logically ANDed with the one's complement (that is, it is bit-flipped) of the umask value. Shown in Table 6.5 is the "truth table" for logical AND operations; for example, 0 && 0 results in 0, 1 && 1 results in 1, and so on.

TABLE 6.5
Logical AND Truth Table

&&	0	1
0	0	0
1	0	1

When you're working with logical AND operations, it is easier to work in binary mode. Table 6.6 illustrates how the default permission value of 666 is "masked" by the umask setting of 022.

TABLE 6.6
Logical AND of One's Complement of umask Values with Default Permissions

	U	G	O
umask setting of 022	000	010	010
One's complement of the umask value	111	101	101
Default permission of 666	110	110	110
Applying logical AND	---	---	---
Result	110	100	100
Decimal value	6	4	4

As mentioned earlier, what if your umask is 027? The subtraction concept isn't applicable now, is it? The "proper mechanics" discussed here show that the resulting permission setting is 640, as illustrated in Table 6.7.

TABLE 6.7
File Permission Setting Using a umask of 027

	U	G	O
umask setting of 027	000	010	111
One's complement of the umask value	111	101	000
Default permission of 666	110	110	110
Applying logical AND	---	---	---
Result	110	100	000
Decimal value	6	4	0

SLES sets the default umask value (022) in /etc/profile. Therefore, when a user starts a shell (such as by logging on to the server), this value is automatically set. Furthermore, a new child process gets the umask value (and other shell information) from its parent process. However, after the process is spawned, it is free to change its shell environment, such as the umask setting— and these changes are *not* propagated back to its parent or other existing child processes. If you want to change your umask, you can include the command umask *mask_value* in your home directory's .profile or one of the configuration files used by the shell (such as .bashrc) so that it takes effect whenever you log in or start a new shell.

Keep in mind that with a umask of 022, system applications (such as vi and mkdir) will create files with 644 (rw-r--r--) permissions and directories with 755 (rwx-r-xr-x). The world could read (thus copy) the newly created files and directories. This may not be a good idea if you also have guest users from outside your company accessing your server. A better default umask setting is 027. Such a umask would eliminate all world access to any newly created files and directories. You can later selectively make some available to the world using chmod.

CAUTION

Any user or process may set the umask for its shell. So, even if you put in the more restrictive umask 027 in /etc/profile, any user can easily override it with a less restrictive setting. Because umask is a built-in shell function, you cannot easily restrict it from general use; you need to create a custom shell by compiling the modified source code to do that. It is best to educate your users that the more restrictive setting is in everybody's best interest and should not be changed.

SLES includes a number of tools to help you maintain system file and directory permission integrity. For instance, the `seccheck` (SUSE Security Checker) package can report on executables that are group- and/or world-writable. YaST includes a Local Security Configuration module (Control Center, Security and Users, Security Settings; or `yast security` from a terminal session) that configures the level of file permissions as Easy, Secure, or Paranoid. And you can use SuSEconfig to set or reset file permissions accordingly—using specifications according to `/etc/permissions.*`.

Special File Permissions

In addition to the basic permissions discussed earlier, you can also set three special permission bits on files and directories:

- **SUID bit**—Generally referred to as the SUID bit because of the name of the API call used, this bit changes the user ID on execution. When a program is executed with the SUID bit set, the process will have the same rights as the owner of the file being executed.

- **SGID bit**—Generally referred to as the SGID bit because of the API call used, this bit changes the group ID on execution. It operates the same as the SUID bit but inherits rights of the group of the owner of the file. If set on a directory, it means that when a new file is created in the directory, the new file's group owner will be the same as the directory's group owner.

NOTE

Because of shell scripts' inherent lack of tight security, Linux has disabled the SUID/SGID support for them: You can set the bits, but they have no effect. Should you have the need for a SUID/SGID script, use Perl instead. See `man perlsec` for more information.

- **Sticky bit**—In older Unix kernels, this bit was used to trigger a program to "stick" in memory after it is finished (so the next time the application is executed, it is already in memory); now this usage is obsolete with the advent of virtual memory. When set on a directory, the sticky bit ensures nonroot users can only delete files they own in that directory. The sticky bit is applicable only to the world permission setting of a directory; it has no effect when applied to a file.

NOTE

Often, the SUID bit is used by system applications or scripts so that the process may access system resources as root. On the other hand, the SGID bit is not frequently used by system programs but is mostly used by system administrators to set up shared directories.

CAUTION

You should closely monitor programs and scripts that set the SUID and/or SGID bit. It is quite common for a hacker to exploit some vulnerability and then leave behind a root SUID program in place as a backdoor. The key here is to use applications such as Tripwire (see Chapter 12, "Intrusion Detection"), Bastille, and seccheck (see Chapter 13, "System Security") and keep track of your system!

To set any of these three special permission bits, chmod requires a fourth digit. This value is specified as the most significant (left-most) digit, and its possible values are listed in Table 6.8. For example, chmod 1777 testDir means the owner, group, and world have full read, write, and execute rights to testDir, and the sticky bit is also set for the world permission. The ls output would look like this:

```
Athena:/home/admin # chmod 1777 testDir
Athena:/home/admin # ls -l testDir
drwxrwxrwt  2 root admin 48 2005-01-19 17:35 testDir
```

TABLE 6.8
Special Permission Mode Codes

OCTAL DIGIT	BINARY VALUE	DESCRIPTION
0	000	SUID, SGID, and sticky bits are not set
1	001	Sticky bit set
2	010	SGID bit set
3	011	SGID and sticky bits set
4	100	SUID bit set
5	101	SUID and sticky bits set
6	110	SUID and SGID bits set
7	111	SUID, SGID, and sticky bits are set

The corresponding chmod command using a textual value is chmod a+rwx,o+t testDir. The symbols for the special modes displayed by ls reflect whether the corresponding execute bit is also set. For example, if the sticky bit is set but the world's execute bit is not set, a symbol T is displayed instead of t. Table 6.9 summarizes the special mode symbols displayed depending on the execute bit setting.

TABLE 6.9
Special Permission Textual Representation

	EXECUTE BIT NOT SET	EXECUTE BIT SET
SUID	--S --- ---	--s --- ---
SGID	--- --S ---	--- --s ---
Sticky	--- --- --T	--- --- --t

NOTE

When you set these special permission modes using their textual values in chmod, use lowercase characters, such as s and t, and not the uppercase ones. The case distinction is used by ls to display the different permission combinations.

Security Implications of SUID/SGID

It is worth discussing the need for SUID and SGID programs and scripts in the Linux/Unix world, even when they can be Trojan horses left behind by a hacker. First, consider the /etc/passwd file. Only the file owner (root) has write access (rw-r--r--) to it. Yet as an ordinary user, you can modify the contents of this file, albeit in a very limited way, using the passwd and chsh commands.

An examination of the permission bits of the /usr/bin/passwd program shows that both the SUID and execute bits are set (rwsr-xr-x) for the file owner. This indicates that the passwd utility is a root SUID program: It's a SUID program because of the s flag in the permission bits, and it's a root SUID program because root owns the file. Thus, when anyone runs the passwd program, the user *temporarily* gains the privileges of the root user—but only for the duration of the program's execution and only from within that program. Without such a mechanism, many system administration tasks can become unnecessarily complex due to the security implications. For instance, how would you effectively secure the /etc/shadow file and yet allow users to update their own passwords?

On the other hand, the SUID API call can be used to *lower* a user's privileges instead of increasing them. For instance, for an IP-based service to bind to one of the privileged ports, it needs to run as root. However, after the port is bound, the application no longer needs to have root privileges; it can use the SUID call to change the process's UID to that of a nonprivileged user. Or a program may run as root, but it can spawn processes that run at a lower privileged level for security reasons. An example is the Apache web server; its suEXEC utility (see http://httpd.apache.org/docs-2.0/suexec.html) executes CGI and SSI programs as user wwwrun and group www (the default setting on SLES 9) instead of as the owner of the main Apache process, which generally runs as root.

NOTE

For an application to be a SUID program, it must make the SUID or similar API call (there are a number of variants of the SUID call), *and* the file permission bit must be set as such. Simply setting the SUID bit on a program does not automatically make it a SUID program.

There's an identical mechanism for group ownership. For instance, if you examine the permissions for /usr/bin/uucp, you'll see s flags for both the user and group (r-sr-sr-x). Thus, when you run uucp (Unix-to-Unix CoPy), you temporarily gain the rights of the owning user (uucp) and the owning group (uucp).

SUID scripts are generally more dangerous than SUID programs. This is largely due to the fact that running a script first invokes a shell. If the script is SUID root, the invoked shell will run with root privileges. It is possible, after the shell is invoked but before the script runs, to interrupt the kernel and replace the file that the shell is going to execute. The replaced file could be any executable shell script, including another shell (which, in this case, would be a root shell). Due to these security implications, Linux systems have long since disabled support for SUID/SGID shell scripts. If you really need a script that does SUID/SGID, develop it using Perl with the *taint mode* enabled.

TIP

When a Perl script file has its SUID and/or SGID bits set, the Perl interpreter automatically enters a paranoid mode and performs a set of special security checks to detect possible tainted data, such as verifying that directories specified in the PATH variable are not writable by others. You can enable this taint mode explicitly by using the -T command-line flag at the beginning of the script, that is, #!/usr/bin/perl -T. This flag is *strongly* suggested for server programs and any program run on behalf of someone else, such as a CGI script. When taint mode is turned on, it is on for the remainder of your script.

You can use applications such as Tripwire, Bastille, and seccheck to automate searching for and reporting on questionable SUID/SGID programs and scripts.

But if you're a consultant who just walked on to a client's site doing a security audit, the following commands could be useful:

- To obtain a list of *all* SUID or SGID files (programs and scripts), use the following:

```
# find / -type f -perm +ug=s -exec ls -l {} \;
```

- To find all root SUID files, use this command:

```
# find / -type f -owner root -perm +u=s -exec ls -l {} \;
```

- Check for a SUID or SGID script only by looking at the first two bytes in the file to see whether they're #! (the so-called *magic bytes*), indicating it's a script file:

```
# find / -type f -perm +ug=s -print0 2> /dev/null | \
perl -n0e 'chomp; open(FILE, $_); read(FILE,$magic,2); \
print $_,"\n" if $magic eq "#!"; close(FILE);'
```

TIP

Keep the number of SUID and SGID programs on your system to a minimum. The main focus here should be on root SUID programs. Nonroot SUID and SGID programs present less of a risk but can still be a source of security breach.

TIP

If you are unsure whether a program or script should have its SUID/SGID bit set, or you have determined that one or more SUID files or directories are unnecessary, disable them with chmod u-s,g-s *name*. Make sure you keep a record of what you have modified so the changes may be reversed at a later time should the need arise.

SGID and File Sharing

With SLES, as long as a user is a member of the group that has group ownership to a file or directory, he or she can access it according to the group permission settings; it doesn't matter if that user's primary group is different. For example, the group owner of the /usr/share/projectDestiny directory is destiny, and the group has been granted read, write, and execute permissions. User carol is a member of the users, audio, video, and destiny groups, and her primary group is users. As long as carol is a member of the destiny group, she will have full access to the projectDestiny directory. The same goes with the other users. However, this has one administrative shortcoming and one security flaw.

Although the destiny members have full rights to the directory, the files they create will bear group ownership corresponding to the primary group of the users. For instance, files created by Carol will bear a group owner of users because that is her primary group. If, at some point, you need to locate all her files relating to the Destiny project that were moved to a different directory (the mv command does not change the ownership information), it would be very difficult, administratively, unless there is some "marker" you can use. On the other hand, if the files Carol created in the /usr/share/projectDestiny directory all have destiny as the group owner, you can easily use the find command to locate them should they be moved. For example, the following command locates all files with user owner carol and group owner destiny that are *not* located in the /usr/share/projectDestiny directory:

```
# find / -path '/usr/share/projectDestiny' -prune -o \
-user carol -group destiny -exec ls -ld {} \;
```

Now, the potential exists for a security backdoor. The default SLES-installed umask is 022, which means world has read and execute permissions to directories; this means world users can see the filenames in there. Carol creates a file in /usr/share/projectDestiny with a permission of 644 (rw-r--r--). Because the file is in a shared directory and may need to be updated by other members of the destiny group, Carol dutifully changes the file permission to 664 (rw-rw-r--) or even to 660 (rw-rw----). However, the file's group owner is users—Carol's primary group. Along comes Eric, who is not with the Destiny project but is in the users group. As long as /usr/share/projectDestiny has the world execute permission bit set, Eric *can* modify Carol's file because of the group ownership.

You can, of course, rectify this potential security hole by removing world access to the directory entirely. However, an easier solution is to use the SGID bit because it solves both the administrative difficulty and the group owner issue concurrently. When the SGID bit is set on a directory, every time a new file is created in the directory, the new file's group owner is set to be the same as the directory's group owner. Therefore, files created by Carol, for instance, will automatically be assigned destiny as the group owner, and can only be modified by Carol or other members of the destiny group. And to keep the world users from snooping around the directory, you can revoke all the world permissions.

NOTE

With ext2 and ext3 type filesystems, a mount option provides the same functionality as setting the SUID bit on directories. When mounted with the grpid (or bsdgroups) option specified, the Linux kernel treats *all* directories found on that ext2/ext3 filesystem as if the SGID bit were set.

TIP

A good group file-sharing scheme is one that uses a dedicated group as the group owner of the directory and the directory's permission mask set as 2770 (rwxrws---). Only users who need to have access to the folder are made members of the group. The user owner of the directory should be the group or project leader.

A SUID Sample Program

Here is a simple program to illustrate how easily you can write a root SUID program. It takes just five short lines of C code:

```c
#include <stdio.h>
main (void)
{
    setuid(0);
    setgid(0);
    system("/bin/bash");
}
```

Assuming you place the preceding lines in a file called become-root.c, you can follow these steps to compile and turn this code into a root SUID program:

1. From a terminal session, compile the preceding C code using the following command (assuming you have the gcc package installed):

   `# gcc -o become-root become-root.c`

2. Set the file's user and group owner to root:

   `# chown root:root become-root`

3. Set the necessary bits using chmod:

   `# chmod u+s,g+s become-root`

You need to perform the last two steps as root.

Now, whenever you run become-root, even as an unprivileged user, your current identity will be switched to root (both UID and GID), and you can verify that identity with the id command. Just type exit to return to the previous identity.

WARNING

You can see from the preceding example how easy it is to create a root SUID program that executes "some command." Some malicious person can easily substitute the "/bin/bash" command for something really nasty such as "/bin/rm -frdv /"! Therefore, if you don't know where a SUID/SGID (root or not) program comes from or what it will do exactly, *do not run it*!

TIP

If you find some file to be suspicious, *do not* execute it. You can dump all the strings in the file and look for some interesting stuff using the strings command like this:

```
Athena:/home/admin # strings become-root
/lib/ld-linux.so.2
SuSE
libc.so.6
system
setgid
_IO_stdin_used
__libc_start_main
setuid
__gmon_start__
GLIBC_2.0
PTRhP
/bin/bash
```

As you can see from the output, strings showed references to setgid, setuid, system, and /bin/bash, suggesting this is a SUID program of some sort. When you use strings, it is relatively easy to figure out what files the binary wants to open, if there are any special messages (such as "Gotcha!" as Trojan horses tend to contain), and so on.

The system() command in the preceding example can also be used to execute a script, and not just commands. Therefore, if you decide that you need a SUID shell script and don't want to use Perl, you can modify the example slightly and use it as a "wrapper" for your script. You may be tempted to pass the script's path and name from the command line so you have a generic wrapper. However, this approach can be dangerous. If some disgruntled user stumbles upon it, he or she could use it to execute some nasty script or command that will ruin your day. It is, therefore, *strongly* recommended that you hard-code the script's path and name in the program instead of passing it as a command-line option. Ensure the script's permissions are set so that they cannot be modified by anyone else except you. Furthermore, keep all your custom SUID/SGID scripts and programs in a "safe" place, as discussed in the next section.

Securing Against SUID Programs

The primary way of interacting with a Linux system is through the filesystem; even hardware devices, such as the terminal console, are represented by a (special) file on the filesystem. Thus, when an intruder gains access to a system, it is desirable to limit what he or she can do with the files available to him or her. One way to accomplish this is to use restrictive filesystem mount options; for example, the nosuid option disallows the SUID and SGID bits from taking effect.

When a filesystem is mounted with the nosuid option, the Linux kernel will ignore any SUID and SGID bits that have been set on files and directories found on that filesystem. You can specify the nosuid option as part of the mount command when mounting a filesystem manually. For example,

```
Athena:/home/admin # mount -o nosuid /dev/hda4 /mnt
```

results in all files and directories found in /mnt having their SUID and SGID bits ignored. But you can use this command instead:

```
Athena:/home/admin # mount -o nosuid,grpid /dev/hda4 /mnt
```

This way, you can enforce implied SGID on all directories. The equivalent entry in /etc/fstab would look something like this:

```
/dev/hda4      /mnt     ext2     defaults,nosuid,grpid   1   2
```

By carefully considering your requirements and dividing up your storage into multiple filesystems, you can utilize these mount options to provide some level of security against rogue SUID programs and scripts. You can further enhance the security by using the nodev and noexec mount options.

In a typical multiuser system, it is unlikely that users will need to execute SUID binaries or create device files in their home directories. Therefore, a separate filesystem, mounted with the nodev and noexec options, could be created to house the users' home directories. In addition, if you've determined that your users will not need to run programs stored in their home directories—a good policy to have because it cuts down on the installation of possible virus-infected or unlicensed programs—you can use the noexec mount option as well. Similar considerations should be given to /tmp and /var. It is unlikely that any process will legitimately need to execute any binaries or access device files from those directories.

TIP

Locking down world-writable directories with noexec, nosuid, and nodev mount options helps prevent the possibility of an intruder leaving a Trojan horse in common directories. The malicious user may be able to install the program, but it cannot actually run, with or without the proper permission settings.

CAUTION

The nodev mount option may break services running in chroot jails. Often, a service needs to access device nodes such as /dev/null and /dev/log. If the filesystem used by the chrooted service was mounted with nodev, such access would be denied, and the service may fail to run to completion.

As a word of warning, do *not* consider a filesystem mounted with noexec to be totally safe. It will prevent an average user from running an executable binary or script from it. However, a seasoned user can still circumvent the restriction by passing the script through its interpreter (such as perl */script/on/ noexec/filesystem*).

In Linux kernels prior to 2.6, you can use the dynamic runtime library linker, /lib/ld-linux.so.* (where * is the version number of the currently available ld-linux.so), to execute binaries residing on such a filesystem. Although this is no longer an issue with the 2.6 Linux kernel (which SLES 9 is based on) and later, it in no way guarantees that no one can run an executable from a noexec-mounted filesystem.

Sticky Business

Traditionally, the sticky bit on an executable binary file tells the Unix kernel that after the concerned application has finished executing, it should remain in the swap space rather than being purged—thus the term *sticky*. This made operational sense when disk access speeds were slow and memory was expensive; keeping frequently used programs in such a state provided shorter program startup times. However, with the development of ever-faster disk drives and memory access technologies (paging instead of swapping, for instance), the sticky bit is no longer required. As a matter of fact, although still supporting its specification via the `chmod` program for backward compatibility, newer versions of Unix no longer respect the flag; Linux never used the flag on files from the beginning.

On the other hand, support of sticky bits on directories is alive in Linux/Unix. A directory with this bit set enables users to rename or remove only those files that they own within that directory (other directory permissions permitting). It is usually found on world-writable directories used to store temporary files (such as `/tmp` and `/var/spool/cups/tmp`) and prevents users from tampering with each other's files. You can use the following command to locate files or directories with the sticky bit set:

```
# find / \( -type f -o -type d \) -perm +o=t \
-exec ls -ld {} \; 2>/dev/null
```

TIP

From a security standpoint, all world-writable directories should have their sticky bit set. If a world-writable directory does not have its sticky bit set, you should consider whether it really needs to be world-writable or whether the use of groups or ACLs (see the next section "Extended File Attributes") will work better for your situation. You can generate a list of world-writable directories that *don't* have their sticky bit set by using this command:

```
# find / -type d -perm -o+w -not -perm -a+t \
-exec ls -ld {} \; 2>/dev/null
```

Extended Attributes

Most of the time, the traditional Linux/Unix file permission system fits the security needs of an organization just fine. However, in today's highly collaborative environment where multiple users need access to files, this scheme can become inadequate or cumbersome to use. The newer Linux kernels introduced access control lists (ACLs) as an extension of the traditional file permission concept. While ACLs do not inherently add "more security" to a system, they do help to reduce the complexity of managing permissions. Supported by the ext2, ext3, ReiserFS, JFS, and XFS filesystems, ACLs provide new ways to apply file and directory permissions without resorting to the creation of unnecessary groups.

You cannot use `chmod` to manipulate these secondary ACLs because they are stored separately from the standard Linux permissions. Instead, you need to use `setfacl` and `getfacl`, as discussed later in this section. Furthermore, to make use of ACLs, both the kernel and the filesystem used must support them.

ACL SUPPORT IN SAMBA

To make Samba as portable as possible, its designers decided against a custom implementation of ACLs. Instead, each Samba server converts Windows ACL specifications (sent via MS-RPC) into a POSIX ACL and then converts that neutral ACL into an ACL that's platform-specific.

If the Samba server's underlying filesystem supports ACLs, and the POSIX ACL can be converted to a native ACL, Windows users can manipulate server-side ACLs on the Samba server using common Windows utilities.

Samba 2.2 and later included support for ACLs, and it will preserve NTFS ACLs rather than mapping ACL permissions to the less-flexible, standard Unix permissions. Native ACL support, in combination with `winbind`, allows a Linux-based Samba system such as SLES 9 to "assimilate" Windows NT and higher users, groups, and ACL permissions.

ACLs are stored as extended attributes (EAs) within the filesystem metadata. As the name implies, they allow you to define lists that either grant or deny access to a given file based on the criteria you provide. ACLs do *not* replace but instead coexist with the traditional permission system; they can be specified for users and groups and are still separated into the realms of read, write, and execute rights. In addition, an ACL may be defined for any user or group that does not correspond to any of the user or group ACLs, much like the "other" mode bits of a file. The ACLs also have what is called an *ACL mask*, which acts as a permission mask for all ACLs that specifically mention a user or a group (so-called *named user* or *named group* ACLs). This mask is similar to the `umask` but not quite the same. For example, if you set the ACL mask to `r--`, any ACLs that pertain to a specific user or group and are "looser" in permission (for example, `rw-`) will be "masked out" and effectively become `r--`.

ACL masks work similarly to the *Inherited Rights Mask (IRM)* used by the NetWare file system, where each named ACL is logically `AND`ed with the ACL mask to obtain an effective ACL; a named ACL can be compared to a NetWare user or group trustee assignment. The main difference here is that in Linux, a named ACL takes precedence over a named group ACL, whereas in NetWare, both assignments are combined to get an overall privilege. For example, Carol belongs to the group users. If there is a named user ACL for username carol and a named group ACL for groupname users, the mode assigned to the named user ACL is compared with the ACL mask to determine the effective ACL; the name group ACL is ignored in this case.

SECURING FILES USING EXTENDED ATTRIBUTES

With ext2/ext3 filesystems, there is an EA called the "immutable" bit. A file with this bit set (using `chattr +i filename`) cannot be modified in any way: It can't be renamed or deleted, no links can be created to this file, and no data can be added to this file. Only a process with the CAP_LINUX_IMMUTABLE privilege or the root user can set or clear this attribute. If a file with the u (undeletable) attribute set is deleted, its contents are saved and thus can be undeleted. See `man chattr` for other EA attributes. (File undelete is not possible on an ext3 filesystem; see `batleth.sapienti-sat.org/projects/FAQs/ext3-faq.html` for an explanation.)

Use `lsattr` to list the EAs on an ext2/ext3 filesystem.

Directories may also contain *default ACLs*, which specify the initial ACLs of files and subdirectories created within them.

To add, modify, or remove ACLs, you use the `setfacl` command. To add or modify an ACL, you use the -m flag, followed by one or more comma-separated ACL specifications and one or more filenames. To delete an ACL, you use the -x flag instead. The general command syntax is

```
setfacl option_flag acl_specification filename
```

There are four general forms of an ACL: one for users, another for groups, one for others, and one for the ACL mask, as shown in Table 6.10. Notice that for the user and group ACLs, the actual user and group names that the ACL applies to are optional. If they are omitted, the ACL will apply to the base ACL, which is derived from the file's mode bits. Thus, if you modify them, the mode bits will be modified and vice versa, as illustrated by the following example:

```
Athena:/home/testuser # touch testfile
Athena:/home/testuser # ls -l testfile
-rw-r--r--  1 testuser users 0 2005-01-12 10:15 testfile
Athena:/home/testuser # setfacl -m g::---,o:--- testfile
Athena:/home/testuser # ls -l testfile
-rw------- 1 testuser users 0 2005-01-12 10:15 testfile
```

TABLE 6.10

ACL Specifications

TYPE	SYNTAX
User	u[ser]:[*username*]:*mode*
Group	g[roup]:[*groupname*]:*mode*
Other	o[ther]:*mode*
ACL mask	m[ask]:*mode*

Consider the following example in which user eric is given read and write access to a file called `report`:

```
Athena:/home/testuser # ls -l report
-rw-rw-r--  1 testuser users 0 2005-01-12 10:25 report
Athena:/home/testuser # setfacl -m u:eric:rw- report
Athena:/home/testuser # ls -l report
-rw-rw-r--+ 1 testuser users 0 2005-01-12 10:25 report
Athena:/home/testuser # getfacl report
# file: report
# owner: testuser
# group: users
user::rw-
user:eric:rw-
group::rw-
mask::rw-
other::r--
```

TIP

In the ls output after the setfacl command, notice the + after the permission bits. This symbol indicates the file has extended attributes associated with it.

The `getfacl` command displays ACLs and other file information. The first three lines show the file's name (`report`), the file's owner (testuser), and the group owner (users). The line `user:rw-` and the lines `group::rw-` and `other:r--` simply reflect the traditional file mode permission bits. The `user:eric:rw-` line is the new, *named user ACL* (where a specifically named user is given an ACL assignment). Assume that Eric is not a member of the group users. This named ACL has just granted Eric read *and* write access to the file. Without the use of ACLs, either Eric would just have read access (as a result of the world permission bits), or you would have to add him to the group users to grant him read/write access.

Now, if you change the ACL mask to r--, the ACL for Eric would effectively become r-- as well:

```
Athena:/home/testuser # setfacl -m m:r-- report
Athena:/home/testuser # getfacl report
# file: report
# owner: testusre
# group: users
user::rw-
user:eric:rw-            #effective:r--
group::rw-
mask::rw-
other::r--
```

As mentioned earlier, directories can have default ACLs that will automatically be applied to files and subdirectories that are created within it. You set default ACLs by prepending a d: to the ACL that you want to set:

```
Athena:/home/testuser # mkdir testdir
Athena:/home/testuser # setfacl -m d:u:eric:rw- testdir
Athena:/home/testuser # getfacl testdir
# file: testdir
# owner: testuser
# group: users
user::rwx
group::r-x
other::r-x
default:user::rwx
default:user:eric:rw-
default:group::r-x
default:mask::rwx
default:other::r-x

Athena:/home/testuser # touch testdir/blah
Athena:/home/testuser # getfacl testdir/blah
# file: testdir/blah
# owner: testusre
# group: users
user::rw-
user:eric:rw-
group::r-x            #effective:r--
mask::rw-
other::r--
```

As you can see here, Eric's ACL has been applied to the newly created file under **testdir**. When the default ACL is set, the **umask** no longer influences the permissions of new files.

In short, ACLs let you maintain fine-grained control over your files. With ACLs, you can avoid the risk of granting privileges too widely.

Data and Filesystem Encryption

So far, we've been concerned mainly with securing *access* to data, and not the actual data itself. At a basic level, file permissions and ACLs enforced by the Linux kernel can protect your files from the prying eyes of other nonroot users on your system. But what if someone compromises your login password or gains root access through one of the security exploits, or simply steals a backup tape or a hard drive or even the whole server?

To guard against these possibilities, you can employ encryption to scramble your data so that a secret password or key is required to unscramble and make it intelligible again. Thus, merely gaining the ability to *read* your files is not enough; an intruder must also have your secret password to make any sense out of the data. There are two ways in which you can protect your data: either selectively encrypt files that need securing or encrypt the whole filesystem on which the data resides.

Most Linux distributions include an excellent encryption software program: the *Gnu Privacy Guard*, also known as GnuPG or GPG. If you are familiar with Pretty Good Privacy (PGP), you'll find GnuPG quite similar but far more configurable. The main program in the GnuPG package is called **gpg** and has more than 100 possible command-line flags.

NOTE

If you want to install GnuPG on your SLES server, it is easiest to use YaST and search for packages with gpg in their descriptions. Visit http://www.gnupg.org for the latest version and online documentation.

Based on OpenPGP (RFC 2440), GnuPG supports two types of encryption: *symmetric* (or secret-key) and *asymmetric* (or public-key). In symmetric encryption, the same key, or password, is used for encrypting and decrypting the data. Public-key encryption, on the other hand, uses two related keys (a *key pair*) known as the public and private (secret) keys. They are related mathematically in that data encrypted with the public key can only be decrypted with the private one, but it is not computationally feasible to discover the private key based on the public key. Therefore, the general usage of asymmetric encryption is that you make known your public key to anyone who is interested in sending you secured information, while you keep your private key to yourself. The sender sends you the data encrypted using your public key, and you decrypt it using your private key. Although other people may have your public key, it cannot be used to decrypt the message.

CAUTION

Before using a public key to encrypt sensitive information to send to someone, make sure that the key actually belongs to that person. GnuPG allows a key to be *signed*, indicating that the signer vouches for the key. Signing works in much the same way as the SSL certificate sent by a web server to your browser where a trusted root certificate is used to verify the authenticity of the SSL certificate.

You can also make your public key available to others via a key server (which acts as a trusted third party). You can submit your public key to one of the many key servers available on the Internet. Two such servers are www.keyserver.net and pgp.mit.edu. Remember that even though you may have retrieved someone's public key from a well-known key server, you should check the key fingerprint with the owner before totally trusting it.

Symmetric encryption is much simpler to use because you only need to use the same key for encrypting and decrypting. Public-key encryption requires some setup, at the very least generating a key pair, but it is more flexible. For instance, it allows others to send you encrypted data without having to first agree on a shared secret key. Therefore, symmetric encryption is often used for safeguarding your own data that is generally not shared with others, and asymmetric encryption is often used when sensitive data is to be transmitted between different parties.

It is beyond the scope of this chapter to go into the details of GnuPG, such as key and trust management and key servers. We refer you to the documentation. The following examples serve to illustrate how you can use it to protect your data files:

- To encrypt a file with a (symmetric) secret key using GnuPG, use the following:

  ```
  Athena:/home/admin # gpg -c filename
  ```

  You will be prompted for the key, and the encrypted file will have a .gpg suffix—for example, filename.gpg.

- To encrypt a file using the recipient's public key, use this command:

  ```
  Athena:/home/admin # gpg -e -r recipient_key_id filename
  ```

  Note that you need to have already added the recipient's public key to your "key ring" (key database) before you can use it. You can encrypt a file for more than one recipient by including additional -r key_id switches to the command.

TIP

You should include yourself in the recipient list by specifying your own public key at encryption time (-r *your_key_id*). Otherwise, you would *not* be able to decrypt the file yourself.

- To decrypt an encrypted file, use this command:

  Athena:/home/admin # **gpg** *filename*.**pgp**

  You will be prompted for the password if the file was symmetrically encrypted or the private key if it was asymmetrically encrypted. The resulting decrypted file will be named *filename*. If you specify the -d switch, the output is sent to **stdout**, which you can redirect to a file or use as pipe input to another program.

- To use GnuPG's asymmetric encryption to encrypt all of Tasha's accounting-related files on the server so only she and you can decrypt them, use the following command:

  Athena:/home/admin # **find /accounting -user tasha -type f **
  -exec gpg -e -r *tasha_key_id* **-r** *your_key_id* **{} \;**

Because of the number of option flags available, you can choose from a wide variety of programs that either use or support GnuPG encryption to make your life easier when using GnuPG. Some GUIs (such as KGpg for KDE desktops and Seahorse for GNOME) simplify your key management tasks to just a few mouse clicks. There are also many Mail User Agents (MUAs) that let you encrypt and sign your email messages seamlessly. You can find a comprehensive list of these and other utilities at http://www.gnupg.org/(en)/related_software/frontends.html.

If you have many files to encrypt or have files transparently encrypted without user intervention, it may be easier to set up an encrypted filesystem. If you have any removable drives on your server, such as hot-swappable hard drives or USB devices, filesystems on them should be encrypted to guard against theft. SLES 9 includes the capability of an encrypted filesystem out of the box.

You can set up encrypted partitions either during initial server installation or later. You can create an encrypted virtual filesystem at any time after the server has been installed because it fits nicely in an existing partition layout. To encrypt an entire partition, you need to dedicate a partition for encryption in the partition layout. The standard partitioning proposal as suggested by YaST does not, by default, include an encrypted partition. You need to add it manually in the partitioning dialog box.

VIRTUAL FILESYSTEM

Linux allows you to take an ordinary disk file; format it as an ext2, ext3, or Reiser filesystem; and then mount it, just like a physical drive—through the help of loopback devices. (A loopback device is a special device that allows you to mount a normal file as if it were a physical device.) After it is mounted, you can then read and write files to this newly mounted "device" as if it were a filesystem residing on a real hard drive. Because it is just a file, you can also copy the complete filesystem to another computer and use it there.

During the server installation phase, the YaST expert dialog box for partitioning offers the options necessary for creating an encrypted partition. Follow the same steps as you would to create a typical partition, but ensure you select the Encrypt File System check box before clicking Next. You will be asked for a password required to mount the filesystem; the operating system will prompt you for this password at server boot. If no password was provided or a wrong password was entered, the encrypted filesystem will not be mounted. If the encrypted filesystem should be mounted only when necessary, check Do Not Mount During Booting in the Fstab Options dialog box.

WARNING

If you forget the password, you cannot mount the filesystem and access its data.

If you want to convert an existing filesystem into an encrypted filesystem, follow the same procedure as just described, but select the desired partition and click Edit instead of Create. Note that this conversion will destroy all existing data on the partition!

For an existing system that has available free disk space, instead of converting an existing partition to be encrypted, it may be best to create a virtual encrypted filesystem. You accomplish this from the same YaST disk partitioning dialog box. Instead of selecting Create or Edit, select Crypt File. In the Create New Loop Device Setup dialog box (see Figure 6.3), enter the path to the file to create along with its intended size. Modify the proposed settings for formatting and the file system type as necessary. Then specify the mount point and decide whether the encrypted filesystem should be mounted during boot.

If you want a commercially supported alternative, BestCrypt for Linux (http://www.jetico.com) is an option.

FIGURE 6.3
Creating a virtual encrypted filesystem.

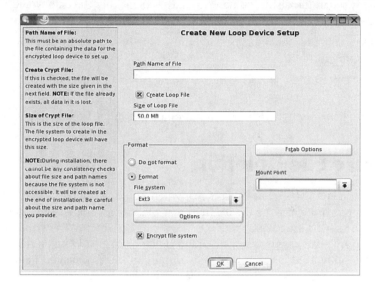

NOTE

A number of free encrypted filesystem implementations are also available:

- EncFS (Encrypted Filesystem module for Linux;
  http://arg0.net/users/vgough/encfs.html)

- CFS (Cryptographic File System; http://www.crypto.com/software)

- TCFS (Transparent Cryptographic File System; http://www.tcfs.it)

Be aware that not all of them have been tested with the 2.6 Linux kernel, which
SLES 9 uses.

You should consider the following potential drawbacks before deploying
filesystem encryption on your servers:

- When an encrypted filesystem is mounted, you must supply the
  passphrase that was used to create the filesystem. Therefore, if you set up
  any encrypted filesystem to automount at boot time, someone needs to
  be at the server console to enter the passphrase (which makes remote
  management challenging).

- You can set the encrypted filesystem not to automount at server boot but
  mount it at a later time. However, this means the users will not have
  access to this filesystem until it is mounted.

- When the encrypted filesystem is mounted, anyone with the proper permissions can read and write data to the disk at any time *transparently*. It's only when the disk is unmounted and "stolen" that the data would be useless.

- Depending on the implementation, the tape backups may be in unencrypted form.

- If the passphrase is forgotten, everything is lost or inaccessible.

Therefore, before you implement, invest some time in up-front planning work.

Secure File Deletion

One thing many users often forget is that when you delete a file, it isn't actually gone. Even if you overwrite the file, reformat the drive, or otherwise attempt to destroy the stored information, chances are it can be recovered. A typical data recovery service costs only a few thousand dollars, so depending on the type of information involved, it might well be worth an attacker's time and money to have it done. The trick is to scramble the erased data by repeatedly flipping the magnetic bits on the disk (the 1's and 0's) so that, when finished, no traces of the original data remain.

The following Linux tools can perform secure file deletion:

- Wipe (http://wipe.sourceforge.net)
- ArticSoft Command Line Scriptor combined with PGP or GnuPG (http://www.articsoft.com/open_pgp_command_line.htm)
- BCWipe for Unix (http://www.jetico.com)
- Shred (included with SLES 9; installed as part of the core system)

The following shows the verbose output when **shred** is used to securely delete a file:

```
Athena:/home/admin/test # shred -uzv myFile
shred: myFile: pass 1/26 (random)...
shred: myFile: pass 2/26 (aaaaaa)...
shred: myFile: pass 3/26 (db6db6)...
shred: myFile: pass 4/26 (000000)...
shred: myFile: pass 5/26 (bbbbbb)...
shred: myFile: pass 6/26 (555555)...
```

```
shred: myFile: pass 7/26 (888888)...
shred: myFile: pass 8/26 (492492)...
shred: myFile: pass 9/26 (6db6db)...
shred: myFile: pass 10/26 (cccccc)...
shred: myFile: pass 11/26 (222222)...
shred: myFile: pass 12/26 (999999)...
shred: myFile: pass 13/26 (random)...
shred: myFile: pass 14/26 (b6db6d)...
shred: myFile: pass 15/26 (444444)...
shred: myFile: pass 16/26 (ffffff)...
shred: myFile: pass 17/26 (111111)...
shred: myFile: pass 18/26 (666666)...
shred: myFile: pass 19/26 (777777)...
shred: myFile: pass 20/26 (249249)...
shred: myFile: pass 21/26 (dddddd)...
shred: myFile: pass 22/26 (eeeeee)...
shred: myFile: pass 23/26 (924924)...
shred: myFile: pass 24/26 (333333)...
shred: myFile: pass 25/26 (random)...
shred: myFile: pass 26/26 (000000)...
shred: myFile: removing
shred: myFile: renamed to 0000000
shred: 0000000: renamed to 000000
shred: 000000: renamed to 00000
shred: 00000: renamed to 0000
shred: 0000: renamed to 000
shred: 000: renamed to 00
shred: 00: renamed to 0
shred: myFile: removed
```

Bear in mind that some of these secure deletion applications work only on certain types of filesystems. For example, shred is not effective on a journaled filesystem such as ReiserFS. Furthermore, even though a file has been shredded from the disk, copies may still exist on (tape) backups.

TIP

If you are to retire a hard disk from your server, either by throwing it out or donating it to a school or charity, ensure you first completely and securely wipe the data off the drive. You can use something like Darik's Boot and Nuke (DBAN; dban.sourceforge.net), Acronis Drive Cleanser (www.acronis.com/enterprise/products/drivecleanser), or Active@ KillDisk (www.killdisk.com/downloadfree.htm) for such purposes.

Journaled Filesystems

Although they are not directly related to the actual "security" aspects of data access, the safety and stability of a filesystem play an important role in data security. You can implement the tightest security known on the planet, but if you, as the data's legitimate owner, cannot access it due to a filesystem failure, security is a moot issue.

Every file's data stored on a Linux/Unix filesystem must be consistent with the attributes, or *metadata*, associated with it. The metadata includes such information as the file type, permissions, owners, size, time stamps, and pointers to data blocks in a partition. This metadata is stored in an *inode*. The problem with maintaining information about a file separate from the actual contents of the file is consistency. In other words, a file's metadata must correctly describe the file before the file can be accessed.

The system kernel always writes the data before the metadata because it otherwise has no idea where on the disk the data will be stored. Data loss could result if an unexpected system crash happens after the data is written but before the metadata is recorded because you have no idea where on the disk the data was stored without the metadata information. This problem gets even worse if the kernel was writing the metadata areas, such as the directory itself. Now, instead of one corrupted file, you have one corrupted filesystem; in other words, you can lose an entire directory or all the data on an entire disk partition. On a large system, this can mean hundreds of thousands of files. Even if you have a backup, restoring such a large amount of data can take a long time.

NOTE

Whenever a Linux server is ungracefully shut down, the system goes through the fsck routine to check the disk for errors and attempts to correct any inconsistencies upon server restart. This process can be very time consuming (much like VREPAIR on a traditional NetWare volume), especially given today's large-capacity disks. This check is also forced once every so many bootups, to make sure everything is working properly.

A journaled filesystem addresses this problem by maintaining a log of metadata information. In a nutshell, the journal is a redo log of changes made to the filesystem. In a system crash, when the filesystem goes down before the sequence of changes is complete, the log can simply be "replayed" to fix resulting inconsistencies. Therefore, if system uptime and performance are important, you should use journaled filesystems. A number of such filesystems are available for Linux, including ext3 (basically ext2 with journaling), ReiserFS, XFS, and JFS. The default filesystem used by SLES 9 is ReiserFS.

NOTE

To learn more about the various filesystems, visit
www.tldp.org/HOWTO/Filesystems-HOWTO.html.

There are, however, two things to keep in mind when using a journaled filesystem, such as Reiser:

- **Additional memory requirement**—The various methods employed by journaled filesystems to keep track of files and their corresponding metadata generally require more memory overhead than the traditional nonjournaled filesystem, such as ext2. To allow for larger individual files (up to 8TB), the newer filesystem uses 64-bit file-access and file-locking system calls, instead of 32-bit ones. As a result, extra memory is required.

- **Security implication**—Because the journal keeps track of data modifications, it is a little treasure chest of information about your data; "interesting" information may be found in the log files. As a result, secure delete utilities such as shred would not be effective. Therefore, if security is a priority, a nonjournaled filesystem, such as ext2, should be your choice.

SLES 9 supports a number of different filesystems, and you can mix and match them for your needs. For instance, your users' home directories may be on a ReiserFS filesystem (default for SLES 9), but the users' confidential data can be on an encrypted ext2 filesystem.

Summary

This chapter reviewed the basics of traditional Linux filesystem permissions (such as the SUID and sticky bits) as well as some advanced topics such as access control lists, pros and cons and the potential dangers of root SUID programs, and data and filesystem encryption. In the next chapter, you'll find out how to monitor your SLES server performance and learn about basic system management techniques.

## CHAPTER 7

System Management and Monitoring

The main focus of this chapter is to introduce you to a number of processes that should be included in daily checks of the server environment. The level of attention given to a specific system depends on the system being managed. Some long-established static systems may require little attention. Other, newer, or more dynamic systems may need to be monitored much more closely. Only time will tell how much monitoring you need to do. Keep in mind, however, that the older, more static systems are also running on older hardware. Monitoring their health is just as important, if not more so.

This chapter describes the following topics:

- Common Linux commands
- A review of the root directory
- Health checks and system monitoring
- System tuning opportunities

It is impossible to eliminate all aspects of hardware failures from an environment. Applying redundancy such as RAID for disk subsystems and, when possible, clustering will enhance the robustness of the services offered. In the following sections, we look at a number of techniques that you can use to monitor a system's health. Proper monitoring allows you to take more proactive measures when logs indicate resource consumption issues or problematic hardware.

Common Linux Commands

In the following sections, we look at a number of the basic commands you will use in the day-to-day management of your server. You can use these commands in conjunction with each other to gain quick access to detailed information on a process or an event. The output from the various commands can be piped through tools such as `grep` to further refine the scope of the information.

Basic Commands

A Linux server can be conceptually subdivided into three main categories. Though this subdivision is not rigorous, we have categorized the basic commands into these distinct areas of interest: system control, the filesystem, memory, and processes.

A number of these commands have been used in examples throughout this book. Table 7.1 provides a quick synopsis of the most commonly used commands, and we expand on a number of them in upcoming sections within this chapter. You can find a more detailed explanation of the various command-line parameters for each in the `man` and `info` pages.

TABLE 7.1
Commonly Used Linux Commands

SYSTEM CONTROL

COMMAND	PURPOSE
init	Allows you to quickly change the runlevel of the system. Not commonly used. `init` was covered in more detail in Chapter 3, "Booting and Shutting Down the Server."
shutdown	Shuts down the system in an orderly fashion. It allows for a message to be displayed to all users and provides for a time delay in the shutdown as well as the opportunity for a reboot.
reboot	Performs a quick restart of the system. This command actually calls shutdown but does not allow for the same parameters.

FILESYSTEM

COMMAND	PURPOSE
df	Returns information of the current disk utilization at the filesystem level. The `-h` flag returns results in "human" readable units of kilobytes, megabytes, or gigabytes.
du	Returns the disk utilization for a file or a directory. The `-h` flag returns results in "human" readable units of kilobytes, megabytes, or gigabytes.

TABLE 7.1
Commonly Used Linux Commands (continued)

FILESYSTEM

COMMAND	PURPOSE
find	Locates files within a directory structure.
fuser	Identifies the user and the process ID currently using a file. This command is particularly useful when you are looking for users who have a volume mounted on the system.
ln	Creates links to other files on the system. This allows for a file to be seen in more than one directory structure at a time. All pointers, however, reference the same file within the filesystem, allowing for a single version to be maintained.
lsof	Lists all currently opened files on the system.
ls	Provides a listing of the files in the target filesystem or directory. Common arguments are -l for a long format, including file sizes; -a to include all hidden files in the list as well; and -t to sort the output by date/time.
mount	Returns information on the current mount points, their underlying format (ext3, reiserfs), and their default options and permissions.
rm rmdir	Removes (deletes) files. The rmdir command is used to remove empty directories.
stat	Returns detailed information about a file including the dates it was created, last accessed, and last modified.

MEMORY MANAGEMENT

free	Displays the current memory utilization and swap file status.
procinfo	Reports memory utilization, although it is more of a process information tool.

PROCESS INFORMATION

ps	Processes status information. A number of parameters can be passed to extract information in a number of formats. By default, this command lists only the process table for the current user.
pstree	Provides a process list in a tree format showing which processes are children and which are their parent.
w	Lists all the processes by users.

Additional Tools

You also can use the following tools:

| | The pipe symbol allows you to control the output from one command and redirect it to the input of another. This extremely powerful tool will be used extensively throughout this book in conjunction with `grep`.

awk   This tool can be used to extract specific columnar information from a file or pipe based on a pattern.

cat   This tool prints the contents of a file to the display.

cut   This tool prints out only selected portions from each line of a file.

grep   This tool searches for information in a file and returns all the lines that match the provided criteria.

head   This tool displays the first 10 lines of a file. The -n parameter can be used to change the number of lines shown.

tail   This tool prints the last 10 lines of a file to the display. You can use the -n parameter to specify how many lines from the bottom of the file should be listed. This command is essential when you are reviewing large log files.

wc   By default, this command counts the number of words in a document or pipe. The parameter -1 changes the default behavior to count lines instead.

The preceding certainly does not provide an exhaustive list of the available commands. As you gain experience using these commands individually, combining the pipe tool with `grep`, `awk,` or `wc` will become second nature.

The root Filesystem

The Linux filesystem is logically one large directory structure. In a default install of SLES, unless otherwise specified, the entirety of the file structure is placed on a single disk partition. Because the / partition is the parent to all other portions of the filesystem, it is called the *root*. When a system is originally installed, the root is populated by directories only. The following directories are present by default:

```
Athena:~ # ls /
.   bin   dev   home   media   opt    root   srv   tmp   var
..  boot  etc   lib    mnt     proc   sbin   sys   usr
```

In Linux, you can add additional disk capacity to a system. To do this, you attach the new disk by mapping its contents into the directory tree and providing a unique directory from which it can be accessed. This directory is called a *mount point*. Adding disk capacity is identical to adding removable media to the system and temporarily associating it with the /mnt directory. In the case of a permanent mount, the disk information is associated with the mount point in /etc/fstab.

In essence, any directory on the system can be associated, either temporarily or permanently, to additional storage. The root of the filesystem is bound to the selected target disk at install time. All the other directories under the root, however, are considered not only directories but possible mount points. In Chapter 2, "Updating the Server," we discussed the addition of extra storage and how it was possible to migrate the contents of /home and /srv from simple directories and convert them to individual disk partition mount points. Table 7.2 lists the directories in the root and summarizes their purpose.

TABLE 7.2
Default Mount Points

MOUNT POINT	PURPOSE
/bin, /sbin	These two directories contain the programs executed when you type Linux commands.
/boot	This directory structure contains the information processed by the boot loader.
/etc	This is the main configuration directory used by the system. It contains most of the configuration files for the standard services as well as the information required for the different runlevels.
/dev	dev contains all the special files needed for the system to recognize the devices connected to the system and the different access methods available for each.
/home	This is where user accounts should be created. It is also one of the most dynamic directory structures and is therefore a prime candidate for segregation to a separate physical device.
/lib	This directory is the main repository for libraries and system modules.
/media	This is the default mountpoint directory for removable media. Media is mounted off subdirectories such as dvd and floppy.
/mnt	This is the default generic mount point provided by the system. It can be used to quickly connect a CD-ROM or USB device without requiring the creation of a mount point directory.

TABLE 7.2
Default Mount Points (continued)

MOUNT POINT	PURPOSE
/opt	This directory houses additional optional software and third-party layered applications.
/proc	This system directory tracks all the processes and system resources. This directory should be left as is; it does not grow very large and is mandatory for a properly functioning system.
/root	This is the "home" directory for the root account.
/srv	This service directory contains the default target (home) locations for the FTP and HTTP services.
/sys	This directory maintains a list of devices currently connected to the system and how they are accessed.
/tmp	This directory stores all the volatile temporary files created by processes at runtime.
/usr	Similar to bin and sbin, this directory mostly houses executables that can be accessed by the end user.
/var	This directory holds additional files that are dynamic in nature. The system stores many of the process log files here. Because this is such a dynamic environment, it is an ideal candidate for moving to a separate large partition.

All these mount points are candidates for conversion to separate physical devices. It is important to note that if the root partition becomes full, the system will no longer be able to log activity or create any temporary files and will simply cease functioning until it can resume these two tasks. It is therefore imperative to prevent this from happening by segregating the more dynamic directory structures, such as /srv, /var, and /home, onto separate physical partitions. Segregating the structures alleviates disk space contention on the root volume. As the system matures, growth of the individual mount points will also be easier to monitor.

Health Checks and System Monitoring

In previous chapters, we described how to install and configure the system and its software components. We also covered the steps required to add users to the system. In the following sections, we monitor how the two interact.

Daily cycle checks of machines and equipment are an important facet of offering robust services. Only by knowing what is going on can you get a feel for what may need attention. The frequency and depth of these checks depend on your comfort level with the system and its importance to the organization. As a rule of thumb, daily checks are a good starting point. Here is a suggested list of what should be checked:

- Machine uptime
- Log review
- Top consumers
- Application checks
- User login activity
- System resource checks

The examples given in this chapter are based on our own personal preferences. They are intended as a quick guide for extracting system information on the fly. The examples are in no way an exhaustive list of the tools available—just our favorites. As you become more knowledgeable with the system, you will almost certainly progress beyond simple commands and move into scripts or third-party layered applications. However, we believe these tools will suffice as a starting point.

Machine Uptime

Though current versions of Linux are very robust, it is important to check how long the system has been running. System reboots can be caused by hardware failures, software failures, or human intervention. If an unscheduled reboot occurred, it is important to find out why.

The `uptime` command provides a quick snapshot of the state of the system, including the current time, the time the system has been running, and user load:

```
Athena:~ # uptime
8:47am  up   3:18,  3 users,  load average: 0.30, 0.29, 0.21
Athena:~ #
```

As this example illustrates, the machine has been running for just over three hours. Because we require our system to be very robust, such a short uptime should lead to some sort of investigation. Typically, this will be due to a scheduled shutdown for hardware maintenance. If this is not the case, a review of the logs might indicate what is going on.

Load averages are supplied to provide a quick verification of the status of the system. Dramatic shifts in load between the 1-, 5-, and 15-minute figures could alert the system administrator to potential problems. Increases can indicate a runaway process, whereas drops in activity can indicate that clients can no longer reach the server.

Log Review

When you are reviewing the health of a system, it is important to look through the logs. Each system component places information in the appropriate log file. This information can be as simple as a time stamp or process milestone marker, or the log may contain information on the pending failure of a hardware component.

You can find system boot information in two ways. First, you can use the dmesg command to examine the content of the *kernel ring buffer*. This buffer contains the most current messages generated by the kernel. At boot time, many of the important hardware discovery phases are logged here. A review of this information yields detailed hardware information on BIOS, memory, disk, and IRQs. The boot information is available in a secondary location that provides yet again more detail. The /var/log/boot.msg file contains all the messages from various sources generated during a system startup. It is a good idea to review these sources periodically to ensure that the expected hardware matches and that no warning messages are present that might affect system performance.

Linux maintains application-specific log files. The location of the log files and their content can be controlled through the /etc/syslog.conf file. In a default install of SLES, you can find all application-specific log information under the /var/log directory structure.

Within this structure, many individual services such as YaST, Samba, and Apache maintain distinct directories of application-specific messages. It is important to review many of these service log files periodically. They can not only reveal local configuration errors within the system, but they also log connection information from all sources.

To identify attack vectors such as infected machines and system probes, you can review connection failure logs. Additionally, you should check Internet-facing machine logs frequently for signs of valid connections requesting nonexistent resources such as login attempts on default account names or requests for invalid web pages.

NOTE

To get an appreciation for the information contained in log files, simply review the Apache failure logs for an Internet-facing machine. The number of errors generated by requests for nonexistent pages can be staggering. A large number of these requests come from script kiddies who launch IIS-specific attacks against Apache servers. Once these individuals discover your site, it is a good idea to keep a vigilant eye on these logs.

It is also very important to check the firewall logs. By default, they are merged into the standard /var/log/messages file. We have stated many times how important it is to offer only services that are required. A periodic review of the firewall logs will expose connection failures. The source of the failure and the nature of the access requested could bring to light misconfigured client machines and possibly exploit attempts. In many instances, infected desktop computers are capable of generating volumes of traffic and probes as the worm or virus tries to replicate. A proper review of server-side firewall logs for internal (trusted network) events is just as important as dissecting the external firewall logs. This topic is explored further in Chapter 12, "Intrusion Detection."

Two log files that you will reference the most often are warn and messages in /var/log. These files contain most of the regular error messages generated by applications and users. Some of the important messages you will want to scan for could be requests for elevated privileges such as

```
Mar 13 11:26:23 Athena sudo: hart : 3 incorrect password
➥ attempts ; TTY=ptst
```

It will take a second to verify that hart is allowed access to sudo and that this user is just having a hard day. On the other hand, if a different username were to show up, it may be an indication of someone trying to gain unsanctioned access.

This section emphasized the importance of log files in tracking system activities. It is important to note that as these log files grow, they will also need to be maintained. Log file retention is essential in guaranteeing that you have a continuous log of system activity.

In the event of an incident that seems to indicate a system compromise, archived logs are essential in tracking down the history of the intrusion. Often, daily reviews of the log files are not possible. Using a utility such as logrotate can ensure that logs are stored in a central location in a manageable format.

Top Consumers

Log files are important for tracing historical events. Unless a process generates a fault or an informational message, it may exist for quite some time unnoticed. As part of your daily exercise, it is a good idea to get a feel for the load on a server. This type of monitoring will help you understand the resource consumption on a typical day, forecast when a resource upgrade may be required, and quickly identify abnormal loads.

You can use the **top** command to generate a dynamic listing of the current processes load of a system. As applications require more resources, they percolate up the list. Listing 7.1 shows an example of the output generated by **top**. The information presented is dynamic; this is, of course, just a snapshot in time.

LISTING 7.1

Typical Output from the top Command

```
top - 16:57:05 up 11:27,  4 users,  load average: 0.15, 0.03, 0.01
Tasks:77 total, 1 running, 76 sleeping, 0 stopped, 0 zombie
Cpu(s):0.3% us,0.7% sy,0.0% ni,99.0% id, 0.0% wa, 0.0% hi, 0.0% si
Mem: 190012k total, 185668k used,  4344k free, 31608k buffers
Swap: 570268k total,  8k used,  570260k free,  30012k cached

PID USER PR  NI  VIRT  RES  SHR S %CPU %MEM  TIME+  COMMAND
4514 root 15   0 33796 11m  24m S  0.3  6.5 0:34.42 X
5329 root 15   0 22696 13m  16m S  0.3  7.5 0:14.43 gnome-terminal
   1 root 16   0  588 244  444 S  0.0  0.1 0:04.21 init
   2 root RT   0    0   0    0 S  0.0  0.0 0:00.00 migration/0
   3 root 34  19    0   0    0 S  0.0  0.0 0:00.00 ksoftirqd/0
   4 root  5 -10    0   0    0 S  0.0  0.0 0:00.07 events/0
   5 root 15 -10    0   0    0 S  0.0  0.0 0:00.00 kacpid
   6 root  5 -10    0   0    0 S  0.0  0.0 0:00.09 kblockd/0
   8 root  5 -10    0   0    0 S  0.0  0.0 0:00.01 khelper
   9 root 15   0    0   0    0 S  0.0  0.0 0:01.04 pdflush
  10 root 15   0    0   0    0 S  0.0  0.0 0:00.74 pdflush
  12 root 15 -10    0   0    0 S  0.0  0.0 0:00.00 aio/0
  11 root 15   0    0   0    0 S  0.0  0.0 0:02.14 kswapd0
 160 root 25   0    0   0    0 S  0.0  0.0 0:00.00 kseriod
 203 root 25   0    0   0    0 S  0.0  0.0 0:00.00 scsi_eh_0
 382 root  5 -10    0   0    0 S  0.0  0.0 0:00.00 reiserfs/0
 561 root  6 -10    0   0    0 S  0.0  0.0 0:00.00 kcopyd
```

The **top** command is very useful when the machine appears to be sluggish. A quick glance at its output can reveal whether the situation is due to CPU consumption, excessive swapping, or particular processes running at odd priorities.

The **top** process also lists the name of the running executable. As you become familiar with the most common names, odd user-written application names may appear in the list. By matching the user and application columns, you can quickly identify the rogue application.

Another tool that is very useful is the w command. This command provides a quick summary of who is currently logged on to the system and what programs they are running. On the current system, w returns the following output:

```
Athena:~ # w
 13:39:33 up  9:09,  6 users,  load average: 0.00, 0.05, 0.02
USER     TTY   LOGIN@ IDLE  JCPU  PCPU WHAT
root     :0     04:31 ?xdm? 4:21  0.11s -:0
root     pts/0 04:32 3:08  4.83s 0.41s bash
belandja pts/1 04:43  0.00s 0.84s 0.10s login -- belandja
belandja pts/2 05:24  1.00s 0.39s 0.07s wget http://cnn.com
eric     pts/3 13:36 3:10  0.38s 0.15s vi index.html
hart     pts/4 13:38 1:06  0.53s 0.34s top
Athena:~ #
```

From this, you can get a good idea as to who is currently working on the system, what they are doing, and what type of resource impact they are having on the system.

Application Check

When applications become unresponsive to the end user, it typically does not take a long time for the operations crew to be made aware of the situation. Before you forage through the appropriate log file, though, a quick glance at the running processes might be in order.

One method for checking on the presence of an application is to use the ps command. The Process Status command (ps) generates a list of all the running processes on a system. In addition, you can use modifiers to selectively extract information for the target service. One method for checking on an application is to use the ps command and filter the output through grep:

```
Athena:~ #ps -ef | grep -e telnet
root   5408 5387 0 04:43 ?     00:00:01 in.telnetd: 192.168.1.100
root   5766 5387 0 05:23 ?     00:00:00 in.telnetd: 192.168.1.100
root   5957 5920 0 06:09 pts/1 00:00:00 grep -e telnet
```

In this example, the -e (every process) and -f (full listing format) modifiers were used to qualify the ps verb. The output from the ps verb was then filtered through grep to extract only the records containing the Telnet process. It is important to remember that, in this case, Telnet does not have its own daemon process. It is part of the xinetd server offerings. As such, the preceding command returns existing Telnet connections, not the presence of the actual server process.

A different method for checking the existence of a service is to verify whether their characteristic port is being advertised by the server. Because each protocol, be it `httpd`, `sshd,` or `telnetd`, offers a specific port to the network, you can quickly check for an open listener process on the port. The `netstat` command can list various attributes of a server's networking environment. You can specify the `-l` parameter to list all listeners and the `-p` parameter to identify the program offering the service. The result would look like the following:

```
Athena:~ # netstat -lp | grep -e http
tcp      0    0 *:https   *:*     LISTEN  4601/httpd2-prefork
Athena:~ #
```

By using the process ID, you can find all related processes and identify the routines offering the service:

```
Athena:~ # ps -ef | grep -e 4601
root       4601     1  0 04:31 ?  00:00:00 /usr/sbin/httpd2-prefork -f
➥ /etc/apache2/httpd.conf
wwwrun     4602  4601  0 04:31 ?  00:00:00 /usr/sbin/httpd2-prefork -f
➥ /etc/apache2/httpd.conf
wwwrun     4603  4601  0 04:31 ?  00:00:00 /usr/sbin/httpd2-prefork -f
➥ /etc/apache2/httpd.conf
wwwrun     4604  4601  0 04:31 ?  00:00:00 /usr/sbin/httpd2-prefork -f
➥ /etc/apache2/httpd.conf
wwwrun     4605  4601  0 04:31 ?  00:00:00 /usr/sbin/httpd2-prefork -f
➥ /etc/apache2/httpd.conf
wwwrun     4606  4601  0 04:31 ?  00:00:00 /usr/sbin/httpd2-prefork -f
➥ /etc/apache2/httpd.conf
root       6807  5920  0 13:28 pts/1  00:00:00 grep -e 4601
Athena:~ #
```

Using this approach , you can quickly verify the presence of a service through its process name or port offerings. You can now verify the application-specific log files for possible errors. If none are present, the application unresponsiveness may be due to resource constraints from other processes.

System Resource Check

A server can be thought of as a container for resources. Application programs, in turn, consume these resources. Well-behaved applications start up, allocate a portion of available memory, utilize a moderate amount of CPU, write a controlled amount of information back to the appropriate files, and then terminate.

Of the resources used by an application, only the CPU resource can be thought of as unlimited. Though only so much processing power is available at any moment in time, a well-behaved application consumes only a little bit at a time. The faster the CPU, the faster the job completes. After the job has terminated, the portion of the CPU's time spent processing the application is now available for other processes.

The same cannot be said for memory and disk resources. When their total complement is consumed, no further processing can take place until some of these resources are freed. In most cases, a well-behaved program releases all its allocated memory upon exit. When this does not happen properly, the application is said to have a *memory leak*. If the application is run a sufficient number of times, eventually the memory leak will consume all the available process memory on the machines.

Similarly, applications that create large output data files and log files often consume vast amounts of disk space. Though disk quotas mitigate against user applications from filling the disk, typical services are not constrained in regards to disk space consumption. In the event of a misbehaving client application or an attack, it is quite possible that the service log files consume all available disk space in a partition.

The preceding describes what could be considered the worst-case scenario. Diligence will ensure that these conditions are less likely to happen. The following commands are suggested additions to your daily server health checks.

You can address memory consumption using the **top** command discussed earlier in the chapter. You also can use a number of other commands to determine the current memory demands:

free lists the current amount of free memory on the system. The **-m** parameter lists the amounts in megabytes.

```
Athena:~ # free -m
             total     used     free     shared     buffers     cached
Mem:           185      173       11          0           4         40
-/+ buffers/cache:      128       57
Swap:          556        0      556
Athena:~ #
```

procinfo displays the system status information contained within the **/proc** filesystem. The following is a truncated version of the information returned:

```
Athena:~ # procinfo
Linux 2.6.5-7.97-smp(geeko@buildhost)(gcc 3.3.3 ) #1 1CPU[Athena.]

Memory:      Total       Used       Free     Shared     Buffers
Mem:        190012     181224       8788          0        6000
Swap:       570268          8     570260

Bootup:Sun Mar 13 04:29:44 2005 Load average:0.06 0.09 0.04
➡   1/99 8152
```

Disk space consumption can be tracked using the following commands:

```
Athena:~ # du -hsc /var
215M    /var
215M    total
```

df displays disk usage by mounted filesystem:

```
Athena:~ # df -h
Filesystem            Size  Used Avail Use% Mounted on
/dev/sda2             6.5G  2.9G  3.6G  45% /
tmpfs                  93M  8.0K   93M   1% /dev/shm
/dev/sdb1              14G   45M   14G   1% /home
```

mount, though typically used for adding resources, can be typed without parameters to display a list of what is currently mounted on the system. A systematic review of this information, coupled with the content of /etc/fstab, may identify missing partitions or mount points:

```
Athena:~ # mount
/dev/sda2 on / type reiserfs (rw,acl,user_xattr)
proc on /proc type proc (rw)
tmpfs on /dev/shm type tmpfs (rw)
devpts on /dev/pts type devpts (rw,mode=0620,gid=5)
/dev/hdc on /media/dvd type subfs (ro,nosuid,nodev,
➥ fs=cdfss,procuid,iocharset=ut
f8)
/dev/fd0 on /media/floppy type subfs (rw,nosuid,nodev,sync,
➥ fs=floppyfss,procuid)
/dev/sdb1 on /home type ext3 (rw,acl,user_xattr,usrquota)
usbfs on /proc/bus/usb type usbfs (rw)
Athena:
```

User Login Activity

Several situations require auditing system access. Auditing is not done to invade anyone's privacy but is a requirement for tracking both system performance and application access. Knowing system load, response times, and processes generating the load is important in order to provide satisfactory service. Another reason for tracking users is to facilitate the investigation of spurious and inappropriate activity that might indicate a compromise of the system. This topic will be explored further in Chapter 12. In this section, we examine a number of commands that can provide user access information.

The w or who commands display which accounts are currently logged in to the system. Here's an example:

```
Athena:~ # w
14:33:32 up  2:10,  7 users,  load average: 0.07, 0.11, 0.06
```

```
USER     TTY   LOGIN@ IDLE   JCPU   PCPU  WHAT
ted      tty5  14:29  3:14   0.20s  0.04s perl extract_P2_pulse.pl
root     :0    12:28  ?xdm?  1:53   0.11s -:0
root     pts/0 12:28  3:06   2.33s  0.25s bash
belandja pts/1 12:29  0.00s  1.68s  1.36s ssh -l root 192.168.1.242
root     pts/2 12:30  0.00s  0.73s  0.04s w
pol      pts/3 14:25  6:34   0.40s  0.16s vi start_femtopulse.csh
mark     pts/4 14:31  14.00s 0.62s  0.38s -bash
```

If more information is required for the currently signed-on users, you need to access the information more indirectly. Each user on the running system creates a login session. This login session is the parent for additional child processes. Additional user information can be extracted by accessing the currently active process information. You can do this in a number of ways. Each of the following examples reports information with varying amounts of detail.

pstree displays a tree of processes:

```
Athena:~ # pstree -U pol
sshd???bash???vi
```

ps reports process status:

```
Athena:~ # ps -ef | grep -e pol
root   5786  3244  0 14:25 ?       00:00:00 sshd: pol [priv]
pol    5789  5786  0 14:25 ?       00:00:00 sshd: pol@pts/3
pol    5790  5789  0 14:25 pts/3   00:00:00 -bash
pol    5814  5790  0 14:26 pts/3   00:00:00 vi start_femtopulse.csh
root   6122  5383  0 14:33 pts/2   00:00:00 grep -e pol
```

lsof lists open files:

```
Athena:~ # lsof
COMMAND PID  USER FD   TYPE  DEVICE SIZE   NODE NAME
sshd    5789 pol  cwd  DIR   8,2    592    2 /
sshd    5789 pol  rtd  DIR   8,2    592    2 /
sshd    5789 pol  txt  REG   8,2    288184 83822 /usr/sbin/sshd
sshd    5789 pol  mem  REG   8,2    107122 19361 /lib/ld-2.3.3.so
sshd    5789 pol  mem  REG   8,2    36895  29038
➥ /lib/libwrap.so.0.7.6
sshd    5789 pol  mem  REG   8,2    33263  29436
➥ /lib/libpam.so.0.77
sshd    5789 pol  mem  REG   8,2    13647  19370 /lib/libdl.so.2
.
.
.
sshd    5789 pol  2u   CHR   1,3           42156 /dev/null
```

```
sshd  5789  pol    3u  unix 0xc31a8700       11642 socket
sshd  5789  pol    4u  IPv6 11623            TCP
➥ Athena.UniversalExport.ca:ssh->192.168.1.240:1037 (ESTABLISHED)
sshd  5789  pol    5r  FIFO 0,7              11644 pipe
.
.
.
vi    5814  pol    1u  CHR  136,3                5 /dev/pts/3
vi    5814  pol    2u  CHR  136,3                5 /dev/pts/3
vi    5814  pol    3u  REG  8,33    12288 1048626
➥ /research/home/pol/.start_femtopulse.csh.swp
```

The lsof command returns a great deal of information about the selected user.
A majority of the files listed are standard system libraries and modules.
Depending on the details required, this command may yield too much infor-
mation to be useful.

NOTE

The lsof command will prove itself quite useful in Chapter 13, "System Security."
In that chapter, we will be required to enumerate all files used by a specific application. lsof can perform this task quite easily.

Other commands can be used to extract information indicating when users
accessed the server in the past. This information may be important if you are
trying to find out who was on the system at a specific point in time. The last
command provides information on all logins, their source, as well as the period
of time the session was active. A couple of examples of the last command are
shown here:

```
Athena:~ # last hart
hart pts/1 192.168.1.100    Sat Feb 26 10:08 - down   (13:48)
hart pts/1 192.168.1.100    Sat Feb 26 09:53 - 09:54  (00:01)
hart pts/1 192.168.1.100    Sat Feb 26 08:44 - 09:53  (01:08)
hart pts/1 192.168.1.100    Wed Feb 16 04:38 - 04:39  (00:00)
hart pts/2 Athena.Universal Tue Feb 15 19:49 - 20:20  (00:31)
hart pts/4 192.168.1.77     Tue Feb 15 06:57 - 07:34  (00:37)

wtmp begins Mon Feb 14 19:00:40 2005
Athena:~ #
```

Without specifying a username, it is possible to generate a login log for all
users on the system:

```
Athena:~ # last
hart      pts/1    192.168.1.100    Sat Feb 26 10:08 - down   (13:48)
eric      pts/1    192.168.1.100    Sat Feb 26 10:04 - 10:08  (00:04)
eric      pts/1    192.168.1.100    Sat Feb 26 09:55 - 10:00  (00:04)
```

```
eric      pts/1    192.168.1.100    Sat Feb 26 09:55 - 09:55  (00:00)
belandja  pts/4    192.168.1.100    Sat Feb 26 09:54 - down   (14:02)
hart      pts/1    192.168.1.100    Sat Feb 26 09:53 - 09:54  (00:01)
root      pts/3    :0.0             Sat Feb 26 09:46 - down   (14:11)
belandja  pts/2    192.168.1.100    Sat Feb 26 09:12 - 10:14  (01:01)
hart      pts/1    192.168.1.100    Sat Feb 26 08:44 - 09:53  (01:08)
root      pts/0    :0.0             Sat Feb 26 08:44 - down   (15:12)

wtmp begins Mon Feb 14 19:00:40 2005
```

You can use a separate command to quickly extract the last login times of certain accounts. This can be a quick way to check for unused accounts or accounts that are being used but shouldn't be. Here's an example of the `lastlog` command:

```
Athena:~ # lastlog
Username Port     From              Latest
root     pts/2 athena.universal Sun Feb 27 12:30:43 -0500 2005
bin                            **Never logged in**
daemon                         **Never logged in**
lp                             **Never logged in**
games                          **Never logged in**
man                            **Never logged in**
.
.
.
ldap                           **Never logged in**
dhcpd                          **Never logged in**
belandja 1       192.168.1.100    Sun Feb 27 12:29:40 -0500 2005
eric     2       192.168.1.100    Sun Feb 27 02:23:43 -0500 2005
hart     1       192.168.1.100    Sat Feb 26 10:08:46 -0500 2005
peter                          **Never logged in**
pol      pts/3 192.168.1.240    Sun Feb 27 14:25:20 -0500 2005
mark     pts/4 hermes.universal Sun Feb 27 14:31:03 -0500 2005
ted      tty5             Sun Feb 27 14:29:25 -0500 2005
```

This command provides a listing of all the accounts on the system as well as times they were last logged in to the system and the source of the login. Because of the large number of system process accounts, the list can grow quite large. You might be tempted to parse the output of this command using `grep` to remove all accounts that have never been used:

```
Athena:~ # lastlog | grep -v -e "*Never"

Username Port     From              Latest
root     pts/2    athena.universal Sun Feb 27 12:30:43 -0500 2005
belandja 1        192.168.1.100    Sun Feb 27 12:29:40 -0500 2005
eric     2        192.168.1.100    Sun Feb 27 02:23:43 -0500 2005
```

```
hart      1          192.168.1.100    Sat Feb 26 10:08:46 -0500 2005
pol       pts/3      192.168.1.240    Sun Feb 27 14:25:20 -0500 2005
mark      pts/4      hermes.universal Sun Feb 27 14:31:03 -0500 2005
ted       tty5                        Sun Feb 27 14:29:25 -0500 2005
```

Parsing the output this way is an acceptable practice if you are looking for individual accounts that you know have been active. The raw `lastlog` command does, however, provide additional information about the system process accounts. Verifying that they have not been used for an interactive login could prove quite useful.

Knowing that a specific account was used in an inappropriate manner is one thing. Being able to identify the individual who used the account is much more difficult. Verifying the number of login failures for an account is an important step. Excessive login failures might be an indication of a password hack attack—possibly a successful one. The `faillog` command allows you to check the number of times a login attempt was unsuccessful against each account:

```
Athena:~ # faillog
Username   Failures  Maximum  Latest
root       3         0  Wed Feb 16 03:49:05 -0500 2005 on 0
belandja   0         0  Mon Feb 14 19:02:11 -0500 2005 on 1
eric       0         0  Tue Feb 15 18:06:28 -0500 2005 on 2
hart       0         0  Tue Feb 15 06:57:10 -0500 2005 on 4
```

An indication of a large number of login failures on an account might indicate that the password on the account was hacked. It may also be a ruse. Having a sound account password policy and including the PAM module `pam_tally` to lock out accounts after a set number of failed attempts are important steps you can take. This way, you can mitigate some of the exposure to password-harvesting attacks. This also helps you in ensuring that the person who last logged in to a specific account knew the password.

In this section, you saw numerous methods for extracting user login information. You can use this information to help investigate resource issues. This information can also be used as a starting point in investigating suspect behavior on the system.

System Tuning

The initial performance of a server is based on a number of parameters set by the supplier of the operating system. In the case of SLES, these parameters are chosen to satisfy a broad range of server types. Each service can require different resources. Some services are memory or bandwidth intensive, whereas others are CPU intensive. These various factors are balanced by default to provide a responsive server regardless of its initial tasking.

What cannot be anticipated, however, are the resources available from the hardware supplied. SUSE specifies a number of minimum requirements to provide a stable environment. In most cases, meeting these minimum requirements is not an issue. As resource limits start contributing to performance issues, memory or disk space can be added to a server.

In some situations, however, the tasking of a server is outside the designed norm. In these cases, you must entertain changes to the fundamental assumptions in the original configuration.

In Linux- and Unix-based systems, the core program of the operating system is called the *kernel*. The kernel is built just like any other program. It incorporates within its structure the original assumptions of the configuration team. These assumptions govern which device types are available such as IDE or SCSI disks, how memory will be managed, and if additional modules can be loaded dynamically. Adding and removing capabilities within the configuration of the kernel can increase flexibility and performance.

When such situations arise, you often need to alter the actual Linux kernel itself. This can be done in a couple of different ways. One option is to recompile the kernel to include additional functionality. The preferred method, when available, is to take advantage of the flexibility of the default kernel and simply tune some of its runtime parameters.

Tuning Kernel Parameters

A number of applications have been ported to Linux. Some of them, such as database applications, have resource requirements that are significantly different from those of typical Linux services. To satisfy these needs, you must make changes to the way the kernel operates by tuning application-specific parameters.

In older versions of Unix, these changes required a rebuild of the kernel itself. Though not an insurmountable feat, rebuilding the kernel is certainly a daunting task for someone who has never done it. Luckily, the Linux kernel is flexible and dynamic. Changes to the Linux kernel can be made in real-time without requiring a reboot.

As an example, let's look at the changes required to the Linux kernel for it to be able to run Oracle 10g. These changes are supplied in a script run at install time; for argument's sake, say you want to make these changes manually. The Oracle 10g requirements are shown in Table 7.3.

TABLE 7.3
Oracle 10g SUSE LINUX Kernel Requirements

KERNEL PARAMETER	MINIMUM VALUE REQUIRED (UNITS DEPEND ON PARAMETER)	DESCRIPTION
kernel.shmall	2097152	Available memory for shared memory in 4KB blocks
kernel.shmmax	2147483648	Maximum size of a shared memory segment
kernel.shmmni	4096	Maximum number of shared segments
kernel.sem	250 32000 100 128	Semaphores
fs.file-max	65536	Maximum number of file handles allocated by the kernel
net.ipv4.ip_local_port_range	1024 65000	Required available ports

NOTE

Tuning the kernel is a task that should only be undertaken with great care. Changes made could generate an environment that is unable to function. There are a number of sites on the Internet that discuss the Linux kernel and its parameters. Visit one of these for more information:

http://www.suse.de/~agruen/kernel-doc/

http://www.kernelnewbies.org/

http://www.bb-zone.com/SLGFG/chapter4.html

You can use the sysctl command to query the values currently in use by the running kernel. Specifying the -a switch lists all the parameters. Each individual parameter can be checked using syntax similar to the following:

```
Athena:~ # sysctl kernel.shmmax
kernel.shmmax = 33554432
```

As you can see, this parameter value is well below the minimum required for Oracle. To set the value, use the following syntax:

```
Athena:~ # sysctl -w kernel.shmmax=2147483648
kernel.shmmax = 2147483648
```

This syntax sets the new value for the kernel parameter and acknowledges the new value.

Most typical installations of SLES come with well-configured kernel parameters. It is not necessary to change these values unless the server in question is running an atypical configuration. In most cases, like Oracle, you will be given the necessary minimum values and most probably a script to make the changes. If not, following the procedure shown here, you can check for compliance to the minimum recommended values as well as set the parameters as recommended.

Tuning Filesystem Access

Previously, we discussed how the Linux filesystem is considered one large logical tree. Table 7.2 identifies the directories created under the root in a standard installation. Sometimes, however, the default install does not satisfy your needs.

In Chapter 2, we presented an overview on how to migrate two of the standard directories in the root to a different disk resource. This process is typically performed when the disk consumption in those branches is expected to impact the overall system. When these directories are part of the same physical partition as the root, should they fill all available space, the system would become unresponsive. The process of adjusting the availability of different directories is known as *tuning the filesystem*.

When the disk makeup of a production server is designed, directories with dynamic content such as /usr, /home, and /var are often placed on separate physical disk partitions. When possible, they are also placed on different physical devices to distribute I/O operations. Though modern disk subsystems are very fast, extracting every bit of performance possible is a good practice. One added benefit to placing them on separate physical devices is that in the event of a disk subsystem failure, fewer partitions may need to be restored.

An additional aspect to filesystem tuning is that of granting access to portions of the directory tree. The initial owner and the group membership of a mount point are root. The rights mask allows for nonroot users to access the contents of directories under the mount point. This is a necessary condition when a mount point contains portions of the standard tree.

Previously, we constrained ourselves to the default directory structure in the root of the filesystem. Because this is just a simple directory, there are no set limitations on the creation of additional directories or mount points in the root. Additionally, there are no limitations that state all mount points must be in the root. It is an important system management practice to keep the root as clean a possible, but that doesn't mean it must be pristine. The following two examples explore methods for adding additional storage to a server and limiting access to the new resource.

If a group of research users are working on a collaborative project, they may need to be segregated onto separate storage for the server to reduce their impact on other users. As part of the process, they should have their home directories placed there. Also, due to the nature of the research, only members of the group may have access to the mount point.

This result can be accomplished by specifying a new mount point in the root /research. A number of filesystems permit restricting access to the mounted partition to specific UID and GID. Mount does not support these features for ext3 or Reiser partitions. Access to specific individuals or groups therefore must be restricted a different way. The following steps can serve as a guide to creating a directory structure specific to the research group:

1. Create a group called research for the project.

2. Prepare the new partition using fdisk and mkfs.

3. Create a standard directory named /research for mounting the new resource.

4. Modify /etc/fstab to allow the partition to be mounted at boot time.

5. Execute a mount -a command to verify that the partition is mounted correctly.

6. Change the group membership of the mount point directory using chgrp research /research.

7. Change the access permissions on the mount point directory using chmod 6770 /research.

8. Create containers for the home directories of the users and one for the project data using mkdir /research/home and mkdir /research/project.

9. Adjust the permissions on these directories using chmod 6770 /research/home and chmod 6770 /research/project.

NOTE

In the preceding set of steps, the ownership of the root directory is left as root. This might seem counter-intuitive because you would probably like it to belong to a member of the group.

Making a group member the owner of the directory generates another issue. If the selected individual leaves, his or her account will be deleted and the UID orphaned. Any new account accidentally given the same UID would automatically be granted access.

You could create a placeholder account, set it so that it is not allowed to log on, and make it a member of the group. Since this service account is never used and unable to log in, the UID associated would remain in service. If, however, the account is changed, maliciously or not, access to the information would be granted without any way of tracking the access.

It is best in this case to leave the ownership as root. Individuals will have access to the directory structure through the group permissions.

At this stage, you can relocate existing users to the new location for their home directories by updating their account information and moving the contents of their directories. Existing users will also have to be added to the group research. New users can be created directly into the new structure and added to the research group. The resulting directories will look like the following:

```
Athena:~ # ls -ld /research
drwsrws---  4 root research 4096 Feb 27 06:55 /research

Athena:~ # ls -l /research
total 25
drwsrws---   4 root research  4096 Feb 27 06:55 .
drwxr-xr-x  24 root root       568 Feb 27  2005 ..
drwsrws---   4 root research  4096 Feb 27 06:59 home
drwx------   2 root root     16384 Feb 27 06:14 lost+found

Athena:~ # ls -l /research/home
total 16
drwsrws---   4 root research 4096 Feb 27 06:59 .
drwsrws---   4 root research 4096 Feb 27 06:55 ..
drwsrws---   7 mark research 4096 Feb 27 07:05 mark
drwxr-sr-x  12 pol  research 4096 Feb 27 07:06 pol
Athena:~ #
```

The protection on these directories allows for full access to root and members of the group research. At the same time, all other users of the system are denied access. It is imperative to adjust the backup utility to permit access to the contents of the structure.

NOTE

The man page for mount goes into more detail about the various options available for the various filesystem types. A number of filesystem types allow for the ownership of a mounted volume to be specified by UID/GID. This certainly makes things easier for restricting access. In some cases, however, the ownership of all files is forced to the same user or group as that specified in the mount options. In addition, the robustness of Reiserfs and ext3 are lost. We certainly encourage choosing the more robust filesystem.

Another typical request is for a large dataset to be made available to everyone on the system. The catch is that the dataset must be available in a read-only format. You can accomplish this by creating a mount point off the root—for example, /gisdata—and specifying that the partition in question be mounted using the ro option in fstab. It would look something like this:

```
/dev/sdc1 /gisdata ext3 ro 1 2
```

The resulting directory will be available to all users for read access. If additional information needs to be added to the structure, the partition can be dismounted, remounted on a different mount point with write privileges, and updated. mount can also use the user option to specify an individual who is allowed to mount/umount the mount point. Combined with the sudo granting of mount/umount, the maintenance of the dataset could be delegated to an individual within the user group responsible for the data.

This section examined the splitting of the typical root directory structure across multiple disk partitions. This is often done to segregate dynamic directory structures from the more static ones. Multiple devices also allow for distributing I/O operations, resulting in improved performance. The other aspect of filesystem management is restricting access to certain areas of the directory. This restriction can be applied across the board or to a specific group. The flexibility this capability offers allows you, the system administrator, more granularity in delivering storage to your customers.

Summary

In this chapter, we covered many aspects of system management. Topics such as system backups and user account management are covered in separate chapters. Here, we focused on the day-to-day aspects of maintaining the server.

We reviewed a number of common commands used to extract resource information from the system. Also, we examined the base directory structure of the root directory and explained the contents of the directories. In addition, we suggested a number of steps to help you in your day-to-day monitoring checks for servers. In the case of resource consumption, we also suggested a number of remedies.

PART III

Data Backup and Disaster Recovery

CHAPTER 8

Network Services

One major strength of Linux is in its offering of a wide range of network services. SLES 9 ships with a large number of such services, ranging from network time services to file sharing to web page serving. A detailed discussion of each topic discussed in this chapter is not feasible due to space; entire books are devoted to many of the topics, such as the Domain Name Service (DNS) and Samba. Therefore, the intention of this chapter is to provide you with the bare necessities to get a specific network service configured and running with a basic configuration.

We selected the topics covered here because they provide services to users on your local, private network, and not necessarily services over the Internet. This is why certain topics, such as the Squid proxy server and SuSEfirewall2, are not discussed here. The following topics, however, are discussed in this chapter:

- The xinetd super-server
- The Network Time Protocol (NTP) service
- Email services using Postfix
- FTP servers
- File sharing using NFS and Samba
- Remote management using VNC, XDMCP, and Telnet/ssh
- Network name services using DNS, DHCP, SLP, and Samba
- Web page serving using Apache
- Authentication services using Kerberos, LDAP, NIS, and Samba

There are other services beyond those available with SLES. Novell's Open Enterprise Server (www.novell.com/products/

openenterpriseserver/) provides a number of extra services (such as NetStorage and iFolder) that help bring the Novell and SLES world closer. These extra services are, however, beyond the scope of this chapter.

Angels and Daemons

Because SLES multitasks, there are always some programs running in the background that take care of the system-related tasks, such as executing `cron` and `at` jobs and watching out for and servicing network requests. These background processes are referred to as *daemons*.

THE ORIGIN OF THE WORD *DAEMON*

Some references indicate *daemon* (pronounced *dee-man* or *day-man*) is an acronym for **D**isk **A**nd **E**xecution **Mon**itor. However, the word was actually first used by Professor Fernando J. Corbato and his Project MAC (http://en.wikipedia.org/wiki/MIT_Laboratory_for_ Computer_Science) team back in 1963 to reference the background processes on the IBM 7094 mainframe. The reference was inspired by one of the "thought experiments" about thermodynamics conducted by the famous nineteenth century Scottish physicist James Clerk Maxwell (famous for Maxwell's equations of electrodynamics). In this experiment, Maxwell suggested that there exists an imaginary agent (a daemon) that helped sort molecules of different speeds and worked tirelessly in the background—an apt analogy to the various housekeeping tasks inside a multitasking computer operating system. (Visit http://ei.cs.vt.edu/~history/Daemon.html for more information.)

The Unix community adopted use of the word *daemon*, which in Greek mythology is a supernatural being that exists between gods and men, to describe the various background server processes that serve users (men) on behalf of the kernel (god). As a result, most of the server applications (such as the FTP server) have d appended to their filename—for example, `ftpd`; this serves to separate them from the client applications (such as `ftp` for the FTP client).

Instead of having various server services (such as FTP) started at system initialization time (which would slow down the server boot process) and be dormant until a connection request arrives (taking up unnecessary resources), a special daemon process is started and listens on *all* service ports for the services listed in its configuration file. When a request comes in on a port for which there is an "active" server listed in the configuration file, this monitor daemon starts the appropriate server. Furthermore, this monitor daemon can provide additional security if the service does not. Because of the way this server operates, it is generally referred to as the *super-server*. The drawback of running a frequently accessed service under the super-server is the slight delay caused by the super-server in starting up the service every time it is required.

There are two implementations of this super-server: inetd (Internet services daemon; pronounced *eye-net-d*) and xinetd (Extended Internet services daemon; pronounced *zy-net-d*). inetd has been widely used since the early days of Unix. However, in recent years, xinetd is much more popular due to its extended functions such as access logging, enhanced access control, and IPv6 support. For example, although inetd allows control for TCP connections using Wietse Venema's TCP_Wrappers software (tcpd, which is included on your SLES 9 media), you cannot control UDP connections. Although you can control the rate of connections using inetd, you cannot control the maximum number of instances. This could lead to process table overflow attacks—for example, an effective denial of service (DoS). xinetd does not suffer from these shortcomings. By default, SLES 9 uses xinetd instead of inetd, so that is what we discuss here.

TIP

If you have been using inetd and want to convert over to xinetd, use either the itox utility or the xconv.pl Perl script (both supplied with xinetd, but xconv.pl is generally preferred over itox) to convert your inetd.conf style configuration files to xinetd.conf. Refer to man itox and man xconv.pl for more information.

Configuring xinetd

On startup, xinetd reads several files located in /etc. The main configuration files are /etc/xinetd.conf plus all the files in /etc/xinetd.d. These files specify which daemon should be started for which service. The other files it reads are shared with other daemons and system services and contain more general information about Internet services:

- /etc/services—This file maps port numbers to service names. Most of the port numbers below 1024 are assigned to special (so-called *well-known*) services (see http://www.iana.org/assignments/port-numbers) and are listed in this file. Every time you refer to a service by its name (as opposed to its port number), the name is looked up in /etc/services and the assigned port number is used to process the request.

- /etc/protocols—This file maps protocols to the numbers the kernel uses to distinguish between the different TCP/IP protocols. The list is based on http://www.iana.org/assignments/protocol-numbers.

- /etc/rpc—Similar to /etc/services, this file maps Remote Procedure Call (RPC) services to their ID numbers and common names.

Generally, you don't need to touch any of the files in the preceding list. When you do, the likely candidate for changes is /etc/services, where you'll add the port(s) used by some custom daemons not already listed in the file or if you need a specific service to run on a port other than its accepted default for some reason.

You can configure services supported by xinetd in two ways: using YaST or working directly with the configuration files. Although YaST provides a friendly user interface, you can modify certain options only by editing the configuration files directly. Therefore, we cover both procedures here.

To access the xinetd configuration module in YaST (see Figure 8.1), select Control Center, Network Services, Network Services (inetd). Alternatively, you can access this module directly by using yast2 inetd or yast inetd. Note that some of the menu text shows inetd even though you are using xinetd.

FIGURE 8.1
The xinetd configuration screen.

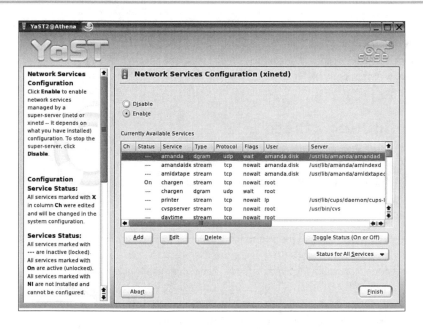

The top of the screen shows whether the super-server is running (Enabled) or not (Disabled). The list box on the screen shows the defined services and their current run status. Of particular interest are the columns labeled Ch, Status, and Server.

TIP

You can check to see whether xinetd is running by using the command /etc/init.d/xinetd status or the following:

```
Athena:/home/admin # ps ax | grep xinetd
32369 ?        Ss      0:01 /usr/sbin/xinetd
20857 pts/8    R+      0:00 grep xinetd
```

The first line shows xinetd is currently running as a detached system process (that is, no terminal attached) and its process ID (PID) is 32369. Similarly, you can use the same command to determine whether any of your service daemons are running by substituting xinetd with the name of the daemon, such as in.telnetd.

The Status column shows whether the daemon is running (On) or not (---); NI means YaST knows about the package, but the package is not installed and therefore cannot be configured. If you toggle the status of the daemon (from On to Off), an X is placed in the Ch column to indicate the status of this daemon has been changed; if the Ch column is blank, the service's status has not been altered. Remember to click Finish for the new status settings to take effect.

TIP

Instead of enabling or disabling one service at a time, you can click Status for All Services and then select to either enable or disable all services with a single click.

The Server column shows the name of the daemon and the path it is running from. Some of the network services do not have a server listed under this column because xinetd provides several simple services internally through the use of built-in routines. These services are:

- ECHO—This service is mostly used as a debugging tool to send any datagrams received on TCP or UDP port 7 from a source back to that source. The risk with this service is that someone can overload the server via the ECHO service, amounting to a DoS attack. RFC 862 (http://www.ietf.org/rfc/rfc862.txt) describes the ECHO service.
- DISCARD—This service is also known as SINK or NULL. It is simply a data blackhole because it throws away any datagrams (TCP or UDP) it receives on port 9. RFC 863 (http://www.ietf.org/rfc/rfc863.txt) describes the DISCARD service.
- SYSTAT—Listening on TCP/UDP port 11, the SYSTAT (better known as ACTIVE USERS or just USERS) service simply sends a list of the currently

active users—users currently logged in—on the host. All inputs are ignored. RFC 866 (http://www.ietf.org/rfc/rfc866.txt) describes the USERS service.

- DAYTIME (human-readable time)—In UDP, after the daemon receives a datagram on port 13 (which can contain any data), it sends back the current date and time in ASCII format. In TCP mode, on receipt of a datagram and after the connection is established, the service sends the date and time in ASCII format and closes the connection:

```
Athena:/home/admin # telnet localhost 13
Trying 127.0.0.1...
Connected to localhost.
Escape character is '^]'.
15 JAN 2005 07:08:42 EST
Connection closed by foreign host.
```

RFC 867 (http://www.ietf.org/rfc/rfc867.txt) describes the DAYTIME service.

- NETSTAT—Also known as the Who Is Up protocol, NETSTAT listens on (TCP and UDP) port 15 and returns information about the server's network information, such as routing tables and connection data. This service reveals a wealth of information about the system's structure that can be used to later hack the system. As a result, this daemon is no longer listed in the /etc/services file in most Linux/Unix distributions available today, and the protocol is obsolete.

- QOTD—Listening on port 17, the Quote of the Day service (also known as the QUOTE protocol) simply sends a short message back to the client either via TCP or UDP without regard to the input. RFC 865 (http://www.ietf.org/rfc/rfc865.txt) describes the Quote of the Day service.

- CHARGEN (character generator)—In UDP mode, CHARGEN (also known as the TTYtst or Source protocol) generates random characters in one UDP packet containing a random number (between 0 and 512) of characters. In TCP mode, the daemon sends a continuous stream of TCP packets after a connection is made on port 19, until the session closes. Any data received (either in TCP or UDP mode) is discarded. A potential DoS attack is spoofing an IP address and causing two devices to send random traffic to each other. RFC 864 (http://www.ietf.org/rfc/rfc864.txt) describes the CHARGEN service.

- TIME (also known as Unix Time; machine-readable time, in the form of the number of seconds since midnight, January 1, 1900—the Epoch)—This service works similarly to the DAYTIME protocol, but instead of returning the information in ASCII form, it sends the time back as a 32-bit binary number. It can also receive time data from another host; this was the standard way to set up time servers for a Unix network before the advent of the Network Time Protocol (NTP). Port 37 is used. RFC 868 (http://www.ietf.org/rfc/rfc868.txt) describes the TIME service.

- FINGER—Also known as the NAME protocol, the FINGER daemon listens on port 79 and returns a status report on either the system at the moment or about a particular person in depth. In recent years, this service has been mostly offered through its own daemon (fingerd) instead of the built-in support in inetd/xinetd. RFC 1288 (http://www.ietf.org/rfc/rfc1288.txt) describes the FINGER service.

When inetd is initially installed, all defined services are disabled by default. Enable only the services that you absolutely require so you minimize any security weaknesses that may be exposed by a given service.

Most of the network daemons offer you the option to set them to run either as standalone applications or to be invoked by xinetd on demand. Although the setup with xinetd saves resources in the time the service is not used, it creates a delay for the client. The daemon for this service has to be loaded and probably has to initialize itself before it's ready to serve the request. You should give considerable thought about which services you want to run as standalone applications and which ones you want to be called by xinetd.

For instance, you would likely want to run a web server such as Apache as a standalone service instead of having it invoked by xinetd whenever a client request comes in on port 80. Apache needs a relatively long load time, and you don't want your clients waiting too long while your website loads. Apache is highly optimized to run in standalone mode, so you probably don't want it to be spawned by xinetd. On the other hand, a service such as Telnet (whose daemon is in.telnetd) that enables logins from other machines doesn't need much time to load. That makes Telnet a good candidate for being invoked by xinetd.

Use the following procedure to add a new service to be managed by xinetd:

1. In the Network Services Configuration dialog box, click Add.
2. In the Add a New Service Entry dialog box (see Figure 8.2), fill in the service name and optionally the RPC Version (if the daemon is an RPC application). Then select the desired socket type, protocol, flags, and user and group the service will run under. Enter the complete path for the location of the daemon and specify any optional command-line arguments for the daemon. Optionally, enter identification comments about this new service.

FIGURE 8.2
Adding a new `xinetd`-managed service.

3. If the new server is to be enabled right away, ensure the Service Is Active box is checked.

4. Click Accept to save the entry.

5. Click Finish to save the changes and signal `xinetd` to use the new configuration.

6. If the new service uses a nonstandard port or one that is not already listed in **/etc/services**, you need to update the file to include the new service name, its port number, and the transport type.

CAUTION

Do *not* use any embedded whitespace in the service name (such as `Password self service`) because YaST stops parsing the name at the first whitespace.

WHAT IS RPC?

RPC (*Remote Procedure Call*; sometimes called *Open Network Computing,* or ONC) is a technique for constructing distributed, client/server-based applications initially developed by Sun Microsystems for its Network File System (NFS). It is based on extending the notion of conventional, or local, procedure calling so that the called procedure need not exist in the same address space as the calling procedure: The two processes may be on the same system, or they may be on different systems connected over a network. By using RPC, programmers of distributed applications avoid the details of the interface with the network. The transport independence of RPC isolates the application from the physical and logical elements of the data communications mechanism and allows the application to use a variety of transports.

RFC 1831 (`http://www.ietf.org/rfc/rfc1831.txt`) describes the Remote Procedure Call Protocol Specification Version 2.

The `Wait` and `NoWait` flag selection indicates if the service is single-threaded or multithreaded and whether `xinetd` accepts the connection or the daemon accepts the connection. `Wait` indicates the service is single-threaded and `xinetd` will start the server and then stop handling requests for the server as the service takes over in accepting the connection. After the service dies, `xinetd` will listen for requests on behalf of this server again. The `NoWait` flag indicates the service is multithreaded and `xinetd` will keep handling new service requests and accept the connection.

NOTE

Generally, UDP/datagram services use the `Wait` flag because UDP is not connection oriented. On the other hand, TCP/stream services use the `NoWait` flag.

Normally `xinetd` runs as root. This means any process it spawns also runs as root. However, from a security standpoint, this is generally not desirable because if the process is compromised, it can cause serious damage. The User and Group settings allow you to specify that the daemon will run as a lower-privileged user. You can use either the user/group names or their respective UIDs/GIDs; however, using the names is recommended. If a group name or GID is not specified, the user's primary group is used instead.

CAUTION

`xinetd` must be running as root for the User and Group settings to be effective. Otherwise, it would not have sufficient privileges to switch a service's UID/GID to that of a nonprivileged account/group.

Under the User column in the Network Services Configuration dialog box, you see, for instance, *name.name* for some services, whereas others have only *name*. Where *name.name* is shown, the first is the actual username, and the second is the group name. For example, the amanda service's User column shows amanda.disk. That means the service runs as user amanda and group disk. Similarly, the User column for the printer service is just root. So this service will run as root, and its primary group is specified in /etc/passwd (and YaST shows the Group as --default--; see Figure 8.2).

The /etc/xinetd.conf File

The main configuration file for xinetd is /etc/xinetd.conf. The xinetd.conf file, shown in Listing 8.1, contains only the default service settings plus a reference to the /etc/xinetd.d directory, where the other service configuration files are stored.

LISTING 8.1
The Default /etc/xinetd.conf File

```
#
# xinetd.conf
#
# Copyright (c) 1998-2001 SuSE GmbH Nuernberg, Germany.
# Copyright (c) 2002 SuSE LINUX AG, Nuernberg, Germany.
#

defaults
{
        log_type        = FILE /var/log/xinetd.log
        log_on_success  = HOST EXIT DURATION
        log_on_failure  = HOST ATTEMPT
#       only_from       = localhost
        instances       = 30
        cps             = 50 10

#
# The specification of an interface is interesting,
# if we are on a firewall. For example, if you only want
# to provide services from an internal network interface,
# you may specify your internal interfaces IP-Address.
#
#       interface       = 127.0.0.1

}
includedir /etc/xinetd.d
```

Instead of cluttering `xinetd.conf` with entries for various services, this file simply refers to an include directory using the `includedir` directive, where each file in that directory corresponds to a defined service. However, instead of using additional files, you can put the service definitions in `inetd.conf`.

In general, the names of the files in `/etc/xinetd.d` match those of the services. This makes them easier to identify. However, having matching names is not a requirement. One example is the `printer` service: There is not a file called `printer` in `/etc/xinetd.d`. Instead, this service is defined in a file called `cups-lpd`. Therefore, if you are adding services to `xinetd` by manually creating files, you can call them anything you like—but having the filename match the service name is helpful.

NOTE

When you create a new service using YaST's Network Services Configuration dialog box, YaST creates a file corresponding to the service name in `/etc/xinetd.d`. This is another reason why you should not use embedded whitespace in service names because it makes accessing the files a little more cumbersome: You would need to put quotation marks (either single or double) around the name due to the embedded whitespaces.

Each service description is in the following format:

```
#comment for the service
#more comment lines
service servicename
{
     directive = value
     directive += value
     directive -= value
}
```

Using =, the values on the right are assigned to the directive on the left. The += appends values to an already-defined directive. Without it (that is, using =), earlier directives are overwritten. This symbol can also be used to spread access lists, for example, over multiple lines. The -= removes an existing value from the directive.

The following is the basic minimum set of directives required for a service:

```
service servicename
{
     disable       =
     socket_type   =
     protocol      =
```

```
        wait         =
        user         =
#       group          =
        server       =
#       server_args    =
}
```

The `disable` directive indicates whether the service is active (`disable` = `no`) or not (`disable` = `yes`). If `disable` is not specified, its value defaults to `no`, meaning the service is active. The `group` directive allows you to specify the group (thus GID) under which the service will run as. If not specified, the service will run using the default group of the UID that the service runs as. Although the `server_args` directive is not required by `xinetd`, most daemons require at least one command-line switch to control behavior.

NOTE

Because the Network Services Configuration dialog box is designed to handle both `xinetd` and `inetd`, its interface does not provide any means to edit directive values other than those listed here as the minimum set. Therefore, if you want to include additional directives (such as access control, discussed in the next section), you need to edit the file containing the service definition to manually add the required directives.

Each service inherits the directives defined in the `defaults` section in `xinetd.conf`, unless specifically modified within that service's definition. Now let's consider the following sample service definition:

```
#Example service
service foobar
{
        disable         = yes
        socket_type     = stream
        protocol        = tcp
        wait            = no
        user            = dummy
        group           = dumdum
        server          = /var/sbin/foobard
        server_args     = -log
        log_type        = SYSLOG mail notice
        log_on_success  += USERID
        log_on_failure  += USERID
        instances       = 15
}
```

When you take into account the directives in the `defaults` section (see Listing 8.1), the effective directives values for the `foobar` service are as follows:

```
disable        = yes
socket_type    = stream
protocol       = tcp
wait           = no
user           = dummy
group          = dumdum
server         = /var/sbin/foobard
server_args    = -log
log_type       = SYSLOG mail notice
log_on_success = HOST EXIT DURATION USERID
log_on_failure = HOST ATTEMPT USERID
instances      = 15
cps            = 50 10
```

Here, the values for `log_type` and `instances` are superceded by new values, and `USERID` is added to `log_on_success` and `log_on_failure`. Because `cps` (connection per second) is specified in `defaults` and is not in `foobar`'s definition, `defaults`' `cps` value is used.

Sometimes it is much more convenient to start or stop a service from the command line instead of YaST. You just need to do the following:

1. Using an editor, open the file containing the service's definition in `/etc/xinetd.d` and add the directive `disable = yes` to stop it. To enable the service, either comment out the `disable = yes` line or change it to `disable = no`.

2. Use `ps ax | grep xinetd` to determine `xinetd`'s process ID.

3. Send the `xinetd` process the `SIGHUP` signal using the `kill` command: `kill -SIGHUP` *pid*. (You can also use `killproc -SIGHUP /usr/sbin/xinetd` instead.)

The `SIGHUP` (hang up) signal causes a hard reconfiguration for `xinetd`, which means `xinetd` rereads the configuration file, starts any new services, and terminates the daemons for services that are no longer available. Alternatively, you can use `/etc/init.d/xinetd reload` (or `/etc/init.d/xinetd force-reload`) instead of the `kill` command. You can also use `/etc/init.d/xinetd` to start and stop `xinetd`—for instance, `/etc/init.d/xinetd start` or `/etc/init.d/xinetd stop`.

YaST does not allow you to set advanced settings, such as `log_type` or `instances`, in a service configuration file. Therefore, you need to resort to using a text editor. After modifying the configuration file, you need to restart `xinetd` by sending it the SIGHUP signal so the new settings take effect. If changes were made using YaST, YaST will automatically restart xinetd after you click Finish.

TIP

Instead of /etc/init.d/xinetd, you can use /usr/sbin/rcxinetd instead because it is just a symbolic link to /etc/init.d/xinetd, a shell script. As a matter of fact, you will find rcxinetd referred to often in the documentation; using it instead is probably more convenient because /usr/sbin is in root's PATH setting, while /etc/init.d is not.

Applying Access Control

You need to realize that xinetd controls connections, not packets. As such, while it would break a TCP connect() attempt from a host that is prohibited from connecting to a service, it will *not*, and could not, break "stealth" scans such as a FIN scan. Therefore, don't rely on xinetd to be a firewall to prevent port scanning. A resourceful hacker will be able to use this information to gather access control lists for your various services. If you see your log file showing very short connection durations (zero or just a couple of seconds) made sequentially to your active services, chances are good that someone is doing a connect()-type port scan against your server.

NOTE

In a FIN scan, scanner software, such as nmap, utilizes TCP packets with the FIN flag set to scan for open ports on a host. nmap and other security assessment and intruder detection tools are discussed in Chapter 12, "Intrusion Detection."

Access control is fairly simple and easy to implement. You can use these three directives:

- only_from lists the networks or hosts (separated by a space between each entry) from which the service will accept connections. You can use network numbers, such as 10.0.0.0 or 10, or network names (if defined in /etc/networks), including *.UniversalExport.ca or .UniversalExport.ca with this directive. Hostnames and IP addresses of hosts also can be used here. (Refer to man xinetd.conf for a list of supported addressing schemes, including subnet specifications.)

WARNING

If only_from is specified without any values, *all* access will be rejected.

- access_times specifies the time intervals (separated by a space between each entry) when the service is available. An interval has the form *hour:min-hour:min*. Connections will be accepted between the listed time window. If access_times is not specified, there is no time restriction. The times are specified using the 24-hour clock format.

TIP

Unless you can use the host's security features to lock down its IP address or use DHCP to assign a static address to a given host, it is more secure to specify networks and subnets instead of individual host addresses when setting up the only_from and no_access directives. And if you are restricting access from outside your network, use domain names whenever possible because many ISPs use a range of subnets that may change from time to time.

By default (as specified in the defaults section of xinetd.conf), successful and failed connection attempts are logged to the /var/log/xinetd.log file. This file should be reviewed periodically for failed attempts from prohibited or unknown hosts and networks, as well as successful connections from unknown sites. The following is an excerpt from /var/log/xinetd.log showing both successful and failed attempts for a number of services:

```
05/1/14@09:17:18: START: telnet from=10.4.4.4
05/1/14@09:17:31: EXIT: telnet status=1 duration=13(sec)
05/1/14@11:09:21: START: telnet from=10.4.4.4
05/1/14@12:15:16: EXIT: telnet status=1 duration=3955(sec)
05/1/14@16:28:05: FAIL: echo-stream address from=10.4.4.4
05/1/14@16:28:05: START: echo-stream from=10.4.4.4
05/1/14@16:28:05: EXIT: echo-stream status=0 duration=0(sec)
05/1/14@16:28:26: START: echo-stream from=10.3.3.4
05/1/14@16:28:43: EXIT: echo-stream status=0 duration=17(sec)
05/1/14@16:29:49: FAIL: echo-stream address from=10.4.4.4
05/1/14@16:29:49: START: echo-stream from=10.4.4.4
05/1/14@16:29:49: EXIT: echo-stream status=0 duration=0(sec)
05/1/14@17:06:18: START: chargen-stream from=10.4.4.4
05/1/14@17:06:23: EXIT: chargen-stream status=0 duration=5(sec)
05/1/14@17:15:08: START: telnet from=127.0.0.1
05/1/14@17:15:08: EXIT: telnet status=1 duration=0(sec)
05/1/15@04:43:46: FAIL: echo-stream address from=10.4.4.4
05/1/15@04:43:46: START: echo-stream from=10.4.4.4
05/1/15@04:43:46: EXIT: echo-stream status=0 duration=0(sec)
```

TIP

If you're interested in just the failed attempts, you can easily display all related entries by using grep:

```
Athena:/home/admin # grep -i fail /var/log/xinetd.log
05/1/14@16:28:05: FAIL: echo-stream address from=10.4.4.4
05/1/14@16:29:49: FAIL: echo-stream address from=10.4.4.4
05/1/15@04:43:46: FAIL: echo-stream address from=10.4.4.4
```

Security Considerations

You should be sure that you need xinetd before you set it up. A client machine that primarily acts as a workstation has no need to run xinetd because the client machine is not meant to provide any services for the network. Similarly, if your SLES server runs a dedicated service, such as DNS, there is also no real need to run xinetd. Whether you use it is basically a question of security. Using xinetd on machines on which you really don't need it may reveal possible entry points for intruders. xinetd-enabled services such as telnet and rlogin can be used to exploit your machine. This doesn't mean that those services are generally insecure, but they may be a first source of information for potential hackers trying to enter your system.

When you are using xinetd, enable only the services that are absolutely required. Typical diagnostic services such as echo and chargen can become targets for DoS attacks because their use diverts CPU resources away from other processes that will cause problems for the connected networks and Internet services dependent on that server.

Network Time Services

Accurate timing plays an important role in any multithreaded computer operating system. The system kernel schedules processes, and then it processes events based on time. The system time is also used for time-stamping log entries, application transaction records, email messages, security certificate management, and so on. However, unless your server has a built-in atomic clock, to keep proper time, the system clock must regularly be corrected for drifts. You can perform the correction manually or have the system clock updated automatically via some time protocol over the network. SLES 9 includes Network Time Protocol (NTP) software (xntp v4 package) to assist you in obtaining an accurate time from the Internet as well as a way to provide the same correct time to other servers and clients on your internal network. In this section, we discuss how to set up your NTP client and cover setting up an NTP server for your internal network. First, let's look at some background information.

NOTE

For internal networks, it is customary to set up a time server to provide times to the local systems and have that time server obtain its time setting from one of the well-known Internet time sources, such as the U.S. Naval Observatory.

CAUTION

We cannot stress enough how important it is that the correct time is maintained on your servers. Even if you have only one server that is running Apache (see "Web Services" later in this chapter), having the correct time is essential for secure HTTP connections. Security certificates used for HTTPS connections (or other applications that use a certificate) often contain both "not valid before" and "not valid after" dates. Should your server's time be inaccurate, it could prevent a certificate from being installed or used. And if your web server also offers e-commerce functions, such as shopping carts, accurate time-stamping of transaction records is essential.

You can adjust your server's time in a number of ways based on external NTP time sources. The NTP software suite includes two applications for setting the system's time via NTP: `ntpdate` and `ntpd`. At first glance, it seems `ntpdate` would be the preference because it is simple to set up and use. In its simplest form, the syntax is

```
ntpdate timeserver_1 timeserver_2 timeserver_3 …
```

where *timeserver_x* are either the DNS names or IP addresses of NTP time servers. `ntpdate` must run as root on the local host. It queries each of the listed servers (multiple samples are taken to obtain an averaged time), determines the time differences between itself and each of the time servers, and sorts them into groups. The largest group of time servers with an identical time (within certain limits) is deemed to possess the "correct time," and `ntpdate` sets the local time to that of the first server's in that group. The drawback here is the way in which the new time is applied by `ntpdate`.

Time adjustments are made by `ntpdate` in one of two ways. If the time difference is ±128 ms or more, `ntpdate` will simply "step" the local time to match that of the NTP server's. If the time difference is less than ±128 ms, `ntpdate` will "slew" the time by making small incremental adjustments until the times match. As you can see, `ntpdate` could cause a sudden time change that can upset the proper operation of some applications, such as `cron`. Although it takes a little more work to set up, the better alternative is to use `ntpd` instead; `ntpdate` is due to be retired from the NTP distribution anyway because all its functions are available within `ntpd`.

CAUTION

You can use the –B switch to force `ntpdate` to always slew the time instead of stepping it for large time offsets. However, if the time difference is much larger than ±128 ms, slewing the clock to reach the correct time could take hours. Additionally, if the difference between the current date and the system date is too large, `ntpdate` can set the year to 1933 due to arithmetic overflow.

NOTE

If you're familiar with the NetWare TimeSync protocol, `ntpdate`'s step operation is exactly the way a Secondary time server (which takes time from a Primary time server or a Reference time server) and a time client behave: The time is adjusted 100% instead of a fraction at a time. The slew operation mirrors the way in which a Primary time server adjusts its time: The time is adjusted by 50% of the difference every time until it is synchronized.

`ntpd` operates by exchanging messages with one or more configured time servers at designated poll intervals. To protect the network from traffic bursts, the initial poll interval for `ntpd` to each time server is delayed an interval randomized over a few seconds. The default initial poll interval is 64 seconds, and, consequently, several minutes can elapse before the local clock is set. (You can reduce the initial delay to set the clock by using the `iburst` keyword with the server configuration command.) By measuring the network roundtrip jitter and local clock frequency drift, `ntpd` will slowly increase the polling interval from 64 seconds to 1,024 seconds (just a little over 17 minutes). Also, if a target time server is unreachable for some time, the polling interval is also increased in step to 1,024 seconds. This helps to reduce network traffic.

NOTE

Much of the SUSE documentation, even the Novell training material to some extent, makes reference to `xntpd`. However, the current NTP distribution documentation uses `ntpd` instead because it reflects NTPv4, while `xntpd` was used for NTPv3. As a matter of fact, you will find on your SLES server that `/usr/sbin/xntpd` is actually a symbolic link to `/usr/sbin/ntpd`. Therefore, we use `ntpd` here.

Under normal conditions, ntpd adjusts the clock in small increments (that is, slewing it) so that the time scale is effectively continuous and without discontinuities. In case of extreme network congestion, ntpd may end up stepping the time; however, this situation is extremely rare because ntpd employs a number of algorithms to try to slew the clock first and steps it only after all recovery attempts have failed.

NOTE

ntpd has a built-in safeguard: If its local time differs by 1,000 seconds (16.67 minutes) or more with that of the time server's, ntpd will immediately exit and log a panic message to the system log indicating an "insane" time source.

Once installed, ntpd is set up to automatically run at server bootup. If, for some reason, it does not, you can use the insserv command as follows:

Athena:/home/admin # **/sbin/insserv /etc/init.d/xntpd**

NOTE

Instead of insserv, you can also use the Runlevel Editor in YaST to enable the service. To access this editor, select Control Center, System, Runlevel Editor or use yast runlevel.

Keep in mind that because both ntpd and ntpdate use port 123, they cannot be run concurrently on the same host.

Configuring the NTP Client

Ordinarily, ntpd reads /etc/ntp.conf at startup time to determine the synchronization sources and operating modes. Although this approach is not recommended because it is cumbersome, you can specify a working, although limited, configuration entirely on the command line, obviating the need for a configuration file. This approach may be particularly useful when the local host is to be configured as a broadcast/multicast client, with all peers being determined by listening to broadcasts at runtime.

CAUTION

The configuration filename for the NTP daemon (ntpd) is ntp.conf, and not ntpd.conf, as you may expect.

The configuration file format is similar to other Linux/Unix configuration files: Comments begin with a # character and extend to the end of the line; blank lines are ignored. Configuration commands consist of an initial keyword followed by a list of arguments, some of which may be optional, separated by whitespace. Commands may not be continued over multiple lines. The default /etc/ntp.conf file as included with the xntp package in SLES 9 is shown in Listing 8.2.

LISTING 8.2
The Default /etc/ntp.conf File

```
############################################################
## /etc/ntp.conf
##
## Sample NTP configuration file.
## See package 'xntp-doc' for documentation, Mini-HOWTO
## and FAQ.
## Copyright (c) 1998 S.u.S.E. GmbH Fuerth, Germany.
##
## Author: Michael Andres,   <ma@suse.de>
##
############################################################

##
## Radio and modem clocks by convention have addresses in the
## form 127.127.t.u, where t is the clock type and u is a unit
## number in the range 0-3.
##
## Most of these clocks require support in the form of a
## serial port or special bus peripheral. The particular
## device is normally specified by adding a soft link
## /dev/device-u to the particular hardware device involved,
## where u correspond to the unit number above.
##
## Generic DCF77 clock on serial port (Conrad DCF77)
## Address:      127.127.8.u
## Serial Port: /dev/refclock-u
##
## (create soft link /dev/refclock-0 to the particular ttyS?)
##
# server 127.127.8.0 mode 5 prefer

##
## Undisciplined Local Clock. This is a fake driver
## intended for backup and when no outside source of
## synchronized time is available.
```

LISTING 8.2

The Default /etc/ntp.conf File (continued)

```
##
server 127.127.1.0  # local clock (LCL)
fudge 127.127.1.0  stratum 10 # LCL is unsynchronized

##
## Outside source of synchronized time
##
## server xx.xx.xx.xx      # IP address of server

##
## Miscellaneous stuff
##

driftfile /var/lib/ntp/drift/ntp.drift #path for drift file

logfile /var/log/ntp       # alternate log file
# logconfig =syncstatus + sysevents
# logconfig =all

# statsdir /tmp/        # directory for statistics files
# filegen peerstats  file peerstats  type day enable
# filegen loopstats  file loopstats  type day enable
# filegen clockstats file clockstats type day enable

#
# Authentication stuff
#
# keys /etc/ntp.keys           # path for keys file
# trustedkey 1 2 3 4 5 6 14 15 # define trusted keys
# requestkey 15   # key (7) for accessing server variables
# controlkey 15   # key (6) for accessing server variables
```

You can make a simple client configuration by adding the list of NTP time servers that you want **ntpd** to contact:

```
##
## Outside source of synchronized time
##
server 10.1.1.1 prefer      # IP of local time server
server time.nrc.ca          # DNS name of Ottawa server
server dense.utcc.utoronto.ca # University of Toronto
#server ntp-1.cede.psu.edu    # Pennsylvania state
#server timex.cs.columbia.edu # New York state
#server tick.jrc.us          # New Jersey state
```

NOTE

The prefer option in the server command indicates that this server's time should be used for synchronization, if all things are equal (such as time jitter) from among the specified set of time sources.

For redundancy, it is recommended that you use three to five NTP sources, located on different networks. When using Internet NTP time servers, select ones that are located geographically close to you but not at the same location. The preceding sample entries show that, in addition to the local time server, ntpd also contacts two other servers located in nearby cities.

TIP

For a list of public NTP time servers, visit http://ntp.isc.org/bin/view/Servers/WebHome. Be sure to read the "Rules of Engagement" (http://ntp.isc.org/bin/view/Servers/RulesOfEngagement) before you select your time sources.

CAUTION

You should ensure the following two lines in your /etc/ntp.conf are *not* commented out or modified:

```
server 127.127.1.0  # local clock (LCL)
fudge 127.127.1.0   stratum 10 # LCL is unsynchronized
```

They provide a fallback using the local system clock as a pseudo time source if none of the NTP sources you have listed are available, due to an ISP service interruption, for example. At the very minimum, the stratum setting should not be set to a value less than 5. (A discussion about stratum can be found in the "Configuring an NTP Server" section later in this chapter.)

If your NTP time source can be reached via broadcast or multicast, you don't need to use server names. Instead, enter either the broadcastclient or multicastclient command in the configuration file. To prevent a rogue time server in the network from changing your server's time, configure the authentication mechanisms listed under the Authentication stuff section in /etc/ntp.conf; refer to /usr/share/doc/packages/xntp-doc/html/authopt.html for details.

NOTE

No man page is available for the NTP distribution. However, you will find an xntp-doc package containing HTML documentation. When you install the package, the HTML files and related FAQs and README files are installed into /usr/share/doc/packages/xntp-doc.

ntpd uses a file (whose name is defined by the driftfile keyword in the configuration file) to record the "drift" (or frequency error) value it has computed. If the file exists on startup, it is read and the value used to initialize ntpd's internal value of the frequency error. The file is then updated once every hour by replacing the old file with a new one containing the current value of the frequency error. Note that the file is updated by first writing the current drift value into a temporary file and then using the rename function to replace the old version. This implies that ntpd *must* have write permission for the directory where the drift file is located, and that file system links, symbolic or otherwise, should be avoided when specifying the value for the driftfile keyword.

ntpd reads /etc/ntp.conf upon startup and then once every hour to look for changes. If ntpd is already running and you made changes to /etc/ntp.conf but do not wish to wait, you can use the command /etc/init.d/xntpd restart (or /etc/init.d/xntpd force-restart) to make ntpd reread the configuration file.

TIP

Instead of /etc/init.d/xntpd, you can use /usr/sbin/rcxntpd because it is just a symbolic link to /etc/init.d/xntpd, a shell script. As a matter of fact, you will find rcxntpd referred to often in the documentation; using it instead is probably more convenient because /usr/sbin is in root's PATH setting, while /etc/init.d is not.

If ntpd isn't running and you want to manually start it, use the command /etc/init.d/xntpd start; to stop it, use /etc/init.d/xntpd stop.

Because of the number of optional keywords possible for the configuration, you will find it is actually much easier to manually edit /etc/ntpd.conf instead of using YaST. But if you insist, there is a YaST module to configure the NTP client; you'll find a package called yast2-ntp-client installed. To access the NTP Client Configuration dialog box (see Figure 8.3) from the Control Center, select Network Services, NTP Client. Or you can open this dialog box directly by using yast2 ntp-client or yast ntp-client.

FIGURE 8.3
NTP client configuration screen.

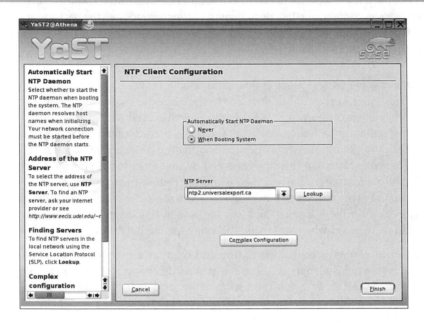

The default dialog box allows you to specify a single host as the time source. To use multiple sources, click Complex Configuration and then use the Add button to create an entry for each desired time server. If you already have at least one time source defined (other than the local clock), the Complex Configuration screen is displayed automatically.

NOTE

One of the options in the Complex NTP Client Configuration dialog box is called Run NTP Daemon in Chroot Jail. chroot jail (or Change root jail) is a way to limit the portion of the file system that the daemon can see; this is similar to using MAP ROOT in NetWare. By default, ntpd runs in chroot jail mode. If, for some reason, you don't want ntpd in chroot jail, edit either /etc/init.d/rcxntpd or /etc/sysconfig/xntp and change the XNTPD_RUN_CHROOTED setting from yes to no.

Refer to Chapter 13, "System Security," for further discussions about chroot jails.

CAUTION

Even if you are running ntpd in chroot jail, the copy of ntp.conf to edit is still the copy in /etc, and *not* the copy in the jail's /etc directory (which, by default, is /var/lib/ntp/etc). That copy is updated automatically by ntpd's startup script.

When you use YaST to set up your NTP client configuration, it also updates the XNTPD_INITIAL_NTPDATE variable (used by ntpd upon system startup to obtain the current date and time information) setting in /etc/sysconfig/xntp. However, if you manually edited /etc/ntp.conf outside YaST, the XNTPD_INITIAL_NTPDATE setting may contain obsolete host data until the next time YaST is used to update the NTP client settings. The following example illustrates the telltale sign of this happening when you manually start or restart ntpd from a terminal session:

```
Athena:/home/admin # rcxntpd start
Try to get initial date and time via NTP from ticker failed
Starting network time protocol daemon (NTPD)            done
```

Ticker is a time source that has been removed from the network, and its server command entry was manually removed from /etc/ntp.conf without using YaST. As a result, /etc/sysconfig/xntp contains the outdated information (XNTPD_INITIAL_NTPDATE = ticker) leading to the failure message.

Configuring an NTP Server

ntpd can function as an NTP client or as an NTP server or as both concurrently. This allows a single server in the network to run ntpd to obtain time from an authoritative time source (either from an NTP server on the Internet or a locally attached reference clock); then it redistributes that information to other servers (running ntpd in client-only mode) internally. This reduces traffic to the external time source and ensures all NTP clients use a common time source.

There are two ways in which an NTP client can locate an NTP server. The first method is simply to statically configure either the IP address or the DNS name of the NTP source in the client's /etc/ntp.conf file. The other method is to set up the NTP time server to broadcast or multicast its time onto the network and configure the clients to listen for the broadcasted/multicasted time information.

To run ntpd with broadcasts or multicasts, add the broadcast *address* command to the configuration file. In broadcast mode, the *address* should be the broadcast address on (one of) the local network(s), such as 192.168.1.255. To enable multicast mode, the *address* should be 224.0.1.1 (for IPv4) or ff05::101 (site local, for IPv6)—the addresses assigned to NTP. Multiple `broadcast` commands may be specified to support multiple local network interfaces or multiple multicast groups.

Before you allow `ntpd` to act as a time source, you must ensure the server has the correct time. In most cases, you accomplish this by obtaining its time from one or more of the standard Internet NTP servers. This also can be done with reference clocks. The NTP distribution includes hardware drivers for more than 40 radio and satellite clocks and modem services that can be used as reference clocks. A list of supported drivers can be found in `/usr/share/doc/packages/xntp-doc/html/refclock.html`. It is also possible to use an otherwise "undisciplined" local clock as a primary or backup time source. The following discussion presents information on how to set up a reference clock, using the local clock as an example.

NOTE

Many radio reference clocks can be set to display local time as adjusted for time zone and daylight saving mode. When used with NTP, the clock must be set for Coordinated Universal Time (UTC) only. The OS kernel performs the conversion to local time, so the fact that the clock runs on UTC will be transparent to the users.

The clocks are specified in `/etc/ntp.conf` as though they are real-time servers on the network using the `server` keyword. For this purpose, they are assigned special IP addresses in the form 127.127.$t.u$. In the address, t specifies the clock type and u is a unit number in the range 0–3 that distinguishes multiple instances of clocks of the same type. For example, the server's hardware clock will have a pseudo IP address of 127.127.1.0.

NOTE

You can find a list of supported clock type values (t) in `/usr/share/doc/packages/xntp-doc/html/refclock.html`.

Normally, the individual drivers have special parameters that describe their configuration details. The `refclock.html` file mentioned in the preceding note provides links to the different driver pages describing these parameters. For instance, a TimeBrick DCF77 receiver module uses the Type 8 Generic Reference Driver (PARSE). But because this Type 8 driver supports a number of different receiver modules, you need to include additional parameters to tell the driver which specific receiver module you are using. The complete server command for a TimeBrick DCF77 receiver module would be

```
server 127.127.8.0 mode 6
```

With the exception of the local clock, most of the radio reference clocks require support in the form of a serial port or special bus peripheral. You need to associate the clock driver to the particular hardware device by manually creating a symbolic link between them. For example, if you have a TimeBrick DCF77 receiver connected to your server's serial terminal port 1 (/dev/ttyS1), link the TimeBrick's clock device (/dev/refclock-*u*, where *u* is 0 for the first TimeBrick device) to the serial port as follows:

```
ln -s /dev/ttyS1 /dev/refclock-0
```

NOTE

The clock device names are listed on their respective driver pages, under the Synopsis heading at the top of each page.

The local clock driver is also a special case. A server configured with this driver can operate as a primary server to synchronize other clients when no other external synchronization sources are available. If the server is connected directly or indirectly to the Internet, there is some danger that it can adversely affect the operation of unrelated clients. For this, you would configure this driver at a stratum greater than any other likely sources of time (say 3 or 4) to prevent the server from taking over when legitimate sources are still available.

By default, the stratum for this driver is set at 5, but can be changed by the fudge configuration command and/or the ntpdc utility. As a matter of fact, the default /etc/ntp.conf sets its stratum to 10.

WARNING

You should *never* configure an NTP time server that might "devolve" to use its local clock to use multicast mode or broadcast mode.

The following summarizes the procedure necessary for setting up an NTP time source:

1. If using a hardware reference clock, configure and connect the device to your server per manufacturer instructions.

2. Update /etc/ntp.conf with the appropriate server 127.127.*t*.*u* command to support the installed clock.

3. Create a symbolic link between the clock device name and the hardware device driver.

4. Configure the startup scripts to run ntpd upon server boot using either insserv or the Runlevel Editor in YaST.

5. Start up or restart ntpd for the updated ntp.conf to take effect.

Troubleshooting Tips

Most of the time, ntpd is a "configure-and-forget" utility, especially if you are running it in the time consumer (a.k.a. client) mode. The most common oversight when it comes to using public NTP time sources is due to your firewall setting: NTP requires UDP port 123 to be opened in *both* directions. Unlike other client/server-type protocols such as Telnet, where the client uses a high-numbered port (1024 or higher), both the NTP client and server use port 123.

Sometimes the problem may be a misconfigured ntp.conf entry causing ntpd to obtain its time from a wrong server, or something has gone astray with the time source itself. The NTP distribution includes a couple of utilities that are helpful in verifying the correct operations of ntpd running in time server mode: ntpq (NTP query) and ntpdc (a special NTP query program utility). The ntpq program implements the Mode 6 control message formats defined in the NTP specification (http://www.ietf.org/rfc/rfc1305.txt). The ntpdc program, on the other hand, implements additional functions not provided for in the NTP standard. Both programs can be used to inspect the state variables defined in the specification and, in the case of ntpdc, additional ones intended for serious debugging. In addition, ntpdc can be used to dynamically reconfigure and enable or disable some functions while the ntpd is running.

Both ntpq and ntpdc can be run either in interactive mode or controlled using command-line arguments. For quick troubleshooting, it is easiest to run them using the -p switch; the following shows sample output from ntpq:

```
Athena:/home/admin # ntpq -p
```

remote	refid	st	t	when	poll	reach	delay	offset	jitter
LOCAL(0)	LOCAL(0)	10	l	7	64	1	0.000	0.000	0.002
dense.utcc.utor	.INIT.	16	u	–	64	0	0.000	0.000	4000.00

NOTE

You can run either ntpq or ntpdc on the server itself or from another machine elsewhere in the network (by specifying the host address on the command line; the default is localhost).

The first column of the output (immediately before the remote host name) contains the "tally code" character, which indicates the status of the associated host that is a result of the clock selection process. A * means the server is the current time source with which system time is compared; a + shows the host is a candidate for the clock-combining algorithm; a - indicates the host is discarded by the clustering algorithm. You can find further information about the different tally codes in the `ntpq` documentation (`/usr/share/doc/packages/xntp-doc/html/ntpq.html`).

NOTE

To provide fault tolerance, a time server usually operates with a number of remote servers. NTP uses a set of algorithms to refine the data from each peer separately and to select and combine the data from a number of sources. First, a "short list" of time sources is created using a clock-selection process that checks for their sanity and computes a confidence level for each source. Ordinarily, the members of this set could in principle provide correct time; however, due to various error contributions, not all can provide the most accurate and stable time. The job of the clustering algorithm, which is invoked at this point, is to select the best subset of the survivors providing the least variance in the combined ensemble average, compared to the variance in each member of the subset separately. You can find detailed discussions of the various algorithms used by NTP, such as for clock selection, clustering determination, and clock-combining procedures, in RFC 1305 (`http://www.ietf.org/rfc/rfc1305.txt`).

The following summarizes the meaning of the rest of the columns:

- `remote` shows the hostname or IP of the remote machine. (If you run `ntpq` with the `-n` switch, IP addresses will be displayed instead of DNS names.)
- `refid` identifies the time source to which the remote machine is synced. If it shows an IP address or a hostname, that server is being synchronized with another NTP server. In the preceding example, it shows `tick.nrc.ca` is being synchronized with a GPS clock.

NOTE

Until the stratum of the remote host is identified (that is, not 16), the `refid` column displays a four-character string called the *kiss code* as a way to help debug the situation. Some of the common kiss codes are INIT (has not yet synchronized for the first time), AUTH (server authentication failed and is waiting for a retry), and DENY (access denied by remote host). You can find a detailed list of kiss codes in `/usr/share/doc/packages/xntp-doc/html/debug.html`.

- **st** shows the stratum of the remote machine. A stratum of 16 means "unsynchronized," or the status cannot be determined. A stratum value of 0 is best, but you will never see one displayed by **ntpq**.

NOTE

In the world of NTP, stratum levels define the distance from the reference clock. A stratum-0 time source has a reference clock, such as a radio clock or its own cesium clock. Stratum-0 servers *cannot* be used on the network. Instead, they are directly connected to computers that then operate as stratum-1 servers. The basic definition of a stratum-1 time server is that it is directly linked (not over a network path) to a reliable source of UTC time (a stratum-0 server). In turn, a stratum-1 time server acts as a primary network time standard.

In essence, the farther away a time server is from a stratum-1 server, the higher stratum level is assigned to that time server. As you progress through different strata, there are network costs (transmission delays) involved that reduce the accuracy of the NTP server in relation to UTC. A stratum-1 time server will typically be less than a millisecond off from UTC. Over the Internet, because of network delays, a stratum-2 time server could be 10–100 ms off from UTC, and each subsequent time server will add an additional 10–100 ms of inaccuracy. For most applications, obtaining your time from a stratum-2 server is more than sufficient.

- **t** shows the type of communication method used: **u** = unicast, **m** = multicast, **1** = local, **-** = unknown.
- **when** displays the number of seconds since the last poll of the remote machine.
- **poll** gives the polling interval in seconds.
- **reach** shows the "reachability register" in octal, with bits entering from the least significant (rightmost) end. A peer is considered reachable if at least one bit in this register is set to one.

  This is a "rotating" register, meaning it tracks the last eight poll requests. For instance, a decimal value of 276 (binary pattern 10111110) means that out of the last eight polls, two (including the very latest poll attempt) received no response from the remote machine.
- **delay** shows the time delay (in milliseconds) to communicate with the remote.
- **offset** shows the offset (in milliseconds) between local time and that of the remote.

- **jitter** gives the observed time error (in milliseconds) of the system clock with the remote as an average of RMS (root mean square) time differences. (In pre-NTPv4, this column was called **dispersion**.)

Another handy troubleshooting tool included in the NTP distribution is **ntptrace**. It determines where a given NTP server gets its time from and follows the chain of NTP servers all the way back to their master time source. If **ntptrace** is run with no arguments, it starts with localhost. Here is an example of the output from **ntptrace**:

```
Athena:/home/admin # ntptrace
localhost: stratum 16, offset 0.000000, synch distance 0.000000
time.nrc.ca: stratum 2, offset 0.002815, synch distance 0.03061
toc.nrc.ca: stratum 1, offset 0.002153, synch distance 0.00156,
➥refid 'PPS'
```

On each output line, the fields are (left to right):

- Host name
- Host stratum
- Time offset between that host and the local host as measured by **ntptrace**—this is why it is not always zero for localhost
- Host synchronization distance and (only for stratum-1 servers) the reference clock ID

All times are given in seconds.

For additional troubleshooting and debugging tips, such as enabling debug and verbose output for **ntpd**, consult the NTP distribution's HTML documentation, especially **/usr/share/doc/packages/xntp-doc/html/debug.html**.

Email Services

If you are familiar with any one of the Unix distributions, such as SunOS or BSD, you will know about Sendmail (**http://www.sendmail.org**), the de facto email application for Unix platforms for so many years. Sendmail has been ported to many non-Unix operating systems, including OpenVMS, Windows, and Macintosh OS X. However, this is not to say that Sendmail is ideal software because it is fairly complicated to implement correctly and configure. It relies on obscure syntax invoked in text-based configuration files that are run through a macro processor. It's also closely tied to Unix conventions and standards, necessitating a significant knowledge base in both.

TIP

If you plan on tackling Sendmail, you'll want to make sure you have a good resource for installing and configuring the server. The *sendmail* book (ISBN 1-56592-222-0) from O'Reilly & Associates, coauthored by Sendmail developer Eric Allman, is considered to be the definitive guide on the subject.

SLES 9 ships with several mail servers, among them Sendmail and Postfix. Developed by Dr. Wietse Venema of IBM's Thomas J. Watson Research Center (Yorktown Heights, New York), Postfix attempts to be a fast, easy-to-administer, and secure replacement for Sendmail. SLES 9 installs Postfix by default, even for a base system configuration. Therefore, the discussion in this section is about Postfix.

NOTE

Two other favored email server software packages (commonly referred to as Message Transfer Agents or MTAs) among the Linux/Unix community are Qmail (http://www.qmail.org) and Exim (http://www.exim.org). However, they are not included with SLES.

WARNING

The Postfix package conflicts with those of Sendmail and Exim. Therefore, if you have Postfix installed, it must first be uninstalled before installing Sendmail or Exim. (If you install, for instance, Sendmail via YaST, the dependencies check will warn you of the conflict and permit you to specify a resolution action.)

One of the best things about Postfix is that it can be set up quickly and easily without sacrificing security. The following steps lead you to a Postfix quickstart:

1. Install the Postfix package (using YaST or rpm) if it is not already installed. You can find it on your SLES CD1 or download the latest version from http://www.postfix.org.

NOTE

If you are installing Postfix from the source tarball, you should be aware that the INSTALL file and many of the readme files (in the README FILES directory) use backspace characters to emulate bold text. Depending on your terminal's setting, you may see text similar to P^Hpo^Gos^Hst^Htf^Hfi^Hix^Hx instead of Postfix, and so on. You will definitely see these characters if you open the file in a text editor, such as vi. Instead, you can point your browser to the html directory for the HTML version of the same files.

2. Open /etc/postfix/main.cf with a text editor and set the parameter myhostname to the fully qualified domain name (FQDN, in DNS-speak, which is your server's hostname plus the domain name) of your host, as shown in this example:

```
myhostname = Athena.UniversalExport.CA
```

NOTE

The main.cf file provides a decent amount of documentation, and often you only need to read the description to get an understanding of the configuration parameter. But if you need more information, a full set of documentation is located in /usr/share/doc/packages/postfix.

When you are adding or modifying a parameter, first scroll to the end of the file to see whether it is already defined there. The installation procedure puts many of the default settings there instead of spreading them throughout the file.

3. Set the parameter myorigin to the name of your domain because it specifies the domain that locally posted mail appears to come from. Enter the following line verbatim:

```
myorigin = $mydomain
```

where $mydomain contains the value of myhostname minus the first component, which will be UniversalExport.ca in our example here. If not defined, myhostname will be used instead.

4. Set the parameter mydestination as follows (enter this line verbatim):

```
mydestination = $myhostname, localhost.$mydomain, $mydomain
```

This line specifies a list of domains for which this server considers itself the final destination; that is, it will not relay mail addresses to those domains elsewhere.

5. Unless your mail server is a top-level server with access to the Internet, you will want to set the relayhost parameter to point to an appropriate mail relay. The relay is typically the next one up the chain toward getting out to the Internet. You can use either an IP address or DNS name, but using an IP address is safer in the case of a DNS outage. A typical format would look like this:

```
relayhost = 10.0.0.1
```

There is no default for this parameter.

CAUTION

You should do some careful planning prior to using the relay features of any MTA. For instance, to reduce email spam, most MTAs have restrictions on whom they will relay mail for.

6. Save and close `main.cf`.

7. Edit or create `/etc/aliases` with a text editor and add these lines:
   ```
   root: peter
   postmaster: root
   mailer-daemon: postmaster
   ```

   The last two entries redirect mail destined for both mailer-daemon and postmaster and forward it to root. You can optionally redirect root's mail to an unprivileged account.

TIP

RFC 2142 specifies a list of standard email addresses that should be implemented; some of them are abuse, hostmaster, and security. You should add these to your `/etc/aliases` file and redirect the email to the appropriate party. In addition, any system accounts found in `/etc/passwd` should have their email redirected to root for security purposes.

8. After updating the aliases file, execute the command `/usr/sbin/ postalias hash:/etc/aliases` to update the Postfix alias database.

9. Start the Postfix daemon using either the command `/etc/init.d/ postfix start` or `/sbin/rcpostfix start`.

NOTE

Notice that the `rc` version of `/etc/init.d/postfix` is located in `/sbin` and not in `/usr/sbin`, like many other packages.

In nine simple steps, you have installed, configured, and started the Postfix SMTP services for your SLES server and its local name domain. Your users can use it to send mail locally as well as out to the Internet. However, for inbound SMTP mail, you need to configure your DNS server to point your domain's MX record to this server. (See the "Network Name Services" section later in this chapter for details on how to do this.) It is a good idea to configure a valid "MX" record for your mail server so that your users can receive any bounced or undeliverable messages.

CAUTION

The preceding procedure is just enough to get Postfix working, but it probably isn't enough to secure this package fully, especially if you are connected to the Internet. Therefore, it behooves you to spend some time going over the various Postfix features, such as configuring access control for mail relaying, content inspection and "graylisting" for general spam and virus detection, TLS encryption and authentication, and address verification, in the Postfix documentation.

TIP

SpamAssassin (http://spamassassin.apache.org) is one of the most popular antispam packages available. You can find step-by-step instructions on how to get Postfix to use both SpamAssassin and Anomy Sanitizer (a virus blocking system) at http://advosys.ca/papers/postfix-filtering.html.

To set up Postfix to run automatically on server bootup, use the insserv command as follows:

```
Athena:/home/admin # /sbin/insserv /etc/init.d/postfix
```

NOTE

To configure Postfix using YaST, make sure the yast2-mail, yast2-mail-aliases, and yast2-mail-server packages are installed. Also, you need to first enable the LDAP Support Active option in the YaST DNS Server module.

TIP

You can test your Postfix configuration using one of the included email clients, such as KMail or even mail (from a terminal session). For KMail, create an Outgoing account under the Network configuration, specify SMTP as the transport type, and use localhost for the hostname. If you use mail, no special configuration is required. To send a message using mail, simply use mail *username*, and you will be prompted for additional information, such as subject.

Telnet is often used to test mail servers (or other types of services, such as HTTP). The following illustrates how you can send a simple email message using Telnet:

```
# telnet athena 25
Trying 127.0.0.1...
Connected to localhost.
Escape character is '^]'.
220 Athena.UniversalExport.ca ESMTP Postfix
```

```
EHLO ws1.UniversalExport.ca
250-Athena.UniversalExport.ca
250-PIPELINING
250-SIZE 10240000
250-VRFY
250-ETRN
250 8BITMIME
MAIL FROM: root
250 Ok
RCPT TO: root
250 Ok
DATA
354 End data with <CR><LF>.<CR><LF>
TO: root, tasha
FROM: root, tasha
SUBJECT: Test mail via telnet

This is a test mail sent via telnet.

.
250 Ok: queued as 9C71D25D72
quit
221 Bye
Connection closed by foreign host.
```

The resulting message as viewed using the `mail` program looks like this:

```
From root@Athena.UniversalExport.ca  Mon Mar 14 06:28:52 2005
Return-Path: <root@Athena.UniversalExport.ca>
X-Original-To: root
Delivered-To: root@Athena.UniversalExport.ca
Received: from ws1.UniversalExport.ca (localhost [10.20.4.1])
 by Athena.UniversalExport.ca (Postfix) with ESMTP id 9C71D25D72
 for <root>; Mon, 14 Mar 2005 06:28:19 -0500 (EST)
To: root@Athena.UniversalExport.ca,
➥ tasha@Athena.UniversalExport.ca
From: root@Athena.UniversalExport.ca,
➥ tasha@Athena.UniversalExport.ca
SUBJECT: Test mail via telnet
Message-Id: <20050314112819.9C71D25D72@Athena.
➥UniversalExport.ca>
Date: Mon, 14 Mar 2005 06:28:19 -0500 (EST)
Status: RO

This is a test mail sent via telnet.
```

One of the most common routes for (software) virus "distribution" is via email. Included with SLES 9 are AMaVIS (**A Ma**il **Vi**rus **S**canner, `http://amavis.sourceforge.net`) and AVMailGate (`http://www.hbedv.com`) to help you protect your system. The packages are called `amavisd-new` and `avmailgate`, respectively, on the SLES media and are automatically installed when you install Postfix. Note that AMaVIS requires you to have a virus scanner already installed; refer to `/usr/share/doc/packages/amavisd-new` for more details.

The following are some examples of commercial antivirus solutions that may meet your requirements:

- BitDefender for Postfix (`http://www.bitdefender.com`)
- Sophos Anti-Virus for Linux (`http://www.sophos.com`)
- Kaspersky Anti-Virus Business Optimal (`http://www.kaspersky.com`)
- F-Prot Antivirus for Linux (`http://www.f-prot.com`)

File Transfer Services

The File Transfer Protocol (FTP) is probably *the* most common means of copying files between servers over the Internet. Most web-based download sites use the built-in FTP capabilities of web browsers, and consequently, most server-oriented operating systems usually include an FTP server application as part of the software suite. Linux is no exception. There are a large number of different commercial and free FTP servers available for Linux/Unix. The following are some examples:

- NcFTP Server (`http://www.ncftp.com/ncftpd`); commercial
- ProFTPD (`http://www.proftpd.org`); free, GPL-licensed
- Pure-FTPd (`http://www.pureftpd.org`); free, BSD-licensed
- glFTPd (`http://www.glftpd.com`); free
- vsftpd (`http://vsftpd.beasts.org`); free, GPL-licensed
- wu-ftpd (`http://www.wu-ftpd.org`); free

The Trivial File Transfer Protocol (TFTP) also is often used to supply boot images on the network to facilitate remote booting of diskless workstations. TFTP servers are also used to provide images for network devices (such as routers and switches) to obtain firmware updates. You can save device configuration data to a TFTP server as well. Similar to FTP servers, a number of TFTP servers, such as `atftp` by Jean-Pierre Lefebvre (`ftp://ftp.mamalinux.com/pub/atftp`) and `tftp-hpa` (`http://www.kernel.org/pub/software/network/tftp`), are available for various Linux/Unix distributions.

This section shows you how to set up an FTP server using the Very Secure FTP Daemon (`vsftpd`) and Pure-FTPd (`pure-ftpd`) packages included in SLES 9. In addition, we cover ways to set up a TFTP server using the standard TFTP server, `in.tftpd`, included with SLES 9; `atftp` is also included with SLES 9 but is not discussed here.

Using Pure-FTPd

Pure-FTPd is pretty much a command-line–driven application. All its options are to be specified on the command line. You can get a full listing from its `man` page (`man pure-ftpd`) or by typing the following at a terminal prompt:

`pure-ftpd --help`

You'll find that Pure-FTPd uses all 26 letters (both upper- *and* lowercase) plus a few numerals for switches. The following list briefly explains some of the more commonly used options:

- `-A` will `chroot` everyone but root.
- `-b` tells `pure-ftpd` to ignore some standards to deal with broken clients such as Internet Explorer.
- `-B` starts the standalone server in the background (that is, in "daemonized" mode), which is the same as running `./pure-ftpd &`.
- `-c` `#` limits the maximum number of clients to `#`; the default is 50.
- `-C` `#` limits the number of simultaneous connections from the same IP address to `#`; the default is 50 (or the maximum number of clients).
- `-e` allows only anonymous users. This option is mutually exclusive with `-E`.
- `-E` allows only authenticated users (that is, disables anonymous FTP access).
- `-H` prevents resolving a client's IP address into a DNS name (so 10.58.2.5 will be logged instead of `ws2.UniversalExports.ca`). This can speed up connections significantly, and it helps to reduce (reverse-DNS) bandwidth usage on busy servers, especially on public FTP servers.
- `-j` creates the user's home directory if one doesn't exist. This allows home directories to be created on demand. This option is especially useful when used in conjunction with something other than Unix-based

authentication, such as LDAP (see -1 option next): Just insert a new entry in the database, and the account is ready to go. No need to create any directory for that user: It will be automatically created the first time he or she logs in.

- -1 *authentication_method:filename* enables a new authentication method and specifies the file containing authentication data. The method can be one of the following:

  - unix for standard (/etc/passwd) authentication

  - pam for PAM authentication

  - ldap:*LDAP_config_file* for LDAP directories

  - mysql:*MySQL_config_file* for MySQL databases

  - pgsql:*Postgres_config_file* for Postgres databases

  - puredb:*PureDB_database_file* for PureDB virtual user databases

  - extauth:*path to pure-authd socket* for external authentication handlers

  PAM is assumed by default if the server was compiled with PAM support, and Unix is assumed by default otherwise. The SUSE version has PAM support included.

  Multiple authentication methods can be specified concurrently. For instance, you can run the server with -1puredb:/etc/pwd.pdb -1mysql:/etc/my.cf -1unix. The users will first be authenticated from a PureDB database. If this method fails, a MySQL server will be queried. If the account is still not found, standard Linux accounts will be scanned. Authentication methods are tried in the order you give the -1 options. Refer to the README.LDAP and README.MySQL files in /usr/share/doc/packages/pure-ftpd for information about the built-in LDAP and SQL directory support, or visit http://www.pureftpd.org/documentation.shtml.

- -R disallows the use of the chmod command. This is a nice security feature because users are not able to change file permissions on files uploaded by others or those that are available for download.

- -S *host,port* specifies the IP address and port that will accept incoming connections. This option is useful if the server has multiple NICs and you wish to limit FTP traffic to just one. This option can be used only in standalone mode.

- -u *#* doesn't allow UIDs below *#*. If you specify -u 1, the root user will be denied access, which may be a good idea.

- -U *umask_for_files:umask_for_dirs* changes the mask used when creating new files or directories. The defaults are 133 for files (readable but not writable by other users) and 022 for directories (same as files but with the execute bit on). For instance, if new files should be readable only by the user that uploaded those files, use 177:077.

- -X disallows user access to files and directories whose name begins with a period (.), such as .hosts.

As you can imagine, all these possible command-line switches equate into a very long, hard-to-remember command-line string. Therefore, the best way to set things up is to use the "configuration" file, /etc/pure-ftpd/pure-ftpd.conf.

The pure-ftpd.conf file isn't used as a configuration file in the traditional sense. That is, pure-ftpd doesn't read this file on startup. Instead, you specify the desired options, using keywords instead of command-line switches, and their settings in the file. And then you run a Perl script, /usr/sbin/pure-config.pl, which reads the configuration file, translates the options into the equivalent switches, and then launches pure-ftpd with those parameters. Alternatively, you can use /etc/init.d/pure-ftpd start to run pure-ftpd, which uses /usr/sbin/pure-config-args instead to parse the configuration file.

Other than the fact that keywords are easier to understand than the command-line switches, the use of pure-ftpd.conf also offers some security. The ps aux command would reveal the command-line switches used to launch an application, so the use of a configuration file will hide from the users what settings are being used for pure-ftpd.

NOTE

Both /usr/sbin/pure-config.pl and /usr/sbin/pure-config-args are Perl scripts. The only difference between the two is the instruction at the end of the files. /usr/sbin/pure-config.pl launches pure-ftpd using the exec command, while /usr/sbin/pure-config-args simply returns the parsed switches; instead, the launching of pure-ftpd is accomplished by the startproc command in /etc/init.d/pure-ftpd.

TIP

Instead of /etc/init.d/pure-ftpd, you can use /usr/sbin/rcpure-ftpd because it is just a symbolic link to /etc/init.d/pure-ftpd. Using it instead is probably more convenient because /usr/sbin is in root's PATH setting, while /etc/init.d is not.

After you have established which switches to use, you need to decide how to run `pure-ftpd`: Do you want to launch it from `xinetd` or have it run automatically, independent of the super-server, at server startup? On a lightweight, multipurpose system on which you don't anticipate large numbers of concurrent FTP users, you may want to run `pure-ftpd` from `xinetd`; this way, the daemon will be started only when an FTP user tries to connect. This means `pure-ftpd` won't consume any system resources except when being used. Also, whenever you modify `/etc/pure-ftpd/pure-ftpd.conf`, the changes will automatically be applied the next time a user connects, without your having to perform additional administrative tasks because the daemon will run with the new settings when it is invoked by `xinetd`. The other advantage is that you can use the access control and logging features of `xinetd` to provide additional security.

TIP

Your specific needs may vary, but a good set of command-line switches for pure-ftpd is

-A -B -b -C 5 -c 25 -E -H -R -u 1 -X

There are two disadvantages of using a super-server here. The first, and foremost, drawback is the performance hit. For a busy FTP server, it is very inefficient to start `pure-ftpd` repeatedly in a short period of time and parse the configuration file every time. Users will notice a delay when trying to connect. The other disadvantage is that some of the `pure-ftpd` features, such as -S, are available only in standalone mode. Therefore, on a dedicated FTP server or one on which there will be frequent or numerous FTP connections, standalone mode works best.

To run `pure-fptd` under `xinetd`, ensure there is a configuration file for it in `/etc/xinetd.d`. A file called `pure-ftpd` should have been placed there during the installation, so you can simply edit it to reflect your needs. If it is not there, create one that contains the following information either manually within an editor or via YaST:

```
service ftp
{
        socket_type  = stream
        server       = /usr/sbin/pure-ftpd
        server_args  = `/usr/sbin/pure-config-args
➥/etc/pure-ftpd/pure-ftpd.conf`
        protocol     = tcp
        user         = root
        wait         = no
        disable      = no
```

```
# access control if needed
#     only_from   =
#     no_access   =
#     access_times =
}
```

CAUTION

Depending on how you made package selections during the SLES server installation, you may have multiple FTP server packages installed. If this is the case, you will notice multiple FTP services listed in the inetd/xinetd configuration screen in YaST. Make sure you enable the correct service by first looking at the Server column and noting the name of the binary being used. It would make for a more secure and cleaner system if you uninstall the other unused FTP services.

Instead of using the configuration file, you can specify the necessary switches, such as server_args = -A -i -s -E. If you leave out or comment out the server_args keyword, pure-ftpd will run using its default settings by listening for incoming connections on every interface, all IP addresses, using the standard FTP control port (21).

CAUTION

Pure-FTPd's online documentation indicates signal SIGUSR2 is to be used for hard reconfiguration of xinetd. However, this hasn't been the case for versions of xinetd since 2.3.9 (released in October 2002). Because SLES 9 ships with xinetd-2.3.13-39.4, you should use SIGHUP for xinetd.

To set up pure-ftpd to run in standalone mode automatically upon SLES boot, use insserv as follows:

Athena:/home/admin # **/sbin/insserv /etc/init.d/pure-ftpd**

In this mode, you need to make use of the /etc/pure-ftpd/pure-ftpd.conf file.

SETTING UP FOR ANONYMOUS FTP

If a user called ftp exists in /etc/passwd (which it does by default on SLES 9) and its home directory is reachable, Pure-FTPd will accept anonymous login, as ftp or anonymous. Files have to be located in the home FTP directory. There is no need for bin, lib, etc, and dev directories in the home directory, nor any external programs, such as `ls` (Pure-FTPd does not execute any external programs and has a built-in `ls` utility). Note that you don't need to `chown` the public files to ftp, but you should do so for the writeable directories (such as `incoming`).

One of the features of Pure-FTPd is its provision for users that are not defined in `/etc/passwd`. These users are called *virtual users* and can access the server via FTP only. This is a nice feature if you do not allow anonymous FTP access and don't want these FTP-only users to be able to log in to your SLES server via non-FTP means. Pure-FTPd virtual user information is stored in a PureDB database and is managed using the `pure-pw` utility. Refer to `/usr/share/doc/packages/pure-ftpd/README.Virtual-Users` or `http://www.pureftpd.org/README.Virtual-Users` for details.

Lastly, if you are tired of using command-line switches to manage Pure-FTPd, a couple of packages provide a nice GUI interface. For KDE users, there is KcmPureFTPd (`http://1kr.sourceforge.net/kcmpureftpd`); Figure 8.4 shows the Users configuration dialog box. For GNOME fans, take a look at `PureAdmin` (`http://purify.sourceforge.net`); Figure 8.5 shows an example of its User Manager dialog box.

FIGURE 8.4
KcmPureFTPd's Users configuration tab.

FIGURE 8.5
PureAdmin's virtual user manager.

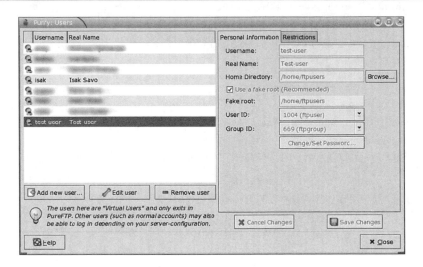

There is also a browser-based virtual user administration tool called User Manager for PureFTPd (see Figure 8.6). Developed by Machiel Mastenbroek using PHP scripts, this tool makes it easy to create, modify, or delete virtual Pure-FTPd users from any type of client workstation. To download the software or for more information about this free software, visit http://machiel. generaal.net/index.php?subject=user_manager_pureftpd.

NOTE

At the time of this writing, Pure-FTPd version 1.0.16 has added *experimental* support for encryption of the control channel using SSL/TLS security mechanisms. With the option enabled, usernames and passwords are not sent as cleartext; neither are other commands sent by your client nor replies made by the server. However, the data channel is *not* encrypted by SSL/TLS. Refer to /usr/share/doc/packages/pure-ftpd/README.TLS or http://www.pureftpd.org/README.TLS for details.

Using vsftpd

vsftpd (Very Secure FTP Daemon) is a secure and extremely fast FTP server. It has a rich feature set similar to that available in Pure-FTPd. For example, it provides the following:

- Virtual IP configurations

- Virtual user support

- The capability to run standalone or under a super-server

- Powerful per-user configurability

- Bandwidth throttling

- Per-source-IP configurability

- Per-source-IP limits

- IPv6 support

FIGURE 8.6
User Manager for PureFTPd.

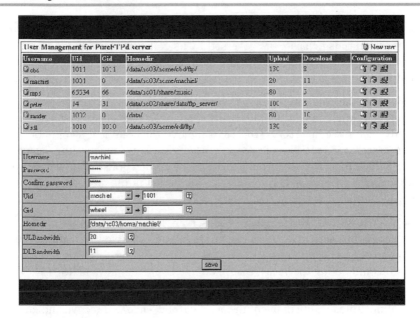

Beginning with v2.0.1 (v2.0.0 was not released), vsftpd includes SSL/TSL integration. Unlike the experimental SSL/TLS support for only the control channel (port 21) provided in Pure-FTPd, vsftpd offers full support for *both* the control and data channels. Therefore, if you need to offer a secure FTP server solution, vsftpd should be at the top of your list for consideration. Because of its high performance and tight security, vsftpd is in use by a large number of Internet sites, such as `ftp.suse.com`, `ftp.redhat.com`, `ftp.gnu.org`, and `rpmfind.net`. You can find out more at `http://vsftpd.beasts.org/#performance` and at `http://vsftpd.beasts.org/#security`.

NOTE

The version of `vsftpd` included on the SLES 9 media is 1.2.1, and you need at least version 2.0.1 (released in July 2004) for SSL/TSL support. You can download the latest version from `http://vsftpd.beasts.org/#download`, or you can find the latest RPMs for SUSE at `http://rpmseek.com`.

You need to have OpenSSL installed to be able to use the SSL/TSL options. If you don't already have OpenSSL installed on your server—you should since it is part of the base runtime package—or want to use the most current version, you can download the latest tarball from `http://www.openssl.org/source`.

Unlike many other FTP daemons (and especially in contrast to Pure-FTPd), *all* aspects of `vsftpd`'s behavior are governed by its configuration file, `/etc/vsftpd.conf`. Its sole command-line option is to specify a different configuration file.

`vsftpd` reads the contents of `vsftpd.conf` upon startup, so you have to restart `vsftpd` each time you edit the file for the changes to take effect. For a quick test drive, simply edit `/etc/vsftpd.conf`, remove the comment symbol (#) before `listen=YES`, and execute `/usr/sbin/vsftpd`. This launches the daemon in standalone mode, ready for immediate client connections. Without any other modifications, except for `listen=YES`, this file uses a number of default settings that you should be aware of:

- `vsftpd` runs as an anonymous FTP server. The configuration file's `anonymous_enable` directive can be set to `NO` to disable this feature. You also need to simultaneously enable local users to be able to log in by uncommenting the `local_enable` directive and set its value to `YES`.

- This file allows only anonymous FTP downloads, and not uploads. To allow uploads, uncomment the `anon_upload_enable` directive and ensure it is set to `YES`.

- This file doesn't allow anonymous users to create directories on your FTP server. You can change this by modifying the `anon_mkdir_write_enable` directive.

- This file logs FTP access to `/var/log/vsftpd.log`. To change this to a different file or location, modify the `xferlog_file` directive.

- `vsftpd` expects files for anonymous FTP to be placed in the `/var/ftp` directory. You can change this by modifying the `anon_root` directive.

CAUTION

With anonymous FTP, there is always the risk that users will discover a way to write files to your anonymous FTP directory. The result is that you risk filling up your /var filesystem if you use the default setting. It is best to make the anonymous FTP directory reside in its own dedicated filesystem.

The directives listed in /etc/vsftpd.conf are by no means exhaustive. For instance, the performance-tuning settings, such as the following, are not included:

- max_clients limits the maximum number of concurrent client connections.

- max_per_ip restricts the number of concurrent connections from the same source IP address.

- anon_max_rate determines the maximum rate of data transfer per anonymous login.

- local_max_rate governs the maximum rate of data transfer per nonanonymous login.

You can find detailed descriptions of all supported directives and their default values using man vsftpd.conf or online at http://vsftpd.beasts.org/vsftpd_conf.html.

WARNING

vsftpd is very strict about its command syntax. Putting any whitespace between the option keyword, the = sign, and the value is an error. For example, anonymous_enable=YES is valid, whereas anonymous_enable = YES is not.

As with the case of Pure-FTPd discussed earlier, you have to decide if vsftpd should be launched standalone upon server boot or via xinetd. Should you choose to use xinetd, a default configuration file is installed as /etc/xinetd.d/vsftpd, and its contents are as follows:

```
service ftp
{
      socket_type        = stream
      protocol           = tcp
      wait               = no
      user               = root
      server             = /usr/sbin/vsftpd
#     server_args        =
```

```
#      log_on_success += DURATION USERID
#      log_on_failure += USERID
#      nice            = 10
       disable         = yes
}
```

To enable **vsftpd** for **xinetd**, change the **disabled = yes** entry to **disable = no** or comment out the entry. Also, ensure the **listen=YES** directive in **/etc/vsftpd.conf** is commented out. To run **vsftpd** as standalone, on the other hand, make sure you have set **listen=YES** and **background=YES** and then add **/usr/sbin/vsftpd** to the server startup script.

NOTE

There is no /etc/init.d/vsftpd or /usr/sbin/rcvsftpd shell script. To manually start vsftpd, simply run /usr/sbin/vsftpd. To stop it, you can use the kill or killproc command. You can create a custom init script for vsftpd using /etc/init.d/skeleton as a template. Save a copy of this file under a new name and edit the relevant program and filenames, paths, and other details as needed. After you do this, use insserv to install the new script.

Using the Standard TFTP Server

Setting up a TFTP server using **in.tftpd** is fairly easy and straightforward. Use the following steps to configure and secure your TFTP server settings:

1. If the TFTP package is not already installed, use YaST or RPM to install it.

2. Create a directory where the TFTP files (such as boot images) will reside. Set the directory's ownership and permission as follows:
   ```
   Athena:/home/admin # mkdir /tftpimages
   Athena:/home/admin # chown nobody:nobody /tftpimages
   Athena:/home/admin # chmod 777 /tftpimages
   ```

   Change the directory's permission to **744** if network devices are not to upload images to the **/tftpimages** directory.

3. Edit or create **/etc/xinetd.d/tftp** so the file looks similar to the following:
   ```
   service tftp
   {
           socket_type = dgram
           protocol    = udp
           wait        = yes
           user        = nobody
   ```

```
    server      = /usr/sbin/in.tftpd
    server_args = -c -s /tftpimages
    disable     = no
    per_source  = 10
    cps         = 100 5
}
```

You should also include access control directives, such as `only_from` and `access_times`, to the preceding file to help tighten security.

TIP

Since TFTP has no build-in security (such as authentication), you should include xinetd access control directives such as access_from and no_access to restrict which systems can access your TFTP server. For additional security, you may want to configure ipchains rules on the server that runs the TFTP server to control access to UDP port 69. Refer to Chapter 13 for more information about ipchains.

4. Start or restart `xinetd` for the TFTP server configuration to be read by using `/etc/init.d/xinetd start` or `/etc/init.d/xinetd restart`.

TFTP server activities are recorded in `/var/log/messages`, and you can zero in on the `in.tftpd`-related entries by using `grep`:

Athena:/home/admin # **grep -i tfptd /var/log/messages**

Network File-Sharing Services

Besides making files available to users logged in locally, often you also need to make files and directories transparently available to other servers or to remote workstations. And these other servers and workstations may or may not be running Linux. To make this file sharing possible, SLES supports both the Network File System (NFS) and Samba network file-sharing protocols.

NFS is a protocol originally developed by Sun Microsystems in 1984 and defined in RFC 3530, as a Unix-based file system that allows a computer to access files over an IP network as easily as if they were on its local disks. NFS is available for a wide range of computer hardware running different operating systems to share files and disk storage. At around the same time, the *Server Message Block* (SMB) protocol was created by Dr. Barry Feigenbaum at IBM Corporation. It was later extended and used by IBM, 3Com, Intel, and Microsoft as the communications protocol for network file sharing between

DOS, Windows, and OS/2 operating systems. Today, Microsoft Windows uses SMB, better known as the *Common Internet File System* (CIFS), which utilizes NetBEUI (NetBIOS Enhanced User Interface) over TCP, as the standard network file sharing mechanism. Like NFS, a number of CIFS implementations are available for a wide variety of operating systems, including NetWare. Samba is an open source implementation of CIFS that runs on Unix/Linux platforms but speaks to Windows clients like a native. It allows a Unix/Linux system to move into a Windows "Network Neighborhood" without causing a stir. Windows users can happily access file and print services without knowing or caring that a Unix/Linux host instead of a Windows server is offering those services. In short, NFS and Samba are two different methods in which you can share your server's disk storage with other systems over the network. The choice of which package to use depends on your network environment. If you have Windows workstations and servers, Samba would be a good choice. Or if you mostly have Unix/Linux-based systems, NFS would be a good option.

As mentioned at the beginning of this chapter, because of the complexity of NFS and Samba, rather than delving into the details, we simply supply the bare essentials you need to quickly set up a simple NFS server and Samba server. You can learn more about each of these protocols from other published documents, such as

- RFC 3530: Network File System (NFS) version 4 Protocol
- RFC 2624: NFS Version 4 Design Considerations
- RFC 2224: NFS URL Scheme
- *NFS Illustrated* (ISBN 0201325705)
- *The Definitive Guide to Samba 3* (ISBN 1590592778)
- *The Official Samba-3 HOWTO and Reference Guide* (ISBN 0131453556)

Setting Up an NFS Server

A computer can be both an NFS server and an NFS client. Here, we concentrate on the NFS server aspect where your SLES server will make available (export) its files and directories over the network (via port 2049) to NFS clients.

The NFS daemon is integrated into the SLES kernel, so no installation is required; all you need to do is configure and then activate it. The main functionality is handled by the **nfsd.o** kernel module, and **/usr/sbin/rpc.nfsd** is the user-space application that is treated as a "filesystem" and initiates the NFS server process; the **/usr/sbin/rpc.mountd** application is used for NFS client operations.

TIP

There are two quick ways to check whether the NFS server is active. First, you can use the ps command:

```
Athena:/home/Admin # ps aux |grep nfsd
root     7680  0.0  0.0     0     0 ?     S   10:48  0:00 [nfsd]
root     7681  0.0  0.0     0     0 ?     S   10:48  0:00 [nfsd]
root     7682  0.0  0.0     0     0 ?     S   10:48  0:00 [nfsd]
root     7683  0.0  0.0     0     0 ?     S   10:48  0:00 [nfsd]
root     7684  0.0  0.0     0     0 ?     S   10:48  0:00 [nfsd]
root     7706  0.0  0.1  2588   692 pts/3 R+  10:49  0:00 grep nfs
```

If the NFS server is running, you will see a number of [nfsd] processes. Another method is to use the lsmod command, which shows what kernel modules are currently loaded in a user-friendly format:

```
Athena:/home/Admin # lsmod | grep nfsd
nfsd                   106184  5
exportfs                10368  1 nfsd
```

The first column shows the name of the modules, followed by the size of the module (in bytes), followed by a number that indicates how many instances of that module are currently active; if the number is zero, that means the service is not active.

NOTE

Under the NFS protocol, only one user at a time has write access to a file, and this access is controlled by the NFS file-locking daemon (/usr/sbin/rpc.lockd).

All NFS server configuration information is stored in /etc/exports. This file contains an entry for every directory that you intend to share with NFS client machines. Each entry defines how the directory is shared.

The general form of an exports entry is

directory_name [host_1[(option_list)]] [host_2[(option_list)]] ...

where *directory_name* is the directory that you want to export, *host_x* indicates a machine (using IP address, DNS name, or network name, such as *.UniversalExport.ca) that can mount the exported directory, and *option_list* is a comma-separated list of option keywords.

WARNING

If no options are given, the default export is read-write to all hosts. If no host-name is provided, it means any machine can mount this exported directory. Consequently, you should *never* export a directory without specifying at least one option in the *option_list*.

The following is an example of an /etc/exports file:

```
# A sample /etc/exports file
/            hermes(ro,root_squash) castor(ro,root_squash)
/home        *.UniversalExport.ca(rw,no_root_squash)
/var/ftp     (ro,all_squash)
#end of /etc/exports file
```

In this example, the first entry exports the entire filesystem to servers Hermes and Castor, where it will be read-only, and the root users on Hermes and Castor do not have root privileges on this exported filesystem. The second line exports /home to all hosts in the UniversalExport.ca domain where users have read-write access to their home directories, and the root users on these hosts have root privileges on this exported path. The last entry exports /var/ftp (the default anonymous FTP directory used by vsftpd) as read-only to the world and executes all requests under the nobody account.

After you have modified the /etc/exports file, you can start or restart the NFS server by using the /etc/init.d/nfsserver start or /etc/init.d/ nfsserver restart command. You can also use /usr/sbin/rcnfsserver instead of /etc/init.d/nfsserver. To configure the NFS server to start automatically on server boot, you need to enable *two* system init scripts for it to work:

```
Athena:/home/admin # /sbin/insserv /etc/init.d/nfsserver
Athena:/home/admin # /sbin/insserv /etc/init.d/portmap
```

The portmapper, which uses TCP/UDP port 111, is an essential component of Remote Procedure Call (RPC) services, and NFS makes use of RPC. This is why you need to ensure the portmapper process is also started when the server boots. However, you do not have to create a link for /etc/init.d/nfslock (for the NFS file-locking daemon) because it is started automatically by nfsserver.

NOTE

The nfsserver start script looks in /etc/sysconfig/nfs for a variable called USE_KERNEL_NFSD_NUMBER, which is used to determine how many server threads should be started for rpc.nfsd. The default value is 4.

You can also configure the NFS server using YaST. From the YaST Control Center, select Network Services, NFS Server; or from a terminal prompt, use `yast2 nfs-server` (or `yast nfs-server`). When using YaST, you don't need to use `insserv` to set up the startup scripts. You can simply select Start NFS Server from the Configuration of the NFS Server dialog box, and use the Directories to Export to the Others dialog box (see Figure 8.7) to set up the `/etc/exports` file.

FIGURE 8.7
Setting up directory exports.

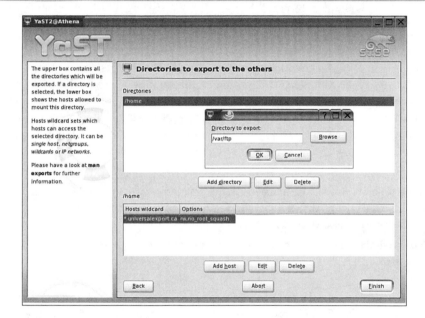

TIP

Sometimes you may need to temporarily export a directory. You can easily do so using `/usr/sbin/exportfs` without having to modify `/etc/exports`. The syntax for `exportfs` is

`exportfs -o option_list host:/directory_name`

where `option_list` is a list of export options and `host` is the remote system. Both are specified in the same manner as `/etc/exports`. To restore the original export state, use `exportfs -r`. See man `exportfs` for more details.

You can easily check to see whether `rpc.nfsd` and its associated modules are running by using the `rpcinfo -p` command. The NFS server registers with the portmapper as nfs while the NFS client shows up as mountd; there may be multiple nfs entries corresponding to the number of NFS server threads. In addition, you can also check to see which NFS client systems have mounted your exported directories by using the `showmount -a` command.

Setting Up a Samba Server

Samba is software package that allows a host to interact with a Microsoft Windows client or server as if it were a Windows file and print server. The Samba package runs on a wide range of operating systems—for example, Linux/Unix, IBM System 390, and OpenVMS. Samba implements Microsoft's Server Message Block (SMB), which is now referred to as Common Internet File System (CIFS), networking protocol. Among the features offered by SMB/CIFS is network file sharing, in much the same way as NFS discussed previously, by means of *SMB shares*, which are covered here. Other Samba features such as Samba authentication services are discussed later in this chapter; a discussion of Samba print services can be found in Chapter 9, "Printing Services."

NOTE

At the time of this writing, Samba 4 is in the development stages and hasn't yet had an initial release. SLES 9 ships with Samba 3, the current stable version. Samba 2.2 was declared end-of-life as of October 1, 2004.

You can find the latest version of Samba at `http://www.samba.org/samba/download`.

A Samba server uses the SMB protocol to share its files and directories with clients using TCP/UPD ports 137 through 139 inclusive. The exported directory is called a *share* and is identified by a *share name*, and Samba clients use this name to access the resource. The share name doesn't have to be the same as the directory name; this allows you to use more descriptive names for the exported directories, which makes it easier for users to find them. To access a share from a Samba client, simply use the Unique Naming Convention (UNC) notation: `//server_name/share_name`.

To set up a basic Samba file server, ensure the `samba` and `yast2-samba-server` packages are installed on your server. You need to install `yast2-samba-server` only if you want to manage your Samba server via YaST. However, you should install `samba-doc` for online documentation. Other Samba-related packages, such as `samba-client` and `libsmbclient`, are available, but they are not required to run a Samba server.

The Samba server consists of three daemons: nmbd, which handles all NetBIOS-related tasks; smbd, which provides file and print services; and winbindd, which resolves user and group information from NT/ADS domains. All of Samba's configuration data is stored in the /etc/samba/smb.conf file. You can either edit this file yourself or do it using YaST or one of the many graphical tools available, such as the web-based interface SWAT (Samba Web Administration Tool) that is included with Samba.

The smb.conf file uses the same syntax as the Windows .INI files. This file consists of sections, which begin with the section name within brackets ([]) on a new line. Each section contains zero or more key/value pairs separated by an equal sign (=).

Although each section in smb.conf represents a user-defined share on the Samba server, you should be aware of three special sections that are predefined:

- [global]—This section contains settings that apply to the whole Samba server, and not to one share in particular.

- [homes]—If this optional section is included in the configuration file, services connecting clients to their home directories can be created on the fly by the server.

- [printers]—This section works like [homes], but for printers. If a [printers] section exists in the configuration file, users are able to connect to any printer specified in the local host's printcap file.

Shown in Listing 8.3 is a minimal smb.conf example.

LISTING 8.3

A Minimal Sample smb.conf File

```
[global]
workgroup = TUX-NET
netbios name = MySambaServer
;The following is the default security setting
#security = user

[junk]
path = /tmp

[docs]
path = /usr/share/doc
#read only defaults to yes so no real need to set it
read only = yes
comment = on-line documentation
```

In Listing 8.3, the default `security` setting in `[global]` tells Samba to use `/etc/passwd` and `/etc/samba/smbpasswd` when validating user passwords. If you have a Windows domain controller or a Windows Active Directory realm set up, you can use them to validate usernames and passwords instead by setting `security = domain` or `security = ads`. If you set `security = share`, no password is required when a client initially connects to the Samba server; however, a password may be necessary when the client tries to access a share.

THE /ETC/SAMBA/SMBPASSWD FILE

`/etc/samba/smbpasswd` is the Samba password file. It contains the username, Unix/Linux user ID, and the hashed passwords of the user, as well as account flag information and the time the password was last changed.

The format of the `smbpasswd` file used by Samba 2.2 and 3 is similar to the `/etc/passwd` file. It is an ASCII file containing one line for each user. Each field within each line is separated from the next by a colon. Any entry beginning with # is ignored. The following is a sample `smbpasswd` record:

```
testuser:6002:XXXXXXXXXXXXXXXXXXXXXXXXXXXXXXXX:
➥XXXXXXXXXXXXXXXXXXXXXXXXXXXXXXXX:
➥[DU          ]:LCT-00000000:
```

The first field contains the username; this name must already exist in the `/etc/passwd` file. The second field holds the UID of the user, which must match the UID for the same user entry in `/etc/passwd`. The third field is the LAN Manager (LANMAN) hash of the user's password, encoded as 32 hexadecimal digits. This is the same password used by Windows 9x systems. If this field's value is equal to 32 X characters, then the user's account is considered disabled and will not be able to log in to the Samba server. The fourth field is also a password field. It contains the Windows NT/2000/XP hash of the user's password. Similar to the LANMAN password hash, if the NT hash value is equal to 32 X characters, then the user's account is considered disabled and will not be able to log in to the Samba server.

The second-to-last field contains account information. The field is bracketed by [and] characters and is always 13 characters in length, including the open and close bracket characters. The contents of this field may be one or more of the following characters:

- U means this is a "User" account, that is, an ordinary user. Only User and Workstation Trust accounts are currently supported in the `smbpasswd` file.

- N means the account has no password (the passwords in the fields LANMAN Password Hash and NT Password Hash are ignored). Note that this will allow users to log on with no password only if `null passwords = yes` is set in the `smb.conf` file.

- D means the account is disabled and no SMB/CIFS logins will be allowed for this user.

- W means this account is a "Workstation Trust" account. This kind of account allows Windows workstations and servers to join a domain hosted by a Samba PDC.

The last field holds the time the account was last modified. It consists of the characters LCT- (Last Change Time), followed by a numeric encoding of the Unix time in seconds since the epoch (1970) that the last change was made. Any additional colon-separated fields after this LCT field are ignored.

NOTE

All share names that end with a dollar sign ($) are hidden; they do not normally appear when a user displays server resources (such as using the NET VIEW *SambaServername* command from a Windows workstation). This also applies to such shares hosted on an SLES Samba server.

You can specify several options for each of the [*share*] sections. The most commonly used ones are as follows:

- read only = yes/no specifies whether the client can create, delete, or modify any files on the share. The default is read only = yes. (You can use writeable = yes instead of read only = no.)

- guest ok = yes/no indicates whether a password is required to access this share. The default is guest ok = no, which means that a password is required. With guest ok = yes, it means that no password is required. (You can also use public = yes, an older and more vague form of guest ok = yes, and public = no, which is synonymous with guest ok = no.)

- guest account = *username* is the username that will be used to access services specified as guest ok = yes. The user must exist in the password file (of whatever service is used to authenticate the users). The default is nobody.

- comment = *description* provides a description of the nature of the share, which helps users to select the correct resource to access.

- hosts allow = *host1*, *host2*, ... specifies one or more machines that are allowed to access the share. The default is all hosts are granted access.

- hosts deny = *host1*, *host2*, ... specifies one or more machines that are not permitted to access the share. Localhost (127.0.0.1) is always granted access, but you can use hosts deny = localhost to block it.

Refer to man smb.conf or the documents found in /usr/share/doc/ packages/samba for a list of all supported options and the use of macros in the configuration file.

AN ANONYMOUS READ-ONLY SERVER CONFIGURATION

You can very easily and quickly set up a document server using Samba so that anyone within your organization can have access to the shared information. The following configuration file illustrates the minimal settings required:

```
[global]
workgroup = TUX-NET
netbios name = DocumentServer
security = share

[docs]
path = /usr/share/doc
read only = yes
guest ok = yes
# limit access to your internal network
hosts allow = *.universalexport.ca, 10.0.0.0
comment = on-line documentation
```

If you set the security level to share and allow guest to the docs share, your users can access this share without using a password. For instance, from a Windows 2000 workstation, all a user needs to do is enter the following:

```
net use i: \\documentserver\docs
```

After you have created the configuration file but before you start the Samba daemons, run /usr/bin/testparm to validate the contents of your smb.conf file. If testparm runs correctly, it will list the loaded services. If not, it will give an error message. Make sure it runs correctly and that the services look reasonable before proceeding. The command syntax is

/usr/bin/testparm *config_file*

TIP

If you leave out the name of the configuration file, it defaults to /etc/samba/smb.conf. You can, therefore, make a copy of your current smb.conf file, modify it, run testparm against the edited file, and overwrite only the current one if the modified version contains no errors as reported by testparm.

testparm parses your configuration file and reports any unknown parameters or incorrect syntax. The following is the testparm output from checking the minimal smb.conf file shown in Listing 8.3:

```
Athena:/home/admin # /usr/bin/testparm smb.conf.new
Load smb config files from smb.conf.new
Processing section "[junk]"
Processing section "[docs]"
Loaded services file OK.
Server role: ROLE_STANDALONE
Press enter to see a dump of your service definitions

# Global parameters
[global]
        workgroup = TUX-NET
        netbios name = MYSAMBASERVER

[junk]
        path = /tmp

[docs]
        comment = on-line documentation
        path = /usr/share/doc
```

Notice that for [docs], testparm did not display the directive read only = yes even though it is specified in the smb.conf.new file. The reason is that it is the default setting, thus is not shown. Any comment lines (those starting with # or ;) are also not displayed.

TIP

Always run testparm after the smb.conf file has been modified.

After you have verified that smb.conf contains no errors, you can start the SMB server by using the following commands:

```
Athena:/home/admin # /etc/init.d/nmb start
Athena:/home/admin # /etc/init.d/smb start
Athena:/home/admin # /etc/init.d/winbind start
```

You can also use /usr/sbin/rcnmb, /usr/sbin/rcsmb, and /usr/sbin/rcwinbind instead.

NOTE

The nmbd daemon should be the first command started as part of the Samba startup process, followed by smbd. Note that winbindd is *not* necessary to run a Samba server. You need to start winbinddd only when using NT/ADS domains for user authentication. Without winbindd, smbd will use only /etc/passwd and /etc/group to resolve user information.

To start the Samba server automatically on server bootup, create the necessary startup scripts using insserv as follows:

```
Athena:/home/admin # /sbin/insserv /etc/init.d/nmb
Athena:/home/admin # /sbin/insserv /etc/init.d/smb
Athena:/home/admin # /sbin/insserv /etc/init.d/winbind
```

If you have installed the yast2-samba-server package, you can use YaST to manage your Samba server configuration. From the YaST Control Center, select Network Services, Samba Server; or from a terminal session, use yast samba-server or yast2 samba-server. The first time you configure the Samba Server, you will be asked to select a workgroup or domain to which your server belongs and the role of the server within this domain/workgroup (that is, whether it's a primary domain controller).

Once initialized, YaST displays the Shares tab of the Samba Configuration dialog box as the default. Figure 8.8 shows the Shares dialog box when the sample minimal configuration file is used. From this screen, you can add, delete, or modify shares. Using the Toggle Status button, you can make a share inaccessible while leaving its definition in the configuration file so that you can easily reinstate it later.

On the Start Up tab, you indicate whether the Samba server should be active. If you have SuSEfirewall2 installed, this screen also gives you the option to open the necessary ports for Samba: Enable the Open Ports in Firewall check box and then click on Firewall Details to open TCP/UDP ports 137 through 139 inclusive, and TCP/UDP port 445 if you have Windows servers, on all external and internal interfaces. The Identity tab allows you to select the domain/workgroup as well as the role of the Samba server within that domain/workgroup. On the Trusted Domains tab, you can set up NT-style trusts so your server can provide access to the listed domains.

FIGURE 8.8

The Shares tab of the Samba Configuration dialog box.

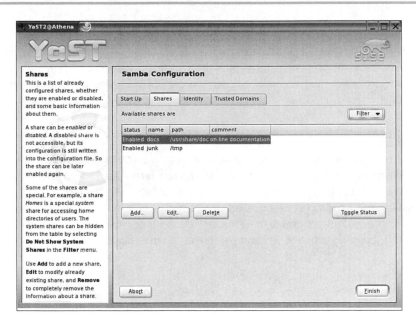

With the Samba server up and running, you can verify whether all your shares are available using the smbclient utility. You should see a list of the defined shares similar to the following:

```
Athena:/home/admin #  /usr/bin/smbclient -NL localhost
Anonymous login successful
Domain=[TUX-NET] OS=[Unix] Server=[Samba 3.0.4-SUSE]

        Sharename        Type        Comment
        ---------        ----        -------
        junk             Disk
        docs             Disk        on-line documentation
        IPC$             IPC         IPC Service (Samba 3.0.4-SUSE)
        ADMIN$           IPC         IPC Service (Samba 3.0.4-SUSE)
Anonymous login successful
Domain=[TUX-NET] OS=[Unix] Server=[Samba 3.0.4-SUSE]

        Server           Comment
        ---------        -------
        MYSAMBASERVER    Samba 3.0.4-SUSE
```

```
Workgroup            Master
---------            -------
TUX-NET
```

The defined shares are listed first, followed by two additional shares called IPC$ and ADMIN$. The IPC$ (Interprocess Communication) share is used by Windows NT and later systems to provide a number of remote system administration services to other networked users. The ADMIN$ share provides remote administration capabilities.

WARNING

In the Windows environment, the IPC$ share is a common target for NetBIOS-based hacking attempts. To protect your SLES Samba server from such attacks, you should at least use hosts allow and host deny directives to limit which machines can have access to your shares. You can put them in the [global] section, making the settings applicable to all shares. If that's not feasible, you can create an [IPC$] section in your smb.conf and put the restrictions there.

Lastly, any servers providing file services should run antivirus software to protect its files from being tampered with. At the time of this writing, SLES 9 includes samba-vscan, a proof-of-concept module for Samba, which uses the virtual file system (VFS) features of Samba 2.2.x/3.0 to provide an on-access Samba antivirus solution. Visit http://www.openantivirus.org/projects.php for more information. If you are looking for a commercial solution, in addition to the ones mentioned earlier in this chapter, BitDefender for Samba (http://www.bitdefender.com) provides on-access virus checking on Samba shared folders.

Remote Management Services

The most common method of accessing a server or configuring its layered application is through the Console GUI. This is mostly done at install time when the machine is first configured. After a server has been moved to a production environment, for purposes other than switching backup media, it is not usually acceptable to allow physical access to the machine. To resolve this problem, a method for providing external access to the server is required. The following sections review a number of alternatives for allowing remote access to a system.

Telnet

In the past, access to computer systems was granted by hard-wiring a terminal device to a server. These devices, commonly known as *dumb terminals*, would allow for rudimentary character-based access. As systems evolved and networks became more prevalent, this terminal access mode was ported to a network-aware application. The result was called a *terminal emulator*, and the protocol it used, for the most part, was Telnet.

The Telnet protocol uses TCP port 23 for conversations between the user's system and the target server. When it is invoked and a conversation is established, the user is presented with a username and login prompt. After the user is authenticated, a login shell is created for the user based on information contained in /etc/passwd.

The Telnet service is part of xinetd. You can enable the service by editing /etc/xinetd.d/telnet and changing the disabled flag to no. This is what the Telnet file should look like in a live environment:

```
service telnet
{
        socket_type     = stream
        protocol        = tcp
        wait            = no
        user            = root
        server          = /usr/sbin/in.telnetd
        disable         = no
}
```

The drawback to the Telnet protocol can be found in the way the packets are sent to the target server. In Telnet, there is no provisioning for protecting the information contained within each packet as it traverses the network. As information is entered in the terminal session, it is broadcasted in cleartext across the network. This includes the original authentication steps, allowing a network eavesdropper to intercept the traffic and collect usernames, passwords, and other sensitive information passed during the conversation. For this reason, the Telnet protocol is considered inappropriate for use.

ssh

A replacement method for accessing servers can be found in an application called Secure Shell (ssh). This protocol communicates over TCP port 22. This application establishes a link between the host and the destination computer, exchanges a series of cryptographic keys, and establishes an encrypted channel between the two machines. This channel is then used to create a login shell for the user. Because the channel is encrypted, the user's data, such as username, password, and so on, is protected from network sniffing. The user can then proceed with system maintenance tasks such as resetting passwords and editing system configuration files, knowing that any information exchanged is secure.

You start **sshd** as a standalone application through **/etc/init.d** and configure it through files contained within **/etc/ssh**. You can initiate the **sshd** service at boot time by using the YaST Runlevel Editor (System, Runlevel Editor). Figure 8.9 shows the service as enabled at boot time.

FIGURE 8.9
Adding **sshd** to run at boot.

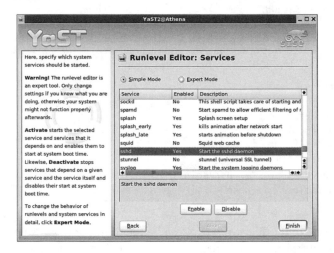

You can connect to a host through **ssh** using the syntax shown here:

```
Athena> ssh -l eric Hermes.UniversalExport.ca
```

In this example, the -l option is used to specify the login account at the remote end. Without this option, **ssh** will use the account name associated with the current session to connect. Once you are connected, an encrypted session is established between the hosts. After an exchange of cryptographic information, you will be asked for the password of the remote account. Once the password has been verified, you will have an encrypted terminal connection. Later in this chapter, you will learn how **ssh** connections can be turned into tunnels for encrypting insecure protocols between hosts.

VNC and XDMCP

Often, it is desirable to run the GUI version of a configuration tool. On systems running the X Windows System environment, two methods are available to provide remote GUI access: VNC and XDMCP.

The Virtual Network Computing (VNC) application provides remote access to an existing GUI desktop. The default install of SLES disables remote management. To permit external users to connect to a server through VNC, you must perform the following configuration steps:

1. Start YaST/YaST2.
2. Choose Network Services.
3. Choose Remote Administration.
4. Select Allow Remote Administration.
5. Restart the display manager.
6. Modify firewall settings appropriately.

WARNING

Beware of the unexpected runlevel switch.

When Allow Remote Administration is selected, you will be prompted to issue the `rcxdm restart` command. Doing so results in the machine switching to runlevel 3. A more gentle way of restarting the display manager would be to log off and on again from the GUI console or issue a reboot command.

The last step involves modifying the firewall. By default, VNC client packages communicate to the server over port 5901. If the client will be connecting from VNC client, this port will have to be opened on the firewall. The version of VNC server bundled with SLES also provides for HTTP/Java connections from client web browsers. By default, VNC provides for HTTP access over port 5801. Enabling this port on the firewall permits access to a Java-capable, browser-based VNC client. The URL for the VNC client would be `http://target_machine:5801`. In our case, this would be

`http://Hermes.UniversalExport.ca:5801`

Both the VNC client and HTTP VNC client are representations of a desktop. It is possible to modify the screen geometry to suit your needs. By default, the geometry is set to a resolution of 1024×768. You can change this setting by modifying the `/etc/xinetd.d/vnc` configuration file. VNC is also capable of offering, on distinct TCP ports, different default screen resolutions. Examples of these resolutions can be toggled on or off by changing the disabled flag from yes to no in the configuration file. The appropriate firewall changes are also required.

XDMCP is the X Display Manager Control Protocol. Whereas VNC represents a virtual desktop, XDMCP allows for a fully functioning desktop to be run on a remote machine. This is often used in environments where X-based terminal sessions are required. The Linux Terminal Services Project uses XDMCP to provide X-based resources to lower-end PCs. Additionally, other platforms that do not support the X Windows System natively can run third-party software and allow them to run an X Windows System desktop. If you enable Remote Administration, XDMCP is enabled alongside VNC. Unlike VNC, however, the firewall configuration changes required for XDMCP to operate properly are significantly more complex. XDMCP requires manual changes to the firewall setting to allow UDP traffic to flow—something the YaST firewall configuration utility does not permit natively.

NOTE

For more information on VNC, you can visit the project home page at
`http://www.uk.research.att.com/archive/vnc/index.html`

Other sites discussing the configuration of VNC include
`http://www.softpanorama.org/Xwindows/vnc.shtml`

`http://www.uk.research.att.com/archive/vnc/sshvnc.html`

`http://gentoo-wiki.com/HOWTO_Xvnc_terminal_server`

Securing System Management Conversations

It is important to secure the communications channel used to make modifications to a server. If this is not done, someone on a network could intercept traffic flow and read the transmitted packets. This form of wiretapping could reveal passwords as well as a number of system configuration parameters that could be exploited.

We have seen that it is more prudent to use a protocol such as ssh over the unencrypted Telnet protocol. The GUI System Management options VNC and XDMCP both transmit their information in cleartext. This means that someone with enough patience would be able to intercept a conversation and reconstruct a session to the point of being able to extract the same information vulnerable under Telnet. It is therefore imperative to secure this link if possible.

To secure links, you can look at additional functionality available through the ssh program. ssh is capable of making an encrypted terminal session to a host as well as create an encrypted tunnel to a host. Over this encrypted tunnel, it is possible to run nonsecure protocols safely. You do this by using the -L option of the ssh command. This turns on mapping of a port on the local machine through the secure tunnel to a port on the target machine. As an example, a user on Athena can create an encrypted tunnel to Hermes for use with VNC by typing

```
Athena> ssh -L 5902:localhost:5901 Hermes.UniversalExport.ca
```

This command maps any connections to port 5902 on the localhost—in this case, Athena—through the encrypted tunnel to port 5901 on Hermes. When the command is executed, an ssh session to the remote host (Hermes) will be created using the currently active username. If the remote username is different, the -1 switch will have to be used to supply the appropriate username. The user will then be prompted for the password for the account on the remote node. When the connection is successful, a shell will be created on the remote machine. This shell must be maintained because it supports the tunnel session.

NOTE

You can also configure your system to support what is known as X forwarding. You can do this by including the -X switch on your ssh command, followed by the X Windows System application you want to run on the remote system.

To run an encrypted VNC connection to Hermes from Athena, the user then executes a VNC session pointing to the port on the local machine representing the local end of the tunnel—in this case, port 5902—as follows:

```
Athena> vncviewer -encodings "copyrect hextile" localhost:5902
```

The local host will recognize the local port as one end of a tunnel and will forward all subsequent packets through the tunnel to port 5901 on the remote end, establishing a secure VNC session. The encoding parameters are used to alter the VNC conversation to tune the information flow between the client and the server, thus enhancing performance.

One direct benefit of this method is to reduce the number of exposed ports on the firewall. Because all communications with the remote host happen through the encrypted tunnel, the conversation is pure ssh traffic and requires only port 22. All the other ports required for VNC can be closed on the target host, masking the availability of VNC altogether. The other advantage is that VNC becomes available only to already-authenticated clients because they had to establish the tunnel in the first place. The only drawback is that a user must authenticate to create the tunnel and then again for the VNC logon screen.

NOTE

ssh tunnels are a great way of securing connections to machines and applications that, by design, do not support encrypted links.

If you think of IMAP or POP, most servers support these through their SSL equivalents. Database traffic, in most cases, is not encrypted. Using this method, you can tunnel your MySQL traffic from your application server to your database server, and the traffic will be transparently encrypted over the wire.

Restricting Connections by IP Address

By definition, servers offer applications to users. In some instances, these applications are accessed remotely over the network through an established port. To reduce the exposure of these services to attacks, it would be beneficial if you could restrict who is allowed to establish a connection. Exchanging authentication credentials is not a complete solution because it is dependent on a pre-existing connection. What is required, therefore, is a method to prevent connections from all but specific clients.

The xinetd super-server allows for the control of the source addresses that are permitted to use xinetd resources. In the default case, it accepts connections from any source IP address. The xinetd configuration file, /etc/xinetd.conf, contains a line that describes valid sources for connections. By default, it is a comment line. If you uncomment the only_from line in the /etc/xinetd.conf file, you can supply a list of IP addresses for valid client machines. In a server environment, this approach is feasible because server addresses are typically static. Placing unique addresses from a DHCP pool in this section could lead to exposing the services to unintended clients.

The following is an excerpt of the xinetd.conf file.

```
defaults
{
        log_type       = FILE /var/log/xinetd.log
        log_on_success = HOST EXIT DURATION
        log_on_failure = HOST ATTEMPT
#       only_from      = localhost
        instances      = 30
        cps            = 50 10

#       interface      = 127.0.0.1

}
```

Changing the only_from line to remove the comment symbol (#) and replacing localhost with a specific list of addresses will restrict all traffic for xinetd to those addresses. Further granularity can be achieved by placing the `only_from` line in the application-specific configuration file in the `/etc/xinetd.d` directory. Using this approach, you can allow `ssh` traffic to a list of hosts while allowing VNC traffic from a different list.

The `xinetd` restriction on IP further reduces the exposure of version harvesting for other utilities such as `sftp`, `echo`, and `telnet`. Because some versions of applications are known to have vulnerabilities, restricting connections—and hence the display of any banner information—reduces the chance of an unwanted machine mining services for information.

In the case of VNC, you could reopen port 5801 on the firewall. With `xinetd`, you can then grant access to unique static IP addresses for selected machines. You would then be able to offer VNC over HTTP to these specific clients.

A Secure System Management Environment

In the previous sections, you saw several different methods for accessing a server to perform system management tasks. Because of the sensitivity of the information typically used in system management, encrypted channels are mandatory.

The `ssh` command was used to create a secure channel through which normally insecure VNC could be used. This allows the system administrator to exploit the benefits of the GUI interface without compromising the security of the session. We also examined how to restrict access to the `xinetd` family of services to specific IP addresses. In a properly switched environment, such restrictions could be used to allow VNC and XDMCP access to specific workstations.

The secure access methods discussed here can be used to facilitate system management and reduce the number of people requiring physical access to the servers themselves.

Network Name Services

A Network Name Service is a mechanism by which a requesting client machine can inquire information about a network-available machine or service. In the following sections, we examine services available under SLES.

Samba

Usually, the Samba software is perceived to be a file and printer sharing application. For it to perform this task, however, a number of factors must be in place. It is not sufficient to simply place a machine on a network to have all its shareable resources automatically available to all.

Samba provides an environment called a *domain* within which machines can be registered. The domain is a network entity and is the main repository for all user and machine information. When a client machine requests a service from a target server, it must first inquire about the server. Using NetBEUI/NetBIOS protocols, a client can find a service provider's name and collect the necessary information to open a connection. After the target computer has been found, a connection request can be made for the resource in question. If the resource exists, the requestor's rights and privileges are checked, and access is either granted or denied. The user's credentials and access rights to the shared resource are stored within the Samba domain.

Service Location Protocol (SLP)

The Service Location Protocol (SLP) allows for a client to generate a network query and broadcast a request for a specific resource on a network. Hosts providing the service can answer the query and provide information as to their whereabouts. You can think of SLP as a decentralized network services name server. However, instead of resolving simple machine names, it provides a bridge between a requested service type and the available systems that provide the service.

The Misc option in YaST has an option called Installation Server. Selecting this function permits you to create an SLP distribution service for your SUSE installation media. You can select the protocol over which the media will be available (HTTP, FTP or NFS). After your installation media has been accepted by the system, subsequent installations can be pointed to this network resource instead of the local CD-ROM drive. Your installations will run more smoothly and not require the constant swapping of CDs.

SLP, however, is not restricted to software-kit distribution. It is also capable of providing network-wide knowledge of file and print servers and mail servers. Many of the applications provided with SLES are SLP aware. Running the SLP browser (which you access by selecting YaST, Network Services) allows you to look for available services on the network.

Domain Name Service (DNS)

The Domain Name Service (DNS) is a TCP/IP-based environment that permits the translation of text-based machine names into their target TCP/IP addresses.

A typical fully qualified domain name (FQDN) reference for a unique machine includes a machine name and a DNS zone to which it belongs. An example could be

`Hermes.UniversalExport.ca`

DNS is essentially a multitiered lookup system, not unlike a series of phone books, that can be used to convert a name into a number.

A phone number is read left to right: country code, area code, local phone number. To find an individual's number, you can look up his last name in the phone book, scroll down to the line with his first name, and find his number. Of course, this is the ideal case. In many cases, many towns are covered by the same phone book. You might also wind up with a number of individuals with the same name.

The case of finding a unique machine on the Internet and locating its address is similar. Instead of a phone book, you have a DNS server. A search for the preceding machine is performed on the local name server; if it recognizes the machine, the DNS server returns the requested information.

If the machine is not recognized, two things can happen. Just like a phone book for Lennoxville, Quebec, is the definitive guide to phone numbers there, a DNS server can be declared as the definitive source for a domain. If the target DNS server is the master server for the zone `UniversalExport.ca`, a message is returned to the users stating essentially "No such host."

If, on the other hand, the DNS server is not the master for the domain in question, it passes the information request to redefined "escalation" servers called *forwarders*. These new target DNS servers also have forwarders, and the query is passed along. Quite quickly, the DNS server with the authority to respond to the query supplies the answer.

In the case of an external machine inquiring about a machine name such as `Athena.UniversalExport.ca`, name resolution happens quite quickly. If only Pollux is the definitive DNS server for the `UniversalExport.ca` zone, the requesting machine's local DNS is unable to answer the query. Its DNS server asks its forwarder whether it can resolve `UniversalExport.ca`. If that does not work, a query for `.ca` will go out. Because this is a root domain, its DNS server knows by default the DNS server address for `UniversalExport.ca`. Pollux will be the target for the next query and will return the proper Internet-facing address.

Before you can set up your DNS server, you need to know the following information:

- The name and address of your local name server (the one you are building).

- The name of the zone you have acquired through your ISP/registrar. In
  our example, this would be `UniversalExport.ca`.

- The address of the name server for your service provider or the IP
  address of a name server you would like your unresolved queries to go
  to.

- The name of the various zones you want your name server to recognize.
  Of course, they must be names that you have the authority to resolve.
  Because we own `UniversalExport.ca`, we may decide to subdivide this
  into `Marketing.UniversalExport.ca`, `Engineering.UniversalExport.ca`,
  and so on.

- If you will be processing mail, the IP addresses and names of your
  Internet-facing mail hosts.

After you have collected this information, you are ready to configure your DNS
server. The simplest way to configure your DNS server is to use the YaST tool.
Under Network Services, choose DNS Server. You then are presented with a
wizard in which you must complete these three steps:

- Configure forwarders.

- Set up DNS zones.

- Tune the server's startup behavior and decide whether you want to enter
  the Expert Configuration menus.

The forwarders and startup steps are fairly straightforward. The startup options
simply define whether DNS should be started when the system boots up.
Forwarders are name servers that are used to further process a DNS request
should the local DNS server be unable to answer a query. Typically, they would
be external DNS servers associated with your ISP.

Determining which queries are passed to forwarders is done through defining
zones. A zone is a definition of a domain of computers for which the local
name server is responsible.

A master zone identifies the current DNS server as the definitive source for
information on the identified domain. Queries for that domain are either
resolved locally, or a failure is sent back to a client.

Slave zones tell the local DNS server which other DNS servers in the organization are responsible for name resolution for the requested domain. Requests for such domains are forwarded to the identified DNS server.

Queries to DNS that are unresolved by the local zone information are passed along to the identified forwarders for processing. By specifying a hierarchy of DNS server, you can control which domains are available to your queries and which are not.

The zone editing stage, however, can require some time to configure properly. There are five main tabs in the Zone Editor, and each tab represents a specific type of record: Basics, NS Record, MX Record, SOA, and Records.

The Basics tab describes who is allowed to extract bulk information from the zone. These bulk queries are called *zone transfers* and are typically not allowed. By dumping the content of a zone, an attacker could learn a great deal about the architecture of your network. If working from a compromised machine within your organization, an attacker could quickly learn about machines resident on your network by simply browsing the DNS entries. It is preferable to leave this setting at None to disallow all types of zone transfers.

The NS Record tab represents the name servers that are responsible for resolving queries to this zone. Though typically only one record is sufficient, a second redundant server could be listed here.

The MX Record tab identifies the zone's mail servers. SMTP mail servers that are forwarding mail to your domain will query the MX records to know which hosts they should be delivering the mail to. Typically, the servers pointed to are not the actual mail servers for an organization. MX records exposed to the Internet are usually perimeter hosts used to accept mail, scan them for viruses and spam, and forward acceptable mail to the internal servers.

The SOA record is known as the "Start of Authority" record for a zone. On the SOA tab, the authoritative server can place stale date ranges on server names, maintain updated serial numbers, and set expiry information on records. The values provided are standard values in common use. This allows for a name passed along to a query to remain in the requestor's cache for a fixed period of time. If a server is moved to a different IP address, the stale date on the requestor's client will force a rediscovery of the new proper address within the described period. This is done to ensure that remote information is kept relatively up to date.

On the last tab, Records, you can define the names and addresses of actual servers on the network. In addition to MX- and NS-type records, the YaST tool allows you to define A and CNAME entries. An A-type record relates the name of a machine with its numeric IP equivalent. A CNAME-type record allows you to define an alias for a machine. As you will see later in the section on the HTTP server, machine alias records can be used to have a single host service multiple web environments.

NOTE

Many more DNS record types are available than those listed in the YaST tool. For a complete list of these record types, refer to RFC 1035. Specifics on all RFCs can be found at http://www.faqs.org/rfcs/.

After you have configured your zones, you can start the DNS service and test your handiwork. Here are a couple of tests you may want to try:

```
Castor:~ # host -l UniversalExport.ca
UniversalExport.ca name server Athena.UniversalExport.ca.
Castor.UniversalExport.ca has address 192.168.1.245
Pollux.UniversalExport.ca has address 192.168.1.244
Hermes.UniversalExport.ca has address 192.168.1.243

Castor:~ # host Hermes.UniversalExport.ca
Hermes.UniversalExport.ca has address 192.168.1.243
```

The -l option request a dump of all the known DNS entries for the requested domain. It is important to control which machines can request a zone transfer of your domain. Only other name servers in your environment should be able to do this. Allowing unrestricted access to zone transfers allows an attacker to get a full list of your machines. It also exposes all your published machines to reconnaissance scans. If you embed the purpose of your machine in the machine name (for example, web1.universalexport.ca), an attacker can concentrate on the appropriate attacks for the specific server.

At this point, you should be able to add your entire server environment to your DNS. Machines within your network can be made to point to your DNS server IP address for name resolution. For all zones for which your server is not capable of resolving, your DNS will forward the request and transparently retrieve the answer. How to quickly set all your workstations to point to your DNS is the topic for the next section.

Dynamic Host Configuration Protocol (DHCP)

In most organizations, the number of desktop workstations greatly outnumbers the complement of the server farm. In a tightly controlled production environment, your ability to assign IP addresses to machines is governed by many factors: whether they are Internet facing, in a particular lab or DMZ, or possibly a server that can be reached only from within the organization. After you have selected the IP address, you can create a DNS entry to allow the clients to connect to the machine by name. The same process applies to all machines that offer services to other machines.

In the case of standalone desktops, there are few, if any, reasons why they should be communicating directly among themselves. Therefore, it is often unwise to register each and every machine in DNS. Furthermore, as the organization grows, maintaining the list of which machine has which address is a horrendous task.

The Dynamic Host Configuration Protocol (DHCP) alleviates many of the problems discussed here. You can use DHCP to provide to requesting workstations all the TCP/IP information they need to be able to function on the network.

In the discussion that follows, we examine a case in which all the internal address space is contained behind a firewall that is capable of Network Address Translation (NAT). We leave up to you the size of your internal subnet, your choice of Class B or Class C, and the way it will be subdivided. If your environment is different and you have a registered range of valid real-world IP addresses, the same concepts will apply.

NOTE

Private subnets are explained further in RFC 1918 and RFC 1466. You can find a copy of these RFCs at `http://www.faqs.org/rf cs/`.

Many companies ship their small business or home router firewalls with a 192.168.x.0/25 subnet preconfigured. Such devices can address as many as 254 machines. Larger companies may opt to use a Class A or B address space if they contain more machines.

Choosing the number of internal private subnets is important because it will govern how "flat" your network is. Selecting multiple smaller subnets may be beneficial in segregating traffic and identifying the origin of spurious traffic.

The bare minimum TCP/IP information a machine requires to talk locally on a network is an IP address and arguably a subnet mask. With this information, all the machines in the current network and the same subnet can be reached by an IP address.

For a machine to talk to machines outside the current subnet, it requires an address for a gateway. The gateway works like a bridge and contains the necessary routing information to target the outbound packet to the appropriate destination. With this additional piece of information, a PC can now talk to other subnets, but only by using the IP address of the target.

The final piece that will allow a client workstation to talk to machines by name is called the Domain Name Server (DNS), which was discussed previously. When you define the IP address of a DNS server, the local machine can translate a fully qualified domain name to a unique IP. Conversations are now possible on a name basis.

In summary, for a PC to function properly on a network, the following information is required:

- IP address and subnet mask
- A gateway address
- An IP address for DNS servers

After you have defined these pieces of information, you are ready to configure your DHCP server. You can start the DHC configuration utility by starting YaST and selecting Network Services and then DHCP Server.

In the initial configuration, you are asked which network card will be providing the DHCP service.

The second step asks you for default gateway and name server IP addresses. You also are prompted for the following information:

- **Domain name**—This is your registered domain name. It will be appended to the workstation's name when it is configured. It will also be the default zone DNS queries will append to requests. In this way, a client can specify a server by name and not require the fully qualified domain name (for example, you can use `Athena` instead of `Athena.UniversalExport.ca`).

- **Time server**—This information allows the client to point to the corporate time server. Identifying the time server is important for a number of protocols and is a good practice. It makes tracking down network events easier and reduces the number of support calls about clocks being out of sync and mail arriving at a PC before the PC's clock reaches the Sent time.

- **Print server**—If you have a corporate print server, you can identify it here.

- **WINS server**—This information allows your machine to automatically register into the Windows Internet Naming Service (WINS). Using this service, machine-user and IP information is collected in a central location to help reduce network queries. WINS uses NetBIOS naming services and is available under Samba/Windows.

The third and final step in the initial setup is to specify a range of TCP/IP addresses available for distribution. The range you choose here can be based on many factors. Single subnet sites may reserve the first 30 addresses for servers, the next 15 addresses for printers, and the rest for dynamic allocation. Other options include having your servers in a subnet, printers and network devices in another, and workstations in yet a third. After you make this decision, you will be required to enter a lower and upper IP address to define the DHCP range.

After configuring, you will be able to start your DHCP server. Changing a client's configuration to permit DHCP and restarting the network services should be all that is required. Your client should now have a valid address in the appropriate pool of addresses.

DHCP allows for the quick configuration of workstations. It also alleviates the tedious task of keeping track of machine-IP pairings. If these pairing are still required, DHCP provides added functionality whereby a network card's MAC address can be registered and matched to a unique IP. Though this is still a tedious task, the data is maintained in the DHCP server itself. It is therefore impossible to allocate the same address twice—something a spreadsheet or paper system is known for.

The MAC address reservation scheme is also useful for quarantine purposes. A questionable machine discovered on the network could have its MAC address reservation point to a quarantine subnet. Such a subnet can be configured not to interact with other subnets, causing the end user to contact the help desk. The help desk staff can then deal with the infected machine without requiring hours of checking from cubicle to cubicle.

DNS and DHCP

You can perform additional configuration steps to more closely tie DNS and DHCP together. Both of these applications are LDAP aware. If a corporate LDAP directory exists, it is possible for these applications to store their information within the structures provided.

An additional feature that has not been discussed here is the linking of information collected by DHCP with the capabilities of DNS. You might want to populate the DNS database with the names and IP addresses of DHCP. SLES allows you to do this using DynamicDNS. This option permits the passing of information from the DHCP server to the DNS server. Auto-registration of the machine name and domain is performed in the DNS environment. This permits hosts to have dynamic IP addresses while retaining the capability to be accessed by name when required.

Web Services

The Apache2 web server is an available configuration option for your SLES server. The Apache2 server is a fully functional and very versatile environment. In a default configuration, Apache2 offers web pages using the HTTP protocol on port 80. If required, a certificate can be incorporated to offer secure web pages using HTTPS on port 443. The following options are available under Apache2:

- Access controls
- Server-side includes
- CGI scripting
- Per-user websites
- Virtual servers (by name or by IP address)

You access the Apache2 configuration menus by selecting the Network Service, HTTP Server options in YaST. In a typical environment, a web server offers content housed in a single structure of directories.

By default, Apache2 on SLES points to **/srv/www/htdocs** as the repository for all centralized web information (see Figure 8.10). Web page requests are pointed to this directory for resolution. Subdirectories can be added within this directory to further segregate content. The directory names then become an integral portion of the requesting URLs. The structure of the website beyond that point is left to the webmaster responsible for the site.

For more dynamic content, you can find a system-wide CGI environment in **/srv/www/cgi-bin**. The web server configuration file defines how documents placed in directories are processed. This specific location is configured to pre-process the requested item through the appropriate scripting engine. Output from the script is then passed back to the requesting client as standard HTML. This allows the website in question to generate dynamic content not normally accessible through raw HTML.

SLES and Apache2 also allow users to publish their own web content. When users are added to a system, they are automatically given a **public_html** directory in their home directory. Web pages in these directories can be accessed by adding **~username** to the default web server path.

An out-of-the-box installation of the HTTP server environment provides a great deal of what a typical website would require. Apache2, however, can provide significantly more functionality. The installed version of Apache2 supports *virtual servers*, which come in two flavors: IP based and name based.

FIGURE 8.10
The default HTTP server configuration.

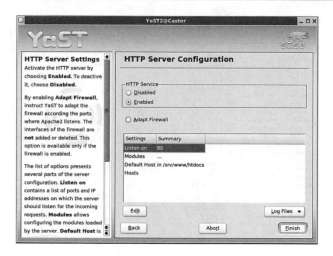

Because it is possible to bind additional addresses to a server's network interface card(s), you can configure an Apache2 server to recognize these addresses.
Each is different and therefore can be associated with a different document
structure, providing a segregated web environment.

You can obtain an equivalent separation of websites by simply identifying the
web server by different names. Additional DNS entries can be made to point
several names to the same server IP address. When Apache2 is asked to invoke
a web session, it looks at the HTTP headers in the request. It then adjusts the
internal server path for returned documents based on the calling URL.

Figure 8.11 shows the configuration of a virtual web server for the Human
Resources department.

Both `Castor.UniversalExport.ca` and `hr.UniversalExport.ca` can be placed in
DNS, resolving to the same TCP/IP address. As the web server receives the
request, it will parse the headers in the HTTP request and transparently pass
the request on to the appropriate document tree. In the case of the default
website (Castor), documents could be processed from its web root in
`/srv/www/castor`. In the case of the Human Resources page, documents will be
viewed from `/srv/www/hr`. Figure 8.12 shows the updated virtual server information in the main HTTP server setup screen.

When websites present general information to a large audience, encrypting the
transmission is often unnecessary. Typically, such websites provide online access
to information easily accessible through other formats of publishing.

FIGURE 8.11

A virtual server configuration for Human Resources.

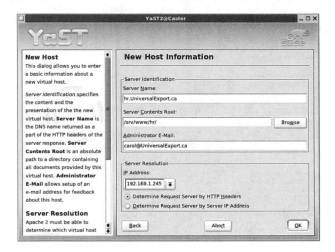

FIGURE 8.12

The main HTTP server configuration page showing available servers.

Sometimes, however, sensitive information is generated by an application residing on a website. The Apache2 server included in the SLES distribution is capable of supporting encrypted HTTP traffic called HTTPS. For your HTTP server to generate HTTPS traffic, a certificate is required. A certificate is a mechanism through which a client can get a certain level of assurance that your server is, in fact, trustworthy. Such a certificate is usually generated by a third-party service that is responsible for establishing your authenticity. When this trusted third party, known as a certificate authority or CA, is satisfied that the identification requirements are met, a certificate can be issued for your server.

If your site requirements are for internal purposes only and not as strict, a self-signed certificate may be all you require. Unlike a certificate from a trusted authority, a self-signed certificate generates a warning message at the client end, indicating the source and type of certificate. The client then needs to decide whether it wants to accept the self-signed certificate.

A self-signed certificate can be generated in two ways:

- Using `/usr/bin/gensslcert` and passing it the appropriate parameters
- Using YaST's CA management option under Security and Users
- OpenSSL

The latter approach provides a more user-friendly interface. Generating a certificate using the YaST CA Management option leverages the CA information provided at build time by the person configuring the server. Assuming your server has not been renamed, the information preexisting in the default CA should be valid.

Selecting the Enter CA option opens a screen of information containing the existing information as well as a button that allows you to view, create, and export certificates. At this stage, it is important to verify that both the server name on the certificate and the email information are correct. After you've done this, you can highlight the certificate and select the Export option.

On export, you need to generate both the certificate and the key information. You can select the Export to File option and export both the certificate and the key in unencrypted PEM format. Using this export function places both the certificate and the key information in the same file. Apache2 expects to find this information in two separate files: `/etc/apache2/ssl.crt/server.crt` and `/etc/apache2/ssl.key/server.key`. At this point, you can manually split the file into two, `cert` and `key`, and copy each portion to the appropriate Apache2 file.

NOTE

The `gensslcert` command automatically splits the generated certificate into the appropriate Apache2 files. The trick is to get all the necessary information on the command line to generate a valid certificate.

You can find the command-line options by typing

`/usr/bin/gensslcert -help`

Pay special attention to the email address field and the fully qualified host name. If they do not match exactly what is configured within Apache2 for the secure site, the certificate will not work.

The following changes are required to create a secure virtual website on an Apache2 server under SLES. Though the YaST interface provides a convenient configuration environment for HTTP sites, configuring for HTTPS seems to work better manually:

1. Ensure that the web services are not running. You can do this by managing the HTTP service in YaST or by issuing the following command:

   `/etc/rc.d/apache2 stop`

2. Create a virtual server environment for the SSL site. The configuration files for Apache2 can be found in `/etc/apache2`. In this directory, you will find a subdirectory called `vhosts.d` that houses the configuration of the various virtual hosts. Copy the template for the virtual SSL site into a configuration file:

   `cp vhost-ssl.template vhost-ssl.conf`

   Edit this new configuration file and ensure that the *ServerName* variable matches the fully qualified server name provided to the certificate. Also, ensure that the *ServerAdmin* variable matches the certificate's default email address.

3. Correct the System Configuration file for Apache2. The system configuration file for Apache2, `/etc/sysconfig/apache2`, is not updated directly by YaST when SSL components are added. You therefore need to verify that the following changes are made:

   - The `APACHE_MODULE` list contains an entry for SSL.
   - The `APACHE_SERVER_FLAGS` is set to `-D SLL`.
   - The `APACHE_START_TIMEOUT` is set to `5`.

4. Tweak the firewall. Because HTTPS runs under a different port than HTTP, you need to modify the server's firewall to accept connections on port 443. If the server will run unsecured web pages in different virtual hosts, port 80 may be required as well.

At this point, a secure site should be available on the server that can be communicated with through HTTPS. If required later or when moving from a staging environment to production, you can insert a certificate from a trusted third-party vendor into the running configuration. This will prevent the clients from dealing with the warnings generated by self-signed certificates.

NOTE

There are many pitfalls in setting up a website to use certificates. If you are using a third-party Certificate Authority, it should have a number of reference articles to help you through the configuration. In many cases, the support staff will walk you through the various steps.

If you use a self-signed certificate, you may require some external resources. Most errors arise from inconsistent spelling of the various names used to generate the certificate. If you are still experiencing difficulties, you may want to visit

```
http://venueserver.rcc.ryerson.ca/index.php?option=com_
content&task=view&id=26&Itemid=40
```

```
http://www.securityfocus.com/infocus/1818
```

```
http://www.securityfocus.com/infocus/1820
```

Configuring most aspects of the Apache2 server is straightforward when you use the YaST tool. The server software allows for a number of various sites to be managed as separate virtual servers. The Apache2 server can also be quickly adapted to support HTTPS.

Authentication Services

In Chapter 5, "User Environment Management and Security," we examined the processes involved with user authentication. We introduced the PAM module system and explored the relationship between the `pam_unix2` module and the `/etc/passwd` and `/etc/shadow` files. Here, we expand on this topic and look at alternate sources that will allow for network-wide authentication of users. As the number of machines increases in an environment, it will become more and more difficult for users to keep track of passwords across multiple platforms. A centralized network authentication mechanism will help alleviate the difficulties of keeping passwords up to date and secure.

Network Information Services (NIS)

The Network Information Services (NIS), formally known as Yellow Pages, provide a Unix-centric client/server environment for controlling usernames, groups, and passwords as well as machine and directory information. In this environment, a master server is created and is configured to accept connections from a set group of client machines.

On the client side, no information is stored in the local `/etc/passwd` file. When an authentication request is made by a user initiating a session, the information is passed along to the master server. The master then either declines the authentication or returns the default directory for the user as well as the list of groups the user belongs to.

In such an environment, users' home directories are often resident on a single server and made available across the network as exported NFS shares.

In terms of PAM, the standard `pam_unix2` module understands and interacts with the NIS environment.

Samba Domains

Samba is an implementation of a group of applications that provide for cross-platform file and print services. It is an open source implementation of the Server Message Block (SMB) and Common Internet File System (CIFS). Both of these protocols were originally defined by Microsoft. Unlike the Microsoft implementation of SMB and later CIFS, Samba is available on a multitude of platforms and native operating systems.

Included in the architecture of Samba is the concept of a domain within which users and servers reside. SLES can be configured to be the primary domain controller (PDC), a secondary (or backup) domain controller (BDC), or simply a member server. In any of these configurations, the authentication process for member SLES servers can be made to point to the central repository of domain accounts.

Unlike NIS, Samba allows for the bridging of the authentication environment across noncompatible operating systems such as OpenVMS, Unix, and Windows.

Lightweight Directory Access Protocol (LDAP)

The Lightweight Directory Access Protocol (LDAP) is a reduced scope implementation of the X.500 directory protocol. LDAP allows for a server or group of servers to share a common repository of information. A typical use for LDAP would be as an address book. Such repositories can contain large volumes of data that need to be accessed in a variety of ways quickly and efficiently. Additionally, LDAP does not demand that all entries contain the same collection of attributes.

As a central store of information, an LDAP server can be accessed by numerous systems simultaneously. Because it is based on an open standard, multiple different applications and platforms can exchange information through a consistent data model. These attributes make LDAP an ideal candidate for sharing account information.

In SLES, the centralized LDAP server can contain not only account information such as username, password, and default directory, but it can also contain information pertaining to DNS and DHCP.

Kerberos

Kerberos is an altogether different method of authentication. In the previous examples and in the case of using the /etc/passwd file, a user is prompted for both a username and password. Both are then sent to the authentication mechanism within PAM that looks at these pieces of information and confirms their correctness. When access to other disparate resources is required, the challenge response mechanism is invoked again and again.

Kerberos is based on a totally different approach. The Kerberos model requires that a server be set aside with the sole purpose of authentication. This server must be a system that the entire infrastructure can trust and must therefore be physically segregated from other servers, have a minimum number of administrators, and have no local users. Kerberos also requires that the network environment be kept time synchronized. One parameter used in the Kerberos environment is time stamps, which prevent information collected at one point in time to be rebroadcast on the network later. Because the information is time-stamped, the rebroadcast data would be considered tainted.

The Kerberos authentication process begins when a new user asks for access to a resource. When this occurs, the following events are put into motion:

1. This user is prompted for his or her username.

2. The client sends the client name to the Kerberos server as well as a request for a ticket.

3. The authentication server collects information on time and IP addresses, generates a random session key, and encrypts this as a key known only by itself and a ticket-granting server. It then takes this encrypted data, a time stamp, and some additional information and reencrypts it in the client's own private key, its password. This new packet of data is sent back to the client.

4. The local workstation then asks the user for his or her password. The password is then used to generate the decryption key for the data packet. Because the user's password is never sent over the network, the chance of its interception is zero.

5. If the decryption is successful, the client now has a copy of the bundle that can be decrypted only by the ticket-granting server.

6. The client can now send this packet to the ticket-granting server to obtain an authentication ticket that is valid for a fixed lifetime.

Kerberos is therefore quite secure. All conversations between the client and server are encrypted. The user's password is never transmitted over the network but is used as the encryption/decryption key for the conversation. Additionally, a portion of the data returned to the client is encrypted by the Kerberos server itself using a private key. Because only the Kerberos server and the ticket-granting server know this key, there are no mechanisms in place through which a client can generate a false ticket.

When a client requests access to a service, the ticket information, a time stamp, and the client IP address are bundled and encrypted with the session key and sent to the target server. The target server can then decrypt the information, verify the validity of the ticket, and grant access.

Summary

This chapter touched on the services available in SLES and provided you with enough information to get the services up and running. At this point, you should have an understanding of the services available through `xinetd` and those governed through `/etc/init.d`. Other topics covered include the services that will most impact on your clients: mail, FTP, web, and file sharing. We also examined different ways of accessing the server for remote management.

Many of the concepts introduced here are quite complex and may require a significant investment of time to understand them completely. The YaST configuration tool is a quick way to navigate through the configurations. For a number of services such as Samba, DNS, and HTTP, additional changes may be required outside the scope of YaST.

In the course of the chapter, we introduced a number of concepts that were not directly tied to the tools. It is imperative to consider the security implications of the configuration options available. Recognizing the benefits of one option over another is important. We hope that the additional topics covered here will help with that understanding.

## CHAPTER 9

Printing Services

In this chapter, we examine how SLES provides services for printing. Historically, printer support on the various flavors of Unix was inconsistent. Manufacturers created drivers for their printers, but often only on a select number of operating systems. This meant that certain printers were supported only on specific platforms.

The Line Printer Daemon (LPD) was used to control the printing of requests on specific queues. Running this application would define the local server as being a print server. Local queues could then be made available to other systems. Clients could then use the LPR application to submit print jobs to a target print server and queue.

The Common UNIX Printing System (CUPS) is designed to be a replacement for the LPD and LPR environments present on these older systems. In SUSE LINUX Enterprise Edition 9 and higher, these older printer environments have been deprecated. Because of this, this chapter focuses only on the features available through CUPS.

All the aspects of producing printed output are tightly related. For purposes of this chapter, we subdivide the printing process into the following sections:

- Printer configuration
- Job lifecycle
- Queue management

Each of these categories will be examined using YaST, command-line tools, and the CUPS web interface.

Printer Configuration

Before information can be printed, the system must be made aware of devices available to produce the required output. When a system knows of the existence of a valid output device, it can make that device available to applications. Printers can be subdivided into two main categories depending on how they are made available to the system: local and network. The following two sections look at each.

Local Printers

Local printers are dependent on physical hardware present within the server. Typical hardware-specific interfaces include parallel, serial, infrared (IrDA), and USB.

Each interface type has a corresponding device file in the /dev directory through which it is accessed. Table 9.1 lists the different interface types and their corresponding device files.

TABLE 9.1
Printer Interface Types and Their Device Files

INTERFACE TYPE	DEVICE
Parallel	/dev/lp0
Serial	/dev/ttyS0, /dev/ttyS1
IrDA	/dev/irlpt0 through /dev/irlpt3
USB	/dev/usb/lp0 through /dev/usb/lp15

Because the interface hardware is resident within the server, the number of local devices that can attach to a single server is limited. An average server comes preconfigured with two serial ports, a single parallel port, and two USB busses spread over four ports. Expansion beyond this requires the purchase of additional hardware.

All these technologies restrict the location of the printing device. The physical length of cable supported by the various protocols forces the printing device to be located within a few yards of the server. Though it is possible to trade off baud rate for distance in the case of serial protocols, this trade-off has serious performance implications. Newer, high-speed printers do not receive data fast enough to maintain their printing speed if they are at the end of a long, low baud rate cable.

The other drawback to co-locating printers with the server is access. In a normal data center environment, users do not have access to the room hosting the server. Access to short-range protocol printers is therefore not possible.

The solution to many of these drawbacks is to push the printer interface hardware outside the data center. This converts the short-range printer technologies discussed here into network-aware solutions.

Network Printers

Network printers, as their name suggests, are accessible only through the network. Such printers are attached through various mechanisms to remote print servers. CUPS supports a number of different network protocols for accessing such printers.

A CUPS server can be configured in either a client or a server role. As a server, it can present a number of local print queues to the network for access by various clients. When configured as a client, CUPS listens to service broadcasts on the network and acquires a list of valid printer destinations.

A Linux server running CUPS also understands LPD, SMB, and IPX network protocols. In such cases, a local printer definition can be made to point to a network server's printer using the appropriate network transport protocols. LPD can be used for accessing queues on non–CUPS-compatible Unix systems as well as a number of commercial print server appliances. The SMB protocol is used to access Samba or Windows server environments, while IPX is used by older Novell networks. In the case of SMB and IPX printing, the local configuration may require a username and password for accessing the remote queues.

Adding a Local Printer

You can add printers to a server using either command-line tools or YaST. The following example shows how to add a local parallel printer to a server using YaST. In YaST, the printer configuration icon can be found under the Hardware menu option. After you select this icon, you are presented with the window displayed in Figure 9.1.

In Figure 9.1, you can see that no printers are currently defined on the server. To create a new printer definition, ensure that the Other (Not Detected) option is highlighted and click the Configure button. This brings you to the next window, as shown in Figure 9.2, where you can choose the type of printer you want to configure. In the current example, add a Canon Bubble Jet 200 to the configuration as a label printer. This device requires a parallel port connection to the host. The local interfaces are shown at the top of the list, and the network-aware protocols are grouped in the lower portion.

Because you are configuring a parallel printer, select the appropriate option shown in Figure 9.2 and click the Next button. In the next window, you can select which parallel port the printer is connected to. Because a typical server has only one parallel port, /dev/lp0, highlight that option and click Next. In the case of a serial, IrDA, or USB printer, you would have to choose the appropriate device.

FIGURE 9.1
YaST Printer Configuration screen.

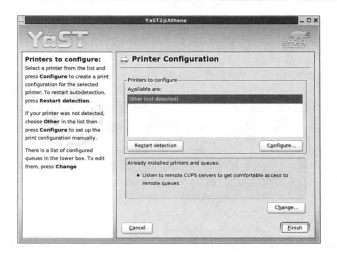

FIGURE 9.2
Printer type definitions.

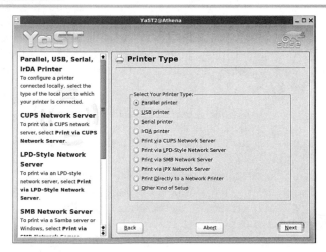

Figure 9.3 displays an example of the next screen that will appear. On this screen, you define the name users will select to gain access to the queue. The use of a good naming standard will prevent a number of lost or misdirected print jobs. This is especially important when some printers are used with special forms such as shipping labels or multipart forms.

FIGURE 9.3

Defining the print queue name and description.

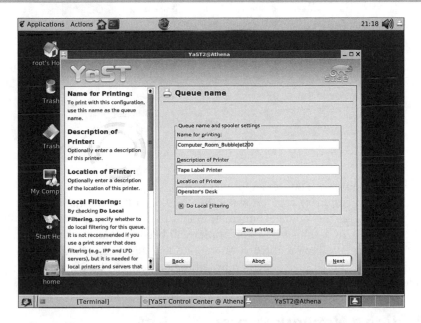

After defining the human-visible characteristics of the printer, you must identify to the server what type of printer is present on the selected port. A sample of this window is shown in Figure 9.4. Each printer has specific capabilities and limitations. Selecting the appropriate printer model will ensure that CUPS can properly translate the user document into a format that can be rendered by the printer.

In Figure 9.4, a large list of manufacturers is shown in the left column. Selecting the appropriate manufacturer presents, in the right column, a list of supported models for that manufacturer. When you select the printer, you are letting CUPS know what your printer is capable of doing. Using this information, CUPS can translate various types of documents into a format compatible with your printer.

FIGURE 9.4
Defining the printer model.

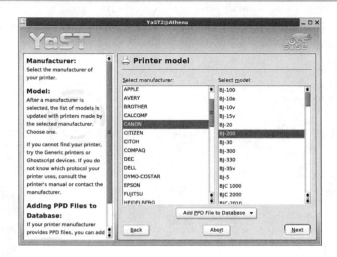

After you choose the appropriate printer model, you are presented with the configuration summary page, shown in Figure 9.5. At this point, clicking the OK button saves the defined configuration into the various files used by CUPS. After the configuration is saved, the printer will become available to the system's users. We explore the fine-tuning of queue restrictions later in this chapter. First, though, let's look at how defining a network-based printer is different.

Adding a Network Printer

In YaST, adding a queue definition on a local server for a network printer is almost identical to setting up a local printer. The main difference encountered in selecting a network-based printer in Figure 9.2 is that the local interface selection option is replaced with a network configuration screen. For an SMB queue, you are presented with a window similar to that shown in Figure 9.6.

NOTE

A workgroup is a collection of machines in a Windows/Samba environment. When a system is configured, it can be placed within a specific workgroup. When you are searching the network for computers, only systems in the same workgroup will be discovered. This permits the segregation of machines based on function.

The drawback to this classification is that, unlike a domain, usernames and passwords are machine specific. Users needing access to multiple machines have to maintain their passwords separately on each.

FIGURE 9.5
The YaST edit printer configuration window.

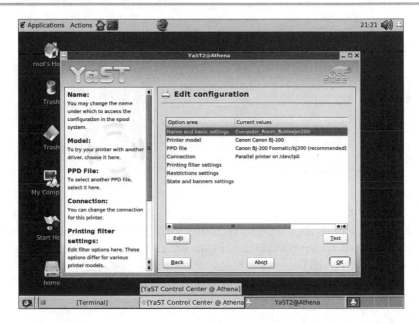

In this configuration screen, the environment and access rights for the target queue must be defined. If required, a username and password must also be included. Because you do not want queue access to terminate should a particular employee leave, you should configure an appropriately hardened service account in the target environment to allow printer-only access from specific hosts.

An additional consideration that must be factored in when configuring remote network printing is access for the appropriate ports through firewalls.

The remainder of the configuration for a network-attached printer is identical to that of local printers.

FIGURE 9.6
Configuration options for an SMB printer.

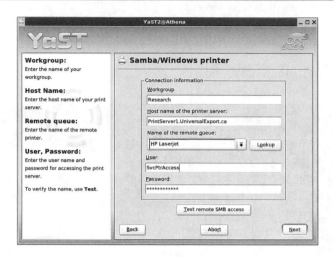

NOTE

Each printer protocol discussed here requires a distinct TCP/IP port. If the protocol is to be used, allowances have to be made with the server firewall configuration. The Telnet and HTTP protocols are generally used to grant access to the local printer's configuration settings. The following table lists the more common ports used for communication purposes with printers.

PROTOCOL	PORT
Telnet	23
HTTP	80
SMB	137,138, 139
LPD	515
CUPS/IPP	631
JetDirect	9100

Print Job Lifecycle

A number of events take place between the time a user requests a document to be printed and when it is sent to the physical device for output. In simplified terms, a print request can be broken down into three main stages:

- Saving all the print information locally for subsequent processing (spooling)
- Translating the information into a format compatible with the printer (filtering)
- Providing the parsed output to the appropriate target device (printing)

All these print job stages are executed without the knowledge of the user requesting the output. Each step, however, must be successful for the operation to produce valid output.

Job Spooling

Each request for a print copy of a document is tagged with a request number. This number allows the system to uniquely track the document data, the destination print queue and filters, as well as job accounting information.

The spooler places a snapshot copy of the requested document in a directory under /var/spool/cups. The document, as well as its various instances in the filtering process, reside in the directory until the job successfully prints. On servers that process a large volume of print jobs, a significant amount of disk space can be consumed by pending print requests.

The spooler is responsible for providing job status information upon request to users, as well as routing the data through the various stages of the printing process.

Job status can be verified either through the CUPS web interface (this is shown later in Figure 9.10) on the print server or through the lpstat command using a terminal interface.

Applying Filters

Printing implementations using the LPR/LPD environment suffer from the lack of cross-platform driver support for various printers. In CUPS, many of the driver issues are solved through abstracting job requirements from the hardware. This is accomplished by a series of conversions that massage the various data formats contained within the print request into a single standard format.

After the data is converted into a standard format, the printing process is reduced to a simple translation from the standard format to one understood by the individual printer.

In CUPS, the standard format is PostScript. The filters used by CUPS are stored in /usr/lib/cups/filter. After a data stream is converted into PostScript, it can then be translated into the required format for the specific printer. Support for specific printers, or printer families, is therefore reduced to providing a single PostScript-aware driver. If the printer is PostScript capable, the file is forwarded to the next step. If it is not PostScript aware, as in the case of the sample Canon BJ200, the file is converted into a raster format compatible with the printer.

Printing the Information

After the data has been massaged into the appropriate format, it is ready to be printed. The last stage in the process involves invoking what is known as a back-end process. This process is responsible for moving the final document version to the printer itself.

In the case of a local printer, the back-end process reports progress, success, or failure of the print job back to the spooler process.

Network print jobs are handled slightly differently than local print jobs. With such jobs, the back-end process is constrained to handing off the document to the spooler service at the remote end. After this is accomplished, the spooler is notified and the local print job is marked as completed. After the hand-off has occurred, however, the local back-end process can no longer report on the status of the spooled job. The remote server also has a method for tracking the now "local" print request. Further tracking at the client end is not possible, but diagnostic information is available on the endpoint server.

Queue Management

CUPS provides for a very robust printing environment. To date, we have examined how to create queues to both local and remote printers. In this section, we concentrate on how these resources can be managed.

Before we delve into managing single queue characteristics, we need to explore some additional functionality available through CUPS.

The CUPS environment allows for additional flexibility when dealing with printers. Built into CUPS is the concept of a printer class. A class within CUPS is a collection of like printers. When a job is submitted to a class of printers, instead of a specific target, the first available printer in that class processes the output. In work areas where a number of similar printers are available, submitting a job to a class prevents small jobs from being queued behind slow printing jobs. As an example, emails could be printed to a class to avoid being stuck behind a large double-sided month-end report.

NOTE

As of the date this book was written, CUPS does not provide any indication of which printer within a class satisfies a print request. It is therefore imperative that like printers be grouped physically close to each other to reduce the amount of time spent going from printer to printer looking for output. This also means that sensitive documents should not sent to a printer class for printing. It is expected that CUPS version 1.2 will support such notifications.

CUPS extends the class construct to what it calls implicit classes. An implicit class is generated when a collection of servers is made to point to the same network printer using the same name. This also assumes that the printer is, in fact, a self-contained network printer, and not a local printer on a vulnerable server. In such environments, the failure of a single print server does not result in the loss of client access to the printer in question. CUPS further extends this concept to actual printer classes. If a job is submitted to a class, any server servicing that class can respond to the request.

An additional feature supported directly by CUPS is the possibility of defining multiple print queues that all point to the same physical printer. In many instances, software such as a web browser can force printout formatting. In some cases, such as with the command line, accessing double-sided print or two-up printing involves remembering a number of switches and parameters for the `print` command. It is possible to define distinct queues that have embedded in their configuration the desired formatting options. This alleviates the requirement of specifying option definitions in individual print requests.

YaST Queue Configuration

Figure 9.5 showed three items at the end of the Options list that do not have entries in the Current Values column. These options are actually placeholders for additional queue configuration options.

The first option is called Printing Filter Settings. Selecting this option allows you to configure how the output will be formatted, what media your output will be printed on, paper size, orientation, and so on. The options available vary from printer to printer. For a simple label printer, few options are available. High-end laser printers allow for the most section options.

When you are configuring multiple queues to point to a single printer, the Printing Filter Settings option allows you to define the default print options at the queue level. You can then present multiple queues to the users, each with its own characteristics.

The second option on the Edit Configuration window is Restriction Settings. By default, queues created on a system are available to all authenticated users. You can use this option to restrict access to specific users or, alternately, deny queue access to all but specific users.

The last option in Figure 9.5 is State and Banners Settings. With this option, you can control whether the printer is available to accept new printing jobs. In addition, if separation pages are required between printing jobs, you can configure pre- and post-job banner pages. For high-volume printing or in the case of the printing of sensitive information, banners can be used to separate jobs and facilitate their handling by the operations staff.

NOTE

Applications such as web browsers or editors often pass their own default printer configuration parameters to the target queue. These options override the configuration parameters set on the queue. The submitted job should print as expected by the software package even though the orientation and size of the output don't match the queue specification.

Command-Line Queue Configuration

All the configuration options available through the YaST interface are available from the command line as well. Unlike the YaST interface, the command-line configuration options are split into two different verbs.

The first printer configuration command is `lpadmin`. This command configures both printers and printer class objects. You can grant access to a specific printer using a single command such as

```
Athena:~ # lpadmin -p Laserjet -u allow:hart,eric
Athena:~ # lpadmin -p Laserjet -u deny:ted,pol
```

In this example, Eric and Hart are granted explicit access to the LaserJet printer, while Ted and Pol are explicitly denied the use of this printer.

Table 9.2 summarizes the parameters that can be passed to `lpadmin`:

TABLE 9.2
lpadmin Parameters

CLASS MODIFIERS

PARAMETER	PARAMETER VALUE	PURPOSE
-c	class	Makes the printer a member of the class. Creates the class if necessary.
-r	class	Removes the named printer from class. Delete the class if it becomes empty.

CONFIGURATION MODIFIERS

-m	model	Sets a standard System V interface script or PPD file from the model directory.
-o	name=value	Sets a PPD option for the printer (for example, Duplex=None).
-o	job-k-limit=value	Fixes the maximum print job size in kilobytes.
-o	job-page-limit=value	Fixes the maximum number of pages printed.
-o	job-quota-period=value	Defines the length of a quota period in seconds.
-u	allow:user,user,@group deny:user,user,@group allow:all deny:none	Controls access to the printer by authenticated username.
-v	device-uri	Defines the printer interface (for example, parallel:/dev/lp0).
-D	Info	Provides a text description of the printer.
-E		Sets the printer to Enabled.
-L	Location	Provides a text string for the printer's physical location.
-P	ppd-file	Defines the filter file to be used for this printer.

After you configure a printer, you can use the lpoptions command to fine-tune the configuration. In contrast to the lpadmin command, the lpoptions command can also be used by an unprivileged user to save customized queue configuration parameters in a personal configuration file.

You can display configuration options for a particular printer by using the –1 option on the command, as the following illustrates:

```
Athena:~ # lpoptions -d Computer_Room_bj200 -1
PageSize/Page Size: *A4 Letter 11x17 A3 A5 B5 Env10 EnvC5
➥EnvDL EnvISOB5 EnvMonarch Executive Legal
PageRegion/PageRegion: A4 Letter 11x17 A3 A5 B5 Env10 EnvC5
➥ EnvDL EnvISOB5 EnvMonarch Executive Legal
Resolution/Resolution: 180x180dpi 180x360dpi 360x180dpi
➥*360x360dpi
Athena:~ #
```

Of course, the more advanced the printer, the larger number of configurable options. As an example, to set the default page size to letter format, you can use the following command:

```
Athena:~# lpoptions -d Computer_Room_bj200 -o PageSize=Letter
```

The `lpoptions` command sets the default queue characteristics for the local user. If the command is executed by the root account, the changes are made system-wide.

Printer Queue Basics

Above and beyond queue configuration verbs are the simple commands used to start, monitor, and stop queues. Though CUPS makes available a number of GUI tools for controlling queues, knowing the command-line versions can often save time and frustrations. This section offers a quick overview of some of the basics.

To submit a file to be printed, you use the `lp` or `lpr` commands. Both take a parameter –d to specify the destination queue name if it is other than the default. Additional parameters are available and documented in the `man` pages. These defaults override the selections defined on the queue. A sample print job could look like this:

```
Athena:~ # lp -d Laserjet -o landscape x-ray.log
request id is Laserjet-9 (1 file(s))
Athena:~ #
```

In the event of a printer malfunction, you often need to power-cycle the printer. If you do not do this correctly, or if the printer contains its own print server hardware, jobs could be inadvertently lost. To prevent this loss, it is often desirable to stop the queue from processing further jobs. To do this, you can use the `disable` command, which is documented in the `man` pages. The use of the -r option is recommended to provide users with a short text explanation of the reason the printer is unavailable. An example is shown here:

```
Athena:~ # disable -r "stuck label" Computer_Room_bj200
```

To check the status of a printer, you can use the lpstat command. If you specify the -t option, all the available status information for the print environment will be printed as well:

```
Athena:~ # lpstat -t
scheduler is running
system default destination: Computer_Room_bj200
device for Computer_Room_bj200: parallel:/dev/lp0
Computer_Room_bj200 accepting requests since Jan 01 00:00
printer Computer_Room_bj200 disabled since Jan 01 00:00 -
       stuck label
printer Laserjet is idle.  enabled since Jan 01 00:00
Computer_Room_bj200-4    root 1024    Sun Feb 27 06:14:41 2005
Computer_Room_bj200-5    root 1024    Sun Feb 27 06:15:20 2005
Computer_Room_bj200-6    root 1024    Sun Feb 27 06:15:44 2005
Athena:~ #
```

To allow printing to resume, you can use the enable command. You need to call the enable command using the fully qualified path to avoid shell confusion with the built-in enable command:

```
Athena:~ # /usr/bin/enable Computer_Room_bj200
```

When the preceding command is performed, printing on this device will resume.

NOTE

To avoid confusion between the different enable commands, it is suggested that an alias be created for the printer enable function. This can be done using the following syntax:

```
Athena:~ # alias penable=/usr/bin/enable
```

This allows you to use the synonym penable instead of having to specify the complete path to the enable command every time. Further, you can place it in your login shell to make this command available at all times. If you want to make this available to all, you can add the alias definition to /etc/bash.bashrc.

The CUPS Web Interface

We have seen that SLES offers both command-line tools and YaST for managing printers, queues, and jobs. Built into CUPS is the ability to manage the printing environment from a simple web browser. Through this web interface, all aspects of the printing environment can be addressed. Using a standard browser, CUPS can be accessed through `http://localhost:631`.

By default, the web interface provides read-only access to the classes, queues, and job information on a server. Before administrative tasks can be undertaken, a username/password pair must be created within the CUPS environment. Individuals who do not have any system management rights on the host can be readily made into CUPS administrators. You can do this by using the command-line verb `lppasswd`, as in the following example:

```
Athena:/etc/cups # lppasswd -g sys -a hart
Enter password:
Enter password again:
Athena:/etc/cups #
```

In this example, a username/password pair was created for managing the CUPS environment. This allows the user named Hart to create new printers and classes and manage print jobs, but only from the local server node. This implies that Hart would need to have a local account and X Windows System access on the server. To extend the management capabilities of the CUPS web interface beyond the local machine, you must make a change to the `/etc/cups/cupsd.conf` configuration files.

The `cupsd.conf` file uses a syntax similar to that used for the configuration of the Apache2 server. Administrative access is based on the access controls defined for the `/admin` portion of the CUPS website. In `cupsd.conf,` the default configuration looks like this:

```
<Location /admin>
#
  AuthType BasicDigest
  AuthClass Group
  AuthGroupName sys

## Restrict access to local domain
  Order Deny,Allow
  Deny From All
  Allow From 127.0.0.1

#Encryption Required
</Location>
```

Additional access can be granted to individual workstations or subnets by inserting additional `Allow From` clauses. Ease of access must be balanced against exposure of the CUPS environment. To add a complete subnet, you can simply add the fourth octect set to a *, as follows:

`Allow From 192.168.1.*`

When a user accesses CUPS through the web interface, he or she will be presented with a browser window similar to that shown in Figure 9.7.

FIGURE 9.7
The main page of the CUPS web interface.

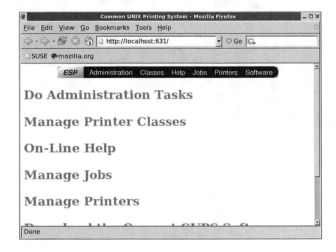

In Figure 9.7, the main menu breaks down the administration tasks into these main sections:

- Administration, for authorized users
- Classes
- Jobs
- Printers
- Help
- Software – access the CUPS web site

The Administration menu option presents a window similar to that shown in Figure 9.8. You must choose this menu option if you need to define new printers or printer classes. The Add function is not found on the various other CUPS menus. Again, the administration page is available only to users who can authenticate using credentials established through the `lppasswd` command.

FIGURE 9.8
The Administration menu for the CUPS web interface.

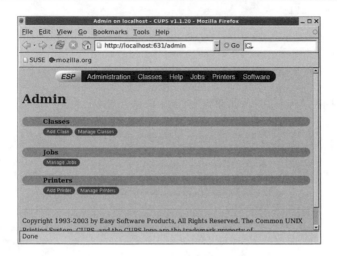

The Class page is shown in Figure 9.9. As with subsequent administration pages, the Delete and Modify options are shown. Access to these selections requires appropriate authentication. Unauthorized users are simply presented with an authorization failure (an HTTP 403 error).

FIGURE 9.9
The CUPS Class page.

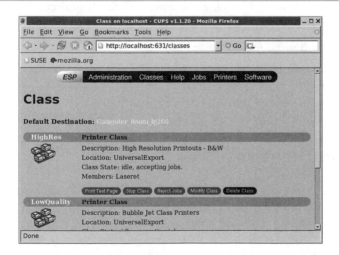

Figures 9.10 and 9.11 complete the series of menu options available under the CUPS web interface. Within the Jobs page, shown in Figure 9.10, you can see information on pending print jobs. Similarly, the Printer page, shown in Figure 9.11, presents configuration information on each printer, status information, as well as a number of management options.

FIGURE 9.10

The CUPS Job management page.

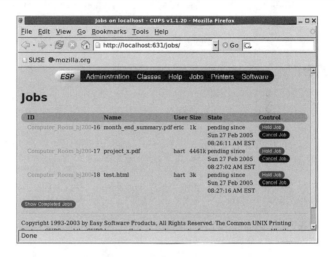

FIGURE 9.11

The CUPS Printer management page.

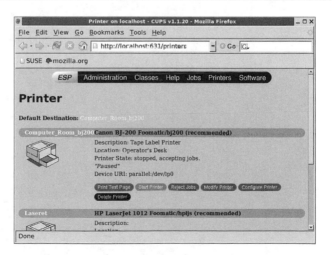

The CUPS web interface into printer configuration management is an important step in easing the support of a distributed printing environment. The CUPS environment incorporates its own administration model. This permits the granting of administration rights to individuals outside the authentication scheme of the hosting server. Users who do not possess any privileges on the host server can therefore be granted administration rights directly within CUPS. This adds an additional layer of administrative burden when implementing an account management policy. It does, however, allow for the delegation of queue management to individuals such as helpdesk staff without the requirement of elevated user privileges on the server.

Summary

In this chapter, we examined the different aspects of printing. SLES provides for a number of different methods for creating and maintaining queues.

Using YaST, we created both a local and a network print queue. We used command-line tools to fine-tune characteristics of these queues and submit jobs.

Throughout this chapter, we saw how the CUPS printing environment has made queue management simpler. Additionally, we examined how the CUPS web interface can be used to remotely manage the printing environment without requiring local access to the print server itself.

## CHAPTER 10

Data Backup and Disaster Recovery

No matter how fault tolerant your server hardware is or if you have implemented the best security measures possible, there is no guarantee that data will never be lost. Sometimes the cause is totally beyond your control—a fire caused by a gas leak, for example, or even Mother Nature (remember the Los Angeles earthquake?). Also, to err is human; even the most experienced users and system administrators make mistakes. Deleting the wrong file or mistyping information into a file (such as /etc/passwd) can cause unwarranted headaches and additional work for yourself or coworkers who need to access the data, or, in the worst case, the deletion renders the whole system unusable. Also, a disgruntled user or malevolent hacker may deliberately remove or corrupt essential data or system files; as a matter of fact, most attacks occur from within the company rather than from without. In all cases, having up-to-date backups would be a lifesaver.

Recovering from a hacker break-in can be tedious work. The problem is that once a system has been compromised, it is essentially impossible to determine everything that has occurred, especially if the system's root account was compromised. Log files and audit trails help, but if the hacker covered his or her tracks well, there will be no telltale signs found. So the best way to quickly recover from any break-in is to use a pristine backup.

To be able to use such a backup, it is of utmost importance that you have developed *and* implemented a reliable data backup and disaster recovery strategy. In this chapter, you learn how to develop a backup plan and how and when to use the standard Linux backup tools, such as **tar** and **cpio**. You also find out how to create and use an SLES rescue floppy disk using YaST.

TIP

If you have a corrupted lilo boot loader, boot your system using the rescue disk and then reinstall lilo on the MRB of your hard disk using the /sbin/lilo -M command.

A Look at Backup Strategies

The purpose of performing backups is to be able to restore individual files or complete filesystems. How often to perform backups, what data should be backed up, and how to rotate backup media are issues that can be confusing.

Exactly how often you should back up which files depends on your system hardware configuration and particular needs. The criterion is, "If the system crashes, how much work are you willing to lose, and how much data can you *afford* to lose?" Remember that in any computing environment, the most valuable component is data, which may be in the form of databases or source code. Ideally, you would want to back up all files on all filesystems every few minutes so that you would never lose more than a few minutes' worth of work. However, this approach is not practical, and there are other ways in which you can achieve this near real-time redundancy without doing backups.

TIP

One option to achieve (near) real-time redundancy, without installing special hardware, is to periodically mirror the data from your server to a backup server using rsync, a file-synchronization utility included with SLES. rsync is discussed later in this chapter.

To examine the problem another way, you might ask this question: "How often should I back up the files?" The more users you have on the system, the more often you should back up the filesystems. A common schedule is to perform a full backup once or twice a week and partial daily backups. In a *full* backup, every single file on every filesystem is backed up, regardless of its creation or modification time. A *partial*, or *incremental*, backup backs up only the files that have been created or modified since the last full backup.

Your backup strategy should be based on a rotation scheme that guarantees complete recovery in case of a disaster, within a reasonable amount of time. The following discussion is based on tape rotation because the most commonly used backup medium today is tape; however, the same principle applies to other storage media, such as rewritable DVDs.

A rotation system distributes both old and new information across several tapes to reduce the risk of being lost due to media failure. The backup and storage media type and media rotation method you choose should take the following into consideration:

- **Backup time window**—How much of a time window do you have when files on the servers are not being updated? Unless your backup software is capable of backing up open files, you need to schedule the job for the time period when no files are being accessed, or you have to make a conscious decision to skip opened files.

- **Amount of data and backup media throughput**—Both the amount of data to back up and the speed at which that data can be written to the backup media will have an impact on your choice of backup methods. For example, if you have 20GB of data to be backed up daily and your backup device is capable of storing only 1GB per hour, performing a full backup will take at least 20 hours. In such a case, doing a daily full backup is probably not a good option, and a daily incremental backup is more appropriate.

- **Media realibility and capacity**—Tapes have a limited lifetime, and constant use of the same tape can shorten its life span. The typical shelf life of a magnetic tape is just a few years, or shorter depending on the environment in which it is stored. On the other hand, tapes have a much higher storage capacity (hundreds of gigabytes) than most other storage media, such as CDs (800MB) and DVDs (4–8GB). Some installations use tapes for short-term storage, and when certain data needs to be retained for an extended period of time, this data is transferred to DVDs. In some cases due to audit requirements, data is backed up directly to CDs or DVDs so they cannot be subsequently modified.

- **File restoration decision**—How many tapes (that is, how much time) will you need to restore information in the event of a complete system failure? (*Always* plan for the worst-case scenario, but hope for the best.) Also, the procedure to restore your filesystems back to a known state (for example, last night) should be as straightforward as possible; you should not have to run through 20 tapes for the task.

- **Storage facilities**—It is general practice that backup archives should be sent to offsite storage facilities for safe-keeping. However, this may not be feasible in all cases, especially with smaller companies. In such instances, you need to consider the question "How many tapes are you physically capable of storing safely and securely onsite?" For instance, your backup tapes should be locked in a fire-resistant safe (one especially designed for tapes and magnetic storage media, and not one for documents). That way, should there be an accidental small fire, the safe can keep the tapes from melting for a few hours and at the same time secure them from theft. However, a typical office safe (22×18×18 inches) has only a small useable storage space (perhaps a couple of cubic feet) due to the thick walls. Alternatives include using bank safety deposit boxes, branch office locations, and even sending your backups home with the company's owner on a frequent basis.

You can choose a number of commonly used media rotation schemes for your backup needs. Two of them, the Grandfather-Father-Son (sometimes known as GFS) and the Tower of Hanoi methods, are discussed in the next section. Because these two rotation systems are based on the traditional incremental and differential backup methodologies, the concepts behind incremental and differential backups are discussed first.

Implementing a Backup Strategy

As previously mentioned, the ideal backup strategy is to do a full backup of all the filesystems frequently. This way, should you need to restore a single file or the whole system, you need to access only the latest backup tape set and go from there. Unfortunately, daily full backups are only possible for small systems where you have enough low system usage time (a backup "window") to create a complete backup. It also becomes expensive to continue purchasing new tapes (because none of the existing tapes can be reused during the archive-retaining time period). For most systems, a combination of full and incremental backups coupled with a tape rotation scheme, where a given set of tapes is reused, is the best option.

NOTE

Always schedule your system backup to take place during a time of little or no user activity—for two reasons. First, backup procedures take up system resources such as CPU cycles and put a high demand on hard disk access. This could degrade the system performance, and in some extreme cases, the backup process can consume considerable resources, resulting in a temporarily denial of service. Second, when users are on the system, there will always be opened files, which are not backed up (unless your backup software has an "open file agent" that handles them). Therefore, to back up as many changed files as possible, during the time that your backup job runs, you should shut down any applications, such as inventory database programs, that keep files open constantly, and you should also restrict user access to files. (Also see the "Database Backups: Cold or Hot?" section later in this chapter.)

The main drawback to incremental backups appears when you need to perform a full system restore. You need to first restore the last full backup and then apply all the incremental backups from that point onward. Therefore, you save some time during the backup process, but the restore phase takes a little longer. In the case of a partial restore, you can easily do that from the incremental backup, but you would have to scan through a number of media to locate the one where the desired data is stored.

There are two types of incremental backups: backup files changed since the last complete backup (often referred to as *differential backups*) or backup files changed since the last incremental backup. Assume that you have set up a backup schedule as listed in Table 10.1.

TABLE 10.1
Sample Differential Backup Schedule

DAY OF WEEK	BACKUP TYPE
Sunday	FB, Full backup
Monday	Differential backup of files changed since Sunday's full backup
Tuesday	Differential backup of files changed since Sunday's full backup
Wednesday	Differential backup of files changed since Sunday's full backup
Thursday	Differential backup of files changed since Sunday's full backup
Friday	Differential backup of files changed since Sunday's full backup
Saturday	No backup (assuming that no one uses the system on weekends)

If you need to restore a file lost on Thursday, you need to access only one tape: either the differential tape created on Wednesday (if the file was changed during the current week) or the full backup tape created on Sunday (if the file was not changed during the current week). To fully restore the system, you need only two tapes: the full backup tape and the latest differential tape. Under this schedule, the backup time gets longer as the week progresses because more and more files need to be backed up. However, it makes restoring files simple. This example is a simplification of the Grandfather-Father-Son rotation method.

NOTE

The main drawback of differential backups is that, as the week progresses, you have more and more changed files to back up as you are backing up files changed since the last *full* backup. Therefore, it is likely that by Friday, your backup time will take twice as long as it did on Monday.

Table 10.2 shows a different backup schedule. This one does a full backup at the beginning of the month, a weekly incremental on Mondays, and a daily incremental for the rest of the week.

TABLE 10.2
Another Backup Schedule Example

DAY	BACKUP TYPE
First of Month	FB, Full backup
Every Monday	Differential backup of files changed since the last full backup
Tuesday	Incremental backup of files changed since Monday
Wednesday	Incremental backup of files changed since Tuesday
Thursday	Incremental backup of files changed since Wednesday
Friday	Incremental backup of files changed since Thursday
Saturday	No backup (assuming that no one uses the system on weekends)
Sunday	No backup (assuming that no one uses the system on weekends)

Using this schedule, restoring files is a little more complicated than it was in the previous example. For instance, to restore a file you lost, you need to do the following:

1. Use the full backup tape if the file wasn't changed during the month.

2. Use the latest differential tape if the file was changed in the previous week but not during the current week.

3. Use the appropriate incremental tape from the current week if the file was changed this week.

The advantage of this sample schedule is that it takes less time per day for the backups because it backs up only those files changed from the previous work-day. The downside is that a little more work is required to restore a file.

The preceding two examples do not take into account multiple tape sets that would be necessary to go back to data from the previous week or month. The Grandfather-Father-Son and Tower of Hanoi rotation systems described in the following sections, on the other hand, use multiple tape sets. These two rotation methods are among the most often used by backup software.

Grandfather-Father-Son Rotation Method

The *Grandfather-Father-Son rotation scheme* (GFS for short) uses three "generations" of tapes (hence, the name), as illustrated in Table 10.3. It uses a total of

21 tapes. Of these 21 tapes, 4 are daily tape sets labeled Monday, Tuesday, Wednesday, and Thursday. Another 4 tapes are weekly tape sets labeled Friday1, Friday2, Friday3, and Friday4; for months that have five Fridays, a fifth weekly tape set labeled Friday5 is used. Also, 12 tapes labeled January, February, and so on through December act as monthly tapes.

TABLE 10.3
GFS Tape Rotation Scheme

	WEEK1	WEEK2	WEEK3	WEEK4
Daily	Monday	Monday	Monday	Monday
Daily	Tuesday	Tuesday	Tuesday	Tuesday
Daily	Wednesday	Wednesday	Wednesday	Wednesday
Daily	Thursday	Thursday	Thursday	Thursday
Weekly	Friday1	Friday2	Friday3	Friday4
Monthly				January

	WEEK5	WEEK6	WEEK7	WEEK8
Daily	Monday	Monday	Monday	Monday
Daily	Tuesday	Tuesday	Tuesday	Tuesday
Daily	Wednesday	Wednesday	Wednesday	Wednesday
Daily	Thursday	Thursday	Thursday	Thursday
Weekly	Friday1	Friday2	Friday3	Friday4
Monthly				February

This rotation scheme recycles the daily tapes the following week (the "sons" because they have the shortest life span), the weekly backup tapes after five weeks (the "fathers"), and the monthly tapes the following year (the "grandfathers").

NOTE

The monthly tapes are full backups, whereas the daily and weekly tapes are incrementals. As to which type of incremental backup (weekly or daily) you use, the choice is up to you. However, you should base your decision on these factors: how large a backup window you have, the amount of data to back up, and the throughput of your backup device.

CAUTION

The daily tapes get the most use; therefore, they are most prone to failure. Check these tapes regularly and often for wear-and-tear before using them.

Tower of Hanoi Rotation Method

The *Tower of Hanoi rotation scheme* is named after an ancient mathematical game of the same name. The rotation scheme is sometimes referred to as the *ABACABA* rotation method, based on the frequency with which tapes are rotated. Five or more tapes are needed in this implementation. To simplify the discussion, five tapes labeled A, B, C, D, and E are used.

NOTE

The French mathematician Edouard Lucas invented the Tower of Hanoi game, sometimes referred to as the Tower of Brahma or the End of the World Puzzle, in 1883.

The basic idea is that each of the five tapes is used at different rotation intervals. For example, tape A is used every other day; tape B, every fourth day; tape C, every eighth day; and tapes D and E, every sixteenth day. Typically, tapes A, B, and C are incremental backups, and tapes D and E are full backups. Table 10.4 shows the rotation pattern.

TABLE 10.4
Tower of Hanoi Tape Rotation Scheme

WEEK1	WEEK2	WEEK3	WEEK4
M,T,W,Th,F	M,T,W,Th,F	M,T,W,Th,F	M,T,W,Th,F
A,B,A,C,A	B,A,D,A,B	A,C,A,B,A	E,A,B,A,C

WEEK5	WEEK6	WEEK7	WEEK8
M,T,W,Th,F	M,T,W,Th,F	M,T,W,Th,F	M,T,W,Th,F
A,B,A,**D**,A	B,A,C,A,B	A,**E**,A,B,A	C,A,B,A,**D**

WEEK9	WEEK10	WEEK11	WEEK12
M,T,W,Th,F	M,T,W,Th,F	M,T,W,Th,F	M,T,W,Th,F
A,B,A,C,A	B,A,**D**,A,B	A,C,A,B,A	**E**,A,B,A,C

Notice that the pattern recycles itself every 31 days (one month), with the use of either tape D or E between the cycles. If you use fewer than five tapes, the cycle repeats itself every 15 days, which doesn't "map" nicely to the requirement of monthly backups. In the case where five tapes are used (as in the example presented here), tapes D and E are alternated in their usage within the cycle, so they are used once every 16 days. This difference is shown in bold in Table 10.4.

Some Tips and Tricks

Having chosen a backup media rotation scheme does not mean you now have a viable backup strategy. You also need to decide what to back up, how often to back up, and how best to keep track and safeguard your backup tapes. The following are some points to consider:

- **Automate your backup.** Most backup software allows you to set up a schedule so that the process initiates itself periodically without manual intervention. This is important because if you need to manually start the backup procedure daily, inevitably there will be a day that you forget because you don't have time, or something happens and prevents you from doing it. And, as Murphy's Law will have it, that is the one day you *will* need a backup!

  If you are using one of the Linux utilities, such as `tar`, for your backup, you can always automate it using one of the other Linux tools, such as `at` or `cron`. They are discussed later in this chapter.

TIP

You might want to get a backup device that holds multiple tapes (or whatever medium)—about twice as much as you require for a backup job—so that you have the option of not changing the tapes for one day.

- **Back up every file.** Do not limit backups to just documents or certain files; you will inevitably need one that was not backed up. Also, having a backup of every file, especially the system files, allows you to rebuild your entire server quickly, should there be a need. Having a pristine copy of your system utilities gives you a way to determine whether an intruder has installed any *rootkits* on your system. Of course, if your old backups contained already-compromised files, you wouldn't necessarily know by comparing existing files to those on the backup. (Refer to Chapter 12, "Intrusion Detection" for more information about rootkits.)

  You can elect to back up documents and files that change frequently (such as those in `/home`, `/etc`, and perhaps `/usr/local`) in your daily incremental backup, and include system files in the full backup. In general, you can safely exclude /tmp, /var/tmp, and /usr/var/tmp from being backed up because they usually only contain temporary files.

If you take intrusion detection seriously, you should also backup your /var/log directory. The log files can be very useful for intrusion situations and for general troubleshooting. However, log files tend to be large, so perhaps you should compress them—using gzip, for instance—before backing them up. Alternatively, you can use a central log server (see Chapter 13, "System Security") so the backup can exclude /var/log should backup media capacity become an issue.

WARNING

You *should* exclude /proc from your backups because it is not a true disk filesystem. Rather, /proc is really just a way for the kernel to provide you with information about the operating system and system memory. For instance, /proc/kcore is a pseudo-file containing the contents of your entire physical memory; backing it up is rather a waste of time and backup media storage space! (More information about /proc can be found in Chapter 7, "System Management and Monitoring.")

You might also want to avoid backing up the /mnt filesystem, unless you need to back up the files from your CD-ROM device, floppy drive, network file shares, or other mounted devices.

- **Make copies of your backup.** Storage media will fail, especially tapes, after prolonged and repeated use. It does not hurt to have multiple copies (or "generations") of your backups, even if they are older copies. When needed, an old copy is better than no copy at all.

  Some backup software includes a tape-to-tape copy feature that you can use to make a duplicate of your backup without having to actually perform another backup.

- **Keep offsite copies.** You never know when a fire, flood, theft, or some natural disaster will make your office inaccessible for days or weeks and your offsite copy is your only readily accessible copy. One option is to keep your current weekly backup onsite (in a fire-resistant safe, for instance) and send the previous week's backup to a secure offsite location.

TIP

There are companies that specialize in secure and climate-controlled storage for both documents and backup media. They often provide a courier service to pick up your new set of tapes and drop off an older set for reuse. Check your local yellow pages. In a pinch, a bank safety deposit box can be a good alternative.

- **Verify your backups.** You need to know whether you can ever restore from your backups. Most backup software has a verification feature; although it adds to the backup time, use it whenever possible. Also, periodically restore a few files at random and verify them yourself.

- **Label all media.** Be sure to label and date all media—tapes, DVDs, whatever—used in a backup. If you have to use multiple items, make sure they are numbered sequentially. If you send backups offsite, document them so you know which tapes are where.

- **Keep track of where your files are located.** As you can see from the Tower of Hanoi discussion, keeping track of which tape to use when can be complicated. Labeling all your media is certainly a starting point. Fortunately, many backup programs logically label the media so that they can detect whether the right one has been inserted. At the same time, the backup software keeps track of what files have been backed up on which tape using its own database. Make sure that this database is backed up as well.

- **Back up your system before making major changes.** When you upgrade your system or make any configuration changes, you should definitely make a backup of at least the / (root), /usr, and /home filesystems (if they are not on the same disk partition), if not a full backup. Although such failures don't happen often, it is possible for a critical library or package not to upgrade properly, crippling your system.

NOTE

A root filesystem generally contains everything needed to support a functional Linux system, such as the following:

- Minimum set of directories, such as /dev, /proc, /bin, /sbin, /etc, /lib, /tmp

- Basic set of utilities, such as sh, ls, cp, mv, and so on

- Minimum set of configuration files, such as rc, inittab, fstab, and so on

- Device files, such as /dev/hd*, /dev/tty*, /dev/fd0, and so on

- Runtime libraries to provide basic functions used by utilities

Before we discuss the actual backup tools, there is one more topic to consider as part of your backup strategy: how best to back up a database application, such as Oracle or MySQL.

Database Backups: Cold or Hot?

When you are backing up files belonging to a database application, such as Oracle or MySQL, or applications that constantly keep certain files open, such as Lotus Notes, you need to give some extra thought than you would when backing up typical documents, such as OpenOffice files. There are two methods of performing a backup on a database: cold and hot. In a *cold backup,* an application is taken offline, which means there's no user access to the data, and the data is backed up; this is the way backups are normally done. In a *hot backup*, on the other hand, the application remains online, and user access is retained while the backup is performed.

A cold backup is usually the optimal solution for those applications that can tolerate multiple hours of downtime to perform the backup. Some applications that used to be backed up cold have now grown so large that the backup cannot be completed during the allotted time window. If a cold backup is still desired, one way is to take a point-in-time "snapshot" of the data, and within a matter of minutes (depending on the size of the data files involved), the application is brought online. The snapshot can then be mounted back onto the application server, or mounted directly to the backup server, and backed up. Total downtime for the application in such a case is the time required to stop the application, perform the snapshot, and then restart the application.

NOTE

To take a snapshot of an application's database, either you need an application that provides this feature, or you need to obtain additional software and/or hardware.

TIP

It is possible to create a *snapshot device* that is an alias for an existing Logical Volume (LV). The snapshot device, which can be accessed read-only, contains a point-in-time image of the LV; in other words, while applications continue to change the data on the LV, this logical device contains the unchanging image of the LV at the time when the snapshot was created. This makes it possible for you to do a consistent backup without shutting anything down or using any special software. This method is independent of any software because it happens in the LV Manager abstraction layer. SUSE has included a Logical Volume Manager since SUSE LINUX 6.3. For details on performing backups using LVM snapshots, see http://www.tldp.org/HOWTO/LVM-HOWTO/index.html.

If you want to perform a hot backup on an application that has constantly open files, the application must have a hot backup feature, and the backup software needs hot backup support for the specific application. Generally speaking, in hot backup mode, instead of writing to the live data, the application queues up the updates in a special file so the backup software can get a complete backup of the database. The special file is backed up next. After this is done, the application is then allowed to apply the queued-up changes to the database, thus bringing everything up to date.

Therefore, to decide whether you should perform a cold or hot backup of your database application files, you need to take the following factors into consideration:

- Can the application data files be backed up cold and not violate their integrity? If not, does the application have a hot backup feature?

- Does your backup software support the hot backup option of that particular application?

- How much of a downtime window do you have to back up this application's data files? Perhaps the window is wide enough for a cold backup, which would make life a lot easier.

If you have small downtime window but have sufficient disk space, perhaps using the Logical Volume snapshot feature is an option.

Backup and Restore Tools

There are a variety of methods of performing backups with SLES. They include the general-purpose command-line tools included with every Linux distribution, such as `tar`, `dd`, `dump`, and `cpio`. Newer Linux distributions, such as SLES 9, include some text-based utilities, such as AMANDA (*Advanced Maryland Automatic Network Disk Archiver*) and `taper`. These utilities are designed to add a more user-friendly interface to the backup and restore procedures. GUI-based utilities are available as well, such as the System Backup and Restore modules in YaST. Finally, many commercial backup utilities are also available, such as BRU, CTAR, ARCserve, Legato NetWorker, and System Backup Administrator. Any one of these backup solutions can provide protection for your valuable data.

CAUTION

When you are selecting a backup utility, ensure it supports the filesystem types that you are using. For instance, Legato NetWorker 7.2 for Linux supports ext2/ext3, ReiserFS, and JFS (Journaled File System), but not XFS.

When deciding on a backup solution, you need to consider the following factors:

- **Portability**—Is backup portability (that is, the ability to back up data from your SLES server and restore it to another server running a different Linux distribution or implementation of Unix) important to you? For example, can you port the backup from SLES 9 to HP/UX? If so, you'll probably want to choose one of the standard command-line tools such as `tar`, `dd`, or `cpio`, because you can be reasonably sure that such tools will be available on any Linux/Unix system.

- **Unattended backup**—Is the ability to automate backups so that they can be performed at regular intervals without human intervention important to you? If so, you will need to choose both a tool and a backup medium that support such a backup scheme.

- **Ease of use**—Is a user-friendly interface important to you? If so, you will likely want to choose a tool that provides either a text- or GUI-based interface. Commercial products may provide the easiest interfaces as well as added technical support.

- **Remote backups**—Do you require the ability to start backups and restores from a remote machine? If so, you'll probably want to choose one of the command-line tools or text-based utilities instead of the GUI-based utilities (unless you have a reasonably fast network connection and the ability to run remote X sessions).

- **Network backups**—Is performing backups and restores to and from networked hosts important to you? If so, you'll probably want to use one of several of the command-line utilities (such as `tar`) that support network access to backup devices, or a specialized utility such as AMANDA or one of the commercial products.

- **Media type support**—Backups can be stored on a variety of media, such as tape, an extra hard drive, ZIP drives, or rewritable DVDs. Consider cost versus reliability, storage capacity, and transfer speed and select a backup application that supports your chosen device type.

TIP

Often, even if your selected tool doesn't have a built-in scheduler to automate and run backups unattended, you may be able to automate such backups by using the `cron` facilities.

In the following sections, we discuss methods for performing backups and restores using the following tools:

- `tar`
- `dump` and `restore`
- `cpio`
- `dd`
- `rsync`
- AMANDA
- YaST's System Backup and Restore modules

Making Tarballs

The `tar` (tape archive) utility is probably *the* most commonly used application for data backup on Linux/Unix systems. Why? Because as with `vi` or `ls`, you can be guaranteed that any Linux/Unix system will have `tar`. Furthermore, this tool has been ported to a wide range of hardware platforms and operating systems. Therefore, if you need your backups to be portable across different versions of SUSE, other Linux distributions, to Unix platforms (such as HP/UX or AIX), other operating systems (such as Windows), or even to mainframes, `tar` would be an excellent choice.

`tar` was designed to create a tape archive (a large file that contains, or "archives," other files). In addition to file contents, an archive includes header information to each file inside it. This header data can be used when extracting files from the archive to restore information about the files, such as file permissions, ownerships, and modification dates. An archive file can be saved to disk (and later copied to tape or transferred to another storage medium), written directly to tape, or transmitted across the network while it is being created.

NOTE

The `tar` archive file is officially referred to as a *tarfile*. However, it is often (affectionately) called a *tarball* instead. Frequently, source codes for Linux/Unix-related applications are available as tarballs on the Internet.

By convention, tarfiles use `.tar` as their filename extension. You will also encounter `.tar.gz` or `.tgz` extensions, which identify `tar` archives that have been compressed using `gzip`.

Although many command-line options are available with `tar`, Table 10.5 shows a list of the most commonly used option switches.

TABLE 10.5
Commonly Used Options for `tar`

OPTION	DESCRIPTION
-c	Creates a new archive. This option implies the -r option.
-exclude *file*	Excludes named files from being backed up or restored.
-f *devicename*	Specifies the output device for the tarfile. If the name is -, `tar` writes to `stdout` or reads from `stdin`, whichever is appropriate. Thus, `tar` can be used as the head or tail of a command pipeline. If -f is omitted, `tar` uses /dev/rmt0. It also checks to see what the TAPE environment variable is set to if no /dev/rmt0 exists.
-j	Filters the archive through the `bzip2` program, which is quite a bit better than `gzip` at compressing text but is quite a bit slower.
-p	Extracts all permission information.
-r	Appends files to a tarball.
-t	Lists the contents of an archive. You can add the -v option to get additional information for the files. The listing is similar to the format produced by the `ls -l` command.
-u	Updates an archive. The named files are added to the tarfile if they are not already there or have been modified since last written to that tarfile. This option implies the -r option.
-v	Turns on verbose mode. Normally, `tar` works silently. This option causes `tar` to show the name (including path) of each file processed.
-V *label*	Adds a (logical) volume label to the archive for identification.
-W	Verifies the archive after writing it.
-x *file*	Extracts, or restores, from an archive. The named files are extracted from the tarball and written to the current directory. If a named file matches a directory whose contents have been written into the tarball, this directory is (recursively) extracted. The owner, modification time stamp, and mode are restored (if possible). If the filename is not given, the entire content of the archive is extracted. Uses the file or directory's *relative* pathname when appropriate; otherwise, `tar` will not find a match.
-z	Filters the archive through the `gzip` program.
-Z	Filters the archive through the `compress` program.

CAUTION

The -r and -u options cannot be used with many tape drives due to limitations in those drives, such as the absence of the backspace or append capability.

NOTE

Some of the `tar` switches have mnemonic equivalence so the switch is more intuitive. For instance, instead of -x, you can use --extract or --get. Refer to the `tar` man pages for more details.

The general syntax for the `tar` command is as follows:

```
tar [options] filename
```

Following are some examples of the use of `tar` in backing up and restoring files:

- Copies all files in /home and below to the archive file called home-directory-backup.tar in the current directory; the verbose mode is on:

  ```
  tar -cvf ./home-directory-backup.tar /home
  ```

- Copies all files in /usr/lib and below to a tarball on a tape drive; verbose mode is on:

  ```
  tar -cvf /dev/st0 /usr/lib
  ```

- Reads the table of contents from tape drive /dev/st0:

  ```
  tar -tvf /dev/st0
  ```

- Extracts *all* files from the tarball located on the tape drive:

  ```
  tar -xvf /dev/st0
  ```

- Extracts all files from the tarball located on the tape drive and places them in /home/temp:

  ```
  tar -xvf /dev/st0 -C /home/temp
  ```

- Extracts only the file called chapter.10 (located in the SLES directory) from the archive located on the tape drive (note that a relative path is used):

  ```
  tar -xvf /dev/st0 SLES/chapter.10
  ```

- Duplicates the contents from the directory /home/peter to the current working directory; file permissions and ownerships are preserved:

  ```
  (cd /home/peter; tar -cpf - *) | tar -xf -
  ```

The parentheses in the command instruct the shell to execute the commands inside them first before piping the output to the second `tar` command.

TIP

You can use the following handy `tar` command in a script (and have it executed by a `cron` job) that backs up your entire system onto the tape drive (/dev/st0). The /tmp directory, /proc pseudo-filesystem, any mounted filesystems in /mnt, as well as Squid proxy server's cache files, and the log file for the `tar` job are excluded from the backup; insert additional --exclude parameters for other directories to be excluded from backup:

```
tar -cvpf /dev/st0 \
-V "full system backup on 'date'" \
-directory / -exclude=mnt -exclude=proc \
-exclude=tmp -exclude=var/spool/squid \
-exclude=home/root/tar.logfile . > /home/root/tar.logfile
```

A logical volume label with the date and time at which the `tar` command was executed is included in the tarball to aid with identification. (If you have many files to exclude, you can place them in a text file, one name per line, and use the -X *file* switch.)

`tar` has a built-in incremental backup option. It uses an ASCII file to keep track of files and directories that were backed up. To use this feature, do the following:

1. Create a full backup of the desired directory or directories using the -g option. For example,
   ```
   tar -czpf /backup/home_full_backup.tgz \
   -g /backup/home_tracking_file /home
   ```

2. Create daily incremental backups using the following commands:
   ```
   tar -czpf /backup/home_monday_backup.tgz \
   -g /backup/home_tracking_file /home
   tar -czpf /backup/home_tuesday_backup.tgz \
   -g /backup/home_tracking_file /home
   (and so on for other days)
   ```

Because you are using the same "tracking" file, `tar` is able to tell what files were previously backed up and when. Subsequent tarballs will contain only files that have been modified or created since the last backup (as recorded in the tracking file).

WARNING

The tar man page describes a -P (or --absolute-paths) switch, which you use to not strip the leading / from pathnames. You should *not* exercise this option as the default mode (to use relative paths) to protect you from accidentally over-writing critical files during a restore operation when you didn't mean to. If you use it, instead of the files going into your current working directory, they are written to the original location!

Archiving Data with cpio

The cpio (copy in-out) program is similar to tar in that it is a general-purpose utility for copying file archives. However, it can use archive files in many different formats, including tarballs. A cpio archive can span multiple tapes or disks, and this capability is a big plus for dealing with large files and filesystems.

cpio operates in one of three modes:

- **Copy-out mode**—cpio -o reads from stdin to obtain a list of filenames and copies those files to stdout together with pathname and status information. Output is padded to a 512-byte boundary by default or to the user-specified block size or to some device-dependent block size, where necessary (as with certain types of tapes).

TIP

A typical way to generate the list of filenames for the copy-out mode is to use either the ls or find command.

- **Copy-in mode**—cpio -i extracts files from an archive, or the standard input (stdin), that is assumed to be the product of a previous cpio -o operation. Only files with names that match patterns are selected. Extracted files are conditionally created and copied into the current directory tree based on the specified command-line switches. The permissions of the file are those of the previous cpio -o command. Owner and group are the same as the current user unless the current user is root. If this is the case, owner and group are the same as those resulting from the previous cpio -o command. Note that if cpio -i tries to create a file that already exists and the existing file is the same age or newer, cpio displays a warning message and does not overwrite the file. (The -u option can be used to force an overwrite of the existing file.)

- **Copy-pass mode**—cpio -p reads from stdio a list of filenames and copies these files from one directory tree to another, essentially combining the copy-out and copy-in steps without actually using an archive.

Similar to tar, cpio uses many command-line switches. Table 10.6 shows a list of the most commonly used options.

TABLE 10.6
Commonly Used Options for cpio

OPTION	DESCRIPTION
-A	Appends to the existing archive. The archive must be specified using either -F or -O. Valid only in copy-out mode.
-B	Sets the I/O block size to 5,120 bytes instead of the default 512 bytes. -B is meaningful only with data directed to or from a character block device such as /dev/st0; thus, it is meaningless in the copy-pass mode. It cannot be used in conjunction with -C.
-C bufsize	Sets I/O block size to bufsize instead of the default 512 bytes. Like -B, -C is meaningful only when using devices such as /dev/st0. It cannot be used in conjunction with -B.
-f	Copies only files that do not match any of the given patterns.
-F file	Uses file for the archive instead of stdin or stdout.
-i	(Copy-in mode) Extracts files from stdin.
-I file	Reads the archive from the specified file instead of stdio. This option is valid only in the copy-in mode.
-o	(Copy-out mode) Reads filenames from stdin and copies those files to stdout.
-O file	Directs output to file instead of stdout. This option is valid only in the copy-out mode.
-p	(Copy-pass mode) Reads filenames from stdin and copies those files to stdout. This option is used mainly to copy directory trees.
-t	Prints a table of contents of the input. No files are created (mutually exclusive with -V).
-u	Unconditionally replaces all files, without asking whether to replace existing newer files with older ones.
-v	Turns on verbose mode. Lists the files processed. When this option is used with the -t option, the table of contents looks like the output from the ls -l command.
-V	Turns on special verbose mode. Prints a dot for each file processed. This option is useful to assure the user that cpio is working without printing out all the filenames.

The general syntax for the `cpio` command is as follows:

```
cpio [options] [filename]
```

Following are some examples of the use of `cpio` in backing up and restoring files:

- Copies the files in the current directory to a `cpio` archive file called `newfile`:

```
ls | cpio -VoO newfile
```

- Prints out the table of contents from the archive file:

```
cpio -tvF newfile
```

or

```
cpio -itvI newfile
```

- Extracts all the files from the archive file into the current directory, over-writing any existing files:

```
cpio -ivuI newfile
```

- Using the copy-pass mode (-p switch), copies or links (the -1 option) all the files and directories from `/home/carol` to the `newdir` directory located in the current path:

```
(find /home/carol -depth -print | cpio -pdlmv newdir) 2>cpio.log
```

The -d switch tells `cpio` to create directories as necessary, -m says to retain the modification times, and -v turns on the verbose mode. All log messages from `cpio` are redirected to the `cpio.log` file in the current directory. Notice that `stderr` redirected as `stdout` is a valid output path, so `cpio` logs messages to `stderr` instead. `Newdir` must exist; otherwise, the `cpio` command will fail.

The choice between using `cpio` or `tar` to perform backups is largely a matter of preference. However, because of the simpler command syntax and wide availability on other operating systems, `tar` seems to be the more popular choice.

Converting and Copying Data Using dd

The `dd` program is another oldie but goldie that does data conversion and transfers. It was originally designed for importing mainframe data to Unix systems. On the mainframe, the data is transferred to tape using the EBCDIC character encoding scheme. To use such data on most Unix machines, `dd` was used to read the tapes and change the coding to ASCII. However, with the availability of TCP/IP on mainframes, `dd` is no longer needed because FTP and other IP-based protocols can do the same job over the network (and eliminate the need for tapes).

dd can strip file headers, extract parts of binary files, and write into the middle of floppy disks; it is even used by the Linux kernel makefiles to create boot images. It can be used to copy and convert magnetic tape formats, convert between ASCII and EBCDIC, swap bytes, and force upper- and lowercase conversions.

WARNING

Because dd works with volume headers, boot records, and similar system data areas, its misuse can potentially trash your hard disks and filesystems. As a result, some people refer to dd as "Destroy Disk" or "Delete Data" because if it is misused, accidentally or otherwise, a disk partition or output file can be trashed very quickly.

One common use of dd today is to create disk images of your filesystems or to rip CD or DVD contents to an ISO image that you can later access (without having to use the CD or DVD again) by mounting the images.

Unlike most of the Linux/Unix commands that use command-line switches, dd uses a keyword=value format for its parameters. This was allegedly modeled after IBM System/360 JCL (Job Control Language), which had an elaborate DD (Dataset Definition) specification for I/O devices.

Most of the time, you need to use only two keywords: if=*infile* and of=*outfile*. Input defaults to stdin and output defaults to stdout if these two keywords are not specified. For instance, to copy one file to another, use the following:

```
Athena:/home/admin # dd if=/etc/passwd of=passwd.backup
4+1 records in
4+1 records out
```

By default, dd copies files in 512-byte records. The preceding output (4+1 records) indicates that four full 512-byte records plus one partial 512-byte record were read and then written. (In this case, /etc/passwd is 2,185 bytes in size.) You can modify the buffer size used, as in this example:

```
Athena:/home/admin # dd if=/etc/passwd of=passwd.backup bs=3000
0+1 records in
0+1 records out
```

The following are some additional sample uses of the dd command:

- To create a disk image of a 1.44MB floppy disk (the bs= specifies the standard geometry of a 1.44MB-formatted floppy disk: 18 sectors of 512 bytes, 2 heads, and 80 cylinders, for a total of 1,474,560 bytes; this results in a single 1,474,560-byte read request to /dev/fd0 and a single 1,474,560-byte write request to /tmp/floppy.image):

```
dd bs=2x80x18b if=/dev/fd0 of=/tmp/floppy.image
1+0 records in
1+0 records out
```

- To write the same disk image back onto a floppy disk:

```
dd bs=2x80x18b if=/tmp/floppy.image of=/dev/fd0
1+0 records in
1+0 records out
```

- To make a complete copy of a partition:

```
dd if=/dev/sda1 of=/backup/boot.partition.image
```

- To make a backup copy of your Master Boot Record (MBR), which is the first block on the disk:

```
dd if=/dev/sda of=/backup/mbr_backup count=1
```

- To make an ISO image of a DVD disk (assuming the DVD drive is /dev/hdc):

```
dd if=/dev/hdc of=/backup/dvd.image
```

To mount an ISO image created using dd for access, use mount -o loop /path/image.name /mountpoint, for instance,

```
mount -o loop /backup/dvd.image /mnt
```

See man mount for additional information.

TIP

Depending on the file sizes involved, it may be advantageous to use a larger buffer size because doing so reduces the number of system calls made and performance improvement may be significant. If the input and output devices are different (say, from a file to a tape), you can use ibs= and obs= to set different buffer sizes for the reads and writes, respectively; bs= sets the same size for both reads and writes.

You can obtain a complete listing of all keywords available by using the
dd --help command.

Using dump **and** restore

The dump program performs an incremental filesystem save operation. It can
back up all specified files (normally either a whole filesystem or files within a
filesystem that have changed after a certain date or since the last dump operation). The output (known as a *dump image* or archive) can be a magnetic tape,
floppy disks, or a disk file. The output device can be either local or remote.
The restore program examines the dumps to recover individual files or an
entire filesystem.

NOTE

On some versions of Unix, dump is referred to as ufsdump, whereas restore may
be called restore or ufsrestore. On HP/UX, fbackup performs similar functions
to dump.

CAUTION

dump works only with ext2/ext3 type filesystems.

dump : **THE GOOD, THE BAD, AND THE UGLY**

A simplistic and primitive tool, dump was designed to work at the inode level,
but it does come with a brilliant feature for incremental archiving. It identifies
newly created or modified files after the previous backup and efficiently stores
them to the dump image very quickly.

NOTE

Every Linux/Unix file has an inode. Inodes are data structures that hold descriptive information about a file, such as file type, permissions, owners, time stamps,
size, and pointers to data blocks on disk. (They act like the Directory Entry Table,
or DET, entries found in NetWare or the File Allocation Table, or FAT, entries found
in Windows.)

For example, suppose a file titled foobar was backed up during the last archiving and removed afterward. On the next incremental archiving, dump puts the
record in the archive as "Hey, there used to be a file foobar at inode xxx, but it
was removed." During a full filesystem restore process, deleted files are not res-
urrected. If you use, for example, tar for your regular incremental backup

tasks and attempt a full restoration one day, you may run out of disk space by trying to restore a large number of files that had been previously removed. With dump, you will never face such a problem because of the way it handles incremental backups.

Incremental backups by dump are controlled by assigning a *dump level* to a particular backup. There are 10 dump levels, ranging from 0 through 9. When a dump of a certain level N is performed, all files that have changed since the last dump of level $N-1$ or lower are backed up. For instance, if a level 2 dump was done on Monday, followed by a level 4 dump on Tuesday, a subsequent level 3 dump on Wednesday would contain all files modified or added since the level 2 (Monday) backup.

NOTE

A level 0 dump would back up the entire filesystem.

The main advantage of dump is that it can simplify your backup strategy because it looks directly at the filesystem rather than from user space (like tar or cpio). For example, you don't have to mess around with scripts that try to figure what has changed since your last backup; therefore, implementing an incremental backup solution is much easier. Another benefit is that you don't have to worry about file permissions or ownerships being lost in the backup and restore process, not to mention the creation time or last-modified time of a file, because this information is included when dump scans the filesystem. The restore program is also simple to use whether you're trying to fully restore a filesystem or just pulling out an important OpenOffice document file that one of your coworkers deleted.

There are a few things that might make dump a poor choice for a backup utility in your environment, however. You should keep these factors in mind before deciding to deploy dump for your setup:

- **Ext2/ext3 filesystem types only**—Because dump is closely tied to the filesystem, it is designed for ext2fs and ext3fs filesystems only. Unfortunately, the default filesystem type used by SUSE is ReiserFS. So, unless you changed the filesystem type when creating your filesystem, dump will be unable to help you. Also, dump works with local filesystems only.

- **Version dependency**—dump is very much a version-dependent program. Sometimes dump is not backward compatible with itself, which means that if you want to restore a dump image that was made with dump-0.4b35, you need to have a copy of the restore binary from that same version available. In an environment where you may be frequently upgrading an operating system (such as to apply security patches) or the versions of software available for it, dump probably is not an ideal solution. One way around this problem is to keep a backup copy of your backup utilities handy on a CD-ROM or a vendor/OS-neutral archive on tape (like tar or cpio).

- **Filesystems *should* be inactive during backup**—The filesystems should be inactive when dump is performing their backup; otherwise, the dump output might be inconsistent (as files may be changed during backup), and restore can get confused when doing incremental restores from dump tapes that were made on active filesystems. It is *strongly* recommended that a level 0 (and perhaps even a level 1) dump be made when the filesystems are inactive, while the other levels may be made with the system in multiuser mode. If you decide to perform a dump in single-user mode, you must choose between convenience or data integrity.

NOTE

A filesystem is considered inactive when it is unmounted or when the system is in single-user mode or at run level 1. (Refer to Chapter 3 for details about run levels.) Of course, if the filesystem is unmounted, you can access it for backup. Furthermore, you cannot unmount the root filesystem; otherwise, you wouldn't have a running system! If you need to back up the root filesystem using dump, boot your system using a rescue disk and run dump from there.

- **Difficult to exclude files and directories from being dumped**— Because dump works directly with filesystems, it is labor intensive to exclude certain files and directories on a filesystem from being backed up by dump.

TIP

You can exclude a file or directory from being dumped in three ways. First, you can use the -e switch to specify the list of inode numbers of the files or directories (determined using stat *filename*) to be excluded. Second, you can place the inode numbers in a file and pass it to dump using the -E switch. Third, you can manually flag the files and directories to be excluded with the d attribute using chattr.

- **Know thy mt commands**—dump doesn't have any built-in capability to manipulate tape storage media like commercial backup software utilities do. This means that if you're backing up to tape, you'll need to become familiar with the mt (**m**agnetic **t**ape) commands and mtx commands if you have a tape changer.

NOTE

The mt utility enables you to manipulate tape drives. With mt, you can rewind, forward, and position the tape, as well as check the drive status. It is a must-have tool if you want to use dump and restore with tape drives. If possible, it is a good idea to prepare a tape for training purposes and practice using it. Some commands of mt are drive dependent, so you should check the tape drive's manual carefully to find out which commands are available for your drive.

Now that you know the good and the bad about dump, we'll briefly discuss how to use dump and restore.

BACKING UP USING dump

The man page for dump includes several command-line switches. Table 10.7 shows a brief summary of the important ones you should be familiar with when using dump.

TABLE 10.7
Noteworthy dump Command-Line Options

OPTION	DESCRIPTION
-[0-9]	Tells dump what level of backup to perform. Full filesystem dumps are level 0 by default, and you can specify nine more levels (1 through 9) that can be used to determine which files are to be backed up. Whenever a dump is made, it will back up only the files that have changed since the last *lowest* level of dump. The default is -9.
-a	Tells dump to try to autosize the dump image. It bypasses all tape length calculations and writes until the device returns an "end-of-media" signal. Normally, you would use this option when you have a tape changer and want to have your dump span multiple tapes, you want to append to an existing dump on a tape, or you're dumping to stdout (so you can pipe it to another command-line utility). This option is also useful when the tape drive has hardware compression.
-A *file*	Archives the table of contents to *file* so it can be used by restore to determine whether a file that is to be restored is in the dump image.

TABLE 10.7
Noteworthy dump Command-Line Options (continued)

OPTION	DESCRIPTION
-f *file*	Tells dump where the dump image goes. It defaults to /dev/tape, and it also checks to see what the TAPE environment variable is set to if no /dev/tape exists. This option is useful if you would like to send the dump to a remote device (/dev/rmt*), a file on the local filesystem (or an NFS mount), or pipe the results back to standard input. To output to stdout, specify a filename of -.
-L *label*	Specifies a label for the dump image. Unfortunately, you have only 16 characters to work with here, so you need to be careful what you use. One suggestion is to use the device name (such as a label of /dev/sda6).
-q	Makes dump abort immediately if it encounters a situation that would normally require user input. This option is useful for scripting automated backups because dump reads its input straight from the tty instead of from stdin, which prevents you from using something like yes no | dump -0au /dev/hda1 in your script. This option did not appear in dump until version 0.4b24.
-u	This option is very important if you are planning to make incremental backups of a filesystem. This option tells dump to update the /etc/dumpdates file, which essentially records the date and time you ran the dump and the level the dump was set to run at. If you forget this, you will *continuously* be doing full level (level 0) backups.
-z[*compression_level*]	Compresses every block to be written on the tape using the zlib library. This option works only when dumping to a file or pipe or when dumping to a tape drive if the tape drive is capable of writing variable length blocks. The (optional) parameter specifies the compression level zlib will use. The default compression level is 2. If the optional parameter is specified, there must be no whitespace between the option letter and the parameter—for example, -z3. You need at least the 0.4b22 version of restore to extract compressed tapes. Tapes written using compression are not compatible with the BSD tape format.

NOTE

dump sends all of its output through stderr, so a command such as the following is valid:

dump -0af /tmp/backup /home 2>/tmp/backup.log

This example sends the dump image to /tmp/backup and causes the stderr output from dump to go to /tmp/backup.log.

Running dump may seem complicated, but it is actually fairly straightforward. A typical command looks like this:

Athena:~ # **dump -0au -L "/dev/hda1: /boot" -f /dev/st0 /boot**

When dump is invoked normally, backup proceeds with some messages printed on the console, as shown in Listing 10.1. It is a good idea to leave this session in the foreground rather than to send it to the background until you are convinced everything works fine. If dump reaches the end of tape or if some error occurs, you will be requested to make some choices in the interactive session.

LISTING 10.1

Sample dump Log Messages

```
DUMP: Date of this level 0 dump: Sat Jan 29 17:03:55 2005
DUMP: Dumping /dev/hda1 (/boot) to /dev/st0
DUMP: Added inode 21 to exclude list (journal inode)
DUMP: Label: /dev/hda1: /boot
DUMP: mapping (Pass I) [regular files]
DUMP: mapping (Pass II) [directories]
DUMP: estimated 11000 tape blocks.
DUMP: Volume 1 started with block 1 at:
➥Sat Jan 29 17:03:55 2005
DUMP: dumping (Pass III) [directories]
DUMP: dumping (Pass IV) [regular files]
DUMP: Closing /dev/st0
DUMP: Volume 1 completed at: Sat Jan 29 17:03:56 2005
DUMP: Volume 1 10940 tape blocks (10.68MB)
DUMP: Volume 1 took 0:00:01
DUMP: Volume 1 transfer rate: 10940 kB/s
DUMP: 10940 tape blocks (10.68MB) on 1 volume(s)
DUMP: finished in 1 seconds, throughput 10940 kBytes/sec
DUMP: Date of this level 0 dump: Sat Jan 29 17:03:55 2005
DUMP: Date this dump completed: Sat Jan 29 17:03:56 2005
DUMP: Average transfer rate: 10940 kB/s
DUMP: DUMP IS DONE
```

The log messages in Listing 10.1 also indicate whether any files (inodes) are skipped. In the example, the log shows inode 21 was excluded from the backup. The reason is that inode 21 turns out to be the journal for the ext3 filesystem; therefore, it doesn't need to be backed up and can be excluded from future backups.

When the `dump` session finishes properly, you can dump another filesystem if enough tape capacity remains.

TIP

It is always a good idea to first check the filesystem's integrity prior to doing a dump, especially when it is a full dump. To do this, after you have entered single-user mode, unmount the filesystems one by one and check them using e2fsck:

`Athena:~ # umount /usr/home; e2fsck -afv /dev/sdd1`

Check all the filesystems that are to be backed up, preferably after unmounting them. Because you cannot unmount the root filesystem, you may want to remount it as read-only to prevent its data (thus the inodes) from being modified and check it with e2fsck:

`Athena:~ # mount -r -n -o remount / ; e2fsck -afv /dev/hda1`

After all the checks are done, remount it again with read-write so that dump can log the backup information:

`Athena:~ # mount -w -n -o remount /`

A simple incremental backup strategy is shown in Table 10.8.

TABLE 10.8
A Simple Incremental Backup Strategy Using dump

DAY	DUMP LEVEL
Day 1	Level 0
Day 2	Level 1
Day 3	Level 2
Day 4	Level 3
Day 5	Level 4
Day 6	Level 5
Day 7	Level 6
Day 8	Level 7

TABLE 10.8
A Simple Incremental Backup Strategy Using dump (continued)

DAY	DUMP LEVEL
Day 9	Level 8
Day 10	Level 9
Day 11	Level 0 (and the sequence repeats)

After Day 2, dump backs up updated files only. And on Day 11, you make a complete backup again and the sequence repeats.

Some people use a more elaborate method, using the Tower of Hanoi sequence, for the dump-level scheduling. This method may employ the following sample sequences:

```
Rotation 1: 0, 3, 2, 5, 4, 7, 6, 9, 8
Rotation 2: 1, 3, 2, 5, 4, 7, 6, 9, 8
Rotation 3: 1, 3, 2, 5, 4, 7, 6, 9, 8
```

In this case, you start with a level 0 dump and then perform daily incremental backups based on the sequence. The pattern repeats itself after 27 days.

Note that under this scenario, each level 0 dump should be made on a new tape and stored at a safe place. For level 1 backups, use two different tapes (or as many as the number of rotations). For other dump levels, one tape per level is sufficient, and they can be reused from one rotation to another.

CAUTION

If you are considering the Tower of Hanoi sequence for your dump-level schedule, pay attention to the section "A Few Words of Caution About Dump Levels" later in this chapter.

RECOVERING DATA USING restore

There are two main methods of restoring files from a dump archive: either interactively (when the -i switch is specified) or through a full restore. You point restore to a dump image, and the selected files are extracted into the current directory. Table 10.9 shows some of the important restore command-line switches.

TIP

A piped combination of dump and restore can duplicate the contents of one filesystem onto another filesystem.

TABLE 10.9
Noteworthy `restore` Command-Line Options

OPTION	DESCRIPTION
-C	Compares the contents of the archive with the current filesystem and no restore takes place. You can use this option to check what has changed since your last backup.
-f *file*	Specifies the archive file. Like dump, it also defaults to /dev/tape and will check the TAPE environment variable if that fails.
-h *directory*	Extracts only the *directory* when specified, rather than its contents.
-i	Performs interactive restoration of specified files. This option also allows you to browse the dump image and flag files or directories to be extracted later.
-r	Allows you to rebuild the filesystem from the dump image. Use this option if you need to do bare-metal recovery from a tape. It expects a clean filesystem (that is, it expects you to have just run mke2fs). This operation is *not* interactive and should not be done unless you intend to actually restore the filesystem itself rather than just extract a couple of files.
-R	Resumes interrupted full restoration.
-s *fileno*	Specifies the position of the archive on the tape. This capability is useful when there are multiple dump images on the same media.
-t *file*	Lists filenames on the backup archive but does not restore them.
-T	Specifies the temporary directory.
-v	Produces verbose output.
-x *file* -X *fileset*	Extracts only the named files from the archive. The uppercase -X instead reads a list of files to restore from a flat ASCII text file.
-y	Does not query on error.

The **restore** utility is not too difficult to use but can be rather tricky when you're dealing with multiple dump images on the same media. Therefore, you should be familiar with it before you really have to use it. The following are two sample **restore** commands:

- Retrieves all the files from the archive in tape media and writes them under the current directory:

  ```
  restore -rf /dev/st0
  ```

- Performs an interactive restoration from the third dump image on the tape media:

  ```
  restore -is 3 -f /dev/st0
  ```

TIP

When you are performing a partial restore interactively, it is recommended that you do *not* restore the files directly to the target directory. Instead, you should first restore the files to an empty temporary directory and then move them to their final locations. That way, you do not run the risk of accidentally overwriting any existing files.

For a full filesystem restore, you should mount a formatted disk first, move to that mount point, and then invoke the `restore` command.

CAUTION

You should be careful about the sequence of the archives to restore. When restoring the full filesystem from the archives with the -r switch, you *must* start with the level 0 archive.

A FEW WORDS OF CAUTION ABOUT DUMP LEVELS

You can save some trouble during a *full* filesystem restore if your dump backups were made of staggered incremental dump levels. The online man page for dump suggests the following method of staggering incremental dumps to minimize the number of tapes.

First, you start with a level 0 backup and then daily dumps of active filesystems using a modified Tower of Hanoi algorithm. The suggested sequence of daily dump levels is as follows:

```
3 2 5 4 7 6 9 8 9 9 ...
```

One thing you need to realize with the dump level logic is that an archive with some level becomes ineffective if a smaller level dump is taken after that. For instance, in the preceding sequence, the level 3 archive becomes "ineffective" when the next level 2 dump is taken because a level 2 dump includes all files backed up under level 3. Similarly, an existing level 5 archive is ineffective after the next level 4 dump. In the extreme case, a new level 0 dump makes all existing archives with level 1 through 9 ineffective.

Therefore, on a full restore, you should skip these ineffective archives. When restoring from dumps made using the sequence presented in the preceding example, you should choose the restoration sequence as follows to obtain the latest status of the filesystem:

```
0 2 4 6 8
```

If you ignore this rule and try to restore the archives following the Tower of Hanoi sequence (that is, 0, 3, 2, 5, 4, and so on), you will encounter the Incremental tape too high error on the restoration of your level 2 archive and then Incremental tape too low errors after that. After you encounter one of these errors, you cannot complete the full restore by any means, and you must restart that restoration from the first step.

NOTE

The generation of ineffective archives by no means diminishes the usefulness of the Tower of Hanoi sequence. It is still an excellent way to preserve many snapshots of the filesystem for a long period with less backup media.

Data Mirroring Using rsync

The rsync (remote synchronization) utility is a replacement for rcp (remote copy), which has many more features. rsync is intended to create copies of complete directory trees across a network to a different system but also works locally within the same machine; it uses a special algorithm (adeptly called the "rsync algorithm") that provides a very fast method for bringing remote files into synchronization. It does this by sending just the differences in the files across the network link, without requiring that both sets of files are present at one of the ends of the link beforehand.

Features of rsync include the following:

- Can update whole directory trees and filesystems
- Optionally preserves symbolic links, hard links, file ownership, permissions, devices, and creation/modification times
- Does not require special privileges to install
- Uses internal pipelining to reduce latency for multiple files
- Can use rsh, ssh, or direct sockets as the transport
- Supports "anonymous rsync," which is ideal for public data mirroring (such as distributing file changes to FTP mirror sites serving open source programs)

rsync supports a large number of command-line switches, but the ones listed in Table 10.10 are used most frequently.

TABLE 10.10

Most Frequently Used `rsync` Switches

OPTION	DESCRIPTION
`-a`	Puts `rsync` in archive mode. This is equivalent to specifying all of these options: `-r` (recursive copying), `-l` (copy symbolic links), `-p` (preserve permissions), `-t` (preserve times), `-g` (preserve group), `-o` (preserve owner), and `-D` (preserve devices).
`-c`	Performs a checksum on the data.
`--delete`	Deletes files that don't exist on the sender side.
`--delete-exclude`	Deletes excluded files on the receiver end.
`-e` *command*	Specifies a remote shell program (such as `ssh`) to use for communication between the local and remote copies of `rsync`.
`--exclude=`*pattern*	Excludes files matching *pattern*.
`--exclude-from=`*file*	Excludes patterns listed in *file*.
`-n`	Performs a "dry run"—shows what would have been transferred, but no actual transfer takes place.
`--progress`	Shows progress during data transfer.
`--stats`	Gives some file transfer statistics.
`-v`	Turns on verbose mode.
`-z`	Compresses data during transfer.

The following are some sample `rsync` command usages:

- Mirrors all home directories to a backup filesystem:

  ```
  rsync -acv --stats /home /backup
  ```

  Notice that in the preceding command, there is *no* trailing slash after /home. If you specify the source path with a trailing slash (such as /home/) as in

  ```
  rsync -acv --stats /home/ /backup
  ```

  all data in the /home directory will be mirrored to /backup but not the directory itself.

- Mirrors root's home directory (/home/admin) to a remote system, Pollux, using `ssh` as the transport:

  ```
  rsync -azcve ssh /home/admin/ root@pollux:/backup/home/admin
  ```

  root@pollux specifies the username (root) and the host (Pollux) to log in to, and /backup/home/admin is the path for the remote directory that `rsync` will mirror the files with.

- Copies root's home directory data back from the remote system:

```
rsync -azcve ssh root@pollux:/backup/home/admin/ /home/admin
```

The sample script in Listing 10.2, found at `http://rsync.samba.org/ examples.html`, backs up a number of important filesystems to a spare disk; this extra disk has the capacity to hold all the contents of the main disk. The first part does the backup on the spare disk, and the second part backs up the critical parts to daily directories.

LISTING 10.2

A Sample Backup Shell Script Using `rsync`

```
#!/bin/sh
export PATH=/usr/local/bin:/usr/bin:/bin
LIST="rootfs usr data data2"

for d in $LIST; do
    mount /backup/$d
    rsync -ax --exclude fstab --delete /$d/ /backup/$d/
    umount /backup/$d
done

DAY=`date "+%A"`
rsync -a --delete /usr/local/apache /data2/backups/$DAY
rsync -a --delete /data/solid /data2/backups/$DAY
```

For more details, consult the `rsync man` page, as well as the detailed documentation found at `http://rsync.samba.org`, home of `rsync`.

TIP

You can find an excellent article titled "Easy Automated Snapshot-Style Backups with Linux and Rsync" at `http://www.mikerubel.org/computers/ rsync_snapshots`.

TIP

rsync is also available for different operating systems, including NetWare (`http://forge.novell.com/modules/xfmod/project/?rsync`) and Windows (`http://www.cygwin.com`).

YaST's System Backup and Restore Modules

The YaST Backup module allows you to create a backup of your data files. The backup created by the module does *not* comprise the entire system, but only saves information about changed packages and copies of critical storage areas (such as the MBR), configuration files (such as those found under /etc), and user files (such as /home). Furthermore, it does not provide any incremental backup features. The Backup module basically provides you with a GUI front end to tar.

To access the Backup module, from the YaST Control Center, select System, System Backup; or from a terminal session, use yast2 backup or yast backup. At the YaST System Backup screen, you can select Profile Management, Add to create different backup profiles that store different backup settings. For example, you can create a profile called MBR Backup that is used exclusively to back up the Master Boot Record and another profile called User Home Directories that will back up all user files.

Figure 10.1 shows the Archive Settings screen where you can specify the name of your tarfile and the archive type (such as a tarball compressed using gzip). Clicking Next takes you to the File Selection dialog box. Here, select the desired option(s) and click Next. (If you want to back up your MBR, click the Expert button for additional settings.) The last screen specifies the Search Constraints. Here, you select the directories and filesystems that you want to be *excluded* from backup. Click Finish to save the profile settings.

FIGURE 10.1
The Archive Settings dialog box.

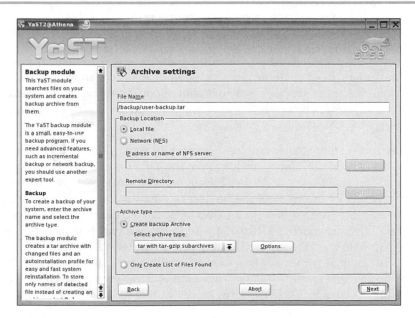

NOTE

If your screen resolution is 800×600, the File Name edit box may be partially hidden if you have the task panel displayed.

If you need to do a one-off backup, you can select the Backup Manually button and walk through the same setup screens described in the preceding paragraphs, but not save the settings in a profile.

To perform a backup, simply select one of the existing profiles and then click Start Backup. YaST takes a few minutes to search through the system for files matching your selection and then creates the resulting archive (see Figure 10.2). The tarball created by YaST has the following "structure":

```
Athena:/home/admin # tar -tvf backup.tar
-rw------- root/root    143 2005-01-14 06:07:42 info/files
-rw------- root/root    136 2005-01-14 06:07:42
➥info/packages_info.gz
-rw------- root/root      6 2005-01-14 06:07:35 info/hostname
-rw------- root/root     17 2005-01-14 06:07:35 info/date
-rw------- root/root      0 2005-01-14 06:07:35 info/comment
-rw------- root/root    127 2005-01-14 06:07:35
➥info/complete_backup
-rw------- root/root  18754 2005-01-14 06:07:42
➥info/installed_packages
-rw------- root/root   1679 2005-01-14 06:07:42
➥NOPACKAGE-20050114-0.tar.gz
```

Instead of the tarfile holding the backed-up files, those files are actually placed in another tarball within the archive, and additional identification information is added. As a result, the YaST System Restore module does not accept a "standard" tarball created by `tar` unless you have packaged the files into the same structure.

The System Restore module enables restoration of your system from a backup archive. To access the Restore module, from the YaST Control Center, select System, System Restore; the Archive Selection dialog box is then shown (see Figure 10.3). (From a terminal session, you can use `yast2 restore` or `yast restore`.) First, specify where the archives are located (removable media, local hard disks, or network file systems). A description and the contents of the individual archives are then displayed, letting you decide what to restore from the archives. There are two dialog boxes for uninstalling packages that were added since the last backup and for the reinstallation of packages that were deleted since the last backup. These two steps let you restore the exact system state at the time of the last backup.

FIGURE 10.2
The Backup summary screen.

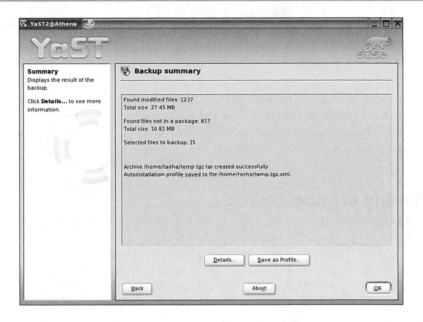

FIGURE 10.3
The Archive Selection dialog box.

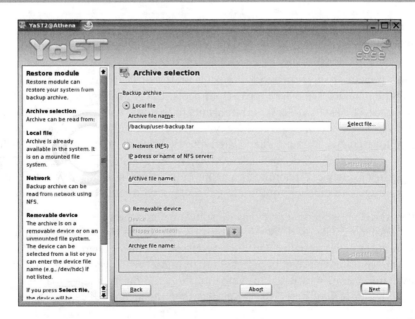

Because it does not support incremental or differential backups, the YaST System Backup module is of limited use. However, it is adequate for quick-and-dirty backups or for small test servers. Also, it has a built-in scheduler (which you access by selecting Profile Management, Automatic Backup), so you can run regular backups at predetermined times in the background.

CAUTION

If your screen resolution is 800×600, the Start Backup Automatically check box is hidden if the task panel is displayed. This makes all the selections on the Automatic Backup Options dialog box inaccessible (grayed out). You need to hide the task panel to access the check box.

Getting to Know AMANDA

AMANDA, the Advanced Maryland Automatic Network Disk Archiver, was originally written by James da Silva while at the University of Maryland at College Park in 1997. This backup system allows a network administrator to set up a single master backup server and back up multiple hosts to a single, large-capacity tape drive. AMANDA uses native `dump` and/or GNU `tar` facilities and can back up a large number of workstations running multiple versions of Linux/Unix. Recent versions can also use Samba to back up Microsoft Windows hosts; no support is available for Macintosh systems at the time of this writing.

NOTE

The current main website for AMANDA is `http://sourceforge.net/projects/amanda`, where you can find the latest version and its source code.

AMANDA provides its own network protocols on top of TCP and UDP instead of using the standard `rsh`, `rdump`, or `rmt` protocols. Each client agent writes to `stdout`, which AMANDA collects and transmits to the tape server host. This allows AMANDA to insert compression and encryption and also gather a catalog of the image for recovery. Multiple clients are typically backed up in parallel to files in one or more holding disk areas as *cache buffers*. A separate tape-writing process keeps the tape device streaming at maximum possible throughput. AMANDA can also run direct to tape without holding disks, but with reduced performance.

Either the client or tape server may do software compression, or hardware compression may be used. When enabled on the client side, software compression reduces network traffic. On the server side, it reduces client CPU load. Software compression may be selected on an image-by-image basis. If Kerberos is available, clients may use it for authentication and dump images may be encrypted. Instead of Kerberos, `.amandahosts` authentication files (similar to

.rhosts) can be used instead, or AMANDA may be configured to use .rhosts (even though the r*-utilities, such as rlogin, are not themselves used). AMANDA is friendly with security tools like TCP Wrappers (ftp://info.cert.org/pub/network_tools) and firewalls.

AMANDA uses standard software for generating dump images and software compression. Consequently, if you have an AMANDA-created tape, but AMANDA is not readily available, you can readily use the normal Linux/Unix tools such as mt, dd, and gzip/uncompress to recover a dump image from the tape. When AMANDA software is available, using the catalog, it locates which tapes are needed and finds images on the tapes. There is an FTP-like restore utility for administrators to make searching online dump catalogs easier when recovering individual files.

There is no graphical interface available for AMANDA; it is totally command line based. As a matter of act, AMANDA consists of a set of command-line utilities. Consequently, you can easily set up cron jobs to run the backup automatically.

AMANDA has configuration options for controlling almost all aspects of the back-up operation and provides several scheduling methods. A typical configuration does periodic full dumps with partial dumps in between. There is also support for the following:

- Periodic archival backup, such as taking full dumps so you can send them to offsite storage.

- Incremental-only backups where full dumps are done outside AMANDA, such as very active areas that must be taken offline, or no full dumps at all for areas that can easily be recovered from vendor media.

- Always doing full dumps, such as for databases that can change completely between each run or critical files that are easier to deal with during an emergency if they are a single-restore operation.

Scheduling of full dumps is typically left up to AMANDA. They are scattered throughout the dump cycle to balance the amount of data backed up during each run. Because there is no human intervention to determine when a full dump may take place, AMANDA keeps logs of where backup images are located for each filesystem. For instance, the Friday tape will not always have a full dump of /home for Athena. Therefore, system-generated logs are essential. The scheduling of partial backup levels is also left to AMANDA. History information about previous levels is kept, and the backup level automatically increases when sufficient dump size savings are realized.

A simple but efficient tape management system is employed by AMANDA. It protects itself from overwriting tapes that still have valid dump images and from writing on tapes that are not allocated to the configuration. Images may be overwritten when a client is down for an extended period or if not enough tapes are allocated, but only after AMANDA has issued several warnings. AMANDA can also be told not to reuse specific tapes.

As you can see, many of the features in AMANDA rival those of many of the commercial backup products, and it's free! If you need to back up multiple systems, take a look at AMANDA. It is included as part of the SLES 9 software.

TIP

You can find an excellent reference on configuring and using AMANDA in Chapter 4 of W. Curtis Preston's book *Unix Backup & Recovery* (ISBN 1-56592-642-0).

Scheduling Backups

As already discussed, backups should be made on a regular basis to be of any use in case of an accident or other emergency. Most, if not all, commercial backup products have a built-in scheduler. If you have elected to use one of the Linux-supplied tools, however, they do not come with schedulers. In this case, you can use cron to execute your backup commands at preset times.

NOTE

While each performs the same task, there are many variants of cron. The version of cron included with SLES 9 is Vixie cron, which is a rather full-featured cron implementation based on AT&T System V's cron. Each user has his or her own crontab file (placed in /var/spool/cron/tabs) and is allowed to specify environment variables (such as PATH, SHELL, HOME, and so on) within that crontab. The actual access to the cron service is controlled by the /var/spool/cron/allow and /var/spool/cron/deny files. Unlike the other cron variants, this version also offers support for the SELinux security module (http://www.nsa.gov/selinux/papers/module-abs.cfm) and PAM. It supports fewer architectures than Dcron (Dillon's cron), but more than Fcron.

System jobs are controlled via the contents in /etc/crontab and the files located in /etc/cron.d. For backup jobs, it is probably best to place the necessary commands in /etc/crontab. The following is a sample crontab entry that performs a backup of /home/project every day at 3:00 a.m. using tar:

```
#mm hh dd mm ww command
 00 03  *  *  * (tar -czpvf /backup/project.tgz /home/project
➡> /home/peter/tar.log)
```

Refer to man 5 crontab for details about the format of cron commands.

Sometimes you may need to run a (backup) command just once, but at a later time. For this purpose, you can use the `at` command instead of `cron`.

The `at` command requires one argument (the time) and accepts a number of options. The command syntax is as follows:

```
at [-q queue] [-bdlmrv] [-f file] time [date | +increment]
```

The output from the commands in *file* (as specified via `-f` *file*) is emailed to the user who submitted the job; `at` executes the command file using `/bin/sh`. The following is a sample `at` command that will make the `backup1` script run 10 minutes from the time it was submitted:

```
Athena:/home/admin # at -f backup1 now+10 minutes
warning: commands will be executed using /bin/sh
job 5 at 2005-1-19 14:24
```

The following example will execute the `backup1` script at 3 p.m., three days from today:

```
Athena:/home/admin # at -f backup1 3pm + 3days
warning: commands will be executed using /bin/sh
job 6 at 2005-1-22 15:00
```

Similar to `cron`, at uses `allow` (`/etc/at.allow`) and `deny` (`/etc/at.deny`) files to control which of the nonroot users may submit `at` commands.

NOTE

The at service (`atd`) is not started by default. You can check to see whether it is currently running by using the command `ps aux | grep atd` and looking for the `atd` process. If it is not running, you can manually start it with `/usr/sbin/atd`. Similarly, you can use `ps aux | grep cron` to ensure the `cron` service is running. If it is not, you can start it with `/usr/sbin/cron`.

For more information about the `at` commands, especially its time syntax, see its `man` page.

Commercial Backup Products

Other than the tools and free utilities included with SLES, a number of commercial backup products are also available. Some notable mentions follow:

- **CTAR**—The Compressing Tape Archiver is an unattended backup/preconfigured command scheduler. It is based on the nonproprietary industry standard `tar` format. CTAR has been around since 1989 and supports a wide range of Linux and Unix systems. Visit UniTrends Software (`http://www.unitrends.com`) for more information.

- **BRU**—The **B**ackup and **R**estore **U**tility family of products is strongly based on `tar` but adds many more features, including both command-line and GUI interfaces. It runs a daemon that manages the backup schedule. BRU supports full, incremental, and differential backups, as well as catalogs, and can save the archive to a file as well as a wide range of storage devices. Like CTAR, BRU has been around for a long time (since 1985), so it has a proven track record. Visit TOLIS Group at `http://www.tolis-group.com` for more information.

- **BrightStor ARCserve Backup for Linux**—ARCserve is an easy-to-use, high-performance, comprehensive data management tool for enterprise networks. Utilizing a browser-based Java GUI, ARCserve makes managing the backup of large servers and heterogeneous networks simple. Full automation of the data management process, including tape rotation, is made easy by the built-in Auto Pilot feature. A number of add-on agents and modules are available to support hot backup of databases (such as MySQL) and applications (such as Apache Web Server). Visit Computer Associates at `http://www.ca.com` for more information.

- **Legato NetWorker for Linux**—NetWorker utilizes a centralized console for configuring and managing all backups and restores, thus reducing the amount of training required across your system. Wizard-driven configuration tools help simplify such tasks as filesystem and device configuration. You can readily implement flexible, automated, calendar-based scheduling, and design separate browse and retention policies at client or defined backup levels to enable more flexibility in managing your data. The user console allows your users to perform ad hoc backups and even browse and recover their own files, eliminating the need for administrator intervention. NetWorker also provides automatic event notification via pager, email, or optional SNMP module. For heavily scripted environments or users wishing to integrate with other applications, NetWorker provides extensive command-line capabilities. A number of modules are also available, such as NetWorker Module for Oracle, which enables you to perform online database backups. Visit EMC Legato at `http://www.legato.com` for more information.

- **System Backup Administrator**—System Backup Administrator (SBA) provides a graphical interface for administration of various types of backups. The rich feature set in SBA allows you to use a single backup product for daily incremental backups, raw partition backups, and full-system backups, along with the necessary boot media. SBA also has some unique system recovery features that are not found in other similar products. For instance, when you are reinstalling a system using new hardware, the configuration is tailored to work with your new hardware configuration. In addition, you can completely recustomize your system during the system installation process by changing filesystem types, adding software RAID devices, converting to LVM partitions, and much more. Visit Storix, Inc., at `http://www.storix.com` for more information.

- **Arkeia Server and Network Backup**—Arkeia offers two Linux backup solutions: Arkeia Server Backup (ASB) and Arkeia Network Backup (ANB). ASB is specifically designed for businesses and enterprise departments that rely on local backups to a single tape drive, and ANB was designed to protect heterogeneous networks with options for backing up to disks and/or tape libraries. Arkeia users can take advantage of a fully integrated wizard for easy setup of basic operations, and the GUI interface provides ready access to various functions and features, including scheduling and email notification. Plug-ins are available to perform online, hot backups of widely used database applications, such as Lotus Notes and MySQL. Visit Arkeia Corporation at `http://www.arkeia.org` for more information.

SLES Boot and Rescue Disks

In the unfortunate event that your SLES 9 system disk is corrupted and no longer bootable, you can still (likely) access the data on the filesystems if you boot with a rescue disk. If you have the SLES CDs or DVD available, you simply boot using the DVD or CD1. At the boot screen, select Rescue System and press Enter. From the language selection dialog box, highlight the desired language and press Enter. When the rescue system starts, log in as root.

NOTE

You can find detailed information about emergency boot and recovery in Chapter 3.

What can you do if your CD-ROM drive doesn't support bootable CDs or you don't have the media handy? If you have the foresight, you can use YaST to create a set of boot or rescue floppy diskettes for just such an emergency.

These floppy disks are helpful if the boot configuration of your system is damaged. The rescue disk is especially necessary if the filesystem of the root partition is damaged. In this case, you might also need the module disk with various drivers to be able to access the system (for example, to access a RAID system).

To access the Create Boot or Rescue Floppies module, from the YaST Control Center, select System, Create a Boot, Rescue or Module Floppy. (From a terminal session, you can use `yast2 bootfloppy` or `yast bootfloppy`.) A dialog box similar to Figure 10.4 is displayed.

FIGURE 10.4
Creating boot and rescue floppies.

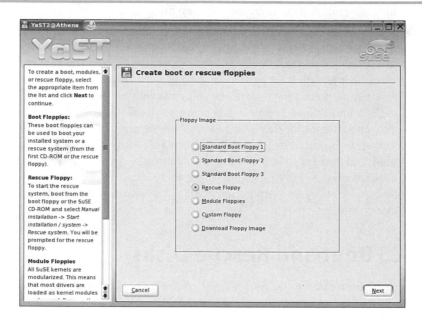

Using this YaST module, you can create the following types of floppy disks:

- **Standard Boot Floppy 1, 2, or 3**—Use these options to create standard boot disks so that you can boot an installed system. You also need these disks to start the rescue system.

- **Rescue Floppy**—This disk contains a special environment that allows you to perform maintenance tasks in your installed system, such as checking and repairing the file system and updating the boot loader.

- **Module Floppies**—Module disks contain additional system drivers that may be required to support hardware access. The standard kernel supports only IDE drives. If your system has SCSI controllers, for instance, you need to load the needed drivers from a module disk to be able to access them. If you select this option and click Next, you are taken to a dialog box for creating various module disks.

- **Custom Floppy**—Use this option to write any existing floppy disk image from the hard disk to a floppy disk.

- **Download Floppy Image**—Use this option to specify a URL and authentication data to download a floppy disk image from the Internet.

To create one of these floppy disks, select the corresponding option on the screen and then click Next. Insert a blank floppy disk when prompted. Click Next again to create the floppy disk. After you have created the necessary disks, label them and store them in a secure location.

Summary

This chapter provided information on how to develop a backup plan and how and when to use various standard Linux backup tools, such as `tar` and `cpio`, to implement a flexible yet reliable data backup and recovery strategy.

Securing Your SUSE Server

## CHAPTER 11

Network Security Concepts

Today, information comes in many forms, and consequently, methods of securing it vary. Instead of dividing information into categories based on content, threat analysis and its protection should be based on methods of processing and storage. These methods can be divided into three general categories:

- **Physical**—Traditionally, information is "physically recorded" (say, in the form of ink-and-paper or electronically in bits-and-bytes) and stored somewhere (for example, in a box, safe, diskette, or hard drive). Therefore, classical security generally focuses on physical protection, such as access control to buildings, server rooms, wiring closets, and so on.

- **Social/Personal**—Many organizations understand the value of their employees, especially the knowledge they hold in their heads and their capability to use that knowledge to corporate advantage.

- **Networks**—Because paper records are bulky, are harder to search for specific data, and have limited a life span, many corporations store much of their information on computers and make it accessible over networks. Documents are stored "somewhere on the net," and users access them through URLs or some specific application (such as a database).

No matter what type of security, it involves prevention, detection, responding to incidents, and monitoring and reviewing measures to reduce perceived risks to acceptable levels. In terms of information security, these measures need to be uniformly applied; they cover various areas such as social/personal (that is, employees), workstations/laptops and the network, and physical access.

THERE'S NO SUCH THING AS COMPLETE SECURITY

Having *complete* security is virtually impossible. If you want something to be *totally* secured, do not permit access to it at all. The weakest link in any security implementation is the users. Your network may be totally isolated from the outside world, but a user can easily make an unauthorized copy of a document by either saving a copy of it or by printing out a hard copy. In the movie *Recruit*, top secret data was copied to a USB thumb drive using a laptop, and then the thumb drive, hidden in a coffee thermos, was smuggled out of the CIA compound. This scenario may sound like Hollywood fantasy, but all the technologies employed in the movie exist: You can purchase a 128MB USB thumb drive the size of a coin for less than $50. Unless your security procedure includes body searches for people entering *and* leaving the premises, confidential data *can* be compromised.

Even if data access is not electronic, you cannot stop someone who has a good or photographic memory from reading a confidential document, leaving the building, and re-creating it later!

Therefore, the effort you spend on security measures should correctly reflect the value of the data you're protecting. There is no point in implementing a $50,000 security solution if the information you're trying to protect is worth only $5,000. Similarly, if the data is worth millions to your competitor, spending a few hundred thousand dollars on security measures may be duly justified.

Because this is a book about servers, we do not cover the security aspects of "people"; in some respects, a company's Human Resources (HR) department should handle staff. Instead, this chapter covers the policies ("rules") that you should have in place to protect your network and to limit physical access to the related equipment. Actual implementations of these rules are discussed in the remaining chapters of this book.

Corporate Security Policies

Even though SLES 9 has been certified to meet the internationally recognized Common Criteria's Evaluation Assurance Level 4+ (EAL4+) security rating, it does not mean your SLES 9 server is automatically EAL4+ rated upon installation: You need to enable the various security options and features. Depending on your specific needs, enabling the full range of EAL4+ settings may be too restrictive. Additionally, these EAL4+ settings apply only to the server's security but do nothing for the overall corporate security. What you need is a set of corporate security policies.

NOTE

For more information about the Common Criteria security rating, see Appendix A, "Security Certifications."

With the ever-increasing dependency on computer technology for ongoing business activities, it is imperative that a company has a plan to protect its computing resources and the data contained therein. This plan is normally part of a *security policy*. A security policy is a document that stipulates the rules for which a company's assets (such as computers) and data are to be configured, maintained, and used. It also identifies the relative value of the company's assets and data. The security policy should be reviewed and updated whenever your organization's business needs, activities, and assets change. Even if everything remains relatively static, the security policy should still be reviewed periodically, perhaps annually, to refresh your and your staff's memory on how things should be done.

SECURITY AND SARBANES-OXLEY

A few years ago, the health-care organizations in the United States were legislated to comply with the Health Insurance Portability and Accountability Act (HIPAA), which protects patient privacy and records. As of April 15, 2005, all U.S. companies also have to comply with the *Sarbanes-Oxley Act*.

The Sarbanes-Oxley Act, more commonly referred to as Sarbanes-Oxley, was named for the two Congressmen who sponsored it. On the surface, it doesn't seem to have much to do with IT security. The law was passed to restore the public's confidence in corporate governance by making chief executives of publicly traded companies personally validate financial statements and other information. President George W. Bush signed it into law on July 30, 2002. All companies have to comply by April 15, 2005.

The law mainly deals with many corporate governance issues, including executive compensation, off-book transactions, the use of independent directors, and so on. IT security was not directly mentioned. However, there is a provision in the law mandating that company executives attest to their companies' having proper "internal controls." As you will readily agree, it's hard to sign off on the validity of data if the systems maintaining it aren't secure.

Sarbanes-Oxley doesn't mandate specific internal controls such as strong authentication or the use of encryption, but if someone can easily get in your system because you have a weak password, that is a sign of noncompliance. Consequently, upper-level management and their security staff need to ensure that proper and auditable security measures are in place and enforced. A set of comprehensive corporate security policies, such as those discussed in this chapter, would go a long way with Sarbanes-Oxley compliance. Even if you are not required to comply with Sarbanes-Oxley or HIPAA (because you are not located in the United States), it is still good business practice to ensure that your data is safe from prying eyes.

NOTE

Providing a thorough study of security policy development or its prerequisite requirements (such as risk analysis) is beyond the scope of this chapter and this book. You can find an excellent collection of security policy templates and related information that can help you to jump-start your security policy development at `www.sans.org/resources/policies`.

Procedures are equally important as policies. Often, policies define *what* is to be protected and what are the ground rules. The procedures outline *how* to protect the resources or how to carry out the policies. For example, a *password policy* would outline password construction rules, rules on how to protect your password and how often to change them. The *password management procedure* would outline the process to create new passwords and distribute them, as well as the process for ensuring the passwords have changed on critical devices. A one-to-one relationship will not always exist between policies and procedures. The remainder of this chapter provides a high-level overview of some specific security policy topics as they pertain to computer networks. Within that context, you will also find some rule-of-thumb procedures that you can incorporate into your own security policies. The following topics are covered in the upcoming sections:

- Physical security
- User accounts
- Strong passwords
- Remote access
- Firewalls

- Acceptable use policy
- Information protection
- Incident response

Following are some other policy topics that you should also consider. Although they are not covered here, some have been discussed in other chapters of this book:

- Email usage and policy regarding email forwarding to offsite addresses
- Data backup, retention, and offsite storage (see Chapter 10, "Data Backup and Disaster Recovery")
- Laptop usage and security
- Wireless security (see Chapter 13, "System Security")
- Change management process

You may already have in place a number of policies that were common practices but were not put down on paper. If someone came in and said, "Show me your policy," you couldn't pull out a document and say, "Here." As a result, some would then say you did not have a policy. To avoid finger-pointing, document all policies.

Physical Security

The first aspect of security, whether computer networking related or not, is physical security. If whatever you are trying to protect isn't physically secure, unauthorized access would be possible regardless of how strict your *other* security measures may be.

Physical security is mostly about common sense, but a few items are often taken for granted, and thus overlooked. The following list describes some of the items that you should consider when implementing physical security for your network:

- Servers and critical network components, such as routers and switches, should be kept under lock and key. Authorized access to the areas where these devices are kept should be restricted to a short list of personnel.
- In situations when extreme confidential data is stored on the server, access to the server room should be possible via magnetic card access only, where each authorized individual has a separate access card. This way, chronological who-entered-when entry records can be maintained.

- Unused ports on your hubs and switches should not be connected to the wiring patch panels. This prevents unauthorized connection of a sniffer, for instance, onto your network from an unoccupied office.

- Server cases should be locked using built-in locks to deter hard disk theft. Although these types of locks are easily picked (without using special tools), someone spotted "fiddling" with the locks would draw attention.

- BIOS bootup passwords can be used on the server. This practice is debatable because most, if not all, administrators find that the password is easily disabled and that it makes autorestart of servers impractical. Some companies actually make a policy that BIOS passwords *not* be used.

CAUTION

Don't confuse the *bootup* password with the *configuration* password. Many networking devices, such as routers, require you to supply a password to make configuration changes. Such passwords *should* be used. As a matter of fact, your password management policy should mandate that the default passwords for such devices be changed before they are put into production.

- If you are using wireless access points, ensure they are not servicing areas outside your office space, such as an adjacent office building. A separate policy on wireless security may be warranted. (See Chapter 13 for more information about wireless security.)

The following are a few items we consider as part of physical security, but some people would instead classify them under the topic "environmental security":

- Servers and critical network components should be connected to uninterruptible power supply (UPS) units to ensure they are not subjected to sudden power spikes and that they are properly and automatically shut down after a prolonged power outage with the help of software such as PowerChute (www.apcc.com/products/management/pcp_linux.cfm). At the very least, power surge protection devices should be utilized. (Policies and procedures should be in place to periodically test the effectiveness of the connected UPS units.)

- Putting UPS units in wiring closets may be unnecessary, but it is a good idea to have the hubs/switches connected to power surge protectors.

- If you have distributed wiring closets on your premises, redundant links should be run between them and the central wiring hub/switch (which is usually located in the computer room), as illustrated in Figure 11.1.

FIGURE 11.1
Redundant links from wiring closets back to the computer room.

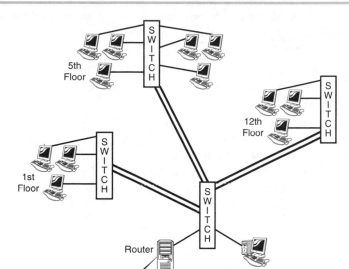

- When wires are run between floors (such as between the 12th floor and the computer room on the 5th floor), they should be placed inside conduits. Depending on the local building safety codes and the type of wiring being used, the conduits may have to be sealed and pressurized with nitrogen gas.

TIP

If your local safety code doesn't require you to use conduits for running wires between floors, it is still a good idea to do so. This will make unauthorized tapping into your network a lot more difficult when the wires located in the shared closet areas are protected inside a pipe.

- Servers and network devices should be placed *off* the floor level. If you have a dedicated computer room, chances are good that you have a raised floor. Otherwise, you should purchase server racks where you can put your servers and network components. At the very least, put them on tables. In more than one instance, we have seen servers or computing devices (such as switches in a wiring closet) being damaged by water, either due to broken pipes or an accidental spill.

- Computer rooms should *not* use water sprinklers for fire-fighting purposes. As a matter of fact, building safety codes in many cities stipulate what non–water-based fire-fighting measure is to be used in such installations.

- Wiring closets should be well ventilated and have temperature sensors that provide you with a warning should their temperature rise past a certain threshold.

Part of physical security policy overlaps that of asset management policy. You need to put in place policies and procedures on when and how a piece of networking hardware is to be installed or removed from the premises. For instance, prior to your moving a server's hard drive offsite for disposal, you should complete the following steps:

- Scrub the drive of all data (see the "Information Protection" section later).

- Update the inventory tracking database.

- Notify the personnel in the appropriate departments (such as Shipping or Front Desk) so they know this specific hard drive is leaving the company property with authorization.

If the hard drive to be disposed of held sensitive information, you may want to be paranoid and go the extra step of having it physically destroyed after scrubbing it of all data. It would be a good idea to obtain a written confirmation from the person or company performing the task, attesting to the fact that the hard drive was indeed destroyed.

User Accounts

A combination of user account and password is the key to your "data kingdom." Therefore, clear policies and procedures must be in place to control their creation and revocation. An employee generally is given a user account to access a company's computing resources in two ways:

- The employee's manager or supervisor submits a request to IT Support, specifying the list of shared folders and databases and the type of access (such as read-only or read-write) required for the user account.

- The account is created via "user account provisioning." User account or identity provisioning is an automated process of creating and enabling access to all needed applications and services for any end user.

There are pros and cons to both approaches. When a new employee joins a company, he or she typically needs access to a variety of accounts and services to do his or her job effectively. It is not uncommon for employees today to have three or four different IDs for services such as group folders stored on network servers, email, enterprise portals, various databases, and more. As a business grows its IT infrastructure with a diverse mix of enterprise applications, systems, and directories, the complexity of managing and securing those resources grows exponentially. The effort of manually giving users access to the myriad disparate systems that they need not only costs the IT department significant time (and thus money), but it opens the door to human errors that may lead to security vulnerabilities in the enterprise's network. On the other hand, because the accounts are not automatically allocated but have to be requested, there is much better control over their creation and dispersion.

As you can imagine, with mid-size to large organizations, the process of managing users' access to applications and services is *very* labor intensive and time consuming: A new employee may have to wait for up to a week to receive all required accesses. To simplify the process, these companies often implement a process known as *identity provisioning*. Based on predefined roles (such as an entry-level marketing sales position), identity provisioning automates the essential tasks of creating and maintaining user accounts and the associated access rights to various resources. This provides huge time and cost savings, as well as rapid deployment of user identities, applications, and services for many companies. One of the main drawbacks of such an automated process is that exceptions to the rules are difficult to handle, and often manual processing is required.

NOTE

For information about Novell's Nsure Identity Manager, visit www.novell.com/products/nsureidentitymanager.

No matter whether you use the manual route or the identity provisioning method, you need to have policies and procedures in place for account termination. This is a *very* important aspect of your user account security policies and procedures. More than 50% of system break-ins can be attributed to user accounts whose owners are no longer with the company, but the accounts have not been disabled or deleted.

Unless an employee's termination is a spur-of-the-moment event, Human Resources (HR) generally knows about it ahead of time. Therefore, your company should have a policy/procedure that when HR is informed of an imminent termination action, the IT department is also informed so that the user's access to company information can be removed at the same time the termination notice is given. When identity provisioning is used, all the user's accounts should be automatically disabled upon HR setting the employment termination flag in that person's record.

Lastly, we would like to add a few words about system accounts that are not used by humans, but by applications. As previously discussed in Chapter 4, "User and Group Administration," and Chapter 8, "Network Services," whenever possible, system services should be run under nonprivileged accounts instead of root. Some package installations create a user account to be used by the package. In all cases, you should ensure these application accounts are not given a useable shell, to prevent them from being used by intruders to access your system. We recommend that you set the shell for these accounts to /bin/false.

TIP

You may want to add /bin/false to the list of available shells in /etc/shell. This way, when YaST is used to create a user, your account creation procedure for application accounts can specify that the /bin/false shell be selected from the drop-down list.

Regardless of how your user accounts are created, either manually or via provisioning, ensure a clearly stipulated set of requirements exists on the minimum amount of user information that must be recorded in the user account record. For example, include location of home directory, groups the user belongs to, GECOS data (if any telephone numbers are to be included or not), and so on.

Strong Passwords

Strong, secure passwords are a cornerstone of an effective security strategy. Passwords ensure that only authorized personnel will be able to gain access to system resources. Unfortunately, this is not always the case. The individuals who are utilizing these resources choose most passwords and, as a result, the words, symbols, or dates that make up the passwords usually have some personal meaning to the users so they are easier to remember. Herein lies the problem. Because of human nature, convenience is often chosen over security. As a result, users choose passwords that are relatively simple. Although this helps them to remember the passwords, it also makes the passwords much easier for hackers to crack. The first line of security defense thus becomes one of the weakest.

NOTE

Hackers will probe a network looking for the weak link that will give them entry, and the most notorious and easiest to exploit is a weak password.

Part of your responsibility, as the system administrator, is to ensure that users are aware of the necessity of maintaining viable secure passwords. This means users must be educated about the importance of strong passwords and ways to implement them, and you need to implement measures that will ensure their passwords are adequately strong. You can accomplish both goals using the same tool as a hacker: a password-cracker.

PASSWORD-CRACKER: A DOUBLE-EDGED SWORD

Some people believe that password-cracking software could be used only for criminal purposes by hackers. This is far from the truth. System administrators can also use password-crackers to ensure that users are implementing strong passwords. You can use password-cracking tools to test the strength of your users' passwords and then notify those users whose passwords are found to be weak.

Users are not the only guilty parties when it comes to choosing weak passwords for convenience's sake; many system administrators are also guilty of the same offense. Because they have a number of passwords to remember, system administrators often pick the same simple password for many applications. Even with PAM-enabled tools, users with root privileges can bypass the strong password enforcement. Couple this with the fact that administrators can modify or remove reminders to change passwords from their own passwords, and you have a serious problem. Finally, system administrators may often take shortcuts in the installation of software or equipment that leave applications with their default passwords. This occurrence is so common that repositories on the Internet list all these default passwords (see "Default Passwords and SNMP Community Names" in Chapter 13). This obviously creates a serious weakness in the security chain.

The two small demonstrations discussed next are usually sufficient to convince users and system administrators alike that weak passwords are *easily* broken. First, provide your users with some simple statistics. In round numbers, assume that brute-force password-cracking software can test 5 million (clear-text) passwords (of any length) per second. This means a four-character password based on a combination of upper- and lowercase letters and the numbers from 0 to 10 (for a total of 62^4 or about 14 million possible combinations) would be broken in no more than 3 seconds. However, as the number of characters in the password increases, the corresponding cracking time increases exponentially, as illustrated in Table 11.1.

TABLE 11.1
Password-Cracking Times Based on Five Million Guesses Per Second

LENGTH	NUMBER OF POSSIBLE PASSWORD COMBINATIONS	CRACKING TIME
1	62	12 microseconds
2	3,844	770 microseconds
3	238,328 (quarter of a million)	50 milliseconds
4	14,776,336 (14 million)	3 seconds
5	916,132,832 (almost one billion)	3 minutes
6	56,800,235,584 (56 billion; 56×10^9)	3 hours
7	3,521,614,606,208 (3.5 trillion; 3.5×10^{12})	8 days
8	218,340,105,584,896 (200 trillion; 200×10^{12})	1.4 years
9	13,537,086,546,263,552 (13 quadrillion; 13×10^{15})	85.85 years
10	839,299,365,868,340,224 (840 quadrillion; 840×10^{15})	53 centuries
11	52,036,560,683,837,093,888 (52 quintillion; 52×10^{18})	330 centuries
12	3,226,266,762,397,899,821,056 (3 sextillion; 3×10^{21})	20.5 million years

Bear in mind that the times listed in Table 11.1 are for cracking clear-text passwords where no computations are necessary. Breaking password hashes in which complex algorithms are involved would take *much* longer.

NOTE

It is worth remembering that certain password-hashing algorithms limit the number of characters in a password. For instance, a DES-hashed password is limited to eight characters in size. Furthermore, depending on the algorithm and the "salt" used for computing the hash, there is a remote chance that two or more different passwords will result in the same hashed value, effectively making the password easier to "crack."

Given the ever-increasing speed of computers and better software algorithms always being developed, these changes give credence to the standard recommendation that a password should be *at least* six to eight characters in size. Furthermore, the password should be composed of printable characters (including symbols such as $ and :) available on the keyboard.

Most of the people presented with the information contained in Table 11.1 instantly understand the need for lengthy passwords. However, they are not always convinced that their "favorite" passwords are vulnerable if the passwords are sufficiently long. At such times, demonstration of a password-cracker, such as Crack or John the Ripper, is necessary. Seeing is believing, and nothing drives the lesson home faster and harder than letting the users see how quickly their "secret" passwords are revealed.

The most popular Linux/Unix password-cracking utility is probably Crack by Alex Muffet (`www.crypticide.com/users/alecm/`). Crack can be configured to periodically run and automatically email a cautionary note to the users with weak passwords, or it can be run in manual mode. Crack can also be configured to run across multiple systems and to use user-defined rules for word manipulation and mutation to maximize dictionary effectiveness. It is probably too much of a program, however, for a novice administrator to master. Another popular favorite is John the Ripper, based on the popular DOS-based Jack the Ripper. Jack had a number of easy-to-use features, and Solar Designer (`www.openwall.com`) took Jack's interface and developed John. As improvements over Jack, John has Crack-like rules, and the software runs on DOS, Windows, and Linux/Unix systems. You can use Crack, John the Ripper, or any of the other available password-crackers for your demonstration. The key point is to convince your users that their passwords *can* be broken and your password policy helps to make their passwords much more difficult to crack; thus, it helps to protect their valuable data.

TIP

The security scripts included with SLES 9 (such as `seccheck`) refer to John the Ripper, but the software is actually not included with the SLES 9 CDs. Instead, John the Ripper is included with SUSE Professional, or you can download it from `ftp.suse.com/pub/suse/i386/9.2/suse/i586/john-1.6.37-21.i586.rpm` or `ftp.suse.com//pub/people/lrupp/john`.

QUICK-START STEPS TO JOHN THE RIPPER

After downloading and installing the John the Ripper RPM package, you can find all the necessary files in `/var/lib/john`. Download the wordlist file from `ftp.suse.com//pub/people/lrupp/john`; additional wordlists (in different languages) can be found at `www.openwall.com/wordlists`, `ftp.ox.ac.uk/pub/wordlists`, and `ftp.cerias.purdue.edu/pub/dict/wordlists`. Concatenate your desired wordlists into a single file and append it to `/var/lib/john/password.lst`.

John works with the `/etc/passwd` file. However, because SLES uses a shadow password file, you (as root) need to "unshadow" it before unleashing John on it:

```
$ cd /var/lib/john
$ unshadow /etc/passwd /etc/shadow > passwords.dat
$ chmod 600 passwords.dat
$ john passwords.dat
```

The chmod command ensures the recombined password file (`passwords.dat`) is accessible only by the owner (root) and no one else; you don't want users to stumble across that file accidentally and make a copy of it so they can perform their own crack.

John runs silently without displaying anything to indicate how it is doing. This permits you to run it as a background task; you may want to use the `nice` command so the process does not hog the CPU too much. When running in the foreground of your terminal session, press any key to obtain a one-line status message telling you the run duration and a few statistics, or press Ctrl+C to abort the session. You can resume an aborted session using the `john --restore` command.

Cracked passwords are written into the file `john.pot`, and the cracked username/password pairs can be shown with the `--show` switch:

```
$ john --show passwords.dat
```

You can instruct John to crack passwords of only certain users or groups with the `--users:` and `--groups:` switches. For instance, to crack passwords only for root and members of the Admin and Helpdesk groups, enter the following:

```
$ john --users:root --groups:admin,helpdesk passwords.dat
```

Running John with no options prints usage information. You can find additional documentation in `/usr/share/doc/packages/john`; the file EXAMPLES contains tips on ways you can use John's features.

The level of security offered by a password is similar to that of a combination lock: If the characters are chosen *truly* at random, one can have millions to quadrillions of possible combinations. Furthermore, the more complicated the method required to turn this combination lock, the longer it takes to crack it. As discussed previously in Chapter 4's "Use a Strong Password-Hashing Algorithm" section, MD5 and Blowfish algorithms are much more CPU-intensive than the default DES algorithm used for hashing SLES passwords. This means given the same six-character password, a password-cracker will take a lot longer to break a Blowfish-hashed password than a DES-hashed one.

Therefore, your password policy should specify a strong hashing algorithm (such as MD5 because it offers a good balance between speed and complexity) to be used for your systems.

The following are some simple guidelines and recommendations you should consider incorporating into your password security policy:

- Do *not* use the default DES password hashing algorithm; use MD5 or Blowfish instead (you can do this either during the server installation (as outlined in the "System Configuration" section of Chapter 1, "Installing SUSE Linux Enterprise Server"), or you can change it later as discussed in the section "Use a Strong Password-Hashing Algorithm" in Chapter 4).

- Make sure user passwords are a minimum of 8 characters long; system administrator passwords should be a minimum of 10 characters long.

- Do not use all punctuation, all digits, or all alphabetic characters for a password; the password should include a combination of punctuation, digits, and letters.

- Use mixed-case letters in passwords.

- Choose a phrase or a combination of words to make the password easier to remember.

- Do not use a word that can be found in *any* dictionary (including foreign language dictionaries).

- Do not use a keyboard pattern such as *qwertyui* or *oeuidhtn* (look at a Dvorak keyboard).

- Do not repeat any character more than once in a row like *zzzzzzz*.

- Do not base the password on information that can be easily determined such as telephone numbers; car license plates; names of friends, relatives, or family pets; or any date.

- *Never* use your account name as its password.

- Use different passwords for different systems, unless a central authentication server (such as LDAP) is used.

- Enforce password aging so passwords are changed regularly; the aging frequency for system administrators should be set higher than for users.

- Do not reuse passwords or attempt to reuse them by appending or prepending a digit or punctuation mark to the old passwords.

- Do not write down passwords; when you must, ensure they are carried on your person and not left out in the open (such as stuck to the monitor or under the keyboard).

TIP

One exception about not writing down passwords may be the root password. Because it is *the* most important password for your server, it needs to be "strong." This means the root password tends to be long (10 characters or more) and hard to remember. Some organizations store a hard copy of the root password in a secure location, such as the company safe or a bank safety deposit box, so there is still a way into the system if the system administrator is unavailable.

- Disable unused or nonlogin application accounts by setting an invalid password hash.

- Do not use default passwords for any applications. Some applications' installation procedures automatically assign a password; change it immediately after installation.

- Do not use default password or SNMP community names for any network devices (such as a router).

- Enforce use of strong passwords by periodically checking for weak passwords using a password-cracker.

A few words of caution about password cracking: Before you actually implement a procedure to check for weak passwords, you should give some thought to how best to conduct password cracking. For instance, it may be worth considering carrying out any password cracking offline to avoid any chance of the password-cracking session being sniffed by unauthorized parties. What's more, password cracking should *not* be undertaken without the proper authorization of senior management (and perhaps notification of the users—something to consult your HR department about). Unless the appropriate notification is given and the required authorization received from management, questions could be raised about the credibility and trust of the person conducting the password cracking. Furthermore, fellow employees may interpret password cracking as a violation of their privacy. This could obviously cause serious problems within the workplace.

WARNING

You should check to ensure that the act of password cracking does not contravene any local laws. In particular, if you are a consultant asked to audit a server for weak passwords, ensure you obtain the proper clearance from the company's senior management in writing prior to even getting a copy of the password file. In some jurisdictions, the possession of the /etc/passwd file belonging to a server that you do *not* manage is considered theft. Therefore, get your authorizations in order before doing any password cracking.

An undiscovered weak password could make everyone's data vulnerable to compromise. Therefore, it is imperative that all aspects of password assurance are included in the password security policy of the organization. The policy should stress the absolute importance of strong, secure passwords and the role of all individual users in maintaining the strength and security of their own passwords. The policy should also outline the steps that the system administrator is expected to follow (such as using strong password hashes and implementing password aging) in ensuring the security of the system through the use of passwords.

Remote Access

With the wide availability of high-speed network connectivity, users and administrators often access corporate computing resources and upload or download files and email messages to or from the office from customer sites or from home using the Internet. As you will read in Chapter 12, "Intrusion Detection," someone can easily eavesdrop on network traffic without being detected because network sniffing is passive. To ensure your data packets are not snooped by third parties while traversing networks that you have no control over (such as your Internet service provider's network or other intermediate connections), you need to have in place a remote access security policy.

In the remote access security policy, you should specify how users are to access company network resources from a remote location. For instance, the policy should specifically indicate that *all* remote access should be made over a virtual private network (VPN) connection. However, this may not be possible for all cases because some ISPs consider VPNs business usage and require the user to pay for a higher cost connection. Therefore, in the absence of VPN, if certain remote access tools such as Telnet and FTP are not permitted, your policy should have a fallback position that lists their acceptable replacements (such as ssh and sFTP, or secure FTP). You can read more about how to secure various remote access protocols in Chapter 13.

Even if you don't access network resources from across the Internet, you should still consider using secure remote access protocols when managing your servers and various network devices from within the office, especially if you use wireless networks. Also discussed in Chapter 13 is the ease in which wireless networks can be monitored from a distance. Therefore, if you manage your network via a wireless connection, someone could sniff your password and later use it to break into your network. Consequently, your remote access security policy should cover all aspects of remote access methods, ranging from Internet access to wireless connections to even modem usage.

Firewalls

Any network that is connected to the outside world, including remote offices, should have a firewall separating the internal network from the external one, as illustrated in Figure 11.2. There are two basic types of firewalls: packet filter firewalls and application-level firewalls.

FIGURE 11.2
Protecting access to an internal network using a firewall.

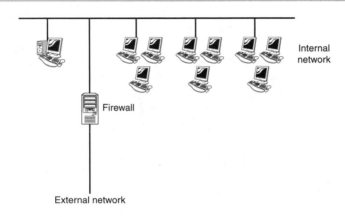

Packet filter firewalls act on IP datagrams running through them by means of rules based on the data found in an IP packet header (source address, target address, source port, target port, and flags). Because packet filter firewalls work with network layer information (see Figure 11.3), they are also known as packet filter routers or screening routers. You use rules to allow or block certain types of data packets from passing through the router (thus, the name *packet filter*). For instance, if you do not want anyone from the external network to access your internal Apache servers, you can specify a rule for the screening router to block all incoming packets addressed to UDP port 80. Another example is that if you don't want your users to access any external FTP servers, simply block all outgoing TCP port 21 packets at the router.

An *application-level firewall* (sometimes referred to as an application-level gateway, ALG, or proxy server) is more "intelligent" than a screening router. An ALG works with all data within a packet, from the IP packet header information down to the actual application data contained within the packet (see Figure 11.4). A typical application-level gateway can provide proxy services for applications and protocols such as Telnet, FTP, HTTP, and SMTP. (Note that a separate proxy must be installed for each application-level service.) With proxies, security policies can be much more powerful and flexible than when using screening routers because all the information in the packets can be used to write the rules that determine how packets are handled by the gateway. It is easy to audit just about everything that happens on the gateway. You can also strip computer names to hide internal systems and evaluate the contents of packets for appropriateness and security; for example, an HTTP proxy can grant or deny access to specific websites based on the URL requested by the clients.

FIGURE 11.3
A packet filter router makes routing decisions based on packet header data.

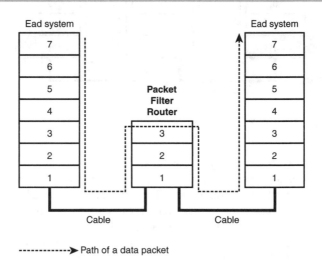

TIP

Firewalls can also be used to protect a department's sensitive, compartmentalized data from being accessed by other departments in the same company. For instance, the Human Resources server may be placed on its own network segment, along with its users, behind a firewall that separates the HR network from the rest of the company.

If you offer publicly accessible services, such as web and FTP servers, it is best not to place those servers on your internal network. If you do, you need to open up ports on your firewall to handle their traffic. There is always a chance that, due to an oversight in your firewall rules or a vulnerability in the firewall software, an intruder may find a way to wander your internal network. Instead, it's better to put such servers in a buffer zone known generally as a *demilitarized zone (DMZ)*.

FIGURE 11.4

An application-level gateway processes the data based on application-related data.

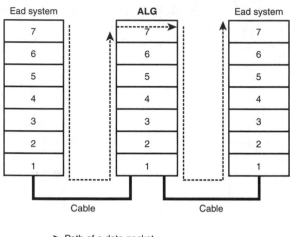

FIGURE 11.4

An application-level gateway processes the data based on application-related data.

------------> Path of a data packet

You can set up a DMZ in two ways, as illustrated in Figure 11.5. Configuration A is the traditional way of setting up a DMZ: The single firewall controls and regulates access to the three networks. This setup has a drawback similar to placing the public servers on the internal network in that the firewall is the single point of vulnerability. After a server offers its services to the public network, it becomes visible to potential attackers. As a result, if an attacker penetrates your (single) firewall, he also has open access to your internal network.

FIGURE 11.5

Two different DMZ configurations.

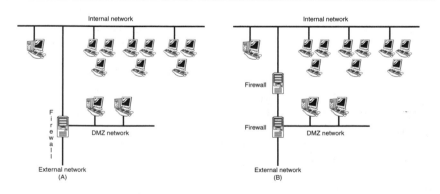

In larger organizations, the DMZ is often composed of two firewalls, as illustrated by Configuration B in Figure 11.5. In this setup, if an attacker is able to compromise the first firewall, he will be blocked by the second firewall, which generally has a much stricter set of rules than the first firewall because the second firewall does not need to deal with traffic directed to the public services. In either DMZ configuration, servers in the DMZ require an increased administration effort in comparison to those in the internal network.

TIP

When you use multilayer firewalls in the DMZ, consider using firewalls from different vendors. For instance, the public-facing firewall may be a Check Point FireWall-1, whereas the second layer is a Cisco Secure PIX Firewall. This way, the intruder would not be able to use the same vulnerability that allowed him to penetrate one firewall on the second firewall.

Consider the following points for inclusion in your firewall or perimeter security policy:

- Describe, in general, how and what perimeter security is maintained; for instance, list what external services users are allowed to access and what services will be denied.

- Indicate who is responsible for checking and maintaining the security.

- Describe how hardware and software changes (such as firmware upgrades) to perimeter security devices are managed and how changes are requested and approved.

- List the procedure to request a firewall device configuration change and how the request is approved.

- Indicate who can grant privileged access to perimeter security systems, and how and who can obtain privileged access.

- Indicate how and who is allowed to obtain information regarding the perimeter configuration and access lists.

- Specify review cycles for perimeter device system configurations.

- If you allow users to access your network remotely, you should require that these remote systems (such as home computers and laptops) have a host-based personal firewall (such as ZoneAlarm) installed.

NOTE

You may want to include wireless access point security as part of your perimeter security policy.

There are very few valid reasons why a member *outside* the security and network support staff would need access to firewall configuration information. Often, in a large organization, a dedicated network security group that is separate from the server and network support staff handles perimeter security (including VPN configuration). Perimeter device configuration information should never be stored on or transmitted to systems of general availability, and it should almost never be printed in hard-copy form.

Acceptable Use Policy

An *acceptable use policy (AUP)* is a set of rules applied by many service providers (such as your ISP) that restrict the ways in which the network may be used and what types of equipment may be connected to the network. For instance, your telephone service provider and ISP will include an AUP as one of the key provisions of their terms of service. You can find an example of an ISP's AUP at www.earthlink.net/about/policies/use.

Acceptable use policy is an integral part of the network security policies. It is often common practice to ask new members of an organization to read and sign an AUP before they are given access to its information systems. For this reason, an AUP must be concise and clear, while at the same time covering the most important points about what users are and are not allowed to do with the computing resources of the organization. It should refer users to the more comprehensive security policy where relevant. It should also, and very notably, define what sanctions will be applied if a user breaks the AUP. Compliance with this policy should, as usual, be measured by regular audits.

NOTE

Although the IT department generally determines the do's and don'ts in an AUP, the penalties to be associated with violations of the don'ts should be made in consultation with the management staff and HR department, and perhaps the Legal department.

The following are some topics, other than the obvious ones (such as no accessing non–business-related websites using company resources), that you should include as part of your AUP:

- Ways the users should safeguard their system passwords and other access tokens (such as magnetic access cards) that would grant them access to the network resources
- Ways to handle data confidentiality.

- Policy regarding software—for instance, users should not copy, install, or remove any application from their company-provided workstations without explicit permission.

- Policy regarding changing of desktop configuration and settings.

- Ways the user can use the company email system—for example, what types of file attachments are permitted and if email and data should be encrypted before being sent.

- Categories of company data that may be taken offsite (such as on a laptop or PDA) and how (for example, whether they need to be encrypted first).

- Rules for using wireless devices.

- Clear policy on how company equipment may be used, if users are provided with such equipment, such as laptops.

- Restrictions on what type of data may be exchanged and how, if you permit users to access your network from home.

- Rules for using packet sniffers, network scanners, and password-crackers.

You should also have an AUP, one slightly different from the end-user version, for contractors and vendors that may be accessing your network. In particular, this variant of the AUP must cover rules for data confidentiality and non-disclosure.

Information Protection

Network security is all about protecting data from being accessed illegally or otherwise altered or compromised over the network. Some of the topics for information protection policy can be considered to fall under AUP and some under the perimeter security topic. However, your corporate information protection policy needs to cover all angles.

The following are some issues and topics you need to take into account when formulating your information or data protection policy. This policy should do the following:

- Define who can have access to sensitive information.

- Have categories of data (or levels of sensitivity) such that users can be granted access based on a need to know, special circumstances, nondisclosure agreements, and so on.

- Define how sensitive information is to be stored and transmitted, such as if the data needs to be encrypted and what types of encryption cipher it should use, or if it should be stored on an encrypted filesystem on the server. Export laws need to be taken into consideration when formulating policy for transmitting encrypted data across country boundaries because certain encryption technologies are not accessible on a worldwide basis.

- Identify on which systems sensitive information can be stored and whether it should be stored using filesystems (such as Reiser) that do not permit undelete.

- Discuss what levels of sensitive information can be printed on physically insecure printers.

- Specify how sensitive information is removed from systems and storage devices, such as degaussing of storage media (such as backup tapes), scrubbing of hard drives (as discussed in Chapter 6, "Filesystem Security"), and shredding of hard-copy output and CDs/DVDs.

- Discuss any default file and directory permissions defined in system-wide configuration files.

- Provide baseline requirements for implementing and using virus protection software.

- Provide guidelines and procedures for reporting and containing virus infections.

- Discuss requirements for scanning email attachments, both inbound and outbound.

- Detail specific policies for downloading and installing software.

- Detail specific policies for the use of thumb/flash memory devices and CD/DVD burners.

- Discuss testing and implementation procedures for new software and software patches.

You should give some extra thought to obtaining, testing, and installing *operating system* software patches. The YaST module offers a feature called YaST Online Update (YOU) that can automatically and periodically check for and apply system software patches (see Figure 11.6).

Good change management practice and common sense, however, say you should never apply changes to a production server without first testing the patches thoroughly. Therefore, part of your information protection policy should identify how server operating system software should be tested and applied. A rollback plan and procedure should be part of the policy.

FIGURE 11.6
Configuring automatic update mode for YaST Online Update.

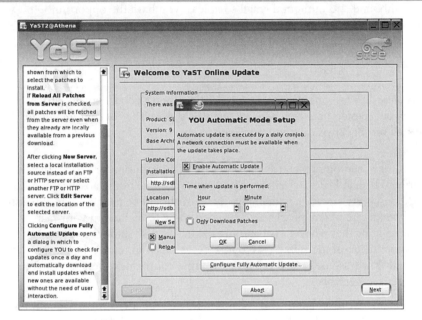

Incident Response

Policies and procedures cannot totally eliminate threats and vulnerabilities to your network; they do, however, help to minimize impact in the event of an attack. We don't want to sound like pessimists, but you need to formulate a policy and procedures on incident handling.

NOTE

Depending on the particular business sector you are in, there may be laws that all system intrusion incidents be recorded and reported to the proper authority, especially in light of the Sarbanes-Oxley law that came into effect on April 15, 2005. Therefore, it is essential that you have a proper incident response policy in place.

For example, in case of an email-based virus attack, you should take necessary measures to minimize the impact on your company. To start, you should block your outbound email until your systems are virus free. In the mean time, if you know the source of the virus-laden email, you can block the source SMTP server and work with that server's administrator to resolve the problem. If you are unable to identify the source, it might be in your best interest to shut down your inbound and outbound email so at least you have the opportunity to decontaminate your systems and not affect other networks by sending them email with a virus attachment.

NOTE

Part of being a responsible network administrator and a good "network citizen" is to not only protect your own network but others' as well by not contributing to viruses, security breas collateral spam, and so on.

If you have laid out a plan to follow in case of an intrusion or attack, the situation will be handled more effectively than it would be in the absence of one. Although every situation is different, the plan should be as thorough as possible to take care of any problems. One good thing to include in your plan is a policy stating that whoever is handling the incident should take very good documentation of the step-by-step procedures taken to return the network to normal. The lessons learned can serve as input for the next iteration of your disaster recovery plan.

An advantage of laying out your plan this way is that it is a proactive approach to solving your problem. From the results of the risk and damage assessment, you will be able to evaluate your options and have more time to plan ahead. Here's one point of caution: Never think that whatever solution you come up with will solve all your problems. Therefore, you need to be prepared for the worst-case scenario.

Your incident response policy should include the following action items:

- Define how to handle anomaly investigation and intruder attacks.
- Specify areas of responsibility for members of the response team.
- Determine what information to record and track and how.
- Specify a list and the order of people to notify and when.
- Define who can release information (for example, the shift supervisor) and the procedure for releasing that information and to whom. This same person may also act as liaison to outside agencies (such as the police or FBI) and organizations (such as the press and the company's business partners).
- Define how a follow-up analysis should be performed and who will participate.

An incident handling procedure is a definite must-have for all organizations. It is impossible to outline responses for all incidents, but you should cover the major types of incidents that might occur. Some sample types are network port scans, Denial of Service attacks, compromised hosts, compromised accounts, and inappropriate use.

Summary

A network security policy is a plan that provides procedures for managing a computing environment. In particular, it gives the system administrator operational guidelines for the environment, such as rules for user account management, system installation procedures, software update processes, the use of security tools, procedures for handling unauthorized access, and so on. The effect of properly using the security policy is a consistent and predictable environment with the added benefit of making anomalies, such as unauthorized access or break-ins, easier to detect.

## CHAPTER 12

Intrusion Detection

Intrusion detection is an aspect of system management that lies, like many others, somewhere between a science and an art form. The main focus in this chapter is on enumerating a number of tools that generate information. This information is about the past and present state of your corporate IT infrastructure. Interpreting the information and understanding what it says are the most difficult parts of the process.

In this chapter, we rehash the ideas expressed in other sections of this book in terms of system hardening. Because servers are created to offer their services, they are exposed to various levels of risk. The task of the various intrusion detection tools is to monitor and, one hopes, maintain the integrity of these hosts.

The topic of intrusion detection is broken down into the following components:

- Reduction of a host's risk
- Network intrusion detection
- Host intrusion detection
- Additional tools of the trade

By the end of this chapter, you should have a good grasp of the different aspects of monitoring for intrusions. In most cases, the best teacher is experience. This is true for both your ability to use the tools and the mindset you have as you work with them.

Defining Intrusions

For the purpose of this chapter, we expand on the standard definition of the term *intrusion detection*. Typically, intrusion detection is understood to be the ability to recognize that, at some point in time, unexpected access to resources was obtained. In most cases, it is assumed that there is a human driving the exploit. A broader, more general definition should also include malware. Though not a pure intrusion, malware can cause significant problems for systems and services.

MALWARE

Malware is defined as a category of software that, by design, attempts to inflict harm or damage to systems. Included in this class of programs are viruses and Trojans.

Other important members of the malware family are spyware, keyloggers, and password grabbers.

In the context of intrusion, malware can often be detected, not by its presence, but by the network traffic it generates.

The most commonly known form of intrusion is that obtained through a known vulnerability in an application. What is less advertised is access obtained by attackers through applications that were inadvertently exposed beyond their intended scope.

As long as there are hackers and requirements for machines to share information, there will be incidents of intrusion. What is important, therefore, is the ability to detect such trespasses and adjust defenses accordingly to mitigate a recurrence. Evaluating the depth of the penetration and the sensitivy of information exposed to the breach is beyond the scope of this chapter. Its importance, however, cannot be overstated. Additional reading on this topic can be found in several places on the Internet. You can find a good article that is a bit Windows centric at `http://www.nsa.gov/snac/support/WORMPAPER.pdf`.

The successful exploit of a vulnerability can only be achieved by first discovering that the target application is available. This implies that in most cases a certain amount of preparatory work, or reconnaissance, is required by the attacker. A proactive approach for preventing intrusions should include watching for reconnaissance scans. It is often impossible to find a single request for service among normal day-to-day traffic, unless of course, it comes from an unexpected source. Diligence in monitoring activities often yields the first hits of an intrusion attempt.

Intrusion detection efforts are typically segregated into two camps; both categories are complementary and must be addressed in a proper detection solution. Tools for managing both of these approaches are covered further in later sections.

The first category is called Network Intrusion Detection Systems (NIDS). This approach requires the deployment of sensors or appliances in strategic locations throughout the network. The sensors passively monitor network traffic for anomalies and can trigger alerts when unexpected events occur.

Similarly, Host-based Intrusion Detection Systems (HIDS) watch for changes on individual hosts. Unlike NIDS, HIDS solutions are, for the most part, not run in real-time. Detecting changes in machine content can therefore go undetected for a period of time.

A complete HIDS and NIDS approach allows for weaknesses in the one technique to be lessened by the other. In many cases, exploited systems start conversations on atypical ports and therefore get caught by the NIDS. If the exploit uses only known, allowed ports, the HIDS system will catch unauthorized changes to the system's content.

Before delving into the various tools available for HIDS and NIDS, we need to examine possible ways to reduce the exposure of systems.

Reducing Your Target Size

At a system level, successful intrusions require access to vulnerable targets. The aim of this section is to ask a number of questions that should be asked for every system on your network. Doing this will help you reduce your overall exposure to exploits.

Several times throughout this book we have discussed the need to run the minimum number of processes possible. If a service is not available on a system, it cannot be exploited. Conceptually, you can think of all the services run on your system as targets. The services that offer up network ports are larger targets because their exposure is greater. Those that only run locally are, in theory, protected by system authentication mechanisms and represent smaller targets. If you add up all the services, the privileges the services are running under, and their exposure, you can get a measure for the total exposure of your system.

A first approach to securing a system is to look at the number of processes running at startup. In the default install of the various flavors of SUSE, great care has been taken to ensure that a full-featured environment is available. Though this provides for maximum flexibility, if not all components are configured properly, it could lead to inadvertent exposure of the system. A process review should be undertaken after a system has been tasked for a specific purpose. Applications not related to the specific tasking of the server should be removed. This reasoning does not just apply to the server environment. Workstations are just as vulnerable to attacks and should therefore be hardened as well.

The second step in reducing exposure is to ensure that your software is kept up to date. Patches and bug fixes occur constantly. It is imperative to replace known defective software as soon as possible. Sometimes, however, a specific fix to one application triggers unexpected incompatibilities in related components. The burden and cost of the development, staging, and production rollover of many fixes often delay their implementation beyond what you, as a system administrator, might deem reasonable. Other avenues should therefore be implemented as well.

NOTE

The YaST firewall configuration tool provides for a quick method for allow-deny rules on specific ports and protocols. It does not allow for more granular definitions for allowed traffic. These definitions have to be implemented directly using `iptables` commands. With such commands, it is possible to restrict the availability of service ports to specific machines, thus further reducing the service's exposure.

The next step in protecting your system is to properly configure the local firewall. In many cases, network-capable services are required for the proper functioning of a local application. As an example, a local database server may require a listener process. If left in the default configuration, the listener may inadvertently be listening for network connections as well as local connections on the loopback address. A properly configured firewall rejects incoming connections before the listener application has a chance to be affected by them. The firewall should not be used as an excuse for an improperly configured application. It is an extra layer of protection. The same is true for many other applications. All systems capable of running a local firewall should do so. Properly configured firewalls don't conflict with business requirements. They are part of a properly configured environment.

After these steps have been performed, they need to be reviewed. As with all aspects of security, everything is a process of continual refinement. Checking a configuration for weaknesses is just as important as, if not more so than, the original security checklist. Vulnerabilities in your defenses are visible to all those who care to look. Verifying the work described here against hardening tools such as Bastille (described in Chapter 13, "System Security") can be quite enlightening.

Vulnerability Assessments

After you have configured your system and believe it is ready for prime time, you need to test it. There are two main categories of tests that should be performed.

The first is a measurement of the target profile your machine presents. This means probing your server for each and every port it presents to the world. In the examples here, we use the `nmap` tool available from www.insecure.org.

The second group of tests involves verifying your server for published vulnerabilities in the services it offers. A number of tools are available to perform this task. In this chapter, we concentrate on the Nessus tool (www.nessus.org).

Both of these tools are present on your SLES distribution media. You should verify that the versions you have installed are up to date. Scanning for vulnerabilities with an outdated tool will leave you with a false sense of security. Verify with the websites shown here that you have the latest software versions and vulnerability signatures.

Both series of tests should be run with your firewall up as well as with your firewall down. While it is comforting to think that the local firewall software will never fail, it never hurts to be cautious. Only by fully testing listener applications will you have a sense of your exposure. If anything, always lean to the side of the paranoid when testing systems.

TESTING VERSUS HACKING!

The tools presented here are excellent professional-grade applications. They can be used to probe your network for weaknesses and vulnerabilities.

Most companies have an explicit policy against running such tools on their production network. Even if such a policy is not written down, any type of vulnerability scanning is considered an attack.

To use these tools, you must receive written permission to conduct your tests. It is also critical that the person giving you permission to run the scans is a recognized agent of the company with the authority to grant such permissions. Also, ensure that strict timelines associated with the scanning event are adhered to.

nmap

The `nmap` tool is a network mapping tool. Designed to scan full networks, `nmap` can return a list of all the ports available on individual machines. It can also be used to probe a single machine for network-accessible ports. Though it can be used in stealth mode, the testing presented here does not have to traverse fire-walls, and we are not concerned about having this scan activity logged. The nmap options used in this section are shown in Table 12.1.

TABLE 12.1
nmap Command-Line Switches

OPTION	MEANING
-sS	Specifies SYN scan. This option establishes half of the standard handshake used by TCP/IP for establishing a connection. It is a little stealthier and does not produce as many log entries.
-sT	Turns on TCP connect() scan. This option creates a full connection to the report port. Each connection shows up in the appropriate application log if it is reachable.
-sV	Turns on version detection. This option triggers additional probes that will be used to get version information on the individual applications hosting open ports.
-P0	Turns off the pinging of hosts for the scan. Because ICMP is often filtered by firewalls, it is not a valid measure for establishing whether a host is present at the specified IP address.
-O	Turns on operating system fingerprinting. Because of the various idiosyncrasies of the various TCP/IP stacks, it is often possible to guess the version of the operating system on the target.
-v	Turns on Verbose mode.
-oN *<logfile>*	Logs the nmap output to **logfile** in text format.
-oX *<logfile>*	Produces an XML logfile.
-p *<port ranges>*	Specifies a comma-separated list of ports to be scanned. Hyphens can be used to identify a range of ports (for example, Oracle Listeners: 1521-1526).
-F	Specifies Fast mode. This option only scans ports that nmap knows about.

The following two examples represent nmap scans of the same server. In the first instance, the firewall is down, and you can see a number of services accepting connections:

```
Athena:~ # nmap -O -n -sT 192.168.1.243

Starting nmap 3.50 ( http://www.insecure.org/nmap/ ) at
➥2005-03-01 08:31 EST
Interesting ports on 192.168.1.243:
(The 1654 ports scanned but not shown below are in state:
➥closed)
```

```
PORT      STATE SERVICE
22/tcp    open  ssh
111/tcp   open  rpcbind
427/tcp   open  svrloc
5801/tcp open  vnc-http-1
5901/tcp open  vnc-1
Device type: general purpose
Running: Linux 2.4.X|2.5.X
OS details: Linux Kernel 2.4.0 - 2.5.20, Linux Kernel 2.4.18
➥- 2.5.70 (X86)

Nmap run completed -- 1 IP address (1 host up) scanned in
➥5.644 seconds
Athena:~ #
```

In this second instance, we have brought up the firewall. As you can see, all but the **ssh** port have been removed from access as expected. Port 113 is accessible but left closed because it is used by some mail services for authentication:

```
Athena:~ # nmap -O -n -sT 192.168.1.243

Starting nmap 3.50 ( http://www.insecure.org/nmap/ ) at
➥2005-03-01 08:40 EST
Interesting ports on 192.168.1.243:
(The 1657 ports scanned but not shown below are in state:
➥filtered)
PORT     STATE  SERVICE
22/tcp   open   ssh
113/tcp closed auth
Device type: general purpose
Running: Linux 2.4.X|2.5.X|2.6.X
OS details: Linux Kernel 2.4.18 - 2.5.70 (X86), Linux 2.4.20
Uptime 0.003 days (since Tue Mar  1 08:37:54 2005)

Nmap run completed -- 1 IP address (1 host up) scanned in
➥77.250 seconds
Athena:~ #
```

What is missing from the second example are ports 5801 and 5901. Referring back to the no-firewall example, you can see that these ports have been enabled to allow remote VNC connections to the server. If this service is not required, the appropriate applications should be disabled. If, however, you want to allow for VNC connections to the server, you could open the ports on the firewall. A more secure option would be to tunnel VNC over **ssh** as discussed in Chapter 8, "Network Services." Such tunneling would require the listeners on the local machine for local connections only.

In both examples, nmap was able to guess that the operating system was a Linux variant. With the reduced number of ports available in the second example, nmap took a lot longer to forge a guess of the remote operating system.

This section shows that it is possible to probe a significant amount of information from a system using nmap. By testing the server with the firewall down, you can inventory the ports offered by the server and ensure that the firewall is tuned appropriately. Keep in mind that the nmap tool is also available to others.

Nessus

The Nessus tool is an open source vulnerability scanner that is composed of both server and client components. This permits a single client workstation to perform testing using several different servers. All the actual communications to the target machine are driven from the server.

The Nessus tool can be used to probe a target machine for services exposed to the network. For each of the ports it finds, it performs a number of tests. Each test is designed to attempt to discover the purpose of the open port and what protocols are supported. The tests also allow for the detection of the application version hosting the port.

Scan results are cross-referenced against a list of known application version vulnerabilities. When this is done, Nessus reports its findings in a number of different formats.

When you are installing SLES, it is possible to include Nessus as one of the components. Before you can use it, however, you must perform a couple of setup steps.

Because the purpose of the Nessus tool is to report back on machine vulnerabilities, the information passed between the server and the client is considered sensitive and should be protected from interception. For this purpose, Nessus encrypts client/server communications. The `nessus-mkcert` command is used to generate the appropriate certificates. When it is invoked, you are asked the following questions:

- CA certificate lifetime in days
- Server certificate lifetime in days
- Your country (two-letter code)
- Your state or province name
- Your location (for example, city or town)
- Your organization

Nessus then creates the appropriate files in /var/lib/nessus/CA. After this is done, you are ready to grant end-user access to the application.

The following shows nessus-mkcert in action:

```
Creation of the Nessus SSL Certificate

This script will now ask you the relevant information to create
the SSL certificate of Nessus. Note that this information will
*NOT* be sent to anybody (everything stays local), but anyone
with the ability to connect to your Nessus daemon will be able
to retrieve this information.


CA certificate life time in days [1460]:
Server certificate life time in days [365]:
Your country (two letter code) [FR]: CA
Your state or province name [none]: Ontario
Your location (e.g. town) [Paris]: Peterborough
Your organization [Nessus Users United]: UniversalExport.ca


-------------------------------------------------------------------
            Creation of the Nessus SSL Certificate
-------------------------------------------------------------------


Congratulations. Your server certificate was properly created.

/usr/local/etc/nessus/nessusd.conf updated

The following files were created :

. Certification authority :
   Certificate = /usr/local/com/nessus/CA/cacert.pem
   Private key = /usr/local/var/nessus/CA/cakey.pem

. Nessus Server :
   Certificate = /usr/local/com/nessus/CA/servercert.pem
   Private key = /usr/local/var/nessus/CA/serverkey.pem

Press [ENTER] to exit
```

Before Nessus can be used, individual accounts called "logins" must be created within it. Using these accounts, users will be able to probe machines for vulnerabilities. Because of the nature of these probes, some being potentially fatal to some services, great care should be exercised when selecting targets and granting access to Nessus.

To grant access to Nessus, you use **nessus-adduser**. When it is executed, you are prompted for

- Login
- Authentication (password/certificate)
- password
- User rules

The login prompt requests the username to be used to establish new client sessions. Authentication can be done by password or certificate. You have to select the appropriate choice for your environment. When you are selecting a login password, ensure that it is sufficiently complex. The user rules section can restrict individuals to specific IP ranges. In most cases, the few individuals allowed to run these scans are granted access to the whole of Nessus.

The following is a transcript of a **nessus-adduser** session. In this example, the user Carol is given the rights to use the Nessus tool to scan all the machines in her branch office (subnet 10.0.17.0/25, which is the short form of 10.0.17.0 netmask 255.255.255.0). Scanning of any other subnets is explicitly denied for this user.

```
Athena:~ # nessus-adduser
Using /var/tmp as a temporary file holder

Add a new nessusd user
----------------------


Login : carol
Authentication (pass/cert) [pass] : pass
Login password :
Login password (again) :

User rules
----------
nessusd has a rules system which allows you to restrict the
hosts that carol has the right to test. For instance, you may
want him to be able to scan his own host only.

Please see the nessus-adduser(8) man page for the rules syntax

Enter the rules for this user, and hit ctrl-D once you are
done : (the user can have an empty rules set)
accept 10.0.17.0/25
default deny
```

```
^D

Login           : carol
Password        : ***********
DN              :
Rules           :
accept 10.0.17.0/25
default deny


Is that ok ? (y/n) [y] y
user added.
Athena:~ #
```

Before the server side of Nessus is invoked, you should perform one important step. Vulnerabilities are being discovered on a regular basis. A list of known weaknesses from the original install CDs will most certainly be out of date by the time you install Nessus. Therefore, before you start Nessus as well as on a regular interval, it is important to update the list of known vulnerabilities. This ensures the validity of the scan results. Nessus uses plug-ins for scanning. These plug-ins are brought up to date using the **nessus-update-plugins** command. At the time of writing, there were more than 7,200 Nessus plug-ins.

After you run the update command, you can start the Nessus server daemon by issuing the following command:

```
Athena:~ # nessusd -D
Loading the plugins... 1224 (out of 7297)
```

After the server has loaded all the plug-ins, the system prompt will return. The client can now be invoked, as follows:

```
Athena:~ # nessus &
```

On startup, the client requires credentials for authenticating against the Nessus scanner on the server side. In addition, if firewalls are in place, allowances for port 1241 will have to be made for client/server communications. The default login screen is shown in Figure 12.1.

The Nessus client interface is composed of a number of tabs. Each tab represents a family of options allowing you to customize your scans. The major tabs are

- **Plugins**—This tab allows you to define the series of tests that will be performed on the selected target.
- **Credentials**—This tab allows you to define valid application accounts (SMB and ssh) to be used to probe for known vulnerabilities available to authenticated users.

- **Scan Options**—On this tab, you can select the number of hosts and tests to run simultaneously. This tab also allows you to select which options are used for port discovery on the target.

- **Target**—You can simply specify a name or address for the target system on this tab. The software also supports defining multiple targets and retrieving a target list from a disk file.

- **User**—User-customized rules can be included using this selection.

- **Prefs.**—This tab permits fine-tuning of the various aspects of the port scanning options. This is also the place where the SNMP community string used for scanning can be changed from public to a more appropriate value. Using this tab, you can also define accounts to be used for insecure services such as FTP, POP, and HTTP.

FIGURE 12.1

The Nessus Client login screen.

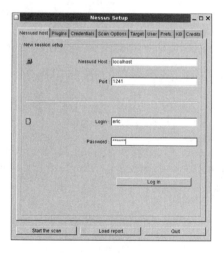

Upon successful login, you are presented with the Plugins tab as well as a warning message (see Figure 12.2). A number of known exploits are Denial of Service exploits (DoS) that cause services to fail. To properly measure the exposure of a system, you must test for the vulnerability using the same approach as the attack. If the system is vulnerable, the service will fail, causing an outage. By default, Nessus disables these tests.

A more detailed version of the Plugins tab is shown in Figure 12.3. In the upper portion of the tab is a list of the different families of tests. If you want to reduce network load and unnecessary alarm, it is best to customize the plug-in selection to match the host type. When you are testing a SUSE server, looking for operating-system–specific vulnerabilities, such as those for Solaris or Windows, is wasteful.

FIGURE 12.2
The Nessus Plugins tab and warning message.

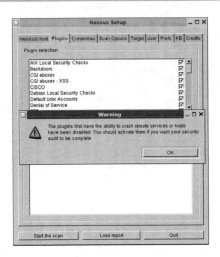

The lower portion of the Plugins tab shows the tests available for a SUSE server. Notice that these are local security checks. This means that if given the proper credentials, Nessus can create a valid **ssh** client session to your server and test for the SUSE vulnerabilities listed.

Selecting the appropriate options for scanning requires a certain amount of fine-tuning. Once you have chosen the appropriate values, you can proceed to the Target tab. After choosing the appropriate target, you can select the Start the Scan button at the bottom of the window.

For the purpose of this section, we have started a number of extra services on the server Athena. We have also selected to run the tests without the local server-side firewall. If the services are present and unprotected, it is best to know whether any vulnerabilities exist.

Nessus will proceed to scan the target for open ports, and for each, it will run a number of tests. A typical report is shown in Figure 12.4. When the report window opens, you are presented with a number of blank panes. Selecting the appropriate subnet in the upper-left pane presents a list of valid scanned hosts in the lower-left pane. Selecting the appropriate host populates the report portion of the window.

FIGURE 12.3
The Nessus SUSE Local Security Checks options.

FIGURE 12.4
A Nessus report for Athena.

Figure 12.4 presents the information gleaned from finding an open Telnet service on the server. Throughout this book, we have discussed using **ssh** over Telnet. In this example, the security warning option in the Severity pane rehashes the perils of using Telnet. The Security Note portion of the Severity

pane presents information that a hacker could collect if Telnet were accessible. From the Telnet banner alone, a hacker can determine not only the flavor of the operating system, but also which version of the kernel it is running.

To reduce this exposure and that of traffic intercept, we have suggested many times replacing Telnet with **ssh**. If you then view the Nessus results for **ssh**, you find the information presented in Figure 12.5. Though **ssh** is a more secure protocol, certain incarnations of the protocols have been found to have weaknesses over time. Currently, **ssh** versions earlier than version 2 are not considered totally safe. In this case, Nessus has revealed that simply turning on **ssh** might leave a false sense of security. Nessus also offers the appropriate configuration changes required to secure the solution.

FIGURE 12.5
A Nessus report for the **ssh** service on Athena.

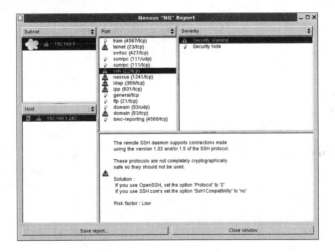

This discussion illustrates how Nessus can be used to probe for vulnerabilities on your servers. Selecting the appropriate scanning options allows for efficient, customized scanning for your infrastructure. It is important to remember that a number of scanning options are known to crash services. Great care should be exercised to restrict the use of such selections.

In most cases, a valid corporate IT policy will prohibit the unscheduled use of scanning tools such as Nessus on the live network. It is not difficult to imagine the chaos that would result from having the uncontrolled use of vulnerability scanners crashing production environments. The next section describes how such scans can be tracked. Whenever possible, a preproduction environment should exist where these tests can be performed on staging servers. This ensures that the soon-to-be-rolled-out changes are secure. If not, the tests will generate downtime in the development section, not in production.

Detecting a Network-based Intrusion

Attackers use application vulnerabilities to gain unauthorized access to systems. We saw in the preceding section how tools such as Nessus help identify vulnerable services and, when possible, recommend ways to remedy the problem. Before attackers can exploit a vulnerable system, they must know it exists.

The following sections examine a number of different methods that can be used to protect a network environment. We also examine techniques that can be used to detect the presence of unwanted guests.

Know Your Traffic, Tune Your Firewall

Applications and users require a transport mechanism for communicating with each other. In a standard network environment, this is handled by using a number of network protocols such as TCP/IP, ICMP, and UDP. For each of these, applications require predefined ports over which the communications will take place.

The file /etc/services contains a number of well-known, predefined protocol-port pairs and the applications they support. If you know the applications that are being run within your environment, you should be able to generate a list of required ports. /etc/services is a static ASCII file used for referencing ports and applications. It does not prevent the binding of services to any specific port. Restricting network traffic flow to only these select ports will reduce your overall exposure. In addition, a proper review of requirements may identify that some services can be restricted to specific clients. Further constraints can be placed on network flow to allow only these conversations.

As an extra level of complexity, some applications initiate conversations only on a specific port. After the appropriate handshake has been performed, the communications exchange is shifted to a different, sometimes random, port.

When you are finished with the application-port mapping exercise, you will have a list of valid client/server/port relationships that are required to support your applications. Layered on top of the business list of ports is the more transparent layer. Protocols such as DHCP, DNS, and NNTP are often forgotten in the application lists. If they are not included at this step in the process, a number of critical applications may fail. The availability of each of these relationships on the network can be controlled by placing the services in question behind an appropriately configured firewall.

Knowing which ports are in use on your network allows you to identify unsanctioned traffic more readily. Keyloggers and password-stealing Trojans often use IRC channels to report their findings to a remote server. If your network doesn't allow chat traffic, you will quickly be able to identify potentially infected machines that use this mechanism.

A properly configured firewall should monitor not only incoming traffic, but it also should be able to monitor and control the port and contents of both inward- and outward-bound packets. If this can be achieved, the first step in mitigating a successful attack has been taken.

Network Intrusion Detection Systems

The preceding section explained how a properly configured firewall allows clients to access only specific target servers. Using such a firewall, coupled with stateful packet inspection, you can be fairly confident that packets reaching the servers contain data that is valid for the target service.

STATEFUL PACKET INSPECTION

A number of firewalls filter traffic based only on the ports used in the conversation. A number of exploits, however, occur when malformed packets are sent to a server over allowed ports.

Stateful Packet Inspection is a tool used to examine information passed between a client and a host. When this tool is enabled, all the packets that make up a single transmission are assembled by the firewall. Once they are assembled, the original message is checked for consistency and correctness of all the appropriate headers. When a packet is considered safe, it is passed along to the target server.

Stateful Packet Inspection also monitors the current state of a conversation between two hosts. If a packet attempts to traverse a firewall claiming to be part of a specific conversation, it is checked against a known list of current connections. If the conversation is active and the packet was expected, it is allowed through.

This process should not be confused with Application Layer packet filtering. Such filtering actually examines the content of the data portion of packets looking for known application-level exploits.

The issue at hand now becomes determining whether the traffic sent to a server is a valid request, and not an attempt to exploit a known vulnerability of the service. Services are exploited when they are sent specially crafted streams of data that cause them to malfunction in predictable ways. As they malfunction, they inadvertently give an attacker access to resources that, in turn, can lead to a system compromise.

A Network Intrusion Detection System (NIDS) is a service that monitors network traffic flow looking for known exploit attempts. In some cases, NIDS is implemented as an appliance; in other cases, as a piece of software. In either case, because NIDS requires access to all network conversations, it must be placed in a network where it can be allowed to intercept all traffic. In most cases, it will therefore require the programming of a switch to allow one port to listen to all traffic.

NIDS inspects each packet and compares the content against a set of known exploits. If a match is found, an alert is generated and the packet is logged. One of the major difficulties in tuning an NIDS environment is determining which alerts are real and which are false positives. There is a fine balance between defining the parameters of an exploit attempt and the necessary resources required to implement a 100% match. Since NIDS must be running in real-time, the processing load of deep inspection of all packet content is not possible. Packet rules configured to recognize particular exploits are therefore potentially prone to incorrectly identify innocent packets as attacks. When they are tuned to an existing environment, however, it is possible to reduce the error rate to an acceptable level. Caution must be taken to find a proper balance between too many alerts versus insufficient protection.

Snort

Bundled with SLES, is an NIDS called Snort. Originally designed as a lightweight NIDS, Snort has become one of the most widely used systems for detecting intrusions. Snort rules are constantly being developed by the Snort community and shared through their website. In addition to using community rules, you also can create your own rules.

Before looking at results from Snort in action, let's first examine how it can be configured to suit your environment. The Snort software can be found in /etc/snort. Table 12.2 lists the files found in this directory.

TABLE 12.2
Snort Configuration Files in /etc/snort

FILENAME	DESCRIPTION
snort.conf	Main Snort configuration file. Used to define network configuration and which rules are loaded at runtime.

TABLE 12.2
Snort Configuration Files in /etc/snort (continued)

FILENAME	DESCRIPTION
threshold.conf	Used to control the logging of rules that are triggered on a frequent basis. Used to reduce the number of alerts from such rules without losing the trigger information.
reference.config	Used to provide URLs for important resources.
classification.config	Definitions of the different alert classes.
gen-msg.map	Text descriptions of the different alert IDs.
sid-msg.map	Text definitions of the different SIDs.
*.rules	Rule definition files.

Though there are many files in the **snort** directory, most of the configuration of Snort is done through **snort.conf**. This file is split into four major sections:

- **Network definition**—This section allows you to define a set of variables that describe the networking environment within which the Snort sensor finds itself. These variables are applied to the rules files as they are loaded. Definitions in this section include the identification of valid servers for specific types of traffic such as SMTP, HTTP, DNS, and so on.

- **Preprocessors**—This section allows you to define if and how related packets are treated. It also allows for the configuration of the way the packets are inspected for content.

- **Logging options**—This section allows you to define where the Snort alerts are to be placed. By default, the alerts go to the system log facility. You can change the behavior here to log to **/var/log/snort** and/or to a database.

- **Rules**—This section allows you to control which rules are activated by the system. Each family of rules is maintained in a separate file. Variables defined in the first section are interpreted and inserted into the rules.

You can activate Snort by running its script in **/etc/init.d**. To have Snort initialized at boot time, you need to use YaST and configure the Runlevel Editor option. By default, the SUSE implementation of Snort can see only network traffic destined to the local host server. You can change this by modifying the Snort startup script in **/etc/init.d** and defining a variable called **SNORT_PROMISC** and setting its value to **yes**. When this is done, Snort will change the mode of the network card to promiscuous. In this mode, Snort can monitor all traffic seen by the network card, and not just the traffic destined for its host system.

When a packet arrives on the interface card that Snort is listening on, Snort intercepts it for analysis. When a packet is found to satisfy the requirements of one of the rules, an alert is issued. An example of such an alert is shown in Listing 12.1.

LISTING 12.1
A Snort Alert Found in /var/log/snort/alert

```
[**] [1:1256:7] WEB-IIS CodeRed v2 root.exe access [**]
[Classification: Web Application Attack] [Priority: 1]
04/16-19:32:41.639229 10.0.131.168:4105 -> 192.168.1.240:80
TCP TTL:113 TOS:0x0 ID:40087 IpLen:20 DgmLen:112 DF
***AP*** Seq: 0x8721649F  Ack: 0x95199331  Win: 0x4470
➥  TcpLen: 20
[Xref => http://www.cert.org/advisories/CA-2001-19.html]
```

In this listing, you see that Code Red attacks are still happening on the Internet. As you can see from this example, Snort registers a fair amount of information in the local log file. Scanning through the log file manually can be a tedious task and prone to missing important information.

Analysis Console for Intrusion Databases

A more flexible tool is required to quickly look at the events triggered by Snort. There are a number of tools for reviewing Snort logs. In this section, we implement a tool called Analysis Console for Intrusion Databases (ACID). This tool can be used to review logged events and present the summarized findings on a web page. Through the web environment, it is possible to drill down using a number of different avenues to obtain event-specific information.

As its name implies, ACID relies on having Snort events collected in a database. The following will help you set up a MySQL repository for your Snort logs as well as implement the ACID tool.

To get ACID running on your system, you need to install the following packages:

- **Snort**—An NIDS tool
- **MySQL**—A logging database
- **PHP**—A web interface scripting language
- **ADODB**—A database access interface
- **JPGRAPH**—A tool that creates charts for websites
- **PCRE**—PERL Compatible Regular Expression library
- **ACID**—An analysis tool

Both Snort and MySQL are included in the original distribution media for your SLES server. If they were not included in the original install, you can add them to your system using the YaST software option. Newer versions of the software are available from their respective websites.

As mentioned earlier, configuring Snort requires making changes to /etc/snort/snort.conf. The version of this file supplied with the default install will suffice for the original install. You may, however, want to modify the /etc/init.sd/snort startup script as mentioned previously to monitor events beyond the local server.

Once snort has been configured and is logging alerts to /var/log/snort/alert, you can proceed with the configuration of MySQL. Similarly to Snort, installing the MySQL database does not enable the startup of the database when the machine starts. To enable this feature and the associated clean shutdown, you must use the YaST Runlevel Editor.

By default, MySQL does not set a local administrator password. To set a password to protect the database, use the following command:

```
Athena:~ # mysqladmin –u root password newpassword
```

The results of a Snort scan should be stored in a Snort-specific database. To create such a database within MySQL, sign into MySQL using the root account just defined and use commands similar to these:

```
use mysql;
create database snort;
use snort;
grant ALL on snort.* to snort@Athena.UniversalExport.ca
➠  identified by 'mspiggy';
grant ALL on snort.* to snort@localhost  identified
➠by 'mspiggy';
exit
```

These commands create an empty database for the Snort alerts. Before you can make Snort point to MySQL, you need to create the tables it is expecting. In the original installation of Snort, a script is provided to create all the required structures. The file containing the script is /usr/share.docs.packages.snort/create_mysql. Enter MySQL using the Snort account this time and execute the preceding script:

```
Athena:~ # mysql -u snort -p
Enter password:
Welcome to the MySQL monitor.
Commands end with ; or \g.
```

```
Your MySQL connection id is 14 to server version: 4.0.18

Type 'help;' or '\h' for help. Type '\c' to clear the buffer.

mysql> use snort;
Database changed
mysql> \. /usr/share/doc/packages/snort/create_mysql
```

This script creates a MySQL database to contain the Snort alerts. You can now proceed to configure Snort to enable logging to MySQL. In the `snort.conf` file, you need to find the section that contains a number of lines beginning with `output database`. In this section, you create a new entry like this:

```
output database: log, mysql, user=snort password=mspiggy
➥dbname=snort host=localhost
```

This allows Snort to log to both `/var/log/snort/alert` as well as the MySQL Snort instance. With this change in place, it is now possible to restart Snort to activate the new logging feature:

```
Athena:~ # /etc/init.d/snort restart
```

The next step is to validate that you are logging events into MySQL. You can verify this by entering the MySQL Snort database and looking for entries in the tables of the Snort instance.

The configuration of the other components can be done quite easily. The PHP install is done through YaST and must include the PHP modules for Apache and MySQL. The ACID tool can be found at the following URL:

```
http://www.andrew.cmu.edu/user/rdanyliw/snort/snortacid.html.
```

ACID REQUIREMENTS

The ACID tool is a great addition to Snort. It's easier to detect patterns graphically than to scan pages of logs visually. The graphical representation of alerts within ACID, coupled with the ability to drill down through the data to a specific event, allows an administrator to quickly determine the source of a threat.

The drawback, however, is that configuring all the components of ACID can be quite challenging. The distribution kit for ACID identifies a number of dependencies. ACID is written in PHP, but specific application hooks must be compiled into the executable. If you want to upgrade your version of PHP, you need to verify that dependencies such as gd and MySQL must be satisfied at compile time.

Though they are a bit tricky to set up, Snort and ACID are essential tools in your NIDS strategy.

Before proceeding any further, you need to secure your MySQL database. By design, database servers are network aware. With MySQL, a listener is created looking for network connections on port 3306. If your Snort sensor is co-located on the same server as your MySQL server, port 3306 need not be made available to the network. You can secure this port by ensuring it is blocked at the firewall level. Snort can log events to the database using the localhost network.

If you deploy a number of Snort sensors throughout your network, you will have to open port 3306 on the firewall. In the preferred scenario, only specific static IP addresses will be allowed to connect through the firewall. In addition, when granting permission to the Snort database, MySQL allows you to specify allowed client hostnames.

Included in the install kit for ACID is the necessary documentation for accessing the other required components. ACID, ADODB, and JPGRAPH are simple to un-tar and move into the default web root, /srv/www/htdocs. It is prudent to trim out all the sample and documentation folders that are not required for the proper functioning of the application. PCRE, on the other hand, requires a compiler environment and must be built through the .configure and make stages. All of this is well documented inside each package.

When all these packages are installed, you should find acid, adodb, and jpgraph-1.16 directories.

The ACID tool relies on a configuration file called acid_conf.php that resides in /srv/www/htdocs/acid. You must edit this file and customize it for your environment. The following variables must be defined to match your installation:

```
$DBlib_path = "/srv/www/htdocs/adodb";

$DBtype = "mysql";

$alert_dbname   = "snort";
$alert_host     = "localhost";
$alert_port     = "";
$alert_user     = "snort";
$alert_password = "mspiggy";

$ChartLib_path = "/srv/www/htdocs/jpgraph-1.16";
```

After saving the modifications for the ACID configuration, you should be able to view your Snort alerts through the web. You can access the web page through http://localhost/acid/acid_main.php. An example of this page is shown in Figure 12.6.

NOTE

Visibility is an important factor to keep in mind when you are deploying web-based tools. When you deploy an ACID website, ask yourself who has access to it. By default, websites are available to anyone who finds them.

Is it acceptable for you to show the world which events tripped your Snort sensor? If an attacker can also monitor your monitoring of network activity, could he change his approach and become more stealthy?

There are a number of steps you might want to take to secure your website:

- You can set up a firewall rule to accept connections only from specific TCP/IP addresses.

- You can also set up a robots.txt file. This keeps spiders from adding your website to Google and other search engines. It does not, however, prevent spiders that do not obey robots.txt files.

- You can enable SSL on the site and configure your web browser to support .htaccess files. This encrypts your HTTP conversations and adds a simple level of challenge-response protection to your site's content.

Keep in mind that the tools you deploy, unless secured, can be used against you.

FIGURE 12.6
The ACID main menu.

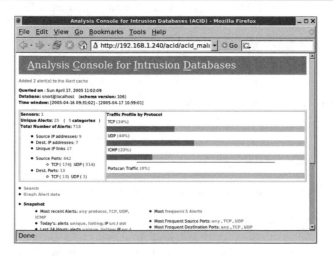

On this page, you immediately get a significant amount of information not immediately apparent from the flat log files. You can quickly see the alert distribution across the various protocols (TCP, UDP, or ICMP). ACID also summarizes the alerts by category, alert type, ports, source, destination, and links.

Figure 12.7 represents the alerts broken down by category. You can see the five separate types of alerts as well as the number of alerts, the number of sources/destinations, and the time span over which the alerts were generated.

FIGURE 12.7
The ACID alert by category menu.

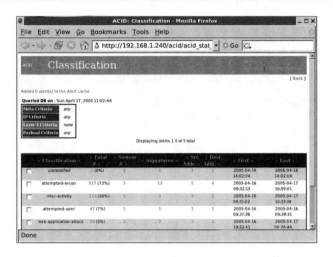

If you want to drill down further, you can find the alert used earlier in Listing 12.1. If you select the 36 members of the web-application-attack category, you can further refine the view of the Snort database down to the event level. After doing this, you can examine the details of the alert in a slightly more readable manner, as shown in Figure 12.8.

The ACID tool allows for a number of additional features unavailable directly through the log file. Since all of the data used by ACID is in MySQL, a number of queries can be launched directly on the database from the Search menu. In addition, it is possible to configure an archive database to keep specific events on file for future reference.

In this section, we discussed the importance of knowing what traffic is flowing across your network. It is important to understand the characteristics of your application-generated traffic. This allows for the appropriate firewall implementations. Traffic that is out of these norms should be refused. If a valid business requirement exists for this new format of traffic, the appropriate changes will have to be made at the firewall level. Measuring out-of-the-normal traffic permits the identification of potentially compromised systems.

FIGURE 12.8
The ACID version of the Code Red example.

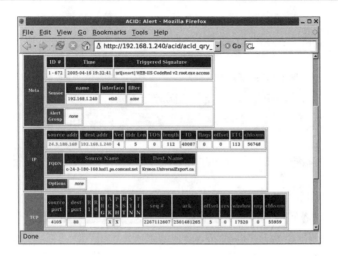

For traffic that does fit within the allowed patterns of traffic, it is still important to remain vigilant. Application exploits will use an application's default port settings when attacking a service. Monitoring the content of the traffic can help determine whether it is malicious.

It is important to also note that, just as in the case for the Nessus tool, many corporate policies may prevent the application of network monitoring tools that actually capture packets.

Detecting a Host Intrusion

In the preceding section, we looked at protecting systems through controlling the network. If attackers cannot reach a system, in theory they cannot compromise it. All servers on a network, however, are there to offer a service. If a vulnerability exists in the code on which the service relies, it may be exploited by an attacker to gain access to the server.

Tools such as Snort and ACID can be used to look for exploit attempts within network packets. If the attacker is using a technique not yet known to these tools, the compromise may go undetected at the network level. In cases such as these, other techniques will have to be employed in an attempt to find possible exploits.

Log Files

One method for looking for traces of an intrusion is to look for clues in log files. Depending on the activity level of the server, this can be a Herculean task. If the attacker was a novice and left traces of his presence, possibly only one log entry in thousands may reflect that fact. If the attack is successful, deliberate modification of the log file could hide any sign of an intrusion.

Placing the log files on a remote syslog server can mitigate against this type of cleanup attempt. Tools such as logsurfer can help sift through the many entries looking for known patterns. The problem is, not all patterns are known, and in many cases the log files are tweaked to erase tracks.

The value of log files should not be dismissed as a valuable tool for detecting intrusions. What they can provide, in some cases, is early warning that an attack is being set up. A careful review of the logs can reveal abnormal login failures from unexpected sources or port scans from other systems. Such information should not be ignored. Repeated failures of a particular service may indicate knowledge of vulnerabilities with the code. A quick check for newer, patched versions should be done.

chkrootkit

As soon as a system is compromised, it is not uncommon for an attacker to install what is commonly known as a *rootkit*. A rootkit is essentially a backdoor environment that allows the attacker to continue to access the compromised system. Often this is done through replacement of known executables with modified versions. This permits the attacker to connect to the system through a more comfortable interface.

Detecting a rootkit can be very difficult. Knowing which executable has been replaced with a hacked version can be almost impossible.

The chkrootkit program has been made available for just such a task and is available for download from www.chkrootkit.org. As new rootkits are discovered, this utility is modified to allow it to detect the subtle nuances in hacked versions of known executables.

Once compiled for your system, the chkrootkit program can be run with the -h flag to receive a list of available options. When run with no flags, it will scan all the executables it knows of and generate a lengthy report of its findings. Portions of such a report are shown here:

```
Athena:~ # ./chkrootkit
ROOTDIR is `/'
Checking `amd'... not found
Checking `basename'... not infected
Checking `biff'... not found
Checking `chfn'... not infected
Checking `chsh'... not infected
Checking `cron'... not infected
Checking `date'... not infected
Checking `du'... not infected
Checking `dirname'... not infected
Checking `echo'... not infected
    .
    .
    .
Searching for HiDrootkit's default dir... nothing found
Searching for tOrn's default files and dirs... nothing found
Searching for tOrn's v8 defaults... nothing found
Searching for Lion Worm default files and dirs... nothing found
Searching for RSHA's default files and dir... nothing found
Searching for RH-Sharpe's default files... nothing found
    .
    .
    .
Searching for LPD Worm files and dirs... nothing found
Searching for Ramen Worm files and dirs... nothing found
Searching for Maniac files and dirs... nothing found
Searching for RK17 files and dirs... nothing found
Searching for Ducoci rootkit... nothing found
Searching for Adore Worm... nothing found
    .
    .
    .
Checking `lkm'... chkproc: nothing detected
Checking `rexedcs'... not found
Checking `sniffer'... eth0: PF_PACKET(/usr/bin/snort)
Checking `w55808'... not infected
Checking `wted'... chkwtmp: nothing deleted
Checking `scalper'... not infected
Checking `slapper'... not infected
Checking `z2'... chklastlog: nothing deleted
Checking `chkutmp'... chkutmp: nothing deleted
```

In the report produced on Athena, more than 100 lines of output were generated. As you can see from this listing, the machine is clean. As expected, however, the sniffer check found that eth0 was in promiscuous mode and that the responsible binary was /usr/bin/snort. Because we knew Snort was running, this was not a problem. If we found something unexpected, it may be an indication of an intrusion.

The chkrootkit utility can be very useful in detecting a number of known backdoors. It can also look for known behaviors of backdoors such as the sniffer example shown in this section. What it cannot guarantee, however, is protection from other modifications beyond its designed scope.

Advanced Intrusion Detection Environment (AIDE)

Tools such as chkrootkit are very good at detecting changes in applications they have been designed to check. Because new backdoor techniques are constantly being developed, however, countermeasures such as these are forever playing catchup.

One approach for detecting unauthorized changes to a system is to take a snapshot of its content on a regular basis. Comparing these snapshots over time can provide a time-lapse reconstruction of changes. Such is the approach taken by applications such as the Advanced Intrusion Detection Environment (AIDE).

TRIPWIRE

One of the first HIDS products available on Linux is called Tripwire. Both free and commercial versions are available. The free version of this tool is included in the SLES distribution.

This product delivers essentially the same functionality as AIDE. It is, however, multiplatform. Based on the architecture of your site, you may decide that you want a common tool for all platforms. In such cases, Tripwire would be an ideal candidate. More information on the Tripwire tool is available from the website at http://www.tripwire.org.

The AIDE utility is a file integrity checker. It does not know about different attack algorithms or how backdoors get implanted on a system. It does, however, know how to keep track of files and notice whether changes have been made.

The main strength of tools such as AIDE is their ability to detect changes in patterns. When a system is built from known, trusted media, it can be considered safe and unexploited. The moment the machine is placed on a network, it is potentially vulnerable to exploits. Before exposing the system, you must record selected characteristics of your files. You will therefore know what they looked like when they were in pristine condition. On a regular basis, you can then compare the same characteristics from the live system with your time-zero snapshot. Changes in the attributes might reflect a machine compromise.

This is essentially what AIDE permits you to do. The behavior of AIDE is controlled through its configuration file `aide.conf`, which contains three different types of directives.

The first line type can be used to set a number of configuration options. With these options, you can set path values for `database`, `database_new`, and `report_url`. Defining these values within the configuration file means they do not have to be defined on the command line.

Macro lines allow you to specify short forms to define which characteristics will be recorded for each file. Attributes such as permission, inode, ownership, time stamps, and hash values for files can be registered in the AIDE database.

The last line type contains directives regarding which portions of the directory structure will be present in the AIDE database. Directories are included in the list using regular expressions. These expressions can allow for portions of directories or even specific files to be ignored.

The following is a portion of the default `aide.conf` file, supplied with SLES, located in the `/etc` directory:

```
#
#     AIDE _Example_ Configuration
#
#
# Configuration parameters
#
database=file:/var/lib/aide/aide.db
database_out=file:/var/lib/aide/aide.db.new
verbose=1
report_url=stdout
warn_dead_symlinks=yes

#
# Custom rules
#
Binlib          = p+i+n+u+g+s+b+m+c+md5+sha1
ConfFiles       = p+i+n+u+g+s+b+m+c+md5+sha1
```

```
#
# Directories and files
#
# Kernel, system map, etc.
/boot                           Binlib

# watch config files, but exclude, what changes at boot time,
➥... !/etc/mtab
!/etc/lvm*
/etc                            ConfFiles

# Binaries
/bin                            Binlib
/sbin                           Binlib

# Libraries
/lib                            Binlib

# Complete /usr and /opt
/usr                            Binlib
/opt                            Binlib
```

In this example, you can clearly see where a number of command-line parameters have been predefined. Also, the BinLib macro has been created to identify the file attributes we would like AIDE to track. A list of the attributes AIDE is capable of tracking is shown in Table 12.3.

TABLE 12.3
Tracking AIDE Attributes

ATTRIBUTE	DESCRIPTION
P	Permissions
I	Inode
N	Number of links
U	User
G	Group
S	Size
B	Block count
M	Modify time (mtime)
A	Access timestamp
C	Creation time (Ctime)

TABLE 12.3
Tracking AIDE Attributes (continued)

ATTRIBUTE	DESCRIPTION
md5	Creates an MD5 sum for the file
sha1	Creates an sha1 checksum for the file
rmd160	Creates an rmd160 checksum for the file
tiger	Creates a tiger checksum for the file
R	Short form for the combination of p+i+n+u+g+s+m+c+md5
L	Short form for the combination of p+i+n+g+u
E	Checks for empty groups
>	Short form for the combination of p+u+g+i+n+s
crc32	Creates a crc32 checksum (if mhash is enabled)
haval	Creates an haval checksum (if mhash is enabled)
gost	Creates a gost checksum (if mhash is enabled)

AIDE can be invoked in four different modes, as listed in Table 12.4.

TABLE 12.4
AIDE Run-Time Modes

MODE	DESCRIPTION
--check	Performs an integrity check on the AIDE database
--init	Creates an initial database based on the aide.conf configuration
--update	Allows for updates to be accepted into the database for approved changes to the system content
--compare	Checks for differences between the databases pointed to by the database_new and database parameters in the configuration file

The --init version of AIDE needs to be run only once. It creates the initial database. Subsequent calls to AIDE should use the --check option. As an example, after configuring AIDE and initializing the database, we manually changed a file in our system. When we ran the check phase, AIDE generated the following:

```
Athena:/var/lib/aide # aide -C
AIDE found differences between database and filesystem!!
```

```
Summary:s
Total number of files=3679,added files=1,removed files=0,
►changed files=4
Athena:/var/lib/aide #
```

Checking the resulting logs revealed this change:

```
File: /etc/php.ini
Size : 38307                    , 38330
Mtime:2005-04-14 03:24:41       , 2005-03-11 18:42:10
Ctime:2005-04-14 03:24:41       , 2005-03-11 18:42:10
Inode:181287                    , 181494
MD5  :EgKatoUTIIWvIAoBiXtOkg==  , 1tmORxHz6pAD1y5Nl8fPpw==
SHA1:HY09wB3q6MXMepohZ+JkP46TKBk=,LF/6gYohtIPCJj3fZqhBhOpuXfc=
```

Though this is a simple example, it provides a fair amount of comfort that AIDE is capable of finding changes.

The AIDE tool was created to allow for a flexible system to provide a consistent and robust method for tracking changes to a server. It is important to remember that, as configured, the AIDE tool stores all its results within the filesystem. Given sufficient time, attackers may realize that AIDE is installed. This would give them ample opportunity to maintain the AIDE database, covering their tracks as they go.

It is imperative that copies of both the configuration file and the databases be kept on offline storage devices. If the databases are kept on read-only mount points, an attacker with root privileges could simply remount the volume, make changes, and switch it back again. Placing the information on CD is a good idea unless the CD is left in the burner. Multiple session CDs could be used to overwrite previous versions of the database. Additionally, leaving the CD in the drive might also allow an attacker to view the configuration file. Once the attacker has that information, he will know exactly where to place the exploit code to make it invisible to your scans.

Though much of this may sound paranoid, any information stored on, or accessible to, a compromised system must be considered tainted. By placing the AIDE files out of reach of the running system, you have a more reliable comparison snapshot.

It is also important to remember that the AIDE database will have to be maintained every time new applications are applied to the system. This includes patches to the operating system and its underlying services.

Additional Tools

A number of other tools can be used to your advantage in detecting possible intrusions. Though not directly related to HIDS or NIDS, a number of these tools are capable of alerting you to out-of-the-ordinary events.

Scan Detection Tools

PortSentry and Scanlogd are examples of applications that can be run on a local host to monitor connection attempts.

Scanlogd is supplied with your SLES distribution. This tool is run as a daemon so that it monitors activity at all times. Because the tool must be able to monitor all possible ports on an interface, including those that are not active, Scanlogd must be started with root privileges. Once activated and access to the interface has been secured, Scanlogd switches to using a local, unprivileged account called scanlogd.

Scanlogd is a passive tool and only listens for connection attempts. If a remote host attempts to connect to a number of ports within a short time window, Scanlogd logs the attempt. Scanlogd then ignores connection attempts from that host for a brief period of time to prevent a logfile-full brute-force attack.

More information on Scanlogd is available in the local man pages. You should verify that your version is up to date by checking the project website at http://www.openwall.com/scanlogd.

The following is a typical Scanlogd entry that can be found in the system log when a host is scanned by a tool such as nmap:

```
Mar 12 03:33:59 Athena scanlogd: 192.168.1.243:63218 to
➡192.168.1.242 ports 5303, 514, 179, 877, 5999,
➡5301, 2112, 1384, ..., fSrpauxy, TOS 00 @03:33:59
```

In this single log file entry, you can determine the source of the scan as well as the ports of interest to the intruder. Using a tool such as logsurfer, an administrator can receive an alert and take appropriate action.

A more advanced tool for monitoring network scans is called PostSentry. This tool is not included in your SLES distribution but is available at http://sourceforge.net/projects/sentrytools/.

PortSentry also runs as a daemon and listens for inbound network connection attempts. This tool can be targeted to listen for access attempts on a specific list of ports or to listen for connections on all but a predetermined list of ports. An additional feature of PostSentry is that it can be placed in-line between a potential attacker and the target host. In this mode, PortSentry can filter packets and packet responses. If you are going to use PortSentry, read the documentation provided with the tool and ensure that you are running the latest version.

MRTG and Cacti

A different approach to detecting unexpected network traffic could include monitoring packet volumes at various interfaces. MRTG (`http://people.ee.ethz.ch/~oetiker/webtools/mrtg/`) and, more recently, Cacti (`http://www.cacti.net/`) are both tools that can be used to quickly display important network characteristics.

It is possible to configure SNMP on various devices to report on traffic statistics. The devices in question could be routers, switches, or network interface cards. Both of these tools rely on a number of processes to harvest the data from the various devices. The data is then massaged by MRTG or Cacti and presented in a graphical format.

SNMP

SNMP is a great technology for monitoring your devices. It does, however, have a number of characteristics that should make you nervous. SNMP is a cleartext protocol for transmitting status information.

Keep in mind that if there is a chance these packets are intercepted, you will be divulging a great deal of information about your network architecture. It will be fairly easy for someone listening to determine which packets belong to routers and which belong to servers.

There have also been a number of serious vulnerabilities discovered in SNMP. You should ensure that you are running the most recent versions available for your separate platforms.

If you decide to run SNMP, ensure that the environment is configured in such a way as to ensure that the information packets do not leak beyond the confines of your local network.

The graphs are presented through the web. Comparison can be made between current traffic loads, trends, and historical data. When a graph indicates that traffic volumes are outside the expected norm, an investigation can be launched.

Properly configured installations of this software can group devices and mimic the actual network topology. It is therefore rather simple to drill down through the graphs and statistics to find the individual machine that is causing the bottlenecks.

Ethereal

An additional tool that can be useful in monitoring network activity is Ethereal. This tool is an advanced packet-capturing tool capable of capturing all the conversations being transmitted across a network. Once conversations are captured, the stream of these packets can be reassembled, and both sides of the network conversation can be viewed. It is therefore possible to reconstruct Telnet and FTP sessions in their entirety. This includes the transmission of cleartext usernames and passwords. It is also possible to reconstruct web pages and binary transfers. Without the proper authority, running Ethereal may be interpreted as wiretapping. For this reason, it may be in conflict with a great many IT policies. In the proper hands, when used with the approval and knowledge of responsible parties, it can be instrumental in tracking down spurious traffic.

When used in conjunction with tools such as MRTG and Cacti, Ethereal can be used to further identify the source of traffic. As an example, assume that a known non-SNMP capable switch is hosting a machine that is causing network congestion. It is difficult to tell which of the hosts is generating the traffic because SNMP is unavailable to generate port-based statistics. Placing an Ethereal sniffer downstream from the switch will quickly identify which device is the most active.

ETHERAPE

An additional tool not bundled with SLES might be of great interest: This tool, called EtherApe, can be downloaded from the project home page at `http://etherape.sourceforge.net/`.

This application monitors network traffic and tracks conversations between hosts. It presents all its information in a graphical mode, tracing actual lines between the different hosts as conversations take place. The more traffic passed between the hosts, the more intense the line is drawn.

EtherApe is also capable of monitoring for specific types of traffic. From the information displayed and the protocols seen, it is fairly easy to deduce the tasking of the multiple hosts.

Again, such network monitoring should be done only with the written consent of the owners of the network.

Additionally, because Ethereal can capture whole conversations, it can be used to reconstruct network events. As you can imagine, the amount of traffic carried over a network is tremendous. Ethereal allows for the selection of packets for particular conversations and filters for specific traffic types. It is then possible to reconstruct whole sessions and examine the individual packet content.

ETHEREAL HOME PAGE

Your SLES installation comes with a version of Ethereal. Information on how to run it can be found in the local man pages.

You will probably want to visit the Ethereal home page to get an up-to-date version of the product. As new versions are introduced, it will be important to keep up with the documentation supplied. You can find the Ethereal home page at `http://www.ethereal.com`.

Keep in mind that written authorization by a individual who is allowed to give such permission should be obtained before this tool is used on any network.

Ethereal can be quite intrusive in terms of data privacy. Packets containing cleartext data can easily be reconstructed and sensitive information divulged. This is why most corporate IT security policies emphatically state that such applications are forbidden. In the proper hands and in the right circumstances, Ethereal can allow you to solve a myriad of network issues.

Summary

After reading this chapter, you should have a good comfort level with the concept of both host- and network-based intrusion detection systems. The tools presented here are all part of the SLES environment. Deploying these solutions can vastly improve your chances of detecting unwelcome visitors.

The tools presented here are an essential part of a proper HIDS and NIDS environment. On the host intrusion side, you saw tools that are capable of determining whether changes have been made to the content of the filesystem. You also saw other tools that can be used to monitor port scans of your systems.

On the network side, you looked at tools such as Snort and ACID and how you can use them to raise alerts when suspicious traffic is detected. You can watch for abnormal network loads using tools such as MRTG and Cacti. Such traffic can alert you to machines that might be compromised or at the very least are behaving in an unexpected fashion.

All these tools participate together in protecting your environment and contribute to a robust, layered defense against attacks.

The most difficult portion of intrusion detection is fine-tuning the various solutions. Improperly tuned environments generate a large number of false-positive results. This can lead to situations in which valid results are missed. Alternately, solutions that have been overtuned may become blind to a whole family of attack mechanisms.

Patience, vigilance, and a good knowledge of what is supposed to be present on your network infrastructure are the key factors to a successful implementation.

## CHAPTER 13

System Security

Security is always a trade-off between convenience and features on the one hand and being protective and removing unnecessary risks on the other. As the cliché goes, security is inversely proportional to convenience and accessibility. In other words, a "totally secure" system is one that is *not* connected to anything (not to a terminal and most certainly not to a network), no one is ever allowed to use it, and it is never powered on!

TIP

Do you know whether your system has been compromised? Read Jay Beale's article, aptly titled "Detecting Server Compromises," in the February 2003 issue of *Information Security Magazine* (`http://www.infosecuritymag.com/2003/feb/linuxguru.shtml`).

As installed in "normal" mode from most current distributions, Linux tends to be a feature-rich yet very "insecure" operating system. For example, some distributions install an active web server by default. Although this is very convenient—the system can start serving files almost immediately and web-based administrative tools will work right away—it also exposes the system to many sorts of security threats. If a very secure system is your goal, you need to take additional steps to harden it.

NOTE

The process of modifying a system to make it highly secure is known as *hardening*.

NOTE

Realistically, a system should be hardened right after it has been installed and still in a clean state. This is not possible in most cases, and you will probably think of hardening the system after it show signs of being compromised. If this is the case, you should at least check and replace all suspected system utilities (such as 1s and ps) and add-on applications (such as Apache) with known good copies before starting on the hardening process.

This chapter presents you with ideas and theories associated with overall system security, from both a hardware *and* software point of view, starting with an overview of the principles behind system hardening.

System Hardening Principles

The principles of system hardening can be summarized with a single maxim: "Unless explicitly permitted, access is strictly forbidden." In other words, the access to any system service or resource should default to none, unless you specifically allow it. This way, you know what you are opening up and why. It is much more difficult to work the other way around because there is always the slight chance that someone important was missed and later turns out to be a costly oversight. So, the general idea is to install only those packages that the system actually needs and open only those firewall ports that are required by these services. That way, potential intruders can't exploit software that isn't present or running on the system. However, removing a package isn't always possible (due to dependencies) or practical. Therefore, at the very least, unneeded services should be disabled.

The following general tasks are associated with securing the operating system and its services:

- Disable or remove all unneeded services. For services that are required, ensure you are running the latest version.

- Use the secure version of a service daemon wherever and whenever possible. For instance, use **vsftpd** for FTP services instead of one that doesn't support SSL.

- Disable or remove all unused user accounts.

- Keep up-to-date with software updates, for both the operating system and applications, at least in regard to security patches. For SLES servers, you can easily keep them updated using the YaST Online Update (YOU) feature. (Refer to Chapter 2, "Updating the Server," for more details.)

- Harden the Linux kernel using the grsecurity kernel patch (`http://www.grsecurity.net`) to prevent attacks that use buffer overflows and the like. A good starting reference is the "Linux Kernel Hardening" article from the SANS Institute (`http://www.sans.org/rr/whitepapers/linux/1294.php`).

- Specify logging and access control for all services, allowing only the minimum access necessary. Secure and review these logs regularly. (See "Using a Central `syslog` Server" later in this chapter for information on securing system logs.)

- Whenever possible, use `chroot` jail to run a service in a confined directory.

- If at all possible, create a special user to run server processes. For example, run `named` as user named. These accounts should *not* have shell access; for instance, they should be given `/bin/false` as the default shell.

- Restrict access to special system services like `cron` to system administrators.

- Restrict access to root. Administrative tasks should be performed using `sudo` whenever possible.

- Review and remove unnecessary SUID and SGID applications, such as CD burning programs.

- Review and ensure no weak file permissions are assigned to critical system files.

- Remove unnecessary filesystem permissions (such as world-write). Also check for missing sticky bits on world-writeable directories.

TIP

You can use the following `find` command to get a list of all world-writeable directories whose sticky bit is *not* set:

```
find / -type d -perm +o=w not -perm +o=t -print
```

- Remove all compilers (such as `gcc` and `g++`) from the servers. After an intruder breaks into a system, he or she will often copy over the source code of a rootkit so a version specific to your server can be built and installed. If you need compilers, such as for software development work purposes, confine their installation to your workstation.

- Limit the number of daemon processes using the `instances` directive in `xinetd`. Setting limits can help prevent some Denial of Service (DoS) attacks.

- Run a firewall on *each* server so there are no open ports and the only ports that are reachable are those you specifically allowed. The bastion host should have its own packet filtering and access controls in addition to (and not instead of) the firewall.

- Run a system hardening script or utility against your server to ensure all bases are covered. One such utility, Bastille, is discussed later in this chapter.

TIP

After you have hardened a host to your satisfaction, ensure you document its configuration so that it may be used as a baseline for similar systems. Furthermore, a review of the documentation could point out weaknesses that you may have missed the first time around. In addition, should you need to rebuild the server after a system compromise or failure, this documentation can quickly get you back up and running.

You should periodically use security scanners such as those discussed in Chapter 12, "Intrusion Detection," to verify that your servers are secure, especially after any upgrades or patches have been applied; sometimes a patch may inadvertently open a previously closed security hole.

System hardening is not limited to just securing the server operating system and its services. The "system" is composed of more than just the server hardware and the various software packages that run on it. The system also includes *all* associated networking hardware, such as switches and hubs, that provides access to the server. Therefore, you also need to harden your physical network infrastructure.

NOTE

In many situations, the weakest links are the users and their workstations. Therefore, proper user training and education are a must. Be aware that many of the system hardening concepts discussed in this chapter are also applicable to client workstations.

Using a Central syslog Server

One of the important aspects of maintaining network security is keeping and checking various system and application log files. Other than being useful in determining and debugging network problems, the log files can also serve as early-warning indicators of an impending attack: Often you will see "probes" over a period of days or even weeks before an actual penetration attempt takes place.

NOTE

You can find discussions about log file maintenance, log parsing automation, and alerts in Chapter 12.

After an incident has occurred, good logs can help you determine how the attack was launched and what systems may have been compromised. In addition, the logs may even indicate the source (or the "alleged" source) of the intrusion. Because hackers know the values of these log files, they often wipe out or alter the logs, as well as install a Trojan logging daemon, to cover their tracks. To counter this compromise to your system, centralized logging could save the day. After all, if a machine is compromised but the log evidence isn't kept on that machine, it is going to be much more difficult for the intruder to cover his tracks. In addition to the extra level of protection, monitoring the logs for the whole network is also much easier when they are all located in one place.

TIP

By default, `syslog` messages are stored in various files in /var/log. However, you can change the filenames and locations by modifying /etc/syslog.conf.

`syslog` is the tried-and-true workhorse of Unix logging utilities, and it is not surprising that it is also used on Linux. `syslogd` accepts log data from the kernel (by way of `klogd`), from any and all local processes, and even from processes on remote systems. As part of the SLES base system installation, `syslogd` is preconfigured to use the local host as the receiver.

To set up a central `syslog` server, simply start `syslogd` with the -r switch, which tells it to listen for messages from remote machines on UDP port 514. On an SLES 9 server, `syslogd` is set up to automatically start at system boot, and the script used is /etc/init.d/syslog. This startup references /etc/sysconfig/syslog for a few variable settings, including SYSLOGD_PARAMS. Therefore, you should modify /etc/sysconfig/syslog and add -r to the SYS-LOGD_PARAMS line, as follows:

SYSLOGD_PARAMS="-r"

Then restart `syslogd` using the /etc/init.d/syslog restart or /sbin/rcsyslog restart command.

TIP

Do you see a bunch of lines like this in /var/log/messages, about every 20 minutes?

```
Jan  8 00:19:35 Athena -- MARK --
Jan  8 00:39:36 Athena -- MARK --
Jan  8 00:59:35 Athena -- MARK --
Jan  8 01:19:36 Athena -- MARK --
Jan  8 01:39:35 Athena -- MARK --
Jan  8 01:59:36 Athena -- MARK --
```

These lines are generated by the "mark" function (or subsystem) of syslog as a way of "touching base" with the system so that you can (theoretically) tell if syslog has unexpectedly died and stopped logging. Most times, this feature only serves to take up your disk space. Unless you are having trouble with syslog, you probably don't want this feature active. To turn off the mark function, add -m 0 to the SYSLOGD_PARAMS setting in /etc/sysconfig/syslog and then restart syslogd. (When -m isn't specified, the default value is 20 minutes.)

The next step is to instruct the clients to forward their syslog traffic to the central log host. You accomplish this easily by adding a single line in each client's /etc/syslog.conf file:

```
*.*        @loghostname
```

If this is the only line in the configuration file, *all* messages will be sent to the remote host, loghostname. Otherwise, the log messages will be stored both locally (as per the settings in the rest of the configuration file) and remotely for safekeeping. If you do this, it would be fairly easy to develop a script that uses grep or a similar tool to extract particular lines from the remote copy and compare to those from the local copy. Any data mismatch would indicate possible tampering.

Alternatively, you can arrange for selected message categories (known as *facilities*, in syslog-speak) to be sent to a remote server while keeping other message types local. Consider the following two entries:

```
auth,authpriv.warning     @loghostname
auth,authpriv.!warning    /var/log/messages
```

The first line instructs syslog to send any auth (mainly security events) and authpriv (access-control–related events) messages whose priority is warning or higher to the remote logging host, loghostname. The second line tells syslog to store the rest of the auth and authpriv messages locally in /var/log/messages.

Hardening the Central Syslog Host

One drawback of remote logging is that the stock syslogd does not provide any means of authentication or access control with regard to which remote hosts a receiving syslog server should accept the logs from. An attacker can determine, with relative ease, whether you have a central syslog server. For example, the attacker can read the /etc/syslog.conf file on the system he compromised or simply sniff for UDP traffic that is using port 514. After the attacker finds out that information, he may also choose to compromise your central syslog server to modify the log files and cover his tracks. Or he may simply flood it with bogus syslog messages until it runs out of disk space and stops logging.

TIP

You may want to consider running a dedicated syslog server that has no other active services except for the syslog daemon running. Furthermore, you can block UDP port 514 on your Internet-facing firewall so your syslog host cannot be easily flooded from the outside; of course, this wouldn't help much if it is done inside your network, after the intruder has exploited one of your servers.

TIP

A more paranoid setup is to disable all logins to the central logging host except for the console. That way, to access the logs stored on this server, the person needs to have physical access.

As a precautionary measure, at the very least, you should consider running syslogd via xinetd. This way, you can use xinetd's access control feature (such as the only_from list) so syslogd will log messages only from trusted hosts. Alternatively, you can set up some local firewall filtering rules using iptables.

Ideally, you would want to use a syslog daemon that uses TCP instead of UDP communication so that data delivery is reliable and you don't risk losing logging information. Furthermore, with TCP traffic, you can use something like ssh or stunnel (http://www.stunnel.org) to secure the traffic between your syslog daemons. You can do this using a replacement syslog daemon called syslog-ng (syslog new generation).

NOTE

syslog-ng v1.6 is included on your SLES 9 media. By default, the traditional syslog is installed instead of syslog-ng, but you can easily install syslog-ng via YaST. You can download the latest version from http://www.balabit.com/downloads/syslog-ng.

NOTE

Also included with SLES 9 is a package called evlog (Enterprise Event Logging). evlog implements a syslogd-compatible logging service that is in compliance with draft POSIX Standard 1003.25, "System API—Services for Reliable, Available, and Serviceable Systems." Visit http://evlog.sourceforge.net for more information.

syslog-ng uses /etc/syslog-ng/syslog-ng.conf for configuration information. The structure of this file is vastly different from that used by syslog. You may find that configuring syslog-ng takes a little more work than configuring syslog, but that is a reflection of its flexibility. The configuration file consists of five sections: options{}, source{}, destination{}, filter{}, and log{}. Syntactically, syslog-nf.conf is very similar to C and other structured programming languages: Semicolons terminate statements; whitespaces are ignored and may therefore be used to enhance readability. The following is a sample syslog-ng.conf file:

```
options {use_dns(yes); chain_hostnames(yes);};
source s_location {internal();};
destination d_loghostname {tcp("myloghost" port(514));};
destination d_local {file("/var/log/messages");};
filter f_auth_messages {facility(auth, authpriv)
    and level(warning .. emerg);};
log {source(s_location); destination(d_local);};
log {
    source(s_location);
    filter(f_auth_messages);
    destination(d_loghostname);
    };
```

This file instructs syslog-ng to perform the following tasks and sets up this information:

- The file resolves the IP address of the sender to the hostname via DNS and shows names of all hosts that have handled the log message.

- The source of the logs is internal to the server (that is, from syslog-ng itself).

- Two destinations have been defined. One is a remote logging host, myloghost, and the other is a local file.

- A filter is set up to log only auth and authpriv messages whose priority is warning or higher.

- All messages (of any type or priority) are stored locally in the /var/log/messages file.

- Messages of the type auth and authpriv and whose priority level is warning or higher (because of the filter called f_auth_messages) are sent to the remote logging host.

When you gain an understanding of the various keywords, you will find that it's actually much easier and simpler to configure syslog-ng than syslog due to the more readable syntax.

TIP

You can use the logger command-line tool to test your syslog/syslog-ng configuration. The syntax of logger is simple:

```
logger -p facility.priority "message"
```

You can use the following shell script to send test messages to the kernel facility for each of the eight priorities:

```
#!/bin/sh
for i in {debug,info,notice,warning,err,crit,alert,emerg}
do
        logger -p kern.$i "Test kernel message, prio $i"
done
```

The following messages are logged to /var/log/messages:

```
Mar  5 16:07:33 Athena logger: Test kernel message, prio debug
Mar  5 16:07:33 Athena logger: Test kernel message, prio info
Mar  5 16:07:33 Athena logger: Test kernel message, prio notice
Mar  5 16:07:33 Athena logger: Test kernel message, prio warning
Mar  5 16:07:33 Athena logger: Test kernel message, prio err
Mar  5 16:07:33 Athena logger: Test kernel message, prio crit
Mar  5 16:07:33 Athena logger: Test kernel message, prio alert
Mar  5 16:07:33 Athena logger: Test kernel message, prio emerg
```

In addition to being a diagnostic tool, logger is especially useful for adding logging functionality to shell scripts.

Although syslog-ng is much more secure than syslog, an intruder can still find out that there is a separate logging server because of the configuration files and take it out of commission using some form of DoS attack or perhaps hijack or divert the log traffic by forging addresses. Lance Spitzner of the Honeynet Project (http://www.honeynet.org) suggested an interesting—not hack-proof, but conceptually very interesting—stealth logging method. Using this method, you hide the real logging destination from an intruder's view by using a host that does *not* have any network protocols (such as TCP/IP) bound to its network card.

A Stealth Logging Host

The operational theory behind a stealth logging host is based on the fact that syslogd receives messages passively as syslog messages are sent using the connectionless (one-way) UDP protocol; the sending hosts don't require an acknowledgment or any form of reply from syslogd when they send a syslog message. Therefore, you configure the syslog.conf files on the sending hosts to use a bogus but valid IP address for the remote logging host. That is, the IP address must be valid for the network numbering scheme you're using, but it should not be in use by any host on your network. For the host that is acting as the central logging host, you set up a network sniffer, such as Snort, to passively capture data packets destined for UDP port 514 (the syslog protocol port) off the wire.

NOTE

You cannot use tcpdump for stealth logging because it filters data packets based on packet headers, and not the data payload instead.

Mick Bauer wrote an excellent article titled "Stealthful Sniffing, Intrusion Detection and Logging" in the September 2002 issue of *Linux Journal* detailing how to use Snort, running in stealth mode, to act as syslogd. You can find an online version at http://www.linuxjournal.com/article/6222. As you can see in the comments at the end of the article, stealth logging is not a hack-proof solution, but it does introduce some possibilities.

If you are intrigued with the idea of a stealth syslog host but don't want to go through the trouble of setting up Snort or a packet sniffer, you may want to give passlogd a try. passlogd is a purpose-built syslog message sniffer that runs on a host without any open ports. You can find the latest version at http://www.morphine.com/void/src.html.

NOTE

The stealth logging technique works for both syslog and syslog-ng. However, the method does not work with syslog-ng if you secure the syslog message endpoints with ssh or stunnel and the like because the traffic that would be captured by the packet sniffer would be encrypted. passlogd does not work with syslog-ng if syslog-ng is configured to use TCP instead of UDP; however, you can easily set up Snort to look for TCP port 514 instead of UDP port 514.

Regardless of whether you are using stealth logging, if you use a central logging server, you should set up a monitoring system so that you are *immediately* alerted if this logging server is down for any reason because it could be a prelude to an intrusion.

Avoid Logging in As Root

By design, the root user has access to everything on a system. It is the workhorse account and must be used to perform the more intricate and dangerous tasks on a system. You might be tempted to use the root account all the time because it permits unfettered access to all the commands necessary for maintaining a system. The downside is that using it all the time also eliminates the warning flag the system generates when something dangerous is about to happen.

In the normal course of events, the system warns a typical user that he or she does not have the necessary privileges for performing a certain function. The warning serves two purposes: Restricting access to parts of the system (or particular functions) and identifying the command requested can have significant repercussions. If the root account is used, many of these warnings are suppressed, and possible repercussions are not flagged. A simple keystroke can turn a simple command into a disaster.

It is therefore a good system management practice to use the root account as little as possible. It is also important to keep the root account restricted to a minimum number of individuals and locked down to the console. Auditing the use of a generic account such as root is difficult if not impossible. There are few business reasons for numerous individuals to have complete access to all the directories and files on a system. In a mission-critical system, it is not uncommon to have only one individual allocated to root.

In Chapter 5, "User Environment Management and Security," we explored the use of the su and sudo commands as appropriate replacements for the root account. When appropriate, the su command can be used to attain root access to the system. Access to the su command can be restricted and requires knowledge of the root password. Once granted, however, this level of access is equivalent to the root user and should therefore be strictly controlled. A more granular method for granting elevated privileges is to use the sudo environment. Within `sudo`, permission to individual commands can be granted allowing the users to perform the tasks they need to perform while restricting them from unnecessary access.

To see how to replace root access with `sudo` access, explore the following example. In many cases, users need to bulk-upload information to a server. In these cases, you may need to grant physical access to the server and provide a mechanism for mounting the volume.

If an operator is available and has the time, he or she could mount the volume for the user, move the data from the CD to the appropriate target directory, and then reset the permissions on the files.

More typically, the user would be responsible for moving the data. By default, SLES does not allow users to mount removable media. There are two ways of working around this situation. The first is to change the definition of the `/dev/cdrom` mount point in `/etc/fstab` to allow the addition of the `user` option. With this flag, nonprivileged users can *mount* and *umount* the CD at will. The problem with this solution is that it grants access to the CD drive to all users on the system. This may or may not be a satisfactory solution.

A more refined approach is to grant, through `sudo`, the right to use the `mount` command. In this way, you can selectively target specific users with the appropriate rights to access specific devices without having to grant access to all users.

Though the root account must be used in some situations, many more instances can be satisfied by using `sudo`. Restricting assess privileges enhances the robustness of the server. If a business practice requires a user to have enhanced access, other mechanisms are available to satisfy the need rather than sharing the root account.

Securing Network Services

Other than hardening the Linux kernel itself, you must also secure any network services that expose your server to the outside world. In the early days of computing, systems were accessed via hardwired (dumb) terminals or remote job entry devices (such as punched card readers). But with the advent of local area networks and development of various TCP/IP-based applications, computers today are accessed mostly using intelligent workstations and high-speed networks (either local or remote), meaning client workstations and the server interact in a collaborative manner. As a result, server-side applications (generally referred to as services) must be robust and be tolerant of any errors or faulty data provided by the clients. At the same time, because the communication pathway between the clients and the server may cross publicly accessible devices (such as routers on the Internet), there is also a need to protect the data from being "sniffed."

Some of the concepts and their applications have already been covered in previous chapters but are reviewed here in the context of securing network services. The following topics are discussed in this section:

- Hardening remote services by using secure protocols when a public network separates the communication pathway between client and server.

- Preventing service processes from having access to data they do not need. This can also be achieved by using UML or `chroot` jails as detailed in a later section of this chapter.

- Granting system processes only the absolute minimum number of rights for them to function correctly. This ensures that the application and its configuration files are only accessible to the appropriate UID/GID.

- Reducing the risk of DoS attacks by blocking undesired data packets from reaching the services. Inappropriate packets should be dropped at the router and firewall levels, preventing them from reaching the server. The local machine firewall would then not have to deal with them, thus reducing the CPU load on the server and the network load on its segment.

- Hardening your network infrastructure.

- Addressing wireless security concerns.

Hardening Remote Services

As illustrated in Chapter 12, it is *very* easy to set up and attach a data sniffer, such as Ethereal, to a network and *passively* capture transmissions between two devices such as user login names and passwords. The most troubling issue here is not the ease in which a sniffer can be employed to snoop on your data, but the fact that it can be done *without* your knowledge.

When users are communicating with your server from a remote location across public networks (such as the Internet or via a wireless network), there are many (too many) junctions where a sniffer may be placed. Chances are remote that someone would specifically target you for a data snoop. However, it is not uncommon that in data centers of your ISP network, traffic is monitored so they can identify bottlenecks and dynamically reroute traffic as necessary. You have no way of knowing how this captured data would be used or what type of security they use to safeguard it from nonauthorized access. By the same token, even the network within your organization is not totally safe from snooping.

For instance, an outside vendor may come in to troubleshoot one of its products and hook up a sniffer, or one of your summer interns may decide it's "fun" to see what goes on across the wire. Or if you have wireless networks in-house, they can be vulnerable (see the "Wireless Security" section later in this chapter). Therefore, it pays to be somewhat paranoid when you are accessing your server from across a network, remote or otherwise.

ACCIDENTAL DATA SNOOP

A number of years ago as part of an annual network health check, we connected a Token Ring sniffer to the network at a financial institution (with blessings from the network administrator and senior management). The main purpose was to check on token rotation times, the number of purge frames, error frames, and so on. However, one of the groups was implementing a new database server and was having some performance trouble, and we were asked to help look into it.

With the sniffer in hand, we looked at how the client software was querying the database server and found that due to a bug in the API, the client software was performing certain table searches by rows instead of columns. While reviewing the captured traces for the final report, we found one more bug in the software: It did not encrypt the user password before sending it on to the server for authentication!

Because data snooping, "accidental" or otherwise, can lead to involuntary disclosure of sensitive data, you should write into your corporate security policy and make known to all users (including vendors) that any unauthorized use of a sniffer will have severe consequences.

If you are somewhat concerned about the confidentiality of your data as it traverses your internal network or travels across public networks, you should consider securing, at the very least, the following remote access services:

- **Telnet and r*-utilities (such as rlogin)**—These services should be disabled, and ssh should be used instead. You can find details about setting up ssh in Chapter 8, "Network Services."

- **Remote control applications (such as VNC)**—If you must use such an application, if it runs over ssh (like VNC can), do so. If not, you should set up access over a VPN link at the very least. You can find details about setting up VNC in Chapter 8.

- **FTP**—Traditional FTP login and data transfer are not encrypted. Because most of the time you use the SLES username and password for FTP download from your server, sending the username and password in clear-text is not a good idea. Instead, you should use something like `vsftpd` as your FTP daemon (refer to Chapter 8), enable SSL support, and use a secure FTP client such as `sftp` or `PSFTP` (`http://www.chiark.greenend.org.uk/~sgtatham/putty/download.html`).

- **Email**—The problem here is two-fold. First, although there is an authen-tication extension for SMTP service (RFC 2554), it is not in wide use. Therefore, data transfers between SMTP servers are mostly performed in cleartext. Consequently, anyone sniffing SMTP traffic may find out confi-dential information about you, your correspondent, and your company. Second, when you download email from your mail server to the worksta-tion using POP3 or similar protocols, it is in cleartext as well. To protect your email from being snooped, you should use an email client that sup-ports encryption (for example, see `http://www.gnupg.org/(en)/related_software/frontends.html#mua`). At the very least, manually encrypt your messages and file attachments using something like GnuPG before sending them.

Although you can access all the preceding services securely using a VPN link, it is not always feasible because you need a VPN client installed on your worksta-tion. There are going to be situations when you need to remotely access your server at work from some workstation that does not have a compatible VPN client. Therefore, it is best to secure the remote services, and when you can also use VPN, you get double the security.

Limiting Rights of Services

Every process on a system is executed under the context of an account. If you sign onto a server and launch a text editor, in theory, the executable instance of the text editor has access to all the files and directories that you would normal-ly have access to. This doesn't sound unreasonable and, in fact, for you to be able to save your file after the edit session, it is a requirement.

If you extrapolate this situation to a typical multiuser system, the situation becomes fairly complicated. In addition to all the interactive sessions from users and their respective `cron` jobs, a system also runs a number of services. Each one of these tasks has access to portions of the system.

As a system administrator, you need to understand the exposure presented by these processes. In the case of a simple text editor, little is exposed to damage other than the user's files. If the user happens to be root, however, the default process privileges can have serious implications in the event of human error.

The same situation arises for all processes. By default, user processes are fairly well contained. Their access to the system is limited to their own account's environment. If a user were to run a program under his or her own credentials, any damage caused by coding deficiencies within the routine would be limited to the access rights of that user's account. For unprivileged users, the damage is restricted by the limitations of the account.

The question is, What happens in the case of a privileged account? There is simply no mechanism available for the operating system to know the difference between an event triggered by mistake and one initiated by design. If a coding error in an application triggers the deletion of files in a directory, there is little to prevent the event. The more privileged the account running the faulty application, the higher the potential damage. It is therefore imperative to ensure that each and every process running on a server is executed with the most minimal privilege possible.

An additional layer of complexity results from placing your server on a network. So far, we have discussed deficiencies within a program running locally on a system and their possible impact. After a server is placed on a network, the services it presents are exposed beyond the confines of the local system. This greatly enhances the possibility that a coding deficiency in any service can be exploited from sources external to the machine. Additionally, the service is exposed to the network where it could be exploited without requiring local credentials.

Many such exploits are common today. In some cases, the remediated code is made available in short order. In most cases, however, there is a significant lapse of time between the discovery of the vulnerability and a patch. It is important to reflect on the fact that vulnerabilities are "discovered" and to understand that this implies they were present and dormant for an extended period of time. What happens to a system during the period leading up to the discovery is unknown. It is quite possible that in some cases the vulnerability was exploited by external sources for a significant amount of time before it was "discovered." Similarly, a system administrator may need to reflect on what can be done between being made aware of a possible problem and the availability of a patch.

One of the most important factors in reducing the amount of exposure to a vulnerability is to contain services within accounts with minimal privileges. In more recent versions of Linux, this is configured by default.

SLES is installed by default in such a way. A review of the accounts in /etc/passwd reveals individual accounts for running most services. In the case of an account such as sshd, it is used only to provide ssh services to the server. It is a local account on the machine and because it has no real login directory, it cannot be used to log in locally. This is in sharp contrast to the Telnet service available through xinetd. Though disabled by default in /etc/xinetd.d/telnetd, it can be enabled by simply changing the appropriate flag. When initiated at xinet startup, the resulting service will, by default, run under the root account. If a vulnerability in Telnet were to be discovered and exploited, the access privilege granted to the attacker would be equivalent to root.

An additional group of processes that should be examined are those that run under cron. In most cases, individuals run housekeeping jobs under cron. These tasks run in their user context, and few system-wide concerns are involved. You should closely scrutinize cron jobs that run under accounts that possess elevated privileges. Consider, for example, a script used to back up a special application. In some cases, a client group may require pre- and post-backup steps to be performed. You may be approached to run a customized script: /home/accounting/close_day.sh before the backup and /home/accounting/open_day.sh when the backups are done. Though this point may be obvious, these scripts must be moved to a location that is not user modifiable and audited for content before they are included in the nightly backup processes. If they are simply called by the nightly cron job, they will be executed in the same context as the backup process. If they are left in a location where they can be changed, there is little to prevent the introduction of a script error killing the nightly backups. In the worst-case scenario, the script could be used by someone to gain backup-level privileged access to the system.

All processes running on a system can have direct impact on the overall health of the server. Application bugs and vulnerabilities are a direct threat to the information and resources provided by the server. Because these vulnerabilities are present in the applications themselves, the local firewall policies cannot be applied to mitigate against this threat. It is therefore imperative to scrutinize the accounts under which processes are run to evaluate a server's exposure from both internal and external sources.

Using chroot **Jails and User Mode Linux**

In the preceding section, we examined the importance of minimizing the impact unknown vulnerabilities can have on a server. This was done by restricting access to system resources through the selection of appropriate accounts for each process.

In this section, we examine two additional methods of further restricting system exposure. Both chroot jails and User Mode Linux (UML) are containment techniques. These methods provide a closed environment within which the application is run, segregating it from the rest of the system. Both chroot and UML provide such environments, but their approaches are vastly different.

chroot

A chroot jail is based on the concept of moving a process from the original system environment and isolating it within a separate, parallel environment. As the process is initiated, it is provided with an alternate environment within which it will run. This environment is made up of a complete directory structure that mimics the standard file system.

Before you can port an application into the jail, you need to know the resources the application requires to run. In the case of a statically linked executable, the list of extra files needed could be very short. If, however, the application to be run requires access to a number of libraries, things can get quite complex. In the case of a chroot'ed web service, additional applications such as Perl or PHP may need to be placed in the target tree. To create a chroot file structure, you must perform the following:

1. Create an isolated directory on a volume on the main server outside any path requiring privileges to access.

2. Create a number of standard directories such as /usr, /dev, /lib, and /etc.

3. Populate the directories with the appropriate files. In the case of the /lib directory, all the libraries required by the application must be copied, or the application will fail at runtime.

4. Ensure the /etc/passwd file in the chroot jail contains the accounts required by the application and not a copy of the live system's password file.

5. Apply the appropriate owneris b and permissions to all content.

The creation of a complete chroot environment for any application is a complex task. The most difficult step is collecting all the necessary library routines required by the applications.

After you have replicated the tree structure, you can launch the application with the command

Athena> **chroot /newtree command**

where /newtree is the directory specification for the directory structure created previously. This will now be used as the / directory for the application instance. The command parameter is simply the application that you want to run within the chroot is benvironment.

USER MODE LINUX (UML)

The second method of creating a segregated environment is using User Mode Linux. UML's approach to segregating environments is to create a virtual machine within which the new application is run.

This new virtual machine is, in all respects, a separate Linux installation. Though YaST provides support for the initial portions of the installation, a number of additional steps are required to finalize the configuration. As a separate machine, it needs to have the required software installed. Unlike the chroot installation where directories can be copied, the UML machine instance requires an actual install. Similarly, all account management functions and system hardening are required on the new system as well.

When UML is launched, it loads its own copy of the Linux kernel within the context of the account used to start the service. This provides a complete Linux system to the application. This system is functionally independent of the original system and acts quite literally as a separate machine. The disks provided for the virtual machine are, in fact, large files in the file system of the parent machine. They can be mounted and modified as normal disks on the parent until they contain what is required for the application. Once configured, UML is launched and the new machine takes over the delivery of the service. The virtual machine appears on the network as a separate entity with its own TCP/IP address, accounts, and services.

Both techniques for providing a segregated application environment are non-trivial. They do, however, provide significant isolation of the service being offered and therefore help protect the remainder of the system. The more complex of the two techniques appears to be the chroot path. Though a number of resources are available on the Internet to help configure such environments, finding all the minutia required for an application can be quite tedious. Once completed, chroot does provide for a minimal environment within which an application can run. If a vulnerability is found and exploited, the minimal environment provided will not provide any extraneous utilities that would be an advantage to an attacker.

The UML approach does provide for a complete system environment and therefore requires more diligence in removing applications installed by default. The level of segregation, however, is almost complete and does not allow for any access to the original system's resources. One of the most significant advantages to the UML approach is the capacity for running a different operating system within each virtual machine. This allows for legacy systems requiring older, more vulnerable operating system flavors to be isolated. Also, third-party software that is no longer supported or software that requires specific runtime environments can be hosted virtually until they can be replaced.

NOTE

The concept of creating a UML environment is to separate the hosted application into a separate virtual machine. This is a good thing. It does, however, imply that each UML environment requires individual system management. Hardening, tuning, and account management must be done on each just as if they were physically separate machines.

Packet Filtering Using `iptables`

Historically, servers were placed on internal networks with little worry about exploits. Because corporations had minimal or no direct access to the Internet, there were few chances of compromise. As time marched on, more and more companies became Internet accessible. Today, most companies allow Internet access all the way down to desktop devices.

The increase in access has been fueled by business demands both in terms of internal resources requiring access to information as well as an outward-facing presence for marketing purposes. To protect Internet-facing machines, companies have employed firewalls. A firewall is a device that can be used to restrict network traffic. Restrictions can be placed on the source, destination, or type of traffic involved. In many instances, firewall appliances are used to segregate corporations from the Internet. These appliances often contain proprietary operating systems and command sets. Others use embedded versions of operating systems such as Linux. These types of firewalls are called *edge devices*. Though SLES can be configured to run as an edge firewall, we focus more on the individual server-side implementation.

SLES can be used to implement a local system-level firewall. The firewall configuration can be controlled though YaST. Though YaST only scratches the surface of the potential of the SLES firewall, it is sufficient for most server-side needs.

YaST serves as a tool for modifying what is known as `iptables` rules. `iptables` is the administration tool used to control the firewall configuration. In its simplest form, `iptables` recognizes the following:

- Network interfaces
- Trusted and untrusted networks
- Network protocols such as TCP, ICMP, and UDP
- Network ports
- Packet sources and destinations: `INPUT`, `OUTPUT`, and `FORWARDING`
- Packet disposition: `ACCEPT`, `DROP`, `QUEUE`, and `RETURN`

Combining the different permutations and combinations of these attributes generates a list of rules. These rules govern what happens to a network packet destined for a target server. When rules are applied to a packet, the process is known as *packet filtering*.

Under YaST, selecting Users and Security presents the option for configuring the firewall. YaST understands most of the typical business applications that run on an SLES server:

- HTTP and HTTPS
- SMTP, IMAP (SSL), POP3 (SSL)

NOTE

In a properly secured environment, the number of cleartext protocols should be kept to a minimum. There is little that can be done to encrypt SMTP traffic to hosts beyond your corporate environment. Securing protocols such as IMAP and POP3 with their SSL equivalents will prevent usernames and passwords from being captured through sniffing. It will also protect the content from being seen internally if intercepted between workstations and the server.

- `ssh`, Telnet
- `rsync`

YaST also provides for a more granular approach by allowing individual ports to be opened for less frequently used applications. In the preceding standards list, protocols such as DNS (port 53), Kerberos (port 88), and LDAP (port 389) are missing. If the firewall is enabled on a server and these protocols are required, manual adjustments will have to take place. In the Additional Services section of the firewall configuration, you can accommodate for these requirements.

In addition, third-party software installed on servers can also be made available through the firewall. A simple example of a port rule could allow for port 3306 (MySQL) to be permitted to traverse the firewall. The resulting entry in the `iptables` would look like this:

```
ACCEPT tcp -- anywhere  anywhere state NEW,RELATED,
↪ESTABLISHED tcp dpt:mysql
```

This example was generated using the YaST tool by specifying, in Additional Services, that port 3306 be available for access to external machines. This entry allows traffic for MySQL to reach the local host. In the **INPUT** stream of packets, this rule will be interpreted as shown in Table 13.1.

TABLE 13.1
Interpreting the INPUT Stream of Packets

PACKET	MEANING
ACCEPT	Tells the firewall to let packets matching the following through.
Tcp	Defines the type of packet.
--	Specifies TCP options to filter on. A TCP option is a specific portion of the packet header. No option is specified in this case; therefore all packets should be accepted.
anywhere anywhere	Tells the firewall that packets received from all interface NICs (the first *anywhere*) be allowed to flow to any destination interface NICs (the second *anywhere*).
State	NEW: Packets initiating a new conversation
	RELATED: Packets that are continuations of pre-existing conversations
	ESTABLISHED: Packets that constitute replies to pre-existing conversations
dpt:mysql	Defines which tcp port the conversation will exist on. Keep in mind that we requested port 3306 be opened; the firewall has itself substituted the known-application name for the port number.
	Warning: This does not mean that the traffic is actually MySQL traffic. It means only that the port is typically associated with MySQL.

Though the syntax and order of the rules can become quite complex, YaST provides for a simple, more intuitive interface.

Placing firewalls on local servers above and beyond the edge firewalls might appear as a waste of resources. Many Denial of Service attacks, however, come from internal sources. Viruses, worms, and the like propagate from machine to machine using known vulnerabilities. Though normally a workstation problem, these pests often affect the performance of servers. With a properly tuned firewall, requests for services from unauthorized clients can be eliminated from consideration at the firewall level. This removes the burden of processing from the application level. Consider, for example, the following two cases:

- A number of workstations are infected with a worm that attempts a password hack attempt on accounts on your servers. The worm is smart and assumes that only ssh traffic is allowed to your server farm. Simple enough, it parses the local /etc/passwd file, harvests account names, and then scans the subnets in question for machines answering on port 22. If the firewall is properly configured, it will allow only ssh sessions from specific machines within the data center. Infected machines in the rest of the company would not be able to establish any connections, and therefore, the exposure to password loss is reduced. This also prevents the local sshd from processing numerous bogus password attempts.

- The Internet-facing web server requires MySQL access through an application server. If each machine's firewall is configured appropriately, only the application server will be permitted to talk over port 3306 to the MySQL server. The application server will accept only communications from the web server over a restricted customized port. In this scenario, even if the Internet-facing web server were compromised, the attacker would be unable to access the database directly. This setup might not stop the attack, but the network rules would certainly slow the progress of the attack—long enough for it to be identified, one would hope.

In a server environment, it is imperative to allow traffic only for those services that should be available and, again, only to those clients that require the access. Restricting access to other network-aware applications that might co-reside on the server will further reduce the machine's target profile. An additional benefit to applying filtering rules is that spurious traffic from unauthorized sources never reaches the intended service. This protects the exposed application from possible hacks while reducing the amount of processing time lost to unsolicited connection attempts.

Hardening Your Physical Network Infrastructure

Proper system hardening practice should include securing your networking hardware from being attacked or hijacked for other uses. For instance, your server is useless if your remote users can't reach it over the WAN link because some intruder hijacked your router and changed its configuration. Similarly, if the access infrastructure is not secure and the traffic easily snooped, your confidential company data can be easily stolen or compromised.

Most network administrators are familiar with the concept of using firewalls to block undesired network traffic in and out of a network. However, many have not given much thought to securing the physical aspects of the network, namely the underlying hardware. The following sections cover a few topics related to hardening your physical networking environment.

PHYSICAL SECURITY

Probably the foremost consideration to securing your networking environment is securing physical access to equipment such as the wiring racks, hubs and switches, and routers. Most of the time, these types of equipment are in a wiring closet located strategically behind closed and locked doors. Unlike in the movies, hackers tapping into your network via available ports on the wiring hubs and switches are rare. It is actually much easier instead to use an available network plug found in one of the empty offices, meeting areas, or conference rooms. Or the attack may even be launched from outside your premises if you have wireless access points installed! (See the "Wireless Security" section later in this chapter.)

NOTE

A primer on various common networking devices, such as switches and routers, can be found at http://www.practicallynetworked.com/networking/bridge_types.htm.

Following are some ideas to ponder when you are implementing physical security for your networking infrastructure:

- Wiring racks, hubs, switches, routers, and servers should be under lock and key.

- Consider setting passwords for your server's BIOS as well as the boot loader.

- Given the negligible cost difference between hubs and switches, it is more secure to use switches because they make packet sniffing more difficult (but not impossible, as many would tend to think; see the "Sniffing Switches" section later in this chapter). At the same time, switches provide better network bandwidth management than hubs.

- Networking devices should be connected to power surge protectors, or better yet, uninterruptible power supplies (UPSes) to guard against power fluctuations and short periods of power outages. We have seen damaged hubs and switches resulting in a partially downed network that took hours to diagnose.

- Unused ports should be disabled at the hub or switch, or patch cables not connected. If manageable hubs or switches are used, you should use the management software to periodically check that the unused ports are not suddenly being used without your prior knowledge.

DEFAULT PASSWORDS AND SNMP COMMUNITY NAMES

Many manageable devices, such as routers, switches, and hubs, are shipped with factory-set default passwords, and some are shipped without a password at all. If you fail to change these passwords, an attacker can easily access your device remotely over the network and cause havoc. For instance, Cisco routers are popular, and many corporations use them to connect to the Internet. An attacker can easily use something like Cisco Scanner (`http://www.securityfocus.com/tools?platid=-1&cat=1&offset=130`) to look for any Cisco routers that have not yet changed their default password of *cisco*. After locating such a router, the hacker can use it as a launching point to attack your network or others (while the finger points to your router as being the source).

TIP

You can find many default user IDs and passwords for vendor products at `http://www.cirt.net/cgi-bin/passwd.pl`.

Manageable devices can normally be accessed in a number of different ways—for example, via a console port, Telnet, Simple Network Management Protocol (SNMP), or even a web interface. Each of these access routes is either assigned a default password or none at all. Therefore, you need to change *all* of them to secure your device. If you don't change them, a hacker can get in via one of the unsecured methods and reset the passwords.

Consider this scenario: Your router can be remotely configured either via a Telnet session or SNMP `set` commands. To be able to manage the router remotely from your office or home, you dutifully changed the default Telnet access password. However, because you don't deal much with SNMP, you left that alone. A hacker stumbled across your router, found out its make, and looked up the default username and password. He tried to gain access through Telnet but found the default password didn't work. But by knowing that the router can also be configured via SNMP and knowing that the default read-write community name is *private*, the attacker can change the configuration of the router, reset the Telnet password to anything he wishes, and lock you out at the same time, all by using a simple SNMP management utility.

Before putting any networking devices into production, first change *all* their default passwords, following standards of good practice by setting strong passwords (see Chapter 4, "User and Group Administration," and Chapter 11, "Network Security Concepts"). Furthermore, you should disable any unused remote access methods if possible.

SNIFFING SWITCHES

A switch handles data frames in a point-to-point manner. That is, frames from Node A to Node B are sent across only the circuits in the switch that are necessary to complete a (virtual) connection between Node A and Node B, while the other nodes connected to the same switch do not see that traffic. Consequently, it is the general belief that data sniffing in a switched environment is possible only via the "monitor port" (where all internal traffic is passed) on the switch, if it has one. However, studies have revealed that several methods are available to sniff switched networks. Following are two of these methods:

- **MAC address flooding**—Switches work by setting up virtual circuits from one data port to another. To track what devices are connected (so the data frames can be routed correctly), a switch must keep a translation table (known as the Content Addressable Memory, or CAM) that tracks which MAC addresses are on which physical port. (Each network card is identified by a unique Media Access Control, or MAC, address assigned by the manufacturer.) The amount of memory for this translation table is limited. It is this fact that allows the switch to be exploited for sniffing purposes. On some switches, it is possible to bombard the switch with bogus MAC address data (for instance, using `macof` from the `dsniff` suite; `http://monkey.org/~dugsong/dsniff/dsniff-2.3.tar.gz`) and overflow the translation table. The switch, not knowing how to handle the situation, "fails open." That is, it reverts to function as a hub and broadcasts all data frames to all ports. At this point, one of the more generic network sniffers can be used to capture traffic.

- **MAC address duplication**—All data frames on a network are routed or bridged based on the associated MAC addresses. Therefore, the ability to impersonate another host's MAC address could be exploited. That's just what the MAC address duplication hack does: reconfigures your system to have the same MAC address as the machine whose traffic you're trying to sniff. This is easily done on many operating systems. On a Linux machine, for instance, the `ifconfig eth0` *12:34:56:78:90:AB* command can be used, where *12:34:56:78:90:AB* is the desired MAC address. In a MAC Address Duplication attack, the switch is fooled into thinking two ports have the same MAC address, and it forwards data to both ports.

There are more ways (such as man-in-the-middle method via Address Resolution Protocol [ARP] spoofing) to sniff switched networks. The two methods discussed here simply serve as an introduction and provide a cautionary note that a switched environment is *not* immune to packet sniffing.

Wireless Security

In the past few years, wireless networking (IEEE 802.11x standards; `http://grouper.ieee.org/groups/802/11/`) has become popular for both business and home users. Many laptops available today come with a built-in wireless network card. Setting up your wireless clients is a cinch. It is almost effortless to get a wireless network up and running—no routing of cables behind your desks, through walls or other tight spaces. And no hubs or switches are necessary. Unfortunately, such convenience comes with security concerns—which many people are not readily aware of—and they are discussed next.

NOTE

Wireless LANs (WLANs) can be set up in one of two modes. In *infrastructure* mode (also known as a *basic service set*, or BSS), each client connects to a wireless access point (also frequently referred to simply as an access point, or AP). The AP is a self-contained hardware device that connects multiple wireless clients to an existing LAN. In *ad hoc* mode (or *independent basic service set*, IBSS), all clients are all peers to each other without needing an AP. No matter which mode a WLAN operates in, the same security concerns discussed here apply.

NOTE

802.11*x* refers to a group of evolving WLAN standards that are under development as elements of the IEEE 802.11 family of specifications, but that have not yet been formally approved or deployed. 802.11*x* is also sometimes used as a generic term for any existing or proposed standard of the 802.11 family. Free downloads of all 802.11*x* specifications can be found at
http://standards.ieee.org/getieee802/802.11.html.

LOCKING DOWN ACCESS

Wireless networks broadcast their data using radio waves (in the GHz frequency range), and unless you have a shielded building (like those depicted in Hollywood movies), you cannot restrict physically who can access your WLAN. The useable area depends on the characteristic of the office space. Thick walls degrade the signal to some extent, but depending on the location of the AP and the type and range of antenna it has, its signal may be picked up from outside the building, perhaps from up to a block or two away.

WARNING

With the popularity of home wireless networks, it is *imperative* that you take steps to secure your AP so strangers can't easily abuse your Internet connection. Given the typical range of an AP, someone could be sitting at the sidewalk next to your house and use your AP to surf the Net without your permission or, worse, commit a cyber crime—with your Internet connection being the "source"—all without your knowledge!

Anyone with a wireless-enabled computer equipped with sniffer software that is within the range of your APs can see all the packets being sent to other wireless clients and can gain access to everything they make available. If the APs are acting in bridge mode, someone may even be able to sniff traffic between two wired machines on the LAN itself!

WARDRIVING AND WARCHALKING

One of the techniques employed by security professionals (the so-called "white hats") and would-be-hackers (the so-called "black hats") alike to determine the boundary of a WLAN is called *wardriving*. First automated by Peter Shipley (http://www.dis.org/shipley) during the 1999–2000 period, wardriving is the process of gathering WLAN information (such as locations of APs and their Service Set IDs, or SSIDs) by listening for periodic AP broadcasts using a computer running a *stumbling utility*.

When you wardrive, you ride around in a car while running the stumbling utility on a laptop or even a PDA equipped with a wireless card, and you record beacons from nearby APs. Most stumbling software has the ability to add GPS location information to its log files so that exact geographical locations of stumbled APs can be plotted onto electronic maps. The most popular and well-known stumbling tool is a Windows program called Network Stumbler (often referred to simply as NetStumbler; http://www.netstumbler.com). NetStumbler can sniff for active wireless channels and note any open networks. A similar tool called Kismet (http://www.kismetwireless.net) is available for a number of operating systems, including Linux and Mac OS X.

The *warchalking* concept was conceived in June 2002 by a group of people who have taken to drawing chalk symbols on walls and pavements to indicate the presence of an AP along with its details (such as SSID) so others can easily locate it. Although the idea was intriguing, it failed to catch on in a big way, most likely due to three factors. First, chalk drawings are easily removed or modified, so any information they provide may not be accurate. Second, with the popularity of public WLANs (so-called *Wi-Fi HotSpots*), such as in airports, school campuses, hotels, and even some communities, there isn't much need to rely on chalk symbols to locate public APs; you can look them up easily online—for example, http://www.wi-fihotspotlist.com. Lastly, in most cities, the use of chalk to mark APs is likely to incur the wrath of local authorities for violating antigraffiti laws.

The term *war*, which is used in *wardriving, warchalking,* and so on, was taken from the old hacking practice known as *wardialing*. Wardialing was phoning every extension of a phone network until the number associated with a modem was hit on and recorded. Today, this practice has been replaced by wardriving with the introduction of WLANs.

One simple way of closing a WLAN to unauthorized systems is to configure your AP to allow connections only from specific wireless network cards. Like standard network cards, each wireless network card has a unique MAC address. Some APs allow you to specify a list of authorized MAC addresses. If a machine attempts to join the network with a listed MAC address, it can connect; otherwise, the request is silently ignored. This method is sometimes referred to as *MAC address filtering*.

WARNING

The vendor hard-codes the MAC address (part of which contains a vendor code) for each network card and thus guarantees its uniqueness. Depending on the operating system, however, the MAC address of the wireless card can be easily changed using something similar to the ifconfig command:

```
sniffer # ifconfig wlan0 12:34:56:78:90:AB
```

If an intruder is determined to gain access to your WLAN, he can simply sniff the airwaves passively and log all MAC addresses that are in use. When one of them stops transmitting for a length of time (presumably disconnected from the WLAN), the intruder can then assume the identity of that MAC address and the AP will not know the difference.

Most APs available today allow the use of the optional 802.11 feature called *shared key authentication*. This feature helps prevent rogue wireless network cards from gaining access to the network. The authentication process is illustrated in Figure 13.1. When a client wants to connect to an AP, it first sends an authentication packet. The AP replies with a string of challenge text 128 bytes in length. The client must encrypt the challenge text with its shared key and send the encrypted version back to the AP. The AP decrypts the encrypted challenge text using the same shared key. If the decoded challenge text matches what was sent initially, a successful authentication is returned to the client and access is granted; otherwise, a negative authentication message is sent and access is denied.

NOTE

Other than the shared key authentication, 802.11 also provides for *open system authentication*. The open system authentication is null authentication (meaning no authentication at all). The client workstation can associate with any access point and listen to all data sent as plaintext. This type of authentication is usually implemented where ease of use is the main security issue.

FIGURE 13.1
IEEE 802.11 shared key authentication.

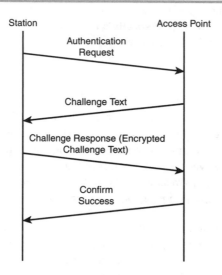

This shared key between the AP and a client is the same key used for Wired Equivalency Privacy (WEP) encryption, which is discussed in the next section.

NOTE

You can also employ IEEE 802.1x Extensible Authentication Protocol (EAP) with specific authentication methods such as EAP-TLS to provide mutual authentication mechanisms. However, such an implementation requires an authentication server, such as Remote Authentication Dial-In User Service (RADIUS), which is not very practical for home, small-, and medium-size businesses. An alternative is to use the preshared key authentication method available in Wi-Fi Protected Access (WPA) for infrastructure mode wireless networks. The WPA preshared key works in a similar manner as the WEP shared key method discussed previously. However, because of the way WPA works (discussed in the following section), the WPA preshared key is not subject to determination by collecting a large amount of encrypted data.

ENCRYPTING DATA TRAFFIC

Part of the IEEE 802.11 standard defines the Wired Equivalency Privacy (WEP) algorithm that uses RC4, a variable key-size stream cipher, to encrypt all transmissions between the AP and its clients. To use this feature, you must configure the AP to use WEP and create or randomly generate an encryption key, sometimes referred to as the *network password* or a *secret key*.

The key is usually expressed as a character string or hexadecimal numbers, and its length depends on the number of bits your hardware will support. At the time of this writing, APs support encryption keys ranging in size from 64 bits to 256 bits. The methodology that manufacturers employ for WEP encryption, however, is not universal and may differ from another. For instance, for a 64-bit encryption key, *most* vendors use a 24-bit randomly generated internal key (known as an *Initialization Vector*, or IV) to trigger the encryption (thus leaving you with a 40-bit key), whereas others may use the full 64 bits for encryption.

NOTE

The 802.11b specification defined a 40-bit user-specified key. Combined with the 24-bit IV, this yields a 64-bit encryption key for WEP. Likewise, a 128-bit WEP uses a 104-bit key, and a 256-bit WEP uses a 232-bit key. This is why user-defined ASCII keys are only 5 bytes in size for 64-bit WEP, 13 bytes for 128-bit WEP, and 29 bytes for 256-bit WEP.

WEP works by using the encryption key as input to the RC4 cipher. RC4 creates an infinite pseudo-random stream of bytes. The endpoint (either the AP or a client) encrypts its data packet by performing a bitwise XOR (logical exclusive OR) operation—a simple and fast method for hashing two numbers in reversible fashion—with the latest section of the RC4 pseudo-random stream and sends it. Because the same encryption key is used at the AP and by the clients, the receiving device knows where they are in the RC4 stream and applies the XOR operation again to retrieve the original data.

If the intercepted packets are all encrypted using the same bytes, this provides a known cryptographic starting point for recovering the key used to generate the RC4 stream. That is the reason a 24-bit random key (the IV) is added to the user-supplied key to ensure the same key is not used for multiple packets, thus making it more difficult (but not impossible) to recover the key. But because the IV is only 24 bits, eventually you must reuse a previous value. By intercepting sufficient data packets, an attacker could crack the encryption key used based on "seeing" repeating RC4 data bytes. The general rule of thumb is that, depending on the key size, about 5 to 10 million encrypted packets would provide sufficient information to recover the key. On a typical corporate network, this number of packets can be captured in less than a business day. If, with some luck—good or bad, depending on your perspective—many duplicate IVs are captured, the key may be cracked in less than an hour.

There exist a few utilities that can recover the WEP key. WEPCrack (http://wepcrack.sourceforge.net) was the first publicly available WEP cracking tool. AirSnort (http://airsnort.shmoo.com) is another such utility. Although both have Linux versions, you will find AirSnort a lot easier to use because the latest version is now a GTK+ GUI application (see Figure 13.2).

FIGURE 13.2
AirSnort cracking a WEP key.

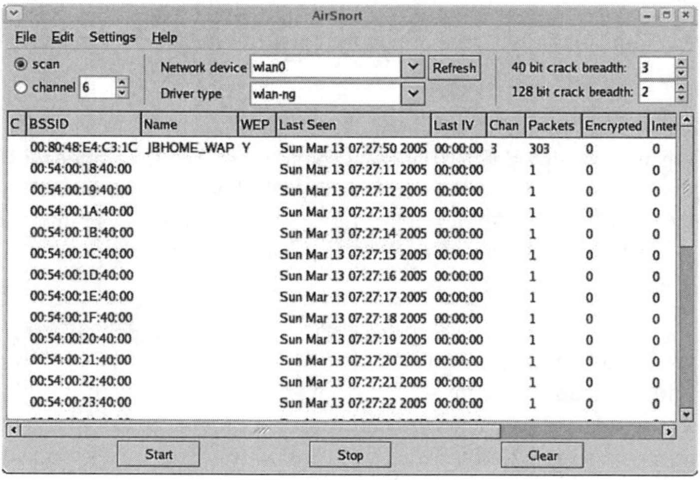

There are a few precautions you can take as deterrence against WEP-cracking, for example:

- Pick a WEP key that is totally random, rather than some word that can be found in a dictionary (much like selecting a good login password, as discussed in Chapter 4). Although doing so will *not* prevent your key from being cracked eventually, it will at least force the attacker to wait until he has captured enough traffic to exploit the WEP weakness, rather than just attempting a dictionary attack against your key. Some vendors will generate a WEP key for you based on a passphrase you supply.

- Use the strongest key available on your hardware. If all your APs and wireless network cards support a 256-bit WEP key, by all means, use it. Although it will not defend against the shortcomings of WEP, a longer key will help deter casual attackers.

NOTE

Quite often, you cannot use the strongest key supported by the hardware because a handful of clients have an older wireless card that supports only 64-bit WEP keys. In such cases, you have to settle for a (weaker) 64-bit key because it is the lowest common denominator, or you might consider upgrading those clients to newer cards. Given the low cost of wireless network cards available today and the potential cost of having your network compromised, you can easily justify the upgrade.

- Use different WEP keys for different APs. Doing this, however, may limit the mobility of your legitimate users within the building. On the other hand, some companies install a WLAN so they do not have to run cables. In such instances, varying WEP keys should not be a hindrance.

- Although it may be administratively intensive, periodically changing the WEP key can serve to deter WEP key cracking. Depending on the frequency with which you change your key, unless the attacker uses the cracked key immediately, he may have to start all over again when he returns, thinking he has gained access to your APs from his previous visit. Depending on the client workstation configuration, you may be able to push out new WEP keys automatically and transparently.

Recognizing the shortcomings of WEP, IEEE 802.11i is a new standard that specifies improvements to wireless LAN networking security. The 802.11i standard addresses many of the security issues of the original 802.11 standard. While at the time of this writing, the new IEEE 802.11i standard is still being ratified, wireless vendors have agreed on an interoperable interim standard known as Wi-Fi Protected Access (WPA).

With WPA, encryption is done using the *Temporal Key Integrity Protocol* (TKIP, originally named WEP2), which replaces WEP with a stronger encryption algorithm (but still uses RC4 ciphers). Unlike WEP, TKIP avoids key reuse by creating a temporary key using a 128-bit IV (instead of the quickly repeating 24-bit IV WEP uses), and the key is changed every 10,000 packets. It also adds in the MAC address of the client to the mix, such that different devices will never seed RC4 with the same key. Because TKIP keys are determined automatically, there is no need to configure an encryption key for WPA.

If your WLAN equipment supports WPA in addition to WEP, by all means, use WPA.

PROTECTING THE SSID

The Service Set ID (SSID) represents the name of a particular WLAN. Because WLAN uses radio waves that are transmitted using the broadcast method, it's possible for signals from two or more WLANs to overlap. The SSID is used to differentiate between different WLANs that are within range of each other.

NOTE

An SSID contains up to 32 alphanumeric characters and is case sensitive.

To connect to a specific WLAN, you need to know its SSID. Many APs broadcast the SSID by default (called a *beacon*) to make it easier for clients to locate the correct WLAN. Some wireless clients (such as Windows XP) detect these beacons and automatically configure the workstation's wireless configuration for transparent access to the nearest WLAN. However, this convenience is a double-edged sword because these beacons also make it easier for wardrivers to determine the SSID of your WLAN.

One of the steps to dissuade unauthorized users from accessing your WLAN is to secure to your SSID. When setting up your WLAN, do not use the default SSID provided by the vendor. For instance, Cisco Aironet APs use *autoinstall* as the default SSID, some vendors use *default* for the default SSID, while some other vendors simply use their company name as the default SSID, such as *proxim*. You can find many wireless vendors' default SSIDs and other default settings at http://www.cirt.net/cgi-bin/ssids.pl.

The SSID should be something *not* related to your name or company. Like your login password, the SSID should be something difficult to guess. Ideally, it should be some random, meaningless string.

CAUTION

Although it is convenient to use the default SSID, it would cause problems if a company or neighbor next to you set up a wireless LAN with the same vendor's access points and also used the default SSID. If neither of you implements some form of security, which is often the case in both homes and smaller companies (sometimes even large organizations where wireless technologies are new to them), and you're both within range of each other, your wireless clients can mistakenly associate with your neighbor's access point, and vice versa.

CAUTION

Many APs allow a client using the SSID of *any* to connect to their APs, but this feature can generally be disabled. You should do so at your earliest convenience.

Unless you are running public APs (such as a community Wi-Fi HotSpot)
where open connectivity is required, if your AP has the feature, it is generally a
good idea to disable SSID broadcasting, even if it doesn't totally prevent your
SSID from being sniffed. Disabling SSID broadcasting (also known as *SSID
blinding*) only prevents the APs from broadcasting the SSID via the Beacon and
Probe Request packets. But in response to a Probe Request, an AP's Probe
Response frame includes the SSID. Furthermore, clients will broadcast the SSID
in their Association and Reassociation frames. Therefore, something like SSID
Sniff (`http://www.bastard.net/~kos/wifi`) or Wellenreiter (see Figure 13.3;
`http://www.wellenreiter.net`) can be used to discover a WLAN's SSID.
Because of this, SSID should *never* be considered a valid security "tool."
However, it can serve as a small roadblock against casual snoopers and "script
kiddies."

FIGURE 13.3
Wellenreiter's main window.

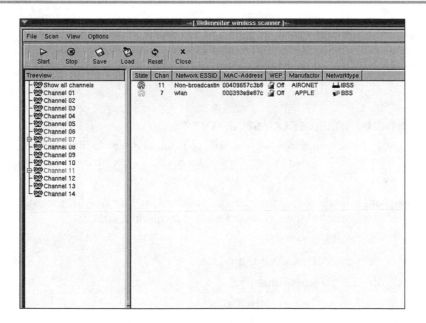

WHAT IS A SCRIPT KIDDIE?

From Webopedia.com, a script kiddie is "A person, normally someone who is not technologically sophisticated, who randomly seeks out a specific weakness over the Internet in order to gain root access to a system without really understanding what it is s/he is exploiting because the weakness was discovered by someone else. A script kiddie is not looking to target specific information or a specific company but rather uses knowledge of a vulnerability to scan the entire Internet for a victim that possesses that vulnerability."

There is one possible countermeasure that you can deploy against SSID snooping: Fake AP (`http://www.blackalchemy.to/project/fakeap`). As the saying goes, "the best hiding place is in plain sight." Fake AP can generate thousands of counterfeit Beacon frames (with different SSIDs) that essentially hide your actual network among the cloud of fake ones. Again, this is not a surefire solution, but it will definitely discourage amateurs and will require an experienced hacker to spend an extraordinary amount of time wading through the bogus beacons to guess at the real network.

CAUTION

You must be *very* careful when using Fake AP because you may unknowingly interfere with neighboring third-party WLANS, which could result in possible legal repercussions. Additionally, the extra traffic generated by Fake AP may decrease your network's available bandwidth.

ADDITIONAL WIRELESS LAN SECURITY TIPS

Other than those steps already discussed, you can take some additional steps to secure you WLAN. The following list summarizes the *basic* precautionary measures you should employ to protect your WLAN:

- Change the default administration password on your APs (this includes the password for the web-based management interface).
- Change the default SSID.
- Disable the SSID broadcast, if possible.
- Enable MAC address filtering.
- Turn off AP's automatic DHCP IP address assignment. This will cause attackers to do extra work to get a valid IP address. If turning off this assignment is not feasible (especially if you have a fair number of users), restrict DHCP leases to the MAC addresses of your wireless clients only.

- Use the highest (common) level of WEP/WPA supported by your hardware; upgrade old hardware to support 256-bit keys if possible.

- Place your APs outside the corporate firewall. This helps to restrict intruders from accessing your internal network resources. You can configure the firewall to enable access from legitimate users based on MAC addresses.

- Use a switch, not a hub, for connecting the AP to the wired network segment. This can help to reduce the possibility of all traffic being sniffed.

- Encrypt your wireless traffic using a VPN, in addition to using WEP/WPA; use encryption protocols for applications where possible (TLS/HTTPS, ssh, and so on).

- If the clients from the WLAN side need access to the Internet, use a proxy server (such as Squid, Novell Security Manager, or Novell BorderManager) with access control for outgoing requests.

- Minimize radio wave propagation to nonuser areas. For instance, orient AP antennas or reduce transmission power, if possible, to avoid covering areas outside the physically controlled boundaries of your facility. By steering clear of public areas, such as parking lots, lobbies, and adjacent offices, you significantly reduce the ability of an intruder to participate on your WLAN. This also minimizes the impact of someone disrupting your WLAN with jamming or DoS techniques.

TIP

You can find a number of wireless intrusion detection systems (IDS) at http://www.zone-h.org/en/download/category=18.

As with fire drills, you should test your WLAN's security on a regular basis using the wardriving tools discussed earlier. It's better to find your own weaknesses (and fix them) than find out second hand from an intruder!

System Hardening Packages

The following are some of the security-related packages included with SLES 9:

- **AIDE**—The Advanced Intrusion Detection Environment is a tool that checks file integrity.

- **Arpwatch**—This tool keeps track of MAC-IP address pairings by monitoring ARP traffic; it can report detected changes via syslog and email.

- **Bastille**—This security hardening tool runs in both interactive and automated modes; it replaces the `harden_suse` script that was previously included with SLES 8.

- **Ethereal**—This is an excellent packet sniffer and decoder.

- **IPTraf**—This tool is a console-based network statistics reporting utility.

- **John the Ripper**—This tool detects weak passwords.

- **ippl**—This IP protocol logger tracks incoming ICMP messages, TCP connections, and UDP datagrams.

- **Logsurfer**—This tool allows log files to be monitored, and when a predefined event is encountered, action (such as an email alert) can be triggered.

- **mon**—This tool monitors the availability of network services.

- **Nagios**—Similar to `mon`, this tool performs periodic checks on the availability of hosts and services; for more information, visit `http://www.nagios.org`.

- **Nessus**—This excellent security scanner can test for and report on more than 900 known weaknesses.

- **nmap**—This tool scans a host and reports on open ports.

- **SAINT**—The Security Administrator's Integrated Network Tool is an enhanced version of the network security vulnerability scanner, SATAN (Security Administrator's Tool for Analyzing Networks).

- **scanlogd**—This daemon can detect and log port scans that are directed at its host.

- **seccheck**—This security-checking script can be executed periodically via `cron` and reports results via email.

- **Snort**—This excellent packet sniffer can also be used as a lightweight network intrusion detection system.

- **tcpd**—This tool provides the `tcp_wrapper` software that `inetd/xinetd` can use to secure network services (such as `telnet` and `finger`) they manage.

- **Tripwire**—This application can monitor filesystems and report on detected changes.

Of all the listed packages, only `tcpd` (thus `tcp_wrapper`) is installed by default as part of the basic runtime system. Most of the other packages will be installed if you select and install the Productivity/Security package group using YaST. Some packages, such as Ethereal, are listed under Network/Security instead.

Automating SLES Hardening

When you secure the operating system manually, you have an opportunity to determine and document what specific features are hardened. However, if you have a large number of servers to secure or need to do this on a regular basis (as a service to customers, for example), it would be much easier if you perform the task using a set of scripts. That way, you can execute them and have the process done for you automatically. This approach has two added advantages. First, the modifications are applied consistently every time. Second, the scripts serve as documentation; by scanning through the scripts, you know what features of the operating system are hardened. SLES 9 includes a number of hardening and monitoring scripts and applications to help make your job easier. Among them is a security setting option in YaST and the Bastille Linux package.

Within the Security and Users option in the YaST Control Center is a security setting control tool called Security Settings. This applet allows you (as root) to define a set of local security configurations, including password settings, user creation settings, console behavior, and file permissions. In the security settings, the default filesystem permissions are set to Easy. This means most system files are readable by root, but not by other users. The more stringent Secure setting restricts the files that can be viewed by root. And the Paranoid setting requires that users who run applications be predefined. A list of the system files, their ownership, and file permissions are predefined in /etc/permissions.easy, /etc/permissions.secure and /etc/permissions.paranoid. You can customize the file permission settings by adding users to /etc/permissions.local. The YaST Security Setting tool performs many of the same functions as Bastille and uses an interactive graphical menu. In most instances, either the Easy or Secure setting is sufficient; select Paranoid *only* if you are sure you need it or that you *are* paranoid.

Bastille Linux (often referred to as just Bastille) is an application (plus a number of configuration scripts) specifically designed to help you harden a Linux/Unix system. Unlike many other script-based packages, Bastille focuses on letting you, the system administrator, choose exactly how to harden your operating system. It runs in either interactive or batch mode. In interactive mode, it asks you questions (see Figure 13.4), *explains* the topics of those questions, and builds a policy based on your answers. It then applies the policy to the system. You can copy the saved configuration file and apply it to other systems.

One of the best features of Bastille is that it actually *educates* you about security (by asking the various questions and telling you why the questions were asked), and helps you make balanced and informed choices. Many users have found Bastille's educational function just as useful as its hardening function. Because Bastille allows you to run through the entire interactive portion without applying the chosen changes, some organizations actually make their new system administrators run through an interactive Bastille session as part of their training.

FIGURE 13.4
Bastille Linux in GUI mode.

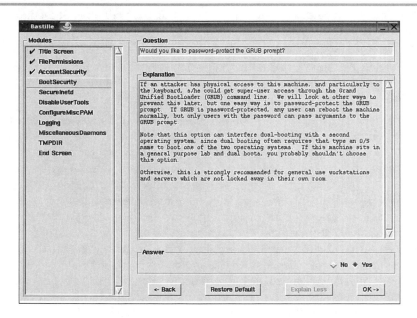

TIP

Bastille Linux has a fairly good undo functionality built in. In essence, running Bastille with the -r switch restores all the configuration files and other OS state settings to exactly where they were before you applied the Bastille policy. Keep in mind that if you just installed Bastille a day ago and haven't changed things much, the undo works perfectly. However, if you installed Bastille on the system six months ago and have made a million manual changes to the system configuration (that Bastille doesn't know about), the undo feature probably won't work so well. Most of the time, Bastille will warn you when this is the case, but you should not consider this as a given.

On SLES, Bastille's related files (such as the OS-specific questions and script files) are installed into `/usr/share/Bastille` and the binary executable, `bastille`, in `/usr/sbin`. No man pages are installed, but you can find a number of `readme` files in `/usr/share/doc/packages/bastille`. Configuration files created by Bastille are stored in `/etc/Bastille`. Bastille runs in text mode (using `ncurses`) or in graphical mode under X (using the Tk graphics toolkit). If you launch `bastille` without any switches, it will first try the GUI mode, with text mode as the fallback. Alternatively, you can use `bastille -x` to force GUI mode or `bastille -c` to force text mode.

Bastille first displays an introductory disclaimer screen to ensure you understand that using *Bastille can help to optimize your system's security but does not guarantee it*. You need to type **agree** and then press Return to get past it; it will not be displayed the next time you run Bastille. (You can reactivate the disclaimer screen by deleting `/usr/share/Bastille/.nodisclaimer`.) You then are led through a series of questions (predefined in `/usr/share/Bastille/Questions.txt`) that you should read thoroughly and understand before answering and proceeding to the next screen. Depending on your server's current configuration, you may not see all the questions.

You should write down the answers you provided to Bastille for future reference and documentation purposes.

NOTE

If you need some guidelines or recommendations to Bastille questions, see "HOW-TO: Bastille Linux 2.1.2," at `http://www.unofficial-support.com/article/how-to/bastille_linux`.

NOTE

The Bastille Linux project (`http://www.bastille-linux.org`) is run by Jon Lasser, Lead Coordinator, and Jay Beale, Lead Developer. The SUSE port of Bastille was made by Niki Rahimi of IBM's Linux Technology Center located in Austin, Texas.

Learning More About Threats

Using the various hardening suggestions presented in this chapter is not sufficient to totally secure your systems from intrusion. The steps presented here and the security precautionary methods you read about last week are like flu shots: They guard against known issues and do not guarantee to be effective against new threats that may be discovered next week. You need to stay current on new threats and their countermeasures.

Script kiddies and casual intruders go for the "easy kill": They look for and exploit security weaknesses that have been widely published. Therefore, other than taking the steps discussed previously in the chapter to secure your systems, you should make sure your systems and networks are not vulnerable to these exploits.

There are a number of well-respected sources of security information, such as the Computer Emergency Response Team (better known simply as CERT, http://www.cert.org), on what a common exploit is. The mailing list BugTraq (archived at http://www.securityfocus.com) is one of the best sources of exploits available for different operating systems, including Linux. In the appendix of this book, you will find a list of websites and mailing lists that can provide you with more information about network security in general, and specific exploits and countermeasures for Linux, and in particular SUSE LINUX, systems. For example, Novell maintains a number of SUSE-specific mailing lists, such as suse-security, suse-security-announce, and suse-sles-e. You can sign up for any and all of them at http://www.suse.com/us/private/support/online_help/mailinglists/index.html.

Summary

In this chapter, we examined a number of methods that can be implemented to protect your server environment. Starting with the premise that if something is not being used, discard it, we further refined our approach by implementing firewalls to restrict network traffic.

Server hardening techniques can be further enhanced by placing exposed applications into containers using tools such as chroot and UML. The resulting compromise of these services restricts the exposure to the containment object.

The number of threats to a computing environment is considerable. Implementing simple physical security measures such as using switches instead of hubs is not sufficient. Network architecture should encompass the physical wiring, the nodes, and the networks (both wired and wireless) used in an organization. Leveraging network subnets and filtering rules can help isolate known allowed traffic patterns within an organization. Out-of-pattern events will therefore become more noticeable and, one hopes, lead to faster investigation. Intrusion detection tools with automatic log file parsing and reporting capabilities should be deployed to provide an early-warning system.

Keeping the target profile of a server environment to a minimum is a continuous process. New applications bring along new features and new vulnerabilities. Old, trusted applications are often found to have long-hidden flaws. Vigilance is the key to properly defending an environment. Knowing where to look for the latest threat vectors is just as important. A number of sources for threat information have been listed throughout this chapter; many more are listed in Appendix B, "Resources."

PART V

Appendixes

Security Certifications

Although often not necessary, selecting a network operating system that has earned a security rating can be advantageous. For instance, if your company has a security-conscious Chief Technology Officer, a network operating system that has an internationally recognized security rating would be an easier sell than one that doesn't. Furthermore, some companies you do business with may require it.

A number of different organizations, including the U.S. government, have defined a set of security requirements that must be met in order for the operating system to be used within those organizations. At the very least, the classifications can be used to help people (primarily the U.S. government and its contractors) in their purchasing decision. Therefore, if your company does business with the U.S. government or its contractors or simply requires the same level of network security, it would be a good idea if your company deployed network operating systems that meet the minimum of these security ratings.

In 1983, the National Computer Security Center (NCSC) assigned a range of security ratings, shown in Table A.1, based on the United States Department of Defense's Trusted Computer System Evaluation Criteria (TCSEC). These ratings, often referred to as the *Orange Book* after the color of the document's cover, measure the degree of protection offered by operating systems, network components, and applications.

NOTE

When a software product, such as a database, is granted a security rating, it is often referred to as a *trusted application*.

TABLE A.1
Orange Book Security Ratings

RATING CODE	RATING NAME
A1	Verified Design
B3	Security Domains
B2	Structured Protection
B1	Labeled Security Protection
C2	Controlled Access Protection
C1	Discretionary Access Protection (this rating is obsolete)
D	Minimal Protection

The TCSEC standard consists of levels of trust ratings, in which higher levels of security build on lower levels, adding more rigorous protection requirements. Although a few *network components* (such as Boeing MILS LAN Version 2.1) have been evaluated A1, no operating system has earned the A1 rating. A number of operating systems such as Hewlett-Packard's HP/UX, Digital's Ultrix, and Silicon Graphics' IRIX have earned B1, B2, and B3 ratings. A number of general-purpose network operating systems, such as Windows NT4 and NetWare 4.11, have earned the C2 rating.

NOTE

You can find a complete list of products evaluated by the NCSC using the Orange Book criteria at www.radium.ncsc.mil/tpep/epl/historical.html.

A similar set of European security criteria, Information Technology Security Evaluation Criteria (ITSEC), was developed in the mid-1990s. Recognizing that an internationally accepted standard is required so that all countries can use one evaluation system, the United States, United Kingdom, Germany, France, Canada, and the Netherlands released a jointly developed evaluation standard for a multinational marketplace in January 1996. This standard is known as the Common Criteria for Information Technology Security Evaluation (CCITSE), usually referred to simply as the Common Criteria (CC).

The CCITSE has a structure closer to the ITSEC than the TCSEC and includes *Protection Profiles* to collect requirements into easily specified and compared sets and a *Security Target*.

A Protection Profile (PP) is a document created by a group of users (for example, a consumer group or large organization) that identifies the desired security properties of a product. Basically, a PP is a list of user security requirements, described in a very specific way defined by the CC. A Security Target (ST) is a document that identifies what a product (known as the Target of Evaluation, or TOE) actually does, or a subset of it, which is security-relevant; it is the basis for agreement between all parties as to what security the TOE offers.

NOTE

For more definitions and explanations of terms used in computer security evaluations, visit www.radium.ncsc.mil/tpep/process/faq.html.

It is often difficult to identify a reasonable set of assurance requirements. The Common Criteria offer a set of predefined assurance requirements, called Evaluation Assurance Levels (EALs). EALs provide a uniformly increasing scale that balances the level of assurance obtained with the cost and feasibility of acquiring that degree of assurance. There are seven hierarchically ordered EALs, as shown in Table A.2. The higher levels build on lower levels, so the higher the EAL rating, the greater the degree of assurance.

NOTE

For more information about Common Criteria for Information Technology Security Evaluation (CCITSE), visit csrc.nist.gov/cc.

TABLE A.2
Evaluation Assurance Levels in Common Criteria

EVALUATION ASSURANCE LEVELS	COMMENTS
EAL1 (Functionally Tested)	The EAL1 rating indicates that the TOE was independently tested to verify its security functions, the TOE functions in a manner consistent with its documentation, and the TOE provides useful protection against identified threats.
	EAL1-rated products are best for situations in which *some* confidence in correct operation is required, but the threats to security are not considered as serious.

TABLE A.2
Evaluation Assurance Levels in Common Criteria (continued)

EVALUATION ASSURANCE LEVELS	COMMENTS
EAL2 (Structurally Tested)	In addition to the EAL1 rating, an EAL2 rating requires that evidence of developer testing and selective results be independently confirmed. The developer must conduct a vulnerability analysis and provide evidence that security functions claimed to operate at certain strength levels meet or exceed those levels. For instance, if the TOE supports 128-bit encryption, the developer must provide evidence to substantiate that feature.
	EAL2 is therefore applicable in those circumstances that require a low to moderate level of independently assured security in the absence of ready availability of the complete development record.
EAL3 (Methodically Tested and Checked)	In addition to the EAL2 rating, an EAL3 rating requires the developer to document the security controls and procedures (including Change Management) employed to protect the TOE during development—for example, how the source code was protected from tampering. Furthermore, the TOE's documentation would be examined to ensure there is no conflicting or misleading information, that it identifies all possible modes of operation, and that it lists all assumptions about the operating environment and requirements for external security measures.
	EAL3 is applicable in those circumstances that require a moderate level of independently assured security and require a thorough investigation of the TOE and its development record.
EAL4 (Methodically Designed, Tested, and Reviewed)	In addition to the EAL3 rating, an EAL4 rating requires validation that the TOE is resistant to vulnerability attacks of "low penetration potentials." In addition to evidence of partial automation of Change Management and problem tracking practices, and implementation of TOE according to strict design documentation, the developer is also required to provide documentation regarding life-cycle support.
	EAL4 is therefore applicable in those circumstances that require a moderate to high level of independently assured security in "off-the-shelf" TOEs.

TABLE A.2
Evaluation Assurance Levels in Common Criteria (continued)

EVALUATION ASSURANCE LEVELS	COMMENTS
EAL5 (Semiformally Designed and Tested)	In addition to the EAL4 rating, an EAL5 rating requires validation that the TOE is resistant to vulnerability attacks of "moderate penetration potentials." The developer must supply an architectural description of the TOE security functions that demonstrate a modular design and that there is minimal interaction among the modules (so that the failure of one security function module will not adversely impact the performance of others).
	EAL5 is therefore applicable in those circumstances that require a high level of independently assured security in a planned development and require a rigorous development approach. An EAL5-rated TOE is generally designed and developed with the intent of achieving EAL5 assurance, where no retrofitting of security modules is required (if retrofitting is required, the components may not integrate nicely).
	EAL6 (Semiformally Verified Design and Tested) In addition to the EAL5 rating, an EAL6 rating requires validation that the TOE is resistant to vulnerability attacks of "high penetration potentials." In addition to evidence of complete automation of the Change Management process, the developer must supply an architectural description of the TOE security functions that demonstrate a layered as well as modular design. An analysis of the documentation is performed to ensure it contains sufficient information for users to detect an insecure TOE.
	EAL6 is therefore applicable to TOEs used in high-risk situations in which the value of the protected assets justifies the additional costs.
EAL7 (Formally Verified Design and Tested)	In addition to the EAL6 rating, an EAL7 rating requires the evaluator to repeat and verify all testing performed by the developer and that a procedure is in place to guarantee that the TOE is not tampered with while en route from the developer to the user.
	EAL7 is applicable to the development of security TOEs for use in *extremely* high-risk situations and/or where the high value of the assets justifies the higher costs.

Today, the Common Criteria standard has replaced TCSEC and ITSEC, and all current network operating system product evaluations are taking place at these new EALs, not at the older levels (such as C2 and so on). In February 2005, SLES 9 running on IBM eServers was granted the EAL4+ rating by astec information security (www.astec.com), one of the few laboratories worldwide officially accredited and licensed to perform evaluations based on the Common Criteria standard. Additional evaluations using a range of IBM and HP hardware platforms are being conducted at the time of this writing.

NOTE

The document titled "SUSE LINUX Enterprise Server (SLES) V9 Security Target for CAPP Compliance," located at www.ibm.com/developerworks/opensource/library/os-ltc-security, contains the security feature specifications of SLES 9 as evaluated for the EAL4+ rating.

NOTE

While EAL*x* is simply a standard shorthand for the set of assurance requirements defined for EAL*x*, products can be evaluated with additional assurance measures. For example, a product (such as SLES) might choose to be evaluated at EAL4 plus *some* additional assurance measures, but not sufficient to be EAL5. Such a combination would be called EAL4+.

You need to be aware that a security *rating* is different from a security *certification*. Operating systems, hardware, and application programs earn ratings, but individual installations must be certified. This distinction is significant. What it means is that you may be running an EAL4-rated operating system, but your site is *not* automatically EAL4-certified. You need to install and configure your system using the same operating system version, patches, and settings as well as the same or equivalent hardware used in the evaluation. Then your system must be inspected and granted that certification by an accredited third party. Furthermore, any changes made, no matter how minor, to an already-certified installation require the whole configuration to be reevaluated to retain the certification.

You will find the system hardening information presented in Chapter 13, "System Security," is complementary to the configuration procedures used for

SLES 9's EAL4+ evaluation. The following summary describes how you should apply computer security certifications toward your network's security needs:

- If you need to run a secure network, select a network operating system that has an EAL rating; you should also consider running EAL-rated workstation operating systems.

- Using an EAL-rated operating system does not automatically give you all the necessary protection. You need to apply the recommended settings as per its security guides. For example, to configure your SLES server to match its EAL4+ settings, follow the procedures outlined in "Common Criteria EAL4+ Evaluated Configuration Guide for SUSE LINUX Enterprise Server (SLES) on IBM Hardware," found at www.ibm.com/developerworks/opensource/library/os-ltc-security. This guide explains how the evaluated configuration was set up and provides information to administrators and users to ensure secure operation of the system.

- EAL4+ settings may be much more than what your environment requires. If that is the case, the configuration guide's recommended settings serve as a starting point to customize your own security requirements.

- Other than using rated operating systems, you may also want to deploy other networking components (such as firewalls) that are EAL-rated. You can find a detailed list at niap.nist.gov/cc-scheme/vp1/vp1_type.html.

You can find an RPM package containing the configuration script and data needed to set up the Common Criteria EAL4 system configuration certified on IBM hardware at http://portal.suse.com/psdb/22e06ee39e67b7064ea5c31de972460c.html. You will need a current SUSE maintenance contract to access this page. Even if you are not using IBM hardware, the script can provide you with insights into the necessary settings to be applied to your server.

Resources

Due to limited space in this book, certain topics (such as Snort) were given only a cursory coverage instead of the in-depth discussion we would have liked. Similarly, certain topics related to basic Linux/Unix usage knowledge were not covered at all. Among the basic tools, a text editor is probably *the* most important one that a Linux/Unix system administrator uses. Therefore, we start this appendix with a brief review of Linux text editors included with SLES 9 and a short primer about vi. In addition, this appendix provides a list of websites and Internet newsgroups where you can locate additional information about SUSE LINUX and Linux-related security issues.

Linux Editors

As you read through this book (especially Chapter 8, "Network Services"), no doubt you have come to the conclusion that *everything* in Linux is configured using one or more text files. These text-based configuration files control how the system boots, what services to run, and even how Apache functions. You can modify many of these settings using the graphical YaST interface, but not all. And what if no GUI were installed on the server or if you needed to administrate the system remotely and a graphical interface was not feasible?

Recall from the first chapter of this book, "Installing SUSE LINUX Enterprise Server," for an SLES server to run efficiently, a GUI desktop should not be installed because the graphical overhead puts an unnecessary load on the system. Therefore, an effective Linux system administrator should be familiar with the operation of text editors. SLES 9 ships with the following text editors:

- **ed**—*The* original Unix line-based editor. It is very useful in scripts.

- **sed**—A stream-oriented (that is, noninteractive) line-based editor. You have to insert commands to be executed on the data at the command line or in a script to be processed; therefore, it is not a text editor in the traditional word processor sense of the term. The **sed** utility works by sequentially reading a file, line by line, and performing all actions specified for the line. The modified line is then sent to the terminal (that is, to **stdout**, which can be redirected) with the requested changes made. The process is repeated until the whole file is processed. As such, **sed** is ideally suited to performing repetitive edits that would take considerable time if done manually.

- **Vim** (**Vi IM**proved) and **gVim**—An enhanced version of the classic Unix screen-based editor, **vi**. **Vim** works in text mode in every terminal, but it also has a graphical user interface (**gVim**) that has menus and mouse support. You can find the latest version of **Vim** at **http://www.vim.org**.

- **gedit**—The official text editor of the GNOME desktop environment. Using the GTK+ and GNOME libraries, **gedit** supports most standard editing features and has a powerful plug-in system to support dynamic function addition. Visit **http://www.gnome.org/projects/gedit** for more information and the latest version.

- **Emacs** (**E**ditor **MAC**ro**S**)—Based on a dialect of the Lisp programming language, **Emacs** is a GNU editor that has a fully integrated user environment and can be invoked either in text mode or GUI mode. Visit **http://www.gnu.org/software/emacs** for the latest version and more information.

- **Kate** (**K**DE **A**dvanced **T**ext **E**ditor)—A native KDE application that is capable of working with multiple documents concurrently, but only a single instance of **Kate** is required. Visit **http://kate.kde.org** for more information.

- **JOE** (**J**oe's **O**wn **E**ditor)—Created by Joseph Allen, this full-screen text editor has the look and feel of the once-famous Micro-Pro WordStar PC editor (where a majority of the commands are based on the Ctrl-K keys and a third key combination, such as Ctrl-K-D to save the document). Visit **http://sourceforge.net/projects/joe-editor** for more information.

You should keep in mind that some of the editors mentioned here, such as **gedit** and **Kate**, will do you little good if the server does not have a GUI desktop installed. And as discussed in Chapter 1, "Installing SUSE LINUX Enterprise Server," not all servers will have a GUI desktop installed because GUIs on a server consume system resources unnecessarily.

Perhaps we are from the old school, but we highly prefer the vi editor (pronounced *vee eye*). Many seasoned Linux/Unix system administrators and programmers echo this same preference because when you become familiar with vi's somewhat unique command syntax, you will find that it is one of the most versatile—although not necessarily the most full-featured—text editors available. The other reason vi is a favorite among the hard-core Linux/Unix users is its universal availability. Other than the fact that you can find an implementation of vi for most operating systems, it is probably the only screen-oriented text editor that you can count on to be "always there" among *all* the Linux and Unix distributions available today. Being able to use vi ensures that you will always have an editor available to you, no matter what version or distribution of Linux/Unix you use.

NOTE

Many modern Linux distributions include Vim in conjunction with or instead of vi. SLES 9 ships with Vim instead of vi. Because Vim falls into the category of being a "vi-clone," knowledge of vi will serve you well in administrating SLES systems.

vi (and thus Vim) has three different "modes" of operation:

- **Visual command mode**—This mode is used to issue short commands (of one character or sometimes a couple of characters) that allow you to manipulate the text or editor environment in a number of ways. You enter it by typing one of the text-entering commands shown in Table B.1 to control how and where text is entered.

- **Data-entry or input mode**—This mode is used for entering text into the editor's work buffer before it is committed to the disk through a save operation, initiated in one of the command modes.

- **Status line command mode**—This mode is also referred to as the "Colon command mode" because you enter this mode from the visual command mode by typing a colon. This mode is used for issuing longer, more complex commands to the editor, such as to save files, quit the editor, set environment variables, and perform more global editor tasks. The commands are echoed back to the user in the status line of the editor (demarcated by a : at the bottom of the screen) and are executed when you press Enter.

NOTE

To switch out of the input mode into the visual command mode, simply press the Esc key. Entering the status line command mode from the input mode is a two-step process: First press the Esc key to enter the visual command mode and then type a colon (:).

vi does not offer you much feedback as to which mode it is currently in. For instance, you may not not realize that vi is currently in the visual command mode and you typed **dd**. Instead of adding two d's to your file, you just accidentally deleted the current line of text. (Fortunately, you can undo the change by using the u command; see Table B.1.) If you are unsure what mode vi is operating in, press the Esc key a few times to place vi in visual mode. Even if you are already in the visual mode, the worst you get is an error beep on the terminal.

TIP

Often new users have difficultly knowing which mode they're working in because vi doesn't really offer much feedback. In a worst-case scenario, press Esc a few times and know that you will be in visual mode. Even if you are already in visual mode, the worst you will get is an error beep.

TABLE B.1
vi Single-Character Commands

TEXT COMMAND	DESCRIPTION
a	Start appending text after the current cursor position.
A	Append text to the end of the current line.
i	Start inserting text to the left of the current cursor location.
I	Insert text at beginning of the current line.
o	Insert a new line below the current line.
O	Insert a new line above the current line.
r	Replace a single character at the present location.
R	Replace text starting at the current position (in other words, start overwriting the remainder of the line).
u	Undo the last change. Undo all the changes to the current line.

CAUTION

vi commands *are* case sensitive.

There is a rather rich set of editing commands in vi. Many of them are two-character combinations, usually with the first character denoting the action (such as deleting) and the second character indicating the type of text object (such as a word or sentence) to be acted on. Table B.2 shows some of the most commonly used vi editing commands.

TABLE B.2
vi Editing Commands

TEXT COMMAND	DESCRIPTION
cw	Change the word at the current cursor position.
D	Delete from the current location to the end of the line.
dd	Delete the current line.
dw	Delete the word at the current cursor location.
x	Delete one character at the current cursor position.
.	Repeat last edit command.
yy	Copy the current line into the memory buffer (known as "yank").
yw	Yank the word under the cursor.
p	Paste the text in the memory buffer (the "yanked" text) at the current cursor position.
P	Paste the yanked text before the current cursor position.
ZZ	Save the changes to disk and exit vi. (You can use :w to write the modifications made so far to disk without exiting the editor.)

TIP

You can precede the editing commands with a number to indicate the command is to be repeated that number of times. For instance, instead of entering dd five times to delete five lines, you can use 5dd instead.

vi, which is a screen-oriented editor, uses the curses library for screen manipulation. That means it works with all supported terminal types, and you can navigate the cursor around the screen using the standard arrow keys. You can move up and down a full screen at a time by pressing Ctrl-B and Ctrl-F, respectively; or, to scroll half a screen up and down, you can press Ctrl-D and Ctrl-U, respectively. Because vi is text-based and does not depend on a mouse, it is most suited for remote management tasks, such as performing file edits over a Telnet or SSH link.

For more information about using vi, you can type :help inside the editor. Other resources include the website dubbed "The Vi Lovers Home page" (http://thomer.com/vi/vi.html) and the book *Learning the vi Editor* (ISBN 1-56592-426-6).

TIP

You can start vi in *read-only* mode (vi -R *filename*). This is useful for viewing long configuration files without the fear of accidentally changing them. vi also has a *recovery* mode (vi -r *filename*) that recovers recent edits after a crash. Vim automatically detects this and displays a message similar to the following:

```
E325: ATTENTION
Found a swap file by the name ".test.txt.swp"
     owned by: tasha    dated: Sun Mar 13 13:20:37 2005
     file name: ~tasha/test.txt
     modified: no
     user name: tasha    host name: Athena
    process ID: 3250
While opening file "test.txt"
          dated: Sun Mar 13 13:20:32 2005

(1) Another program may be editing the same file.
    If this is the case, be careful not to end up with
    Two different instances of the same file when making
    changes.
    Quit, or continue with caution.

(2) An edit session for this file crashed.
    If this is the case, use ":recover" or
    "vim -r test.txt" to recover the changes (see
    ":help recovery").
    If you did this already, delete the swap file
    ".test.txt.swp" to avoid this message.

Swap file ".test.txt.swp" already exists!
[O]pen Read-Only, (E)dit anyway, (R)ecover, (Q)uit,
➥(D)elete it:
```

Website Resources

The Internet is a vast repository of information. Even with the help of search engines such as Google, it is still a daunting task to sort through the various sites for relevant information. One of the biggest challenges of administrating an SLES system (or any server for that matter) is maintaining good security. The following sections identify some of the websites and mailing lists that provide security-related information in addition to what is found in this book.

Security and Linux-Related Websites

The following is a list of URLs to websites containing Linux-related and/or Linux security-related information and applications:

- Intrusion Detection Systems (LIDS), www.lids.org

  Incorporates changes to the kernel mandating that all access to system functions be controlled by ACLs. This ensures that changes are locked out and requires that process-file relationships be specifically described.

- John the Ripper, www.openwall.com/john/

  Password auditing tool. With this tool, you can test to see how closely your user passwords conform to your IT policy document.

- Snort, www.snort.org

  Passive intrusion detection system. Snort listens to network traffic, verifies packet content against a known set of exploit patterns, and can raise a number of separate alarms.

- Nmap, www.insecure.org

  Active, stealthy, port scanning tool. Nmap verifies which ports are visible on a network or system. Using response fingerprints, it can determine the host operating system of the target.

- Ethereal, www.ethereal.com

  Network packet-capturing tool or sniffer. Ethereal can be used to completely reconstruct network conversations. It is useful for detecting inappropriate protocols and attack conversations.

- Tripwire, www.tripwire.org

  Host-based intrusion detection system. Tripwire creates hashes for files that can be compared to baseline values stored offline. The comparison is used to look for unauthorized changes.

- Bastille Linux, www.bastille-linux.org

  Operating system level hardening tool. Bastille Linux can be used to harden a system or simply report on suggestions to further enhance the security on the host.

- CERT (Computer Emergency Response Team), www.cert.org

  Coordination center for information on incidents and known software vulnerabilities hosted at Carnegie Mellon University.

- Internet Security Systems, www.iss.net

  A security services firm offering solutions and assistance on various aspects of network-based threats.

- tcpdump and libpcap, www.tcpdump.org

  These tools are used in conjunction to permit the capture of network traffic for analysis. libpcap allows root to place the network interface in promiscuous mode, and tcpdump captures and formats selected packets.

- Linux kernel source, www.kernel.org

  Source code repository for the Linux kernel and associated modules.

- National Institute of Standards and Technology (NIST) Computer Security Resource Center (CSRC), csrc.nist.gov

  This site hosts a collection of information relating to computer security, guidelines and best-practices documents.

- System Administration, Networking, and Security (SANS), www.sans.org, and The Internet Storm Center, isc.sans.org

  This site maintains a constant real-time eye on the Internet as a whole. Reports are collected and evaluated on live threats and attacks and developing incidents. This is a collaborative vendor-independent project; participation in reporting incidents is encouraged.

- Security Focus's BugTraq, www.securityfocus.com/archive/1

  This site maintains a list of all reported bugs independent of platform or software type.

SUSE-Specific Newsgroups and Websites

The following is a list of URLs to SUSE-related newsgroups and websites hosted by Novell and third parties:

- SUSE Support Database (SDB), portal.suse.com/sdb/en/index.html
- SLES Knowledgebase, support.novell.com/search/kb_index.jsp
- SUSE FTP server (packages and sources), ftp.suse.com/pub
- SUSE product support web forums, support.novell.com/forums/2su.html
- Product support communities where you can find tips, tricks, Q&A, and free tools for various Novell products, including the various SUSE LINUX offerings, support.novell.com/products

- SUSE LINUX software development community, `forge.novell.com/modules/xfmod/community/?susecomm`

- Various SUSE mailing lists, `www.suse.com/en/private/support/online_help/mailinglists`

- Novell-Linux, a third-party website pertaining to Novell Linux Desktop and SLES users, `www.novell-linux.com`

- FAQ for the `alt.os.linux.suse` newsgroup, `www.project54.com/linux/ng/alt-os-linux-suse-FAQ`

- Unofficial SUSE FAQs, how-tos, and guides, `susefaq.sourceforge.net/index.html`

- SUSE security home page, `www.novell.com/linux/security/securitysupport.html`

- Reporting or tracking a bug, `bugzilla.novell.com`

Index

B

I

M

Q - R

S

T

U

X - Y - Z